Imperial Punch-marked Coins
of
Ancient India

Imperial Punch-marked Coins *of* Ancient India

A Case Study of Sarāi Dangri Hoard, Varanasi

Savita Sharma

Aryan Books International
New Delhi

IMPERIAL PUNCH-MARKED COINS OF ANCIENT INDIA
A Case Study of Sarāi Dangri Hoard, Varanasi

ISBN: 978-81-7305-546-1

Published in **2016** by
Aryan Books International
Pooja Apartments, 4B, Ansari Road, New Delhi-110 002 (India)
Tel.: 91-11-23287589, 23255799; Fax: 91-11-23270385
E-mail: aryanbooks@gmail.com
www.aryanbooks.co.in

Designed and Printed in India by
ABI Prints & Publishing Co., New Delhi

Foreword

This monograph on *kārṣāpaṇa*/silver punch-marked coins is interesting from the standpoint of the pertinent questions the author has raised. It is said that in research, to ask the right set of questions is half the work done. The present monograph does just that. Of course, it is not easy to find answers until one delves deep into the problem but questions can arise only if one immerses in the subject.

The monograph traces the beginning of coinage in India, mostly based on the literary data which, though voluminous, does not lead us anywhere if unsupported by archaeology. Our earliest coinage, represented by punch-marked coins, starts from the 6th-5th century BCE. It is predominantly of silver, and the coin denomination is *kārṣāpaṇa*, a term which does not occur in the earliest literature. It appears to have been of West Asian origin, as *kārṣa* was a weight in Babylonia in the second millennium BCE and continued much later in Persia. The term can be divided into *kārṣa* (weight) and *āpaṇa* (Sk. market). Interestingly, the earliest punch-marked coins, the bent-bars, have turned up in the Gandhara region in the northwest, which was part of the Achaemenid Empire. Recent discoveries in Iran and Afghanistan, of bar silver and cut silver, from sites like Nush-i-jahan and Chaman Hazouri deserve our attention inasmuch as bar silver specimens without symbols but confirming to the weight of Persian double *Sigloi* or stater occur in silver hoards. People in the Gandhara region probably stamped them with the typical sun symbol and they became the *śatamānas* of Pāṇini, weighing 100 *rattis*, or 175 grains. From this, cut silver was a short but logical step. Thus, probably the punch-marked coins became current.

Another question raised by the author regarding silver is enigmatic. India is deficient in silver, and there is no dedicated word for it in Sanskrit; the term *rajat-hiraṇya*, meaning white gold, is just descriptive. What is more, silver is impure, because it is supposed to be the 'tears of Rudra'. Why was it then used for the earliest coinage? The answer is not to seek and is to be found in the evidence cited above. It is equally significant that in the post-punch-marked coins period, silver was sparingly used for coinage.

Who issued the punch-marked coins? That is a *yakṣa-praśna*. Attempts have been made but no convincing solution is in sight. Only the minutest analysis of all aspects of punch-marked coins may provide the answer. In Europe, scholars have identified five different tribal groups on the basis of the flaking technique of levallois tools; something on these lines may help.

The author has taken pains in preparing a well illustrated monograph. Catalogue part is not only descriptive but quite educative. Scientific and technical data has also been included in collaboration with metallurgists.

Thus, this monograph comes out as a comprehensive study of p.m.c. and should be of immense help to students and scholars of numismatics. The author deserves to be congratulated for her diligent work particularly at a time when numismatics as a discipline is almost dying.

M.K. Dhavalikar

Contents

Preface

Primitive currencies ranging from the exchange of cattles to *cowries* provide the backdrop to the different methods of exchange prevalent prior to 6th century BCE. The barter system was gradually supplemented by the metal pieces. This medium of exchange led to the introduction of coins as a regular system of currency. India's indigenous coinage is rich and varied, distinguished by regional, cultural and linguistic features and representing imperial and political associations.

Every new discovery of a treasure-trove has something new to add to the mine of knowledge extensively compiled by scholars. Herein lies the value of this monograph containing classification of the coins found in this hoard and revisiting the studies made earlier. The terminology and the metallurgical aspects have been dealt in detail, and the coins have been identified as belonging to various 'Series' classified earlier. There have been many challenges and problems due to the varied nature of the symbolic aspects of the punch-marked coins. This made it necessary to adopt the method of a 're-look' and 're-think', particularly in the light of opinions already expressed. Conclusions vary due to different viewpoints based on studies and researches undertaken by scholars.

Varanasi has been known as the capital of ancient Kasi *janapada* and since long recognized for its age-old cultural and spiritual values and as a trade centre of the Indian subcontinent. It has been attracting a constant flow of devotees, pilgrims, princely merchants, travellers, chroniclers and scholars, resulting in a prolific number of publications highlighting its archaeological and historical importance as well as important numismatic discoveries.

Generally, the treasure-troves when found are shorn of any direct context in terms of period history, even though the location may be historically well known. Their study and analysis also takes a lot of time as the process requires cleaning, proper identification and classification, photography and drawings followed by extensive analytical examination, cross-checking with earlier reports and references. This is the established process for a comprehensive study of coin finds.

An earthen pot containing 333 ancient silver punch-marked coins was found in July 1997, from Sarāi Dangri village, Varanasi while digging the foundation of a primary school building. These coins were handed over to Bharat Kala Bhavan, Banaras Hindu University, Varanasi in 1998 by the District Magistrate of Varanasi. The study of these coins forms the subject matter of this volume. Coins in this hoard, classified as imperial *kārṣāpaṇa*, are datable to circa 4th century to 2nd century BCE, comprising seventy-six varieties. Some important facts surface through this valuable study. Out of these seventy-six varieties, two are unique and analysed for the first time. An attempt has been made to restore a form of six-armed symbol that was unnoticed so far. Finally, the evidence that instead of making smaller coins of small values, the mint or the dynasty legalized the cut of a full coin into two halves. This, however, is only a conjecture. The coins of Series VI are the highest in number, indicating that these coins were in circulation when the hoard was buried. The volume is divided into four parts:

Part I commences with an explanatory introduction outlining the importance of this hoard. This also serves as a comprehensive backdrop of the present study, underlining different views expressed by various scholars on the origin and the period and in establishing their association with different dynasties, who introduced these punch-marked coins, designated as the issues of Imperial Series of Magadha, Śuṅga, Naṅda and Mauryan dynasties and the metallurgical studies of coins indicating the source of metal.

Part II covers classification and cataloguing. Here an attempt has been made to refer to most of the published material and views, with drawings and illustrations of obverse and reverse of each variety in tabulated form. The illustrations—comprising 19 figures and 23 plates in black and white—will help in the appreciation of the coins with particular reference to their identity in the historical evolution. The actual size and thickness has also been tabulated. In addition to the illustration of each coin, their maximum and minimum size in cms and weight in grams are also given in separate tabulated forms. As the entire hoard was found in a good state of preservation, identification was easy.

Part III incorporates the observations on the present study and includes tables of the symbols in detail, as well as a brief description on extra-marks and half-coins.

Part IV comprises appendices on weights and measures, note on fabrication, technique and chemical analysis based on some coins of the hoard, an EDS Report, dispersal of coins, list of hoards and a bibliography.

Hoards were discovered earlier and catalogued individually. Nevertheless, absence of a compiled opus has impeded a comprehensive overview. Therefore, even at the risk of repetition, certain basics are mentioned in the following pages enabling a better perception for the students of numismatics in particular and coin collectors and readers in general.

Bringing out a copious volume of this kind has been a painstaking task and has therefore taken longer time than anticipated. It is, however, a pleasure to place it before the students, scholars and the collectors with the hope that it will be found useful by them. The readers will, hopefully, gain a deeper insight and understanding about this remarkable series of silver punch-marked coins.

Savita Sharma

Acknowledgements

Words can never suitably express the feeling of gratitude that I feel towards friends, colleagues and mentors, who have unhesitatingly contributed in many ways to the value of this monograph-cum-catalogue. I shall be failing in my duty if I do not express my sense of gratitude towards them.

First and foremost, I record my deep appreciation and thanks to Mr. Awanish Awasthi, I.A.S., the then District Magistrate of Varanasi, who made it possible for the hoard to remain with the Bharat Kala Bhavan, Banaras Hindu University (BHU), Varanasi. This gave me the opportunity to study the hoard as in-charge of the numismatic section of the museum.

I am grateful to Late Dr. R.C. Sharma, the then Director and Dr. T.K. Biswas, the Joint Director of Bharat Kala Bhavan, for their encouragement and guidance at various stages of the work. I am also thankful to late Prof. Anand Krishna, who helped me in many ways.

I am indebted to Prof. Vidula Jayaswal, Fellow, Prof. R.C. Sharma Chair, Jñāna-Pravāha, Centre for Cultural Studies & Research, Varanasi, for her valuable guidance throughout the preparation of this volume. Her constant encouragement helped me to get on with my work despite some adverse circumstances upsetting my personal life during the period.

My thanks are also due to Late Dr. Rita Sharma, Curator, Numismatics & Epigraphy, National Museum, New Delhi, who readily provided necessary and related information on the subject as and when required. Unfortunately, she is no more to see the fruits of our labour. I also express my thanks to Dr. Subhash Chandra Yadav, Regional Archaeological Officer, Varanasi and Dr. Vijay Pal Singh, Publication Assistant, Puran Section, Department of Ancient Indian History Culture & Archaeology, B.H.U., who were immensely helpful in procuring relevant documents.

My other colleagues in the museum provided professional services in their respective areas—Shri S. Prajapati for the chemical treatment of the coins, Shri Prakash Rao and Shri P.N. Pancholi for providing photographs, Shri Ram Bhajan Ram for assisting in the classification as well as in recording weight and size of the coins, and Dr. R. Ganeshan in digitizing material on the computer. I sincerely record my appreciation to all of them. Credit is also due to Mr. A.K. Gugalani, Scientific Officer, Department of Metallurgy, I.I.T., B.H.U., for the chemical analysis of coins.

My children, Anu, Vishal and Siddhartha, have remained a constant source of strength and support. My late husband, Shri Sudhir Kumar Sharma, took keen interest in my work, always standing by me and supporting me in every way. I have no hesitation in confessing that but for his omni-presence around me, this volume would not have seen the light of the day.

My sincere thanks are to the university authorities for permitting me to continue working on this catalogue even after my retirement from the museum and to publish it from outside.

Last but not the least, I record my gratitude to Shri O.P. Tandon, former Head of the Bharat Kala Bhavan, who has been my mentor and guide throughout my professional career. He has been helping me at every stage of this work, despite his preoccupations with the Indian Archaeological Society and his other professional interests. I would like to express my sincere thanks to my friend, Shri P.P.P. Sharma, IPS, for his valuable suggestions and encouragement in preparation of this volume. My thanks are also due to Mr. Vikas Vinayaka, student of Christ University, B.C.A., Bangalore, for his help in preparation of this work on computer.

The publisher, Shri Vikas Arya of Aryan Books International deserves a special word of thanks in seeing the monograph through the press. His professionalism and painstaking hard work is commendable.

Abbreviations

AB : *Aitareya Brāhmaṇa*.
AI : *Ancient India*, Bulletin of the Archaeological Survey of India.
Am : *Amaravati Hoard of Silver Punch-marked Coins* by P.L. Gupta.
AIN : *Ancient Indian Numismatics* by D.R. Bhandarkar.
APGM/ Hyderabad : *Punch-marked Coins in the Andhra Pradesh Government Museum* by P.L. Gupta, Hyderabad, 1961.
ARADND : *Annual Report, Archaeological Department of His Exalted Highness the Nizam's Dominion*.
ASB : Asiatic Society of Bengal.
ASIAR : *Archaeological Survey of India Annual Report* by J. Marshall.
AISPMC : *Ancient Indian Silver Punch-marked Coins of the Magadha-Maurya Kārshāpana Series* by P.L. Gupta and T.R. Hardaker.
ASR : *Archaeological Survey Report* by A. Cunningham.
AV : *Atharvaveda*.
Barwani : "Barwani Hoard of Silver Punch-marked Coins in National Museum", by P.L. Gupta in *Numismatic Digest*, New Delhi.
BHU : Banaras Hindu University, Varanasi.
BKB : Bharat Kala Bhavan, Banaras Hindu University, Varanasi.
BMC : *Catalogue of the Coins of Ancient India in the British Museum* by J. Allan, London.
CAI : *Coins of Ancient India* by A. Cunningham.
Ep. Ind. : *Epigraphia Indica*, Delhi.
IA : *Indian Antiquary*.
IMC : *Catalogue of the Coins of Indian Museum*, by V.A. Smith, Calcutta.
JASB : *Journal of the Asiatic Society of Bengal*, Calcutta.
JBBRAS : *Journal of the Bombay Branch of Royal Asiatic Society*, Bombay.
JBORS : *Journal of the Bihar Orissa Research Society*, Patna.
JNSI : *Journal of the Numismatic Society of India*, Bombay, Varanasi.

JRAS	:	*Journal of the Royal Asiatic Society of Bengal of Great Britain and Ireland*, London.
MASI	:	*Memoir of the Archaeological Survey of India.*
NC	:	*Numismatic Chronicle.*
ND	:	*Numismatic Digest*, Anjaneri, Nashik.
NIA	:	*New Indian Antiquary.*
NNM	:	*Numismatic Notes and Monograph.*
NS	:	*Numismatic Supplements.*
Patraha	:	*A Hoard of Silver Punch-marked Coins from Purnea (Patraha)* (*MASI* No. 62) by P.N. Bhattacharya, Archaeological Survey of India, New Delhi.
PHAI	:	*Political History of Ancient India* by H.C. Raychaudhuri.
Rairh	:	*Excavation at Rairh* by K.N. Puri.
RV	:	*Ṛgveda.*
SB	:	*Śatapatha Brāhmaṇa.*
SIC	:	*Studies in Indian Coins* by D.C. Sircar.
Taxila	:	*Punch-marked Coins from Taxila* (*MASI* No. 59) by E.H.C. Walsh, Archaeological Survey of India, New Delhi.
TB	:	*Taittirīya Brāhmaṇa.*
TS	:	*Taittirīya Saṁhitā.*
U.P.T.T.R.	:	*Uttar Pradesh Treasure Trove Report*, Lucknow.

Part I
INTRODUCTION

1

Backdrop

India witnessed early signs of its second urbanisation around 1000 BCE, after a continuous evolution of cultures from Black and Red Ware to Early Historic through Ochre-Coloured Pottery (OCP), Painted Grey Ware (PGW) and Northern Black Polished (NBP) Ware. It resulted in an all-round flowering of an urban material culture by c. 600 BCE. This period also witnessed emergence of an accepted medium of transaction in the form of metallic currency known as 'coins'. Coin, a piece of metal, which facilitates trade within the community, is a mark of high economic development. A coin is of a definite weight, with marks of authorisation by the state or some responsible person, testifying to the weight and purity of the metal and serves the purpose of a medium of exchange. Metals were undoubtedly sought both for their exchange and prestige value but there is no evidence of their value for exchange, prior to 6th century BCE.

Coins replaced the old age barter system under which commodities were exchanged to meet various needs and other primitive practices. In the story of the birth, growth and development of metallic currency with a definite shape and weight and bearing symbols and legend on its face is interwoven the political, social and cultural history of India. The study of Indian coinage, therefore, provides a peep into pages of history. Nay, it remains to this day the only illuminating document in unfolding many dark periods of our history and giving the dynastic chronology of many tribes, clans and kingdoms—big and small. The introduction of coins is rightly considered as a landmark in the history of human civilization. Coins to a very great extent provide the source material for reconstructing history, as these are the most substantial and significant documents and are the best indicators of economic prosperity, social-political strength and stability.

As the complexities of city life grew and with it grew the number of crafts, an urgent need was felt to keep handy a medium of exchange which shook off crudities of barter among various human units, e.g. families, class, tribes, etc. Even using cows as the value of any commodity or service—as was the case during the predominantly rural Vedic habitations—had its own pitfalls. It is not difficult to appreciate how vulnerable the cows (or for that matter any milch animals or draught animals) could be in the face of endemics as far as value sustenance over a longer period was concerned. Any detailed picture of the economic life in those times in the northern parts of India where the punch-marked coins made their first appearance is difficult to perceive due to relative paucity of literary evidence on the subject. That is the backdrop—however sketchy—against which the value of the numismatic finds such as the present one is to be seen.

BACKGROUND: THE VEDIC AGE AND LATER PERIOD

In the *Ṛgvedic* age, the Aryans had already progressed from the pastoral to the agricultural stage. Trade was carried on mainly by barter but cow had become a medium of exchange. In the *Aitareya Brāhmaṇa*, the cow was the most important source of wealth.[1] The *Dakṣiṇā* or the sacrificial fee to *Ṛtvika* is paid in the form of cows.[2] Cows were given as offerings to the Brāhmaṇas and the *Purohitas*.[3] It suggests that in the society of *Aitareya Brāhmaṇa*, metal was hardly used as a medium of transaction or used very rarely. *Niṣka* was not yet elevated to a medium of exchange; it was only once referred to in the sense of a necklace.[4] The use of cow as a medium of exchange had become so much prevalent in society that even in the period of *Sūtras*, when coins had come into use, the cows are referred to as the fee to be paid to the priests.[5] The position of cows in the *Ṛgvedic* period can also be deduced from a passage in the *Ṛgveda*, where ten cows are mentioned as the price of an image of Indra, offered for sale[6] and in another place, a sage declared that he would not sell his image of Indra even for a hundred or a thousand or ten thousand cows.[7] The Bharata's army going out for war is described as impelled by the desire to win the cows.[8] Indra sent his messenger Saramā to trace his stolen wealth, not gold or silver, but the cows.[9]

The pastoral Vedic people reportedly used gold as a medium of their transactions. In the Vedic literature also there are references to metal in general and *niṣka* and *suvarṇa* in particular, signifying metals of high value as unit of wealth and probably with definite weight. These are the first indication of the use of metal in terms of medium for transactions. In order to obviate the problems of accurate weight and right quality, stamping of the metal piece with the mark of a responsible authority evolved. In this way 'coins' came into existence.

TERMS USED FOR VALUABLES

Gold is referred to in the *Ṛgveda* in various forms. It is believed that it was collected in its natural form—'gold dust'—from the beds of the Punjab rivers. It was kept and stored in small bags. We have a reference in the *Ṛgveda* that the ten bags of gold dust, which King Devodāsa offered to his priest along with ten horses, ten garments and ten lumps of gold,[10] were probably ten small bags of gold dust. We have another reference that for safety, gold was stored in troves or pots (*kalaśaṁ nikhāta*) and buried underground.[11] However, gold dust in its natural form is difficult to handle and, therefore, it was melted down and transformed into ingots, which are referred to as *hiraṇyapiṇḍas* in the hymn.[12] It was also used to make different ornaments, used both by men and women. Some of these ornaments are mentioned in the *Ṛgveda* – *Khādi*[13]—used on the arms and the anklets, *Rukma*[14]—sometimes worn on the chest and sometimes on the arms and *Karṇaśobhā*[15]—another word mentioned in the *Ṛgveda*. The word *niṣka* was also referred to as an ornament in a passage where Rudra is described wearing *niṣka* in his *Viśvarūpa* form.[16] Later on, *niṣka* denoted a gold coin equal to four *suvarṇas* or 576 grains.[17]

WHAT IS NIṢKA? AN ORNAMENT? A COIN?

The earliest references of the use of *niṣka* (see above) are found in the *Ṛgveda*.[18] *Niṣka* has been used in different contexts in the *Ṛgveda*. It signified "a gold ornament worn on the neck" as is clear by the epithet *niṣkagrīvā*[19], "having a gold ornament on the neck".[20] The *Atharvaveda* also referred to hundred gold *niṣkas*.[21] It was also used in the sense of a metallic weight equivalent to 320 *rattīs* or 560 grains.[22] Moreover, *niṣkas* were used as a medium of exchange.[23] It is difficult to ascertain the gradual evolution and meaning of the term *niṣka*.[24] However, *niṣka* in the early period referred to neck ornament and hence it would not be unreasonable to infer that this neck ornament was used as a medium of exchange in lieu of cow or grains.[25] Rings were used in Egypt as a medium of exchange. Barker pointed out that: "It is practically certain that the precious metals also have come into use as money only because they were first used as ornaments."[26] Later on, in place of ornament, a piece of metal equivalent to the standard weight was weighed out at each transaction. Chakrabortty suggests that the next step in this regard would be to have ingots of various shapes, preferably globular as in Egypt and Babylon.[27] The Aryans were advanced in the Vedic period to this stage. However, this is a matter of further study as stated by Chakrabortty—"Whether they had these ingots stamped with symbols testifying as to the weight and the purity of the metal, i.e. whether they had succeeded in evolving coins at that early stage."[28] Thomas was the first to draw attention to the passage in the *Ṛgveda* where "a singer celebrates the receipt of a hundred *niṣkas* and a hundred steeds; he could hardly require the *niṣkas* merely for purposes of personal adornment".[29] In another passage, a *Ṛṣi* praises a king for giving him forty thousand *niṣkas* on one occasion and eight thousand on another.[30] These references, though suggest that *niṣkas* served as a sort of currency, however, are yet to be decided. Bhandarkar is tempted to suggest that *niṣkas* were probably the coined money in *Ṛgvedic* age: "Were they coined money or unstamped bullion currency?"[31] He refers to the Hymn 33 of *Maṅdala* II of *Ṛgveda* in support of his view that the *niṣkas* were coined money in the *Ṛgveda*, which was not accepted by the scholars and against the traditional interpretation of Sāyaṇa.[32] Chakrabortty disagrees with the views of Bhandarkar that the *niṣka* were the coined money in the *Ṛgvedic* age and remarked that: "It presupposes the existence of *Niṣka* coins – to the *Niṣka* ornaments; and the fact that there is a reference to ten *Hiraṇyapiṇḍas* (gold globules) cannot establish the proposition that the *Niṣkas* were coins as distinguished from pure bullion because there is no knowing that these were of standard weight equal to each other and circulated as mediums of exchange."[33] He further argued that no gold coin of the punch-marked type had been discovered in India,[34] while thousands of silver and copper coins had been unearthed in various parts of the country,[35] and hence would be better to suspend Bhandarkar's suggestion at this point.[36]

OTHER TERMS FOR METALLIC CURRENCY

Niṣka, an ornament which was used as a medium of exchange in the *Ṛgvedic* period, gradually gave place to a metallic weight equivalent to that particular ornament. Later on, the metallic currency appears to refer to weight. In the *Taittirīya Saṁhitā*[37] and the *Śatapatha Brāhmaṇa*,[38] *Śatamāna* is referred to as a sacrificial fee to the priest. We have another term—*Kṛṣṇala*—in *Taittirīya Brāhmaṇa*[39] and also the *Śatamāna* and both referred to metallic currency as well as the definite weights.[40] *Śatamāna* is based upon a particular unit of weight, i.e. *māna,* and this measure we come across also in the *Ṛgveda*.[41] Das opined that the *māna* refers to a particular kind of coin and it may so far be accepted as a unit of metallic weight, which was used for exchange purposes.[42] Chakrabortty points out that nothing definite can be proposed, as to what the unit really was? He says, "We may be tempted to identify it with *Kṛṣṇala* which is also referred to in the *Brāmhaṇas*, as the traditional unit of measurement as regards metals. But the weight of a Śatamāna as given in Manu is 320 *Kṛṣṇala* and the unit of the Śatamāna, i.e. 1/100 of the metallic weight is not one *Kṛṣṇala* and we are thus faced with an insuperable difficulty, if we try to establish Śatamāna weight on the *Kṛṣṇala* basis."[43] The actual difference in weight of different *niṣkas* had to be taken into account and, therefore, necessity arose for standardisation of the *niṣka*, which should conform to a definite weight of metal. A lump of metal that was one *niṣka* in weight replaced the necklace as a medium of exchange and gradually there appeared lumps of metals, weighing a *niṣka* or its sub-multiples. A *niṣka* of gold is equated to 320 *rattīs*, which was also the weight of a *śatamāna* of silver. It is suggested that a *kṛṣṇala* weighs as much as a *Guñjā* berry and a *śatamāna*, a hundred times the standard weight taken of *kṛṣṇala* of *raktikā*.[44] The smaller unit of weight is *rattī* or *raktikā*. This is also the standard weight for a *niṣka*, equivalent to 320 *rattīs* and a *suvarṇa* 80 *rattīs*, as given by Manu.[45] According to *Śatapatha Brāhmaṇa* and *Taittirīya Saṁhitā*, *śatamāna* was of gold.[46] Manu and Yājñavalkya referred to *śatamāna* as a silver coin only, whereas, in the Brāhmaṇa period, it was also a gold coin.[47]

The references of *suvarṇa* and *śatamāna* alongside *hiraṇya* in two passages of the *Śatapatha Brāmhaṇa*[48] clearly differentiate between the term *hiraṇya* and the two metallic pieces by weight—*suvarṇa* and *śatamāna*. Though Chakrabortty ascribed "– the Śatamāna to the earlier age going back at least to the *Ṛgveda* and *Suvarṇa* to the Brāhmaṇa period when *Kṛṣṇala* became the recognized unit of measurement".[49] He further stated that though it is difficult to determine the unit referred to in the *śatamāna* of the Brāhmaṇa period and the *māna* of the *Ṛgveda*, we have reason to identify it with the *Māñjāḍi*.[50] The *suvarṇa* equals in weight to a *kārṣāpaṇa*[51] and a silver coin of the same weight is referred to in the *Arthaśāstra* of Kauṭilya. The bent-bars of silver, which are stamped to be of high antiquity, approximate in weight to the *kārṣāpaṇa*.[52]

The term *kārṣa*, equal to 80 *kṛṣṇalas or rattīs*,[53] applied to all the metals used for the monetary purpose—when it was adopted for gold, it was called *suvarṇa*—the gold. Generally, *kārṣāpaṇa* was restricted to copper, though in course of time, it became the generic expression for standard coins in all the metals—gold, silver, copper or lead.[54] *Kārṣāpaṇa* weight is practically connected with copper and particularly when it came out as coin, which was believed to be of copper in later literature.[55] Bhandarkar mentioned: "Manu takes kārṣāpaṇa to denote paṇa or coined money which is *tamrika*, i.e. made of copper and is *karṣika*, i.e., one *kārṣa* in weight."[56] He further quoted Thomas: "The Samanta-pasadika while explaining a verse from Patimokkha says about kārṣāpaṇa as follows: *'tattha kahapano ti: Suvanna mayo va rupiyamayo va pakatiko va'*, here *kārṣāpaṇa* is either made of gold, or that made of silver, or the ordinary one."[57] Chakrabortty disagrees with Bhandarkar and suggests that *kārṣāpaṇa* as the unit of copper and not as a coin must be dated back at least to the Brāhmaṇa period.[58] As pointed out by Rapson: "Manu seems to imply that the term was properly applied to the copper *paṇa* weighing a *kārṣa*"—*kārṣāpaṇas tu vijñeyas tāmrikaḥ Kārṣikaḥ paṇaḥ,*[59] while Nārada as quoted in the *Vāçaspatya*, states that the silver kārṣāpaṇa was current in the 'South'-*Kārṣāpaṇo dakṣiṇasyām diśi raupyah pravarttate*[60]— the silver *kārṣāpaṇa* was widely used in south India. *Kārṣāpaṇas* of silver were of 32 *rattīs* based on the *māna* unit and *kārṣāpaṇas* of copper were of 80 *rattīs* or *raktikās* of copper in weight.[61] As also referred to by Manu, *kārṣa* is equal to 80 *rattīs*.[62] The word *kārṣāpaṇa* is derived from *kārṣa*, the weight, and *āpaṇa*, 'custom or use', that is 'the current *kārṣa*'.[63]

KĀRṢĀPAṆA: THE EARLIEST COINAGE

Metal gradually began to serve as the medium of exchange, at first by weight and later as coinage. On the evolution of coinage, the *kārṣāpaṇa* became the medium of exchange, which was used as a general term for coins of copper, silver or even for gold of particular weight. Silver gradually became the main medium of transaction in trade. The earliest coins of ancient India are commonly known as punch-marked coins, as the devices were impressed on the face of the coin by separate punches. A large number of symbols are found stamped on these coins,[64] corresponding to *signati argenti* of the Greek historian Quintius Curtius. The mode of manufacturing these coins was first to get ready a hammered sheet, which was then cut into strips and then cut into pieces of desired weight, which was adjusted by clipping the corners when necessary.[65] This is merely a descriptive appellation from the system of manufacture of these coins. Pāṇini clearly referred in *Sūtra* (V, 2.120) *rūpād āhata-praśaṁsayour-yap* ... where he says, "the word *rūpya (rūpa)* is in the sense of 'struck' (*āhata*), derived from *rūpa*, 'form, nape' with the *taddhita* affix, *ya*, here implying possession; when *rupya* would literally mean 'struck (money), having a form'.[66] The *Aṣṭādhyāyī* has cited that the metallic pieces, stamped (*āhata*) with symbols (*rūpa*)—*ahataṁ rūpam asya rūpyo.....rūpyaṁ kārshāpaṇam*—was the genuine example.[67] According to the *kāśikā,* the symbols on such coins were struck with a punch—*nighatikaśā-tāḍanādritā*.[68] A metal piece, as long as it was not stamped (*ayantrita*), had no use as currency.[69] The earliest coins have no definite shape and were mostly unifaced, do not bear any inscription in contemporary language and almost always struck in silver. These coins are generally marked with 1-5 symbols (and, rarely, with none). These symbols exemplifying animals, hills, trees and human figures followed a definite pattern on the coins, which were always issued under some royal authority.

USE OF SYMBOLS

Symbols have been used by human beings from time immemorial. Since prehistoric days people stamp symbols (*lakṣaṇas*) on the ears of their animals as a mark of their ownership, or even the owners were known by these marks struck on their animals—*paśunāṁ svāmi viśeṣa saṁbandha jñapanārtham, kāśikā*.[70] Some such marks have been cited by Pāṇini in two *sūtras*—*karaṇo varṇa lakṣaṇāt*। (VI, 2.11) and *karṇe lakṣaṇa syāviṣṭā pañça-maṇi-bhinna-chinna-chidra-sruvaḥ svastikasya*। (VI, 3.115).[71] The *Atharvaveda* (VI,141.2-3;XII,4-6), the *Maitrāyaṇī Saṁhitā* (IV, 2-9), the *Mānava Śrauta Sūtra* (IX, 5.1-3) and the *Vārāha Śraut Sūtra-Gonāmika Pariśiṣṭa* have variously listed the practice of branding animals with different types of marks. In the *Mahābhārata* (Vanaparva, 239/4, 240/4), there is a mention of branding cows or calves. The *Arthaśāstra* (II, 29) similarly talks of information to *Gavādhyakṣa* to keep an account of the branded cows.[72] Agrawala referred the system of branding cattle, while dealing with the material available in the *Aṣṭādhyāyī* of Pāṇini and noted some 27 marks (*lakṣaṇa*) from the Vedic literature, which were used for branding the cattles.[73] He pointed out that a few of them resemble the basic symbols seen on the punch-marked coins.[74]

He mentioned a mark called *viṣṭa-karṇi,* which also occurs in the *Maitrāyaṇī Saṁhitā.* Therein, it is referred to as a mark of the cows of Agastya. The mark on the cows of Jamadagini had a lute and *Vaśiṣta*, a stake.[75] The *Aṣṭa-karṇi* of Pāṇini is also found in the *Ṛgveda* (X, 62.7) that is translated as "having sign for (the number) 8 marked on the ear".[76] According to Goldstukar, the use of numerals 5 and 8 as marks of cattle shows that writing was also popularly known during those days.[77] These are some of the common symbols found on the cows and on the punch-marked coins as well:

Sruva () *Svastika* (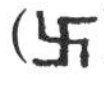) *Aṅkuśa* () *Kuṅḍala* ()

Pliha (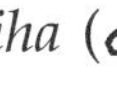) *Bāṇa* () *Mithuna* ()[78]

Cows were one of the main forms of money in prehistoric days. With the evolution of the metallic pieces, it was found necessary to impress some stamps or marks of authority guaranteeing value and the metal contents of the metallic pieces. Stamping of these pieces with marks of recognised authority began for this purpose. State was such an authority that could guarantee the stamped pieces. It is more likely that the earliest coins bore symbols of such authority. However, in the absence of any positive evidence revealing the true nature of the punch-marked symbols, it is difficult to forward a foolproof theory of their identification. However, it can be presumed that a coin has a specific symbol, found generally on all the coins reported from the area. These constant symbols with minor variations can be called state symbols.[79]

PUNCHING OF COINS: SOVEREIGN FUNCTION OR PRIVATE SIGNATURE

The earliest coins of ancient India had the symbols punched on them. A careful study of these symbols provides some clues in identifying the mint, State or locality. But the paucity of records as to the actual provenance of the various types hinders attainment of well-founded conclusions on the subject. The question whether the initiative in producing the coins was taken by the merchants or silversmiths in the interest of commercial trade, or the state, which was responsible for what the society including the merchants, is widely debated by scholars. It can be fairly assumed that punch-marked coinage was privately issued by guilds and silversmiths with the permission of the ruling powers. The marks on the obverse seem to have been impressed by the different bankers, during circulation, and the reverse marks may be regarded as the sign of approval by the controlling authority. Cunningham considered 'several of these symbols' of the punch-marked coins, generally believed to be the earliest Indian issues, as private marks of the money changers.[80] Smith held the view that all the punch-marked coins were the specimens of private issues. According to him, "It is clear that the punch-marked coinage was a private coinage issued by the guilds and silversmiths with the permission of the ruling powers and the numerous obverse punches seem to have been impressed by the different moneyers through whose hands the pieces passed, and the reverse marks may be regarded as the sign of approval by the controlling authority".[81] Rapson is also of the opinion that: "The symbols punched on to the coins on the obverse are supposed to be the marks of money changers, while those on the reverse which are invariably fewer in number and somewhat different in character, may possibly denote the locality in which these coins were issued."[82] Walsh has conclusively proved that Indian punch-marked coins were not "a purely private issues", nor were the marks on them "impressed by the different moneyers through whose hands the pieces passed," (Smith, 133) but a public coinage issued under the authority of the State.[83] Walsh's opinion, which was well attested, contradicts the views shared by Smith (*IMC*, 133) and Rapson (*AI*, 151). Hoards of silver punch-marked coins studied by Spooner,[84] Bhandarkar[85] and Walsh[86] have suggested that the majority of the coins were issued by a central authority, i.e. State, though number of coins have been discovered which appear to be the private issues. According to Allan, "It is true that the punches on them were put on separately and not by a single die, but they were stamped at the same time by the authority issuing them and not from time to time by the private individuals."[87] Banerjea also agrees with Allan's views that: "There is little doubt that the marks were those of a central authority that guaranteed the genuineness of the metal and the correctness of the weight."[88] Chakrabortty (1931) regarded Smith's opinion and says that "practically all or the majority of the coins examined by Smith are surely state issues; but at the same time he maintained that originally the punch-marked coins were being issued by private bankers whose symbols have not yet been recognised by scholars owing to insufficient study and to the fact that the private issues were mostly called back and given the new impress when the state entered into the field."[89] Chakrabortty (2004) quotes the conclusion that Macdonald arrived at from an examination of Athenian coins, "that two wealthy citizens had to supervise the issue of silver for a year, and to meet the cost of mintage out of their own resources, the state supplying the raw material" and observes that this may very well be applied to the conditions in India prior to the state control of currency.[90] He opines that when the coinage was brought under the state control, sometimes the state had to act "through the experts, the private bankers, who were specially fitted for the work and were in a position to help the state with their expert knowledge."[91] Sircar asserted that the minting of coins in ancient India does not seem to have been different from that prevalent in the days of the Peshwas when "coinage was not a monopoly either private or the governmental."[92] In his opinion, there is some evidence to show that all the punch-marked coins were not issued by the state, that some of them were certainly 'issued by guilds and silversmiths' as Smith suggested and that such private coins were in circulation side by side with those issued by the states.[93] A passage in *Viśuddhimagga* of Buddhaghoṣa leads Sircar to suggest that it did not speak anything regarding the symbol of a royal authority manufacturing a particular coin, i.e. *kārṣāpaṇa* and is not associated with the state. He pointed out that the *kārṣāpaṇas* were manufactured by private moneyers with or without the permission of the ruling authority.[94] Buddhaghoṣa describes how a lot of coins (*kārṣāpaṇa*) lying on the tray of a money-changer or goldsmith would strike a child, a rustic and another goldsmith or money-changer differently. The child would simply know that the coins have many symbols (*çitra-viçitra*) on them; and are oblong, square or round in shape; but not those that could be used like gems. The rustic would know all what the child knows and also know that the coins could be used by us for enjoyment like gems, but he would not know the difference among them, which one is genuine or forged. But the goldsmith or money-changer would be in a position to ascertain, after looking at the coins and examining them in various ways, such as hearing the sound they make when they struck, smelling and licking them and taking them in his hand, and he would understand which mint-master (*Āçārya / Āçāriya*) made them and at which village, town, hill or river-bank they were made. The word *āçārya* has been used here in the sense of 'a master goldsmith'.[95] Sircar suggests that:

> The passage makes it abundantly clear that the symbols on the kārṣāpaṇas or punch-marked coins only indicated the place where in a particular piece was made and the goldsmith who made it. Apparently, none of the symbols indicated the State in which it was made or by which it was issued. If there was any such symbol, that would have naturally been regarded as far more important than the others and Buddhaghoṣa could have hardly failed to mention it. Thus the manufacture of the kārṣāpaṇas, referred to in the *Viśuddhimagga* passage, was not directly associated with the state. Of course whether the goldsmith manufactured them with the state's permission is not known from it. The minting of coins from villages is also interesting information supplied by the passage.[96]

Sircar also refers to Bhandarkar, based on the passage, that "every place which issued coinage in ancient India had its own distinguishing mark stamped on it, by observing which the shroff of that age could at once tell from which place any particular coin came."[97]

After studying the two hoards (Patna—107 coins and Gorho-Ghat, Bhagalpur Distt.—58 coins), Walsh found that some of the symbols appeared on the coin "in certain constant and regular groups on the obverse", although other varying symbols were added to these constant groups.[98] Nevertheless, he agreed with Spooner's opinion that the symbols "were not private marks of individual moneyers impressed haphazard from time to time,"[99] through whose hands the coins passed. The symbols stamped "on the obverse represent the issuing authority and constitute the coinage, while those on the reverse would appear to be the private marks of the moneyers through whose hands the coins passed, or in some cases, to indicate locality."[100] Walsh[101] closely examined 58 Gorho-Ghat coins and found those are of three distinct types and appear to belong to three different states. His conclusion tallies with the views of Spooner,[102] who studied 61 punch-marked coins found from Peshawar, Bhandarkar[103] examined 83 punch-marked coins discovered from Besnagar. Such conclusions are also supported by the statement of *Arthaśāstra* that in the Mauryan period, though the coinage was a royal prerogative,[104] sometimes the royal mint could be utilized by the *Naigamas* and *Janapadas.*[105] However, by the time of the Mauryas, we have definite records that the issue of coins was the function of the state under direct control, though some private individuals and different communities were allowed to have struck coins through the royal mints.[106]

HIERARCHY OF SYMBOLS

> It may be suggested, to account for a constant group of marks that one mark may represent state, one the reigning king, one the place where the coin was struck and perhaps one a religious mark recognising the presiding deity; also the master of the mint may have had his mark, which would fix his responsibility for the coin, and additional varying marks may have been those of the *saṅghas*, village, communities, in which the coin was current, affixed at the time the rupiya or the local tax on it was levied on its admission to circulation in that jurisdiction. And the various and unsystematic punches on the reverse would appear to have been the marks of private shroffs and moneyers through whose hands the coin passed in course of circulation.[107]

The marks on the reverse are of entirely different nature. They are less deeply punched and when they correspond to the marks on the obverse, are of a much smaller size. The reverse marks may very well be the marks of the merchants through whose hands the coins passed. But there are certain exceptions; for example, the coins of Taxila, Eran, Banaras, Ujjain, etc. have their peculiar mint marks on the reverse. Nevertheless, the opinion of Rapson may be accepted that the reverse marks are "the official stamp of the local authority and indicate that the coins had been tested and sanctioned within area."[108] The smaller reverse marks that are similar to the marks on the obverse are perhaps "the official marks of the testing authority"[109] and are smaller in order to differentiate them from the original mint marks. Cunningham's suggestion that some of the marks on the reverse stand for the names of the moneyers concerned seems to be plausible.[110] It can be proposed that even if the punch-marked coinage owed its origin to private individuals in early times but in the Mauryan period, the coinage had definitely come under the State control.[111]

Numismatists and historians have known the early silver punch-marked coinage owing to their nomenclature. Made of silver, the punch-marked coins bear a recognized number of symbols of various types, which are punched individually. Their combinations present more than six hundred varieties depicting animate and inanimate objects. These coins are rectangular, circular and sometimes irregular in shape. These bear a group of five symbols on the obverse generally; these are now-a-days recognised as the Imperial Series.

THEORIES ON GENESIS AND DISSEMINATION

A number of coins found in India as early as the 19th century were soon recognised and reported as being the most ancient specimens extant. James Prinsep, for the first time, attracted the world's attention towards this subject. Cunningham recorded several finds of punch-marked coins from various parts of the country, illustrating only a few of them.[112] Later on, Thomas attempted a study of the symbols on punch-marked coins.[113] Theobald (1890) studied these coins and for the first time identified about 200 (277) symbols on these coins.[114] It was believed that the symbols on the coins were made haphazardly without any order or meaning. Spooner (1905) succeeded to establish that the punching of the symbols followed a definite scheme and some royal authorities issued these coins rather than it being 'private money', as had been suggested earlier.[115] A few years later (1913-14) Bhandarkar reached the conclusion after carefully studying some copper punch-marked coins found in excavations at Besnagar, Madhya Pradesh. He suggested that all these coins are the copper *kārśāpaṇas* forming the standard money.[116]

Walsh (1919) studied some hoards of silver punch-marked coins, found in various specified regions in Bihar. He introduced a scheme for the classification of these coins, into classes and varieties.[117] Further, during the course of the study of two hoards (1912 & 1924) discovered at Taxila on the Bhir mound, he was able to place the coins within specific classes and varieties as warranted by grouping of symbols.[118] Durga Prasad was able to distinguish several types of coins based on their weight, a factor which was previously unnoticed. He described the symbols in detail and drew attention towards many different types, with one to four symbols, particularly on the coins of Kosala *janapada*. Additionally, his comprehensive examination of the five symbols on the Imperial Series was a new approach that advanced the study of the subject.[119] Altekar has re-examined the various theories suggested by the scholars of the earlier mintages and established their Indian origin.[120] Sreenivas[121] and Chakrabartti[122] developed a new approach of study, based on fabrication, shape, size and thickness. Aravamuthan[123] studied the punching technique of symbols and showed that it differed in diverse types of coins according to their locality and period.

The earlier studies sparked in due course of time scholarly investigations into fabric, weight, metallurgy and area, period of circulation and ancient nomenclature of these coins. As a result, the study of these ancient coins until today remains a complex ongoing study.

Gupta (1950 onwards) took up the study of punch-marked coins for his doctoral research with the objective of making an integrated study of the coins from the hoards and stray finds housed in the museums all over the country (unpublished thesis, 1959). He based his studies on analyzing and classifying the symbols in a comprehensive, systematic manner thereby determining the sequence of different types and their historical implications. Gupta (*The Amaravati Hoard*, 1963) studied these coins in detail and assigned these coins to the six periods. Nevertheless, later he revised this classification and distributed these coins into seven series. Gupta and Hardaker (*Ancient Indian Silver Punchmarked Coins of the Magadha-Maurya Kārṣāpana Series*, 1985) classified these coins in a chronological order based on the symbols, the recurrence of the symbols in different series, and the historical association of the same in attempt to associate these coins with different dynasties.

The coins of Series I are mainly found in Magadha and Kasi and therefore predate Magadha's conquest of the north Indian plains, Kasi being an exception. The progress of this conquest is not accurately dated: it had begun by c. 546 BCE (Gupta—500 BCE) and Magadha was a dominant power by the end of the reign of Ajātaśatru, i.e. c. 462 BCE (Gupta—c. 460 BCE).[124]

The coins of the Golakpur hoard are the earliest, attributed to the Series I. These coins may be linked with the Bhabhua hoard,[125] which are of quite different weight standard. They suggest that they were current in Magadha, before the beginning of the Imperial Series. The first two symbols of the coins of the Imperial Series, known from the Golakpur hoard, are also seen on the coins of Bhabhua hoard, which suggests that the two series were issued in continuation. The two common symbols on these coins—the Sun and the six-armed symbol (with three arrows and three ovals)—are the constant symbols occurring on the Imperial Series. As such, the coins of the Golakpur hoard may be assigned to Series I.[126]

Coins of Series I may be attributed to Bimbisāra and Ajātaśatru (c. 546-462 BCE). It is believed that the coins of Series II were issued by the successors of Ajātaśatru. Kasi, originally an independent kingdom, was annexed into the Magadha empire during the period of Bimbisāra, but fell to the Kosala state during the time of Ajātaśatru, who later on succeeded to the throne and re-annexed Kasi into Magadha kingdom. Probably, after the annexation, the coins of Series I and Series II were issued in this area, which is evidenced by the discoveries of three hoards–Aurihar, Jaunpur and Rajghat, of Series II—in the area of ancient Kasi. These hoards are (i) the Aurihar hoard – (534 coins) - 404 in the State Museum Lucknow, 111 coins in the Patna Museum and 19 coins (Acc. nos. 548-566) in the collection of the Bharat Kala Bhavan, Banaras Hindu University, Varanasi; (ii) the Jaunpur hoard – (32 coins) – 5 coins in the College of Indology, now the Department of Ancient Indian History Culture and Archaeology, Banaras Hindu University, Varanasi; 20 coins in the State Museum Lucknow and 7 coins in the Bharat Kala Bhavan collection (Acc. nos. 234-240) and (iii) the Rajghat hoard; (*JNSI* (IX) 1) a few coins are preserved in the Prince of Wales Museum, now the Chhatrapati Shivaji Maharaj Vastu Sangrahalaya, Mumbai, of the Rajghat hoard. However, the exact contents of Rajghat hoard are not known. Three more coins are recorded in the collection of the Bharat Kala Bhavan as from Rajghat (Acc. nos. 482-484, year 1936) but it is difficult to say whether these are part of the same hoard. Gupta had studied these coins and reported their well-preserved condition.[127]

A few coins in these said hoards belonged to the varieties noticed on the coins of Golakpur hoard; all other coins belonged to varieties unknown there. This suggests that these hoards followed the coins of the Golakpur hoard. That these coins preceded the varieties not represented in these hoards is evident from the fact that a few coins of the present hoards are found in other hoards in extremely worn condition.[128]

Śiśunāga and his successors probably issued the coins of Series III. Śiśunāga came to the throne of Magadha in about 440 BCE. The Buddhist texts record that the fifth ruler of Magadha, after Ajātaśatru, was deposed by the people and his *amātya* Śiśunāga was placed on the throne. A large number of coins, which are earliest in the Series, attributed to Series III are found to be restruck over the coins originally belonging to Series I and Series II.[129] These double obverse/re-struck coins indicate that these were issued after some political upheaval. According to Gupta, this change of rule is reflected on the coins of Series III, where the symbols 'Hare with three taurines' and 'Palm tree' were used as distinct class-mark and group-mark, respectively.[130]

The Big Bhir mound (Taxila) contains 6 coins of Series I and 16 coins of Series II having the largest number of minute reverse marks and a number of double obverse coins; these are found in extremely worn condition.[131] These are the earliest coins in this hoard. Gupta distinguished these coins into two broad categories: (i) coins having animal symbols and (ii) coins with hill symbol as class mark; he identified them as the coins of Series III and Series IV, respectively. This concludes that the coins with animal symbols were in worn condition and belonged to Series III while those coins carrying hill symbols were either less worn or fresh in look, and belonged to Series IV. The Allahabad, Gorhoghat, Kauniankuttai and Mathura Museum hoards further confirm this conclusion. The coins of Series I – Series III are absent in the Gorhoghat, Kauniankuttai and Mathura Museum hoards (1954-55) – 100 coins; in Allahabad and Mathura Museum hoard (1952-53) – 172 coins and only one coin each of the Series III are known.[132]

The coins of Series IV may be attributed to the Naṅda dynasty, which had established their power over Magadha in c. 364 BCE and extended their empire far and wide in the country. That these coins belong to the period of Naṅda rulers is evident from the discovery of Bhir mound hoard, Taxila (1924), which contains the coins of Alexander the Great and Philip Arideaus (died- c. 317 BCE) almost in mint condition. This indicates that the hoard would have been deposited not before c. 317 BCE but also not much later than this period. In all likelihood, the hoard was buried during the war between Çandragupta Maurya and Seleucus. However, a number of punch-marked coins of Series IV along with a few coins of Series V are found in this hoard. The coins, which belong to Series V, almost in the mint condition, suggest that these were the coins of the latest Series and probably issued by Çandragupta Maurya. It may be assumed, the coins of Series IV are the earlier issues, may be attributed to the Naṅda rulers.[133] It appears that some of the varieties of Series V may have been issued during the period of Bindusāra, the son of Çandragupta.[134] The coins of Series V to VII might been issued by Çandragupta Maurya and his successors.

The Big Bhir mound hoard (1924) had a few coins with a class-mark 'Three-gate', almost in fresh condition and the heaviest among all in the hoard, presumably the latest in the hoard. As such they provide a link for the coins of Series V. The coins of Series V may be distinguished from those of Series I to Series IV and VI on the basis of Gokulavan hoard.[135] A large number of coins with 'Three-gate' symbol are found in this hoard, not noticed in any hoard mentioned above. The Ramna hoard has the coins from Series I to Series IV and includes only one coin known from the Gokulavan hoard. The coins of Series V have the symbols: bull with taurines or fishes within rectangle, stag before a tree in railing, etc. Such coins are also known from the Phetagram hoard along with a few worn coins of Series IV. This discovery has further confirmed this conclusion.[136]

Bindusāra was succeeded by his son Aśoka in about c. 272 BCE, who ruled until c. 232 BCE. The coins of his reign are attributed to Series VI. This recognition is based on the identification of the class-mark 'Three-arched hill with crescent' as royal insignia of the Mauryas.[137] This symbol is also found on the archaeological objects, dated to the Mauryan period.[138] However, the small Bhir mound hoard (1912) contains exclusively the coins of this period. They are all found in mint condition, and must have been issued during the later Mauryan period. This hoard also includes a coin of Diodotus II (c. 248 BCE).[139] It appears that the hoard was deposited towards or soon after the death of Aśoka. It is thus logical to assume that the coins of Series VI could be attributed to Aśoka and his successors.

The coins of Series VII are attributed to the Mauryas and their successors (c. 210-190 BCE). The small size coins, specimens of high standard of workmanship, are clearly distinguished by the absence of sun and six-armed symbols, which are a regular feature of the coins of Series I–VI. Coins attributed to Series VII with bold reverse marks and the symbols indicate a contemporaneity with Series VIb.[140]

NOTES AND REFERENCES

1. *AB*, V. XXII. 9.
2. *The Cambridge History of India* (1922) (I), 99.
3. *AB*, VII, XXXIII, 6; VIII, XXXVIII, 7; VIII, XXXIX, 8.
4. *AB*, XXXIX. 8.
5. *Gohila Grihya Sūtra, Hiranyakesi Grihya Sūtra*. S.K. Chakrabortty (2004), *Indian Numismatics*, 10.
6. *RV*, IV.24.10. - *ka imaṁ daśabhimarmendraṁ krīṇāti dhenubhiḥ* ||
7. *RV*, VIII.1.5. - *mahe çana tvāṁ adrivaḥ parā śulkāya deyām* | *na sahastrāya nāyutāya vajarivo na śatāya śatāmagha* ||
8. *RV*, III. 33.11. - *yadaṅga tvāṁ bharatāḥ saṅtareyuḥ gavyangrāma iṣitaḥ indrajūtaḥ* ||
9. *RV*, X.108. - *imā gāvaḥ sarame yā tvamaiçchaḥ* ||
   The wealth of the Vedic Indians was the cows, which also served as the medium of exchange. However, in all the ancient societies, the medium of transaction was the same. In the Homeric age, the wealth of the Greek society consisted mostly of flocks of cattle. If the *Ṛgveda* refers to an Indra image worth ten cows, the *Illiad* refers to 'Arms worth a hundred kine for arms worth nine.' The Vedic Indians purchased Soma for cows, the Homeric Greeks bought wine for cattle and hide. Early laws of Rome and Draco assessed the fines, not in coins, but in oxen. A.S. Altekar (1953), "Early History of Coinage in Ancient India" *JNSI*, XV (I), 9.
10. *RV*,VI.47.23.- *daśāśvān* daśa *kośāndaśa vastrādhibhojanā*| *daśo hirṇyapiṇḍān divodāsādasāniṣam*||
11. *RV*, I.117.12. - *hirṇyasyeva kalaśaṁ nikhātaṁ* | *udūhathurdarśame aśvināhani* ||
12. *RV*, VI.47.23.
13. *RV*, V.54.11. - *aṅseṣu va riṣṭayaḥ patsu khādayo vkṣaḥsu rukmā maruto ratheśubhāḥ* || I. 168-3 - *hasteṣu khādiḥ kṛtiśva saṅdadhe* ||
14. *RV*, I.166.10. - *bhūrīṇi bhadrā naryeṣu bāhuṣu vakṣaḥsu rukmā rabhasāso añjayaḥ* || VIII. 20.1. - *rukmāso adhi bāhuṣu* ||
15. *RV*, VIII.78.8.- *uta naḥ karṇaśobhanā purūṇi dhṛṣṇu ābhara* | *tvaṁ hi śṛṇavase vaso* ||
16. *RV*, II.33.10. *ahaṙn vibharṣi sāyakāni dhanvāhrnniṣkaṁ yajataṁ viśvarūpam* ||
17. A.S. Altekar (1953), 11.
18. *RV*, II.33.10; VIII.47.15.
19. *RV*, V.19-3.
20. *The Vedic Index*, quoted by A.C. Das (1925), *The Ṛgvedic Culture*, 140.
21. *AV*, XX, 131.6. - *śataṁ niṣkā hiraṇyāyḥ*.
22. D.R. Bhandarkar (1921), *AIN*, 61 & 212.
23. A.C. Das (1925), 140; *AV*, XX.127.3; *Lat. Sra. Sut.*, IX.9.20; *SB*, XI.4.1.1.8; *Gop. Br.*, I.3.6; *The Vedic Index*, 454-55.
24. S.K. Chakrabortty (2004), *Indian Numismatics*, 10. "It is a difficult question to determine the gradual evolution in the meaning of this word. The interpretation, rather the supposition which is put forward, that the idea of a neck-ornament connected with the *Niṣka* is derived from the practice of stringing together in the form of necklace a number of *Niṣka* coins, is taking for granted what has got to be proved. That the ornaments came into use much earlier than coins among the peoples of antiquity goes without saying."
25. "The *Niṣka*, originally a gold ornament, was also at this time a unit of value; and the cow as a unit was probably in course of supersession." *The Cambridge History of India* (I), 137; S.K. Chakrabortty (2004), 11, fn. 19.
26. D.A. Barker (1913), "It is practically certain that the precious metals, also, have come into use as money only because they were first used as ornaments." *The Theory of Money* (The Cambridge Manuals of Science and Literature); S.K. Chakrabortty (2004), fn. 19.
27. S.K. Chakrabortty (2004), 11.
28. *Ibid.*

29. *RV*, I.126.2; D.R. Bhandarkar (1921), Quoted from *The Vedic Index*.
30. *RV*, VIII. 2.41; "....we may reasonably infer that the *Niṣka* of the Vedas had even then, attained so much of a definite and unvarying form, and partial fashioning, as to be suitable for decorative purposes in its current shape, - a deduction which would further imply that the piece itself was understood or admitted to be of a constant and uniform make, and that, in effect, carried its description in its name." E. Thomas, (1874), The Ancient Indian Weights, 34; S.K. Chakrabortty (2004), 11, fn. 21; A.C. Das (1925), 140.
31. D.R. Bhandarkar (1921), *AIN*, 65.
32. *Ibid.*, 67 69, S.K. Chakrabortty (2004), 11.
33. S.K. Chakrabortty (2004), 11.
34. E.J. Rapson (1898), *Indian Coins*, 2.
35. R.B. Whitehead (1922), "The Pre-Mohamadan Coinage of North-Western India", *Numismatic Notes and Monographs* (No. 13), 42; E. Thomas (1874), 43.
36. S.K. Chakrabortty (2004), 11.
37. *TS*, I.7.6.2; I.2.7.7; D.R. Bhandarkar (1921), 58.
38. *SB*, V.5.5.16; D.R. Bhandarkar (1921), 57.
39. *TB*, I.3.6.7; D.R. Bhandarkar (1921), 60.
40. S.K. Chakrabortty (2004), 11.
41. *Ibid.*, 12.
42. A.C. Das (1925), 140.
43. S.K. Chakrabortty (2004), 12.
44. Keith (1922), *The Cambridge History of India*, (I) 137. "The red-and-black berry of the Guñjā plant *(Abrus precatorius* or wild liquorice), which is usually called *Rati* or *Raktika*, the 'Red' and is also known as *Kriṣṇala*, or the 'Black' from a black spot at one end." A. Cunningham (1891), *CAI*, 44.
45. D.R. Bhandarkar (1921), *AIN*, 212.
46. *SB*, XII.2.3.20; *TS*, III.2.6.3; II.5: D.R. Bhandarkar (1921), *AIN*, 57.
47. D.R. Bhandarkar (1921), 180.
48. *SB*, XII.7.2.13; XIII.2.3.2.
49. S.K. Chakrabortty (2004), 13, fn. 38. "But it is difficult to define the objects or the meaning of 'one hundred measures' (Śatamāna), which do not fit in with either of the national metric schemes" – E. Thomas (1874), 12.
50. S.K. Chakrabortty (2004), 13, 46. *Mañjāḍi*, as being the earliest used as a measure of weight. It is a seed of the Adenanthera pavonina, a tree common in most parts of India and Eastern Archipelago. Sir Walter Elliot (1886), *Coins of Southern India*, 47-48; The weight of *Mañjāḍi* – to be a little less than 5-7 grains as suggested by Cunningham and somewhat higher than Elliot's own average weight 4.8 grains, *CAI*, 48; Chakrabortty purposes " ...We can be practically sure that the *Mañjāḍi would* approximate to 5-6 grains and 100 *Mañjāḍi* would give us the Śatamāna of 560 grains or a little less—the closest approximation that we can have, dependent upon the size and the condition of the *Mañjāḍi* seeds." C.D. Chatterjee identifies 'Mañjeṭṭhī', a synonym of the *Māṣaka* according to *Vinayatthamanñjusā,* with the South Indian *Mañjāḍi*. 'Some Numismatic Data in Pali Literature' (1931), *Buddhist Studies*, B.C. Law (ed.), Calcutta, quoted by D.C. Sircar (1968), *SIC*, 101.
51. D.R. Bhandarkar (1921), 90.
52. V.A. Smith (1906), *Catalogue of the Coins in the Indian Museum* (I) (*IMC*), 136; S.K. Chakrabortty (2004), 14.
53. *Ibid.*, 86. *Kārṣa* – "the seed of the Belleric Myrobolan (*Terminalia Bellerica)* known as *amslaka* or *Kārṣa-phala*, that is the *Kārṣa* fruit", A. Cunningham (1891), *CAI*, 45.
54. D.R. Bhandarkar (1921), *AIN*, 77 and 142. "The fact that in latter times kārṣāpaṇa referred to coins in all three metals, clearly points out that the copper coin was the earliest and the most used; and in course of time it became the generic expression for coins; for example in later times the *Rājataraṅgaṇī* speaks of 'dinaras of gold, silver and copper'," [D.R. Bhandarkar (1921) 204] though there is no doubt that 'Dinaras' were nothing but originally the Denarius aureus of the Romans which were imported to India in large numbers when brisk trade was going on between Rome and India. Kārṣāpaṇa was the metallic weight

for copper and gradually of gold and silver, and when its weight system gave place to coins, the honour must properly belong in the first instance to copper. It extended to silver but was based upon a different standard that was peculiar to the precious metals at an earlier age, but not to gold as the total absence of early gold coins would lead us to infer (1921, 91, 94) fn.50. "The copper coins have not the same longevity as the silver and gold coins and this would explain the comparative scarcity of copper kārṣāpaṇas and its subdivisions." E. Thomas (1874), 53.

55. *Ibid.*, 86.
56. *Ibid.*, 81.
57. *Ibid.*; E. Thomas (1874), 42, fn. 2,
58. S.K. Chakrabortty (2004), 13.
59. E.J. Rapson (1908), *Catalogue of Indian Coins—The Andhra Dynasty*, Clxxix, fn. 1.
60. *Ibid.*, fn. 2. "In Southern India the smallest denomination of the copper currency was the *Kāsu*" and "it has also the peneral significance of money, wealth and likewise of coin, as *pon-kāsu* = gold coin, *vella-kāsu* = silver coin, *semba*-(or red) *kāsu*=copper coin." (Sir Walter Elliot, *Coins of Southern India*, 59); Ellis identified *Kāsu* with the Sanskrit *kārṣa*, and they are probably both derived from the same original source.; according to the law books "a *karṣa* or eighty ratis (*raktikas*) of copper is called pana or *karṣa* paṇa." Afterwards it came to be restricted to "a weight of gold or silver equal to 180 grains troy." Quoted by S.K. Chakrabortty (2004), 49.
61. S.K. Chakrabortty (2004), 97.
62. *Laws of Manu*, VIII, 136.
63. A. Cunningham (1891), *CAI*, 45.
64. W. Theobald (1890 & 1901); Durga Prasad (1934), "Classification and Significance of the Symbols on the Silver Punch-marked Coins of Ancient India", *NS* (1934) XLV, 9ff.
65. V.A. Smith (1906), *IMC* (I) 134.
66. V.S. Agrawala (1953), "Ancient Coins as Known to Pāṇini", 37-38; S.K. Chakrabortty (2004), 15; *Numismata Orientalia* (I) E. Thomas (1874), 39, fn. 3.
67. V.S. Agrawala (1953), 37.
68. *Ibid.*, 38.
69. *Uttararādhyayana Sūtra*, XX, 42; V.S. Agrawala (1953), 38.
70. V.S. Agrawala (1969), *Pāṇini-Kālīna Bhāratavarṣa*, (*Hindi*), 217-19.
71. *Ibid.*, 217.
72. *Ibid.*, 217-18.
73. *Ibid.*, 219.
74. *Ibid.*, 218.
75. *Ibid.*, *The Vedic Index*, I.46.
76. V.S. Agrawala (1969), 217-219.
77. *Ibid.*, 218, fn. 2; Goldstuker, *Pāṇini, His Place in Saṅsakṛta Literature*, (*Pāṇini, Saṅskṛta Sāhitya Meṅ Unakā Sthāna* (*Hindi*), 44.
78. Dilip Rajgor (2001), *Punch-marked Coins of Early Historic India*, 17.
79. V.S. Agrawala (1969), 218.
80. A. Cunningham (1891), *CAI*, 58; *Early Indian Indigenous Coins*, D.C. Sircar (ed.), 50-58.
81. V.A. Smith (1906), *IMC*, 133.
82. E.J. Rapson (1914), *Ancient India*, 151 (fn. 65). Although he formerly believed (*Indian Coins*, 3) that the symbols were stamped on the coins from time to time by the authority responsible for their correctness and purity.
83. *JRAS* (1924), 176.
84. *ASIAR* (1905-06), 153.
85. *ASIAR* (1913-14), 220; (1921), 98-99.
86. *MASI*, No.19; *JRAS* (1924), 175.
87. J. Allan (1936), *BMC* (Introduction), xix.

88. *The Comprehensive History of India* (II), Sastri (ed.), 777.
89. S.K. Chakrabortty (1931), *A Study of Ancient Indian Numismatics*, 129 -30.
90. S.K. Chakrabortty (2004), 90; G. Macdonald (1916), The Evolution of Coinage (The Cambridge Manuals of Science and Literature), 18.
91. S.K. Chakrabortty (2004), 90.
92. D.C. Sircar (1968), *SIC*, 105.
93. *Ibid.*, 102.
94. *Ibid.*
95. *Ibid.*
96. *Ibid.*, 103, fn. 1.
97. *Ibid.*, 96; D.R. Bhandarkar (1921), *AIN*, 126, 128.
98. *JRAS* (1924), 176.
99. *ASIAR* (1905-06), 153.
100. *JRAS* (1924), 177. On Patna coins, two marks i.e. discus (Sun), the *chakra*, and the *chatras* (umbrella) bound together in the middle in the form of a circle (six-armed) and the other two marks are found associated with the majority of the coins while the fifth mark is of a more irregular character and vary more frequently. Gorhoghat coins are of three distinct types and appear to belong to three different areas and governments.
101. *JRAS* (1924), 181.
102. Quoted by E.H.C. Walsh, *JRAS* (1924), 179.
103. D.R. Bhandarkar (1921), *AIN*, 98.
104. *Ibid.*, 156; *Kauṭilya Arthaśāstra*, which recommends state's authority of minting coins, as is apparent from the specification of the duties of mint master *(Lakṣaṇādhyakṣa)*, contains a passage which appears to allow the private agencies to issue coins provided they got their coins minted in the royal mint. The passage prescribes a fine of twenty-five *paṇas* if a coin was minted from outside. According to Kangle, "the 25 *paṇas* thus work out as a licensing fee for making coins elsewhere than in a royal mint." *Kauṭilya Arthaśāstra*, R.P. Kangle (ed.), (1963), (II), 125.
105. S.K. Chakrabortty (2004), 92.
106. *Ibid.*
107. *JRAS* (1924), 184.
108. E.J. Rapson (1895), *JRAS*, 874, referred to by Walsh; S.K. Chakrabortty (2004), 92.
109. *JRAS* (1924), 189.
110. Cunningham has suggested that some of the marks on the reverse stand for the names of the moneyers concerned seem to be plausible. He would make the symbol of the Sun to stand "for Surya Das, a 'Snake' for Nagasena, and Elephant for Gajasingh; Bir Deo might have had a solider; Gopal a Bull, and Khajur Varma a "Palm tree (Khajur)." Some of these symbols "may be the emblems of their castes or clans." A. Cunningham (1891), *CAI*, 58.
111. S.K. Chakrabortty (2004), 93.
112. *ASR* (I) 276; (II) 264, 288; (VI) 197-216; (X) 4, 46; (XI) 25, 38, 53-54; (XIII) 40, 145, 164; (XVI) 4, 46; (XVII) 89; (XX) 37; (XXII) 99, 114.
113. *JASB*, 'Ancient Indian Weights', 58; (XXXII), 256; (XXXIX), 14-51.
114. *JASB* (LIX), 182; (LXIII), 73.
115. *ASIAR* (1905-06), 150-55.
116. *ASIAR* (1913-14), 210.
117. *JBORS* (II), 463-94; (II) 172; (XXVI), 169.
118. *MASI*, No. 59 (1939), "Two Hoards of Silver Punch-marked Coins Found in Bhir mound at Taxila", 31-35.
119. *NS* (XLV), 5-60; (XLVII), 51-92.
120. A.S. Altekar (1953), (I), 1-16.
121. *ARANDH* (1920-30), 29-66.

122. *JBBRAS* (XX), *NS*, 83ff.
123. *ASIAR* (1925-26), 15ff; *JNSI* (1948), "Notes on Punch-marked Purāṇas" (X), 1-16.
124. P.L. Gupta & T.R. Hardaker (1985), *Ancient Indian Silver Punch-marked Coins of the Magadha-Maurya Kārshāpana Series* (*AISPMC*), 31.
125. P.L. Gupta (1966), "Chronology of the Punch-marked Coins", *The Chronology of the Punch-marked Coins*, 13; *JNSI* (1947) (IX), 1; P.L. Gupta (1963), *Amaravati Hoard of Silver Punch-marked Coins*, (*Am*), 147.
126. P.L. Gupta (1966), 12; *JBORS* (V), 16ff.
127. P.L. Gupta (1966), 13.
128. *Ibid.*
129. P.L. Gupta (1963), *Am*, 150.
130. *Ibid.*, 151; P.L. Gupta (1966), 17.
131. *JNSI*, XII, 136ff.
132. P.L. Gupta (1966), 13-14.
133. P.L. Gupta (1966), 17; (1963), *Am*, 151.
134. P.L. Gupta (1966), 17.
135. *JNSI*, XXI, 115.
136. P.L. Gupta (1966), 14.
137. *NS*, XLVII, 61-62; P.L. Gupta (1963), *Am*, 151-52.
138. P.L. Gupta (1963), *Am*, 151; P.L. Gupta (1966), 18.
139. "Punch-marked Coins from Taxila", 31ff.
140. P.L. Gupta & T.R. Hardaker (1985), *AISPMC*, 9, 30. Table 7.

2

Terminology

The texts of the later Vedic period (c. 800-500 BCE)—the Saṁhitās, the Brāhmaṇas and the Upaniṣads—allude to the gold and silver pieces. These are the sources enlightening us about the earliest coinage of the period. They do not refer to any copper currency. The terms *kārṣa* or *paṇa,* which denoted copper currency in later times, were probably unknown to the Vedic literature. The golden *niṣka* is mentioned in both the Brāhmaṇas[1] and the Upaniṣads,[2] though rarely. We also find the term *pāda* in the Upaniṣads, which is probably used for either coins or metallic pieces, probably of gold, of some uniform weight. Silver (*rajata*) *niṣka* is mentioned only once in the *Pañçaviṁśa Brāhmaṇa* (XVII.I.14). The class of coins that finds frequent mention in ancient Indian epigraphs and literary sources is the *kārṣāpaṇa. Kārṣāpaṇa,* also known as *Purāṇa* or *Dharaṇa,* the name of punch-marked coins was in circulation throughout India. Many hoards of silver punch-marked coins have been located in sites all over the country. Its widespread availability suggests that it was a standard medium of exchange from about the 6th century BCE. The class of coins which finds frequent mention in ancient epigraphs and literary sources is the *kārṣāpaṇa.*

The term *kārṣāpaṇa* is derived from *kārṣa,* which was regarded as equal to 80 *rattīs* or 146.4 grains. The literary records speak of *kārṣāpaṇa* of gold, silver and copper. Gold *kārṣāpaṇa* was also known as *suvarṇa* or *niṣka,* whereas the silver one was called *purāṇa* or *dharaṇa* and likewise the copper *kārṣāpaṇa* as *paṇa.* The reference to gold *kārṣāpaṇa* was probably for *niṣka*—an ornament of a particular weight. The references to gold *kārṣāpaṇa* or *suvarṇa* or *niṣka* frequently appear in early literature and, in all probability, it was either a piece of metal or ornament of some uniform weight. Silver *kārśāpaṇa—purāṇa* or *dharaṇa*—is, however, variously mentioned as per its weight.[3]

There are some passages in the Vedas, indicating *niṣka* as gold currency. The *Ṛgveda* relates how sage Kakśīvat obtained ten horses and ten or hundred *niṣkas* from King Bhavya—*śataṁ rājño nāthamānasya niṣkān | śatamaśvān prathatānsadya ādam* (I.126.2). In the *Atharvaveda,* a poet is said to describe how his generous royal patron gave him a hundred *niṣkas,* ten necklaces, three hundred horses and ten thousand cows—*ya iṣāya māmahe śataṁ niṣkāndaśa srajaḥ | trīṇi śatāni arvatā sahasrā daśa gonām* (XX.127.3). Altekar suggests that it is possible that the number of *niṣkas*—ten, twenty and thirty—which were received by the priest may have been used for necklaces (*niṣkas*) for personal adornment.[4] In this context he also mentions that the Vedic poets never refer to the gifts in numerical terms (such as 10 or 100)—*khādis* or *rukmas* or *karṇaśobhanas*—as these were only ornaments. They only refer to *niṣkas* and *hirṇayapiṇḍas* as articles received in large numbers.[5] Therefore, the latter—*niṣkas* and *hirṇayapiṇḍas*—must have constituted a category by themselves as different from *khādis* or *rukmas* or *karṇaśobhanas*.[6] When poets pray for ten *hiraṇayapiṇḍas* or hundred *niṣkas*, they apparently ask for 10 or 100 articles of uniform size, value and weight. Gold *niṣkas* and *piṇḍas* are mentioned only in description of gifts. Most of the gifts—usually cows and gold *niṣkas*—were offered only by a few as a rare favour. *Niṣkas* are not mentioned in connection with any sale or trade. Economic transactions of the Vedic age were done through barter. Cows are occasionally mentioned as means of exchange. *Niṣkas* or *hiraṇayapiṇḍas* of definite weight and value; were however not issued under any authority of the state, nor did they bear any symbols or inscriptions guaranteeing their respective values. Price is always mentioned in terms of cows and never in terms of *niṣkas* and hence, the *niṣkas* cannot be taken as coins.[7]

As to gifts, poets sometimes pray for or receive ten jars full of gold—*daśa te kalaśānāṁ hiraṇyānāmadhīmahi* I *bhūridā asi Vṛttrahan* I (*RV*, IV.32.12)—or ten lumps of gold—*daśo hiraṇyapiṇḍān divodāsādasāniṣam* I (*RV*, IV.47.23)—or ten or hundred *niṣkas* of gold—*śataṁ rājño nāthamānasya niṣkān śatamaśvān prayatān sadya ādam*I (I.126.2). In a passage in the *Ṛgveda*, a request is made to Indra to bestow upon the devotee *manās* of gold along with cows and horses—*ā no bhara vyañjanaṁ gāmaśvabhabhyañjayam* I *saçā manā hiraṇiaya* I (VIII.78.2). In another passage, *māna* stands for desire—*dhīrāsaḥ puṣtimavahanmanāyai* (IV.33.2)—*ā yasminmanā havīṁṣyagnau* (X.6.3). Altekar suggests, "It is possible to interpret this passage also as praying that Indra should come with cows and horses along with a golden, i.e. favourable thought for the devotee."[8] He found it very probable that the poet here refers to a golden coin or piece, especially since we know that *minā* was used by the Babylonians to denote a lump or ingot of silver or gold of a definite weight, before regular currency was introduced.[9] *Māna* as a term for weight or a gold coin (currency) is unknown to the later Sanskrit literature, and this passage would perhaps show that the Vedic Indians knew the golden *minās* of Babylonia, probably pronounced as *manās* for which they pray Indra to bring with him. *Manā* as regular weight was foreign to the Vedic India, as is evidenced by the disappearance of the word in later times and literature.[10]

The later Saṁhitās, Brāhmaṇas and Upaniṣads, however, supply scanty information about the coinage/currency of the age. They do not refer to any silver or copper currency. Silver *niṣka* is mentioned only once in the *Pañçaviṁśa Brāhmaṇa* (XVII.I.14) in connection with *vrātya*, used as an ornament.[11] Golden *niṣka* is mentioned both in the Brāhmaṇas and Upaniṣads, though rarely. In the *Gopatha Brāhmaṇa*, Uddālaka Āruṇi, a scholar of Kuru-Panchala, travelled through the land with a *niṣka* attached to his banner, which he was willing to offer to the one who would defeat him in a debate—*Uddālako Āruṇiḥ udīçyānvṛtau dhāvayāñçakāra* I *tasya niṣka upāhito babhūva* I *upavādādvibhyato yo mā brāhmaṇoūçāna upavadiṣyati, tasmā etaṁ pradāsyāmīti* (I.3.16). In a passage of the *Chāndogya Upaniṣad*, a king offers to a sage his daughter along with a thousand cows, a horse and a chariot, a village and a single *niṣka*—*taṁ ha abhyuvāda raikva idaṁ sahastraṁ gavāmayaṁ niṣkoayamasvatarīratha iyaṁ jāyā ayaṁ grāmo yasminnāsse anu eva mā bhagavaḥ śādhi* (IV.7.ff).These are the only instances of the use of *niṣka* in the later Vedic literature. However, these do not conform to its use as coin at the time. Weight was also not mentioned to suggest its value. It appears that it is either an ornament (necklace) or a piece of gold.[12]

The *Śrauta Sūtra* of Kātyāyana, the Buddhist *Tripīṭakas,* the *Aṣṭādhyāyī* of Pāṇini, and also the *Jātakas* give vivid and reliable information about the coinage of the period—c. 550-300 BCE. This information is corroborated by archaeological evidence as well. In the earlier period, gold currencies were mentioned only in connection with gifts from the generous kings and in this period they are referred to in connection with ordinary transactions. The description in the *Vinaya-piṭaka* of Anāthapiṅḍaka (VI.3.1), covering the entire area of the Jetavana with the gold coins is a legendary reference. Pāṇini in the *Aṣṭādhyāyī* refers to several instances of transactions concluded for one, two or three *niṣkas.* The terms *naiṣkikam, dvinaiṣkikam* and *trinaiṣkikam* denoted articles purchased for one, two and three *niṣkas,* respectively—*dvitripūrvānniṣkāt* (V.I.30). The wealth of a person was also expressed in *niṣkas—śata-sahasrāntāçça niṣkāt* (V.2.119). The terms *naiṣka-śatika* and *naiṣka-sahasrika* denoted persons worth a hundred or a thousand *niṣkas.* The terms used by Pāṇini in the *sūtras—Tena krītam* (V.I.37) 'purchased with that' and *Tad-arhati* (V.I.63) 'worth that'—indicate the transaction system of that period. Pāṇini refers to *niṣka* in three *sūtras*—(i) *Asamāse niṣkādibhyaḥ* (V.I.20) *naiṣkika* means 'purchased for' or 'worth' one *niṣka.* Similarly, *pāṇika, pādika* and *māṣika* denoted an article purchased for these coins; (ii) *Dvi-tri-pūrvān-niṣkāt* (V.I.30) refers to the transaction concluded for two or three *niṣkas*—for that terms used are *dvi-niṣkam; dvi-naiṣkikam; tri-niṣkam, tri-naiṣkikam;* and *(iii) śata-sahastrāntāçça niṣkāt* (V.2.119)—one hundred *niṣkas* was called *naiṣka-śatika,* and one thousand *niṣkas* was called *naiṣka-sahasrika.*[13] The *Mahābhārata* also refers to these two categories of wealth—100 and 1000 *niṣkas—śatena niṣkagaṇitaṁ sahastreṇa ça saṁmitam* (*Anuśāsanaparva,* 13.43). Patañjali uses the terms *niṣkadhana* and *śataniṣkadhana*—owner of 1 *niṣka* or 100 *niṣka* pieces—*nahi niṣkadhanaḥ śataniṣkadhanen spardhate* ǀ (V.3.55).[14] The *Kāśikā* adds that it was not usual to add the word *suvarṇa* before *niṣka,* evidently because *niṣka* was already understood as a gold coin—*suvarṇa-niṣka-śatam asy-āst-īty-anabhidhānān-na bhavati* (V.2.119). The *Śatapatha Brāhmaṇa* (XI.4.1.8) states that the *niṣka* offered by Uddālaka Āruṇi to his learned rival Svaidāyana was of gold. The *Kuhaka Jātaka* refers to a farmer bringing his hundred *niṣkas* of gold to an ascetic (*suvaṇṇanikkhasantaṁ* ǀ 89, *Pāli Jātaka,* I.375). The *Vessantara Jātaka* also mentions a thousand *niṣkas* as the amount for the redemption of Vessantara's son (*Pāli Jātaka,* VI.546). *Juṇha Jātaka* refers that a Brāhmaṇa requests to Juṇha Kumāra for more than 1000 *niṣkas—paro sahssañça suvaṇṇanikkhe* ǀ *Pāli Jātaka,* IV.97).[15] According to the *Mahābhārata,* the unit of wealth was reckoned at 108 *niṣkas* of gold—*sāṣṭaṁ śataṁ suvarṇānaṁ niṣkam āhurdhanaṁ tathā* ǀ *Droṇaparva,* (67.10).

The *Bṛhadāraṇyaka Upaniṣad* describes the *Bahudakṣiṇā* sacrifice performed by King Janaka. He offered a tempting prize to the winner—a thousand cows, each having ten *pādas* attached to its horn, that is twenty thousand *pādas,—sa ha gavāṁ sahastramavarurodha daśa daśa pādā eakaikasyāḥ śṛaṅgayorābaddhā babhūvuḥ* (III.1.1-2). It can be suggested that the *pādas* attached to the horns were the metallic pieces of uniform weight, probably of gold.[16] Bhandarkar suggests that 20,000 *pādas* offered by King Janaka were gold coins related to *niṣka.*[17] He also pointed out that this *pāda* coin was the same as Pāṇini referred to in the *sūtra* (V.1.34)—*paṇa-pāda-māṣa-śatādyat.*[18] According to Agrawala, King Janaka offered gold pieces called *pāda* as *dakṣiṇā,* but it is not certain if *pāda* mentioned in the Pāṇini *sūtra* (V.1.34) was a token coin of the gold *niṣka.* He suggests, "From its juxtaposition with *paṇa,* it may as well have been related to the silver *kārṣāpaṇa,* in which Series it is mentioned by Kauṭilya" (*Arthaśāstra,* II.12, 84).[19]Altekar asserted that the *pādas* offered by King Janaka might have been the quarters of silver *śatamānas,* especially because they are known to have been current in Kosala, as shown by the coins of Paila hoard. But we may well presume that a generous king like Janaka would have disdained to offer silver coins as silver was regarded inauspicious; it was believed to have sprung from the tears of Rudra, and hence its use was generally avoided in sacred transactions.[20]

The submultiple *pāda* coin of *niṣka*, however, did exist, as Patañjali referred to it as *pan-niṣka* and *pāda-niṣka—niṣke çopasaṅkhyānaṁ kartavyam* (*Sūtra*, VI.3.56; III.163).[21] Manu defines *niṣka* as equal in weight to four *suvarṇas* or 320 *rattīs—çatuḥ-suvarṇikoniṣkaḥ* (VIII.137). This would make a *pāda-niṣka* synonymous with *suvarṇa*. Since no specimen of either *suvarṇa* or *niṣka* has yet come to light, it is not possible to indicate their relative weights.[22] The *Kāśikā* instances *niṣka mālā*, a necklace of *niṣkas*, as indicative of wealth in coins—*hiraṇya-parimāṇa* । VI.2.55).[23]

The Brāhmaṇas and the Upaniṣads of the period refer to *niṣkas, suvarṇas, śatamānas*, and *pādas*, which were all gold pieces, probably of well known value and weight. Pāṇini also speaks in a *sūtra* (V.I.34)—*paṇa-pāda-māṣa-śatādyat*, clearly indicating submultiples of *niṣka*. The term *pāda*, as it suggests, is a quarter of the weight of either *niṣka* or *suvarṇa* or *śatamāna*.[24] These are mentioned in connection as *dakṣiṇā* to the priests given on special occasions by kings and rich persons. They might have also been used in other transactions, where rare articles of high value were exchanged. It is worth mentioning that while *niṣkas* were primarily mentioned as ornaments and then used as objects of gift, the *śatamānas* and *pādas* were never referred to as ornaments; these were always mentioned as objects of gift or as honoraria to scholars and priests.[25]

Pāṇini does not name *suvarṇa* as coin, but the same is implied in *sūtra* (VI. 2. 55) *Hiraṇyaparimāṇaṁ dhane*, which refers to a person's wealth in terms of coined gold – *dvi – suvarṇa-dhanam* (*Kāśikā*). Kauṭilya refers to *suvarṇa* as a weight equal to one *kārṣa* or 80 *Guñjās* = 150 grains. Agrawala suggests, "From such examples as – *dvi-survaṇa-dhana, adhyardha-suvarṇa, dvi-suvarṇa* (purchased for 1& 1/2 or 2 *suvarṇas*) (V.I.29) it confirms that *suvarṇa* was a coin with a weight of one *kārṣa*."[26]

When *hiraṇya* and *suvarṇa* are found associated together in *Jātakas* and *Arthaśāstra*, the *suvarṇa* denotes bullion and *hiraṇya* coined gold.[27] In the *Sāma Jātaka*, both the words *'hiraññya suvaṇṇa'* are found together—*dāsakammakādayo pi hiraññyasuvaṇṇāgīni gahetvā palāyiṅsu* । (540, *Pāli Jātaka*,VI.69). R. Shamasastry in his translation of Kauṭlya's *Arthaśāstra* has described the term *hiraṇyasuvarṇam*—to mean *hiraṇya* as *pāsā* (bar gold) and *suvarṇa* as coined gold coin.[28] In another *sūtra*, Pāṇini refers to pieces of gold equal to a standard weight—*jātarūpebhyaḥ parimāṇe* । IV.3.153).[29] Such pieces were gold coins, as shown by their example cited in the *Kāśikā* – *hāṭako niṣkaḥ - hāṭakaṁ kārṣāpaṇam* - gold pieces or coins called *niṣka* and *kārṣāpaṇa* struck to a standard weight.[30] Gold *kārṣāpaṇas* are not mentioned elsewhere. Agrawala has pointed out that the reference of *Kāśikā* is either to *suvarṇa* coins of one *kārṣa* weight, or to the much later gold coins of Kedāra Kuṣānas, also referred to by it as Kedāra (V.2.120).[31]

Though the literary references indicate the existence of a gold currency, yet no such specimens of any denominations are found in any hoard. However, Patañjali is probably indicating gold currency when he refers to the purchase of two *droṇa* measures of corn with gold sufficient for it—*dvi-droṇena hiraṇyena dhānyaṁ krīṇāti* ।, or to the purchase of one thousand horses with amount of gold sufficient for—*sahasra-parimāṇaṁ sāhasram; sāhasreṇa hiraṇyena aśvān krīṇāti* । (*Bhāṣya*, II.3.18; I.452).

Specimens of silver and copper *māṣas* are known but *suvarṇa-māṣaka* occurs only in literature. The *māṣa* coin in gold and in copper weighed 5 *rattīs* and, in silver, coins are of 2 *rattīs* as mentioned in the *Arthaśāstra*.[32] The *Udaya Jātaka* mentions a golden dish with *suvarṇa–māṣakas*, a silver dish with the same, and a copper dish with silver *kārṣāpaṇas*, the three being mentioned in order of their diminishing value—*suvaṇṇa-māsakas pūrāṁ ekaṁ suvaṇṇa- pātiṁ* । (458; *Pāli*

Jātaka, IV.106-8). A silver *kārṣāpaṇa* – 32 *rattīs*, was thus lower in value than gold *māṣaka* – 5 *rattīs*—and gold and silver were related in the ratio of about one to seven in the period of *Jātakas*.[33]

During the period of later Saṁhitās and Brāhmaṇas, we come across another gold piece, *śatamāna*, described as golden. *Śatamāna* is described as *vṛtta* in one passage; it suggests it was round in shape and probably, weighed a hundred *kṛṣṇalas* or *rattīs*, i.e. 175 grains as stated by the commentator Karka—*vṛttākārau raktikāśatamānau*.[34] Later on, Manu and Yājñavalkya refer to *śatamāna* as a silver coin weighing 160 *māṣakas* or 10 *dharaṇas*—*dve kṛṣṇale samadharte vijñeyo raupya-māṣakaḥ* I *te ṣoaśa syād = dharaṇaṁ purāṇañ =ç= aiva rājatam* II... *Dharaṇāni daśa jñeyaḥ śatamānas=tu rājataḥ* II *Manusmṛti* (VIII.135-37) – *dve kṛṣṇale rūpya-māṣo dharaṇaṁ śoḍaṣ=aiva te* I *śatamānaṁ tu daśabhir=dharaṇaiḥ palameva tu* II *Yājñavalkyasmṛti* (I.364-65). According to the *Vedic Index* (II, 152), *māna* is referred to as a measure of weight equivalent to a *kṛṣṇala* or *raktikā* in Vedic literature. Thus the weight of *śatamāna* taken literally would be 100 *rattīs*. During the celebration of *Rājasūya* sacrifice at the time of royal coronation, two *śatamānas* were fastened to the wheels of the royal chariot, participating in race, which were later offered as *dakṣiṇā* to the priest—*sa rathavāhanasya dakṣiṇamanvanuṣya śatamānau pravṛttau ābadhnati* I *tasyaitasya karmaṇa etāveva śatamānau pravṛttau dakṣiṇā* II *tau brahmaṇe dadāti* II (V.4.3.24-26). In two other passages in the *Śatapatha Brāhmaṇa* (I.7.6.2; XII.4.2.10), *śatamana* is recommended as a *dakṣiṇā* to the priest. It was believed to insure a life of hundred years to the sacrificer.[35]

Śatamāna, which was referred to in the earlier period as golden, continued to be used in this age also. The *Śrauta Sūtra* of Kātyāyana speaks of hundred gold *śatamānas*, while describing the *Aśvamedha* sacrifice—*śatamānaṁ dakṣiṇā sauvarṇaṁ* (XVI.30)—but later on refers to silver *śatamāna* at one place—*dvadaśakapālānnirvapati bhinnataṅttrān śatamānadakṣiṇān madhyamasya rājataḥ savitre prasavittre*.....I (XVI.45). It shows that around the 6th century BCE, which is generally taken to be the time of the *Śrauta Sūtra*, silver *śatamāna* weighing 100 *rattīs* or 175 grains or 10.6 grams had come into vogue.[36] Altekar supports the suggestion of Agrawala "that the Bent-bar coins in silver which have this weight, correspond to the silver *śatamāna*; especially since the archaeological evidence shows that they were in vogue as early as c. 400 BC".[37]

The *Aṣṭādhyāyī* of Pāṇini (V.I.27) and the *Śrauta Sūtra* of Kātyāyana (XVI. 181-3) contain references to a coin *śatamāna*, but Buddhist texts remain silent. Manu (VIII.136-7) and Yājñavalkya (I.364-5) also refer to *śatamāna* of 320 grains as silver coin. However, Altekar suggests that it was probably a currency for account and not an actual coin in use.[38] The term *śatamāna* is also referred to in the *sūtra* - *śatamāna-viṁśatikasahastravasanādaṇ* I (V.I.27). Pāṇini observed that an article purchased for one *śatamāna* was called *śatamānena krītaṁ śātamānam* I (V.I.27).[39] Neither Pāṇini nor the Saṁhitas ever mentioned *śatamāna* as an ornament; it is always referred to as an object of gift or as a means of exchange or sale. Probably the weight was hundred *raktikās* = 175 grains as its name indicates. *Śatamāna* is also mentioned by Kātyāyana (c. 4th century BCE) but as a gold coin (XX.2.6) it seems to have gone out of vogue in later times.[40] However, there is reference in Kātyāyana's *Śrauta Sūtra* of *suvarṇa* (gold) (*śatamānaṁ dakṣiṇā sauvarṇam* I XX.2.6) and *rājata* (silver) *śatamāna*—*dvādaśa kapālannirvapati bhinnataṅtrān śatamānadakṣiṇān, madhyanasya rājataḥ* II (XX.1.22).

Agrawala suggests on the basis of the *Śatapatha Brāhmaṇa*—*tasya trīṇi śatamānāni hiraṇyāni dakṣiṇā* (V.5.5.16); - *hiraṇyaṁ dakṣiṇā suvarṇaṁ śatamāṇam tasyoktam* (VIII.2.3.2)—that *śatamāna* was a gold coin. Agrawala has also suggested the existence of silver *śatamāna* on the testimony of the *Śatapatha Brāhmaṇa*. He says that in the *Śatapatha Brāhmaṇa*, it is stated: "Gold and silver will be the fee for the sake of variety to correspond to the manifold form of the deity, and that *dakṣiṇā* will be *śatamāna,* since a human being lives for one hundred years."—*rajataṁ hiraṇyaṁ dakṣiṇā nānārūpatayā śatamānaṁ bhavati śatāyurvai puruṣaḥ*। (XIII.2.3.2).[41] This gives a definite reference to a silver *śatamāna* coin of 100 parts, i.e. 100 *rattīs'* weight. Manu refers to silver *śatamāna* as equal to ten *dharaṇas* or 320 *rattīs* in weight (VIII, 137). However, no actual specimen of a silver punch-marked coin conforms to weight of 560 grains.[42] Sircar disagrees with Agrawala's view and suggests, "To be a mere speculation unsupported by any evidence worth the name."[43] Chakrabortty says that the *śatamāna* was a metallic currency, but not actually a coin in the real sense of the term, which is also supported by Sircar: "*Śatamāna* was essentially a metal weight and not a coin in the real sense of the term."[44] Bhandarkar drew attention of scholars to the mention of a coin called *śatamāna* in Kātyāyana's *Śrauta Sūtra* (XV. 181-83), the *Aṣṭādhyāyī* of Pāṇini, Kātyāyana's *vārttika* on Pāṇini (V.I.29); the *Śatapatha Brāhmaṇa* (V.4.3.24 and 26; V.5.516; XII.7.2.13; XIII.2.3.2); the *Taittirīya Brāhmaṇa* (I.7.6.2; I.2.7.3) and the *Vājasaneyi Saṁhitā* (III.2.3; II.3. 11.5).[45] He refers *śatamāna* in the sense of a gold coin and not a silver one. He quoted the following passages from the *Śathapatha Brāhmaṇa*—(i) *suvarṇaṁ hiraṇyaṁ bhavati rūpasya = ev = āvaruddhai śatamānaṁ bhavati śat-āyur–vai puruṣaḥ;* (ii) *hiraṇyaṁ dakṣiṇā suvarṇaṁ śatamānaṁ tasy = oktam,* and observed "it will be seen that here *suvarṇa* is associated with *śatamāna,* and both are called *hiraṇya* or gold."[46] He also pointed out that Sāyaṇa in his commentary on the *Śatapatha* passage explains *śatamāna* as a round plate weighing one hundred *mānas* and takes *māna* to indicate a *rattī*. Sāyaṇa's interpretation of *śatamāna* involves two suggestions: (i) that it was a plate, and (ii) it weighed 100 *rattīs*.[47] As per one of the suggestions of Sāyaṇa, Bhandarkar concedes, "Śatamāna may, however, have been one hundred *mānas* or *guñjā* berries (*ratīs*) in weight as explained by Sāyaṇa."[48] Sircar points out the above statements of Sāyaṇa forming a part of his fantastic interpretation of *śatamana* is the 'evidence' in favour of the coin or metal currency called *śatamāna* being 100 *rattīs* in weight.[49] Kātyāyana mentions *śatamāna* in *vārttika-suvarṇa-śatamānayor = upasaṅkhyānam,* (*Bhāṣya* on V.1.29 - *adhyardha-śatamānam, dvi-śatamānam*) to regularize such formations as *adhyardha-śatamānam dvi-śatamānam,* purchased for one-and-a-half or two *śatamānas,* which suggests that the *śatamāna* was a current coin up to the time of Kātyāyana.[50]

Shastri refers a much earlier reference to the silver *śatamāna* in the *Maitrāyaṇī Saṁhitā* of the *Yajurveda*.[51] He has assigned hoary antiquity to *śatamāna* as a veritable coin on the basis of a reference in the *Maitrāyaṇī Saṁhitā—sauryaṁ ghṛte çaruṁ nirvateñ śuklānāṁ vṛhīnāṁ brahmavarçasa- kāmaḥ śatamāno rukmo rajato'dhastāt syāç śatamāno rukmo harita upariṣṭādih vā asā āditya āsīt* । (II.2.2).[52] Maheshawari Prasad[53] has, however, compared the above passage to the authority of *Bhāradvāja Śrauta Sūtra* (XI.5.19-20) as follows: *dvau rukmau rajata suvarṇau* । *śatamānau bhavataḥ* । only to suggest how two pieces of gold and silver respectively figured in a liturgical procedure and any interpretation of the reference to suggest existence of coinage would be erroneous.

The term *kṛṣṇala* is found in *Taittirīya, Maitrāyaṇī* and *Kathaka Saṁhitās* and in the *Taittirīya Brāhmaṇa*.[54] The *Taittirīya Brāhmaṇa* mentions that one *kṛṣṇala* (*rattī*) was given to each participant in a chariot race at the time of a *Rājasūya* sacrifice as a reward for his services—*kṛṣṇala kṛṣṇala vājasṛdabhyaḥ prayaçṣhati* (I.3.6.7). *Kṛṣṇala* everywhere figures as weight and never as the name of a coin. Altekar suggested that "side by side with *niṣkas, śatamānas* and *suvarṇas* of well-defined weights, gold bars also circulated from which little bits were taken out and given by scale and weight."[55] There is no reference of silver or copper currency in this period. *Niṣkas, suvarṇas, śatamānas* or even *pādas* are nowhere mentioned in connection with the price of common articles.

The other silver denominations of *kārṣāpaṇa* found expression extensively in the contemporary literature. It is worth mentioning here that the *Jātakas* invariably refer to the name of the contemporary current coins as *kahāpaṇa*. The *Aṣṭādhyāyī* uses both the terms *kārṣāpaṇa* (V.I.29) and *paṇa* (V.I.34), whereas the *Arthaśāstra* (II.12,84) mentions only *paṇa* several times. Kātyāyana records one more name for *kārṣāpaṇa*, i.e. *prati*, an article purchased for one *kārṣāpaṇa* being called *pratika-kārṣāpaṇad vā pratiśça* I (V.I.25; II,347). It is also mentioned in the *Mahābhārata*—*pratikaṁ ça śataṁ vṛddhyā dadāsy-ṛṇam anugraham* I 'a relief loan at 1 p. c. interest' (*Sabhāparva*, 5.68). The Nasik cave inscription of Uśavadāta also records 1 *pratika* interest on 2000 and 3/4 *paḍika* on 1000 *kārṣāpaṇas*.[56] *Prati* was a much later name for *kārṣāpaṇa*. Agrawala identified the term *prati* as *kārṣāpaṇa*.[57]

The *Aṣṭādhyāyī* of Pāṇini refers to *kārṣāpaṇa*, in *sūtra* (V.1.29) *vibhāṣā kārṣāpaṇasahasrābhyām*, regulating the forms *adhyardha-kārṣāpaṇam, dvi-kārṣāpaṇam*, purchased of one-and-a-half or two *kārṣāpaṇa* coins, which was the standard medium of exchange from about 6th century BCE.[58] The references to the purchase of articles for one or the other of these suggests that the coins played a vital role in the commercial dealings as early as the time of Pāṇini. The same tradition was followed in the *Jātaka*, Kauṭlya's *Arthaśāstra* and in the *Mahābhāṣya* of Patañjali.[59]

The word *kārṣāpaṇa* is unknown in the Saṁhitās or Brāhmaṇa literature, excepting once in *Samavidhāna Brāhmaṇa* (III.7.9). In the *Ārhīya* section of *Aṣṭādhyāyī* (V.I.19-37), Pāṇini refers to the *kārṣāpaṇa* and its various subdivisions like, *ardha-kārṣāpaṇa, pāda-kārṣāpaṇa, dvimāṣa*, one-eighth *kārṣāpaṇa* (*dvimāṣaka*) and a *māṣa* or one-sixteenth *kārṣāpaṇa*, as standard silver coins of the period.[60] Pāṇini mentions 1/2 as *ardha-kārṣāpaṇa* or *bhāga* (V.I.48) *ardha-śabdo rūpakārdhasya rūhih, Kāśikā* and *bhāga* (V.I.49) *bhāgād yaç ça; bhāgārdhāçça* I *bhāga-śabdo' pi rūpakārdhasya vāçakaḥ*; 1/4 as *pāda-kārṣāpaṇa*, 1/8 – *dvi-māṣa* and 1/16 as *māṣa* (V.I.34)—*paṇa-pāda-māṣa-śatādyat*.[61] Patañjali calls it *pādika*, paid as daily wages to a labourer—*karmakarāḥ kurvanti pādikam-ahar-lapsyāmaha iti* (I.3.72; I.293). Kauṭilya refers to *ardhapaṇa* and Kātyāyana to *ardha* as a coin by itself – *ṭiṭhana ardhāç-ça, Vārttika on* V.I.25, that which was purchased for an *ardha* was called *ardhia* or *ardhikī*.[62] Agrawala suggests that the terms *dvipadikā* and *tripadikā* implied in *sūtra*-V.4.1; *Bhāṣya*, III.362, for these names and *Kāśikā*, on VI.2.65; 3-10; VI.4.130 signifying two and three *pādas*, respectively, do not appear to be an independent coin, but the *pāda* coin preceded by *dvi* and *tri*.[63] The *Mahāsupina Jātaka* mentions *aḍḍha* and *pāda* as current coin names coming after *karṣāpaṇa* – *kahāpaṇ aḍḍha-pāda-māsa-rūpādini-* (I.340).

Agrawala says, "When Pāṇini refers to big sums (V.1.27; 29; 34) without specifying the name of the coin it is silver *kārṣāpaṇa* that is meant as being the standard coin of his time."[64] Buddhist *Tripiṭakas* frequently refer to the term *kahāpaṇa*, i.e. *kārṣāpaṇa*. The *Gaṅgamāla Jātaka* (3I 448) refers to the *kahāpaṇa* and the subdivisions of the *kahāpaṇa*: 1/2-*aḍḍha-kahāpaṇa*, 1/4-*pāda-kahāpaṇa*, 1/8-*dvi-māṣakās*, 1/16-*eka-māṣaka*, and 1/32-*aḍḍha-māṣka*.[65] These coins are named in connection with commercial transactions like sale and purchase and gifts to the Buddhist *Saṅgha*.[66] *Kahāpaṇa* and its subdivisions are mentioned in early *Pāli* texts, such as *Vinaya-piṭaka, Aṅguttara-nikāya* and *Majjhima-nikāya*. The *Vinaya-piṭaka* (VIII.1.1) refers to Ambapallī, a courtesan of Vaisali, who used to charge fifty *kahāpaṇas* for one night, while her rival Śālavatī of Rajgriha used to charge double this amount (V.I.1). The *Majjhima-nikāya* (III.168) mentions the king of Aṅga giving five hundred *kahāpaṇas* every day to the *saṅgha*—*pañça bho udena kahāpaṇasatāni*. The *Aṅguttara-nikāya* refers to a person falling into slavery on account of the debt of one or even half a *kahāpaṇa- idha bhikkhave ekaçço adhakahāpaṇenāpi bandhanaṁ nigaçchati kahāpaṇenāpi...kahāpaṇasatenāpi.*[67] The *Vinaya-piṭaka* (III.49) refers to a *pāda* or quarter *kahāpaṇa* also, when it prohibits the monks from accepting either a *pāda* or anything of the value of *pāda*. The references in the *Jātakas* also indicate that the *kahāpaṇa/kārṣāpaṇa* was then the standard coin of the country.[68]

In a *sūtra* (V.1.21), Pāṇini teaches a suffix after 100 (*śata*) without the name of a coin in the sense of 'purchased therewith'; in *sūtra* (V.1.27) after 1000 (*sahasra*) and in a *sūtra* (V.I.29) after 1500 – *adhyardha-sahasra* and 2000 – *dvi-sahasra*, etc. The *Gaṅgamāla Jātaka,* likewise, mentions big amounts of a hundred thousand and fifty thousand pieces where *kārṣāpaṇa* is understood. Similarly, the *Arthaśāstra* (368) refers, in descending order, to *śata-sahasra, pañçāśat-sahasra, daśa-sahasra, pañça-sahasra, sahasra, śata* and *viṁśati* coins, meant for silver *paṇas*, i.e. *kārṣāpaṇas* (I.69.5; I.404). Patañjali too mentions *śata-sahasra,* coins without using the name *kārśāpaṇa.* He refers to a hundred pairs of *śāris* "purchased for one hundred", i.e. 100 silver *kārṣāpaṇas*—· *śatena krītam śatyaṁ śaṭka-śatam.* On Pāṇini's *sūtra* (V.2.45) – *tad-asminn-adhikam-iti daśāntāḍ-ḍaḥ*, Patañjali definitely says that the phrase *ekādaśaṁ śatam* and *ekādaśaṁ sahasram* are understood to refer respectively to a hundred and a thousand *kārṣāpaṇas* exceeded by eleven. Agrawala further pointed out, "Similarly *śata* in *sūtra* (V.I.34) prefixed by *adhyardha, dvi* and *tri* would refer to 150, 200 and 300 *kārṣāpaṇas*, and the same standard coin is meant in *sūtra* (V.4.2) in such phrases as *dvi-śatikāṁ daṇḍitah*, 'fined two-hundred' (*kārṣāpaṇas*)."[69]

Kauṭilya says: *suvarṇān-Māṣakam=apaharato dvi-śato daṇah* I *rūpya-Dharaṇām=Māṣakam=apaharato dvādaśa-paṇaḥ* I if goldsmith steals, in the process of making coins, one *māṣa*, from the gold coin called *suvarṇa*, he will be fined 200 [*paṇas*] while his fine will be 12 *paṇas* if he steals one *māṣa* from a silver *dharaṇa*. It is interesting to note that *suvarṇa* and *dharaṇa* appear to be used specifically for gold and silver coins and fine accrued for stealing in terms of *paṇa*. On the other hand, a rough estimate can be drawn of the relative value of silver and gold on the basis of the amounts of the fines for stealing one *māṣa* of gold and silver. Thus, the ratio between gold and silver may be roughly 1:16.6.[70]

The *Jātakas* invariably refer to the name of the current coin as *kahāpaṇa*. The *Aṣṭādhyāyī* uses both the names—*kārṣāpaṇa* (V.I.29) and *paṇa* (V.I.34)—whereas the *Arthaśāstra* uses only the term *paṇa*. The other terms—*Viṁaśatika* and *Triṁśatika*—are used in the *Aṣṭādhyāyī* for coins. None of these names – *Śatamāna, Śāṇa, Viṁaśatika* and *Triṁśatika* are found in the *Arthaśāstra* and in the Buddhist texts, but these texts frequently mention *kārṣāpaṇa, paṇa* and *māṣa*. The *Arthaśāstra* also mentions about *paṇa, ardhapaṇa* and *aṣṭabhāga* as silver coins. Kauṭilya refers one-eighth of *kārṣāpaṇa* as *aṣṭabhāga,* an actual coin related to *paṇa* (II.12.84). However, Kauṭilya stated it as a unit of weight in the *suvarṇa* series. A silver *māṣa* was one-sixteenth part of a *kārṣāpaṇa* as referred to by Manu and called it *pādārdha* (VIII.I 404). The *Jātakas* are silent about one-eighth of *kahāpaṇa*.[71] The terms *kahāpaṇa, addha-kahāpaṇa* and *pāda-kahāpaṇa* are frequently used in the early parts of the Buddhist *Tripiṭakas* as silver coins—*detthāvuso kahāpaṇaṁ pi addhaṁ pi pādaṁ pi.*[72] The *Jātakas* also speak about the various names as the sub-divisions of *kahāpaṇas—kahāpaṇas, pāda-kahāpaṇas, çatur-māsaka, tri-māsaka, dvi-māsaka, ek-māsaka* and *aḍḍha-māsaka* in addition to the names referred in Buddhist *Tripīṭakas—eko kahāpaṇo aḍḍho pādo çattāro māsakā tayo dve eko māsako ti puçchi.*[73] The *Aṣṭādhyāyī* implies it *dvi-māṣa* in a *sūtra* (V.1.34) after *paṇa* and *pāda*.[74] Agrawala opines that "to this we can now definitely add the name of the one-eighth and one-sixteenth of *kārṣāpaṇa. Dvimāsha* may also mean two pieces of *māsha* coins or one double piece; for purpose of grammatical rules the form of the word would be the same."[75]

Pāṇini also mentions the term *śāṇa* with its sub-denominations, such as one-and-half *śāṇa - śāṇād-vā* (V.1.35) - *adhyardhaśāṇam, adhyardhaśāṇyam,* two *śāṇas – dvi-śāṇam* or *dvaiśāṇam* or *dvi-śāṇyam* and three *śāṇas – tri-śāṇam or traiśāṇam* or *tri-śāṇyam* (V.1.36) to which Patañjali adds *pañça-śāṇam* and *pāñça-śāṇyam* (*Bhāṣya,* II.350). It appears that *śāṇa* was a popular coin during the period. Pāṇini also refers *śāṇa* as a *parimāṇa,* i.e. 'weight' – *Parimāṇāntasyāsañjñā-śāṇayoḥ* (VII.3.17). Such examples as *dvai-śāṇa,* purchased for two *śāṇas,* indicate it was a name of a coin. Çaraka mentions to *śāṇa* as a weight equal to a one-fourth of *suvarṇa* or *kārṣa* – 20 *rattīs*. However, it is not certain whether it is in reference to a gold *śāṇa*. The *Mahābhārata* clearly speaks about *śāṇa* as a silver coin, which was one-eighth of one *śatamāna—aṣṭau ṣāṇāḥ śatamānaṁ vahanti*. Its weight therefore, was 12 and 1/2 *rattīs* or 22.5 grains.[76]

The term *māṣa* was used both for silver and copper coins. Pāṇini in a *sūtra* (V.1.34) mentions *māṣa* after *paṇa* and *pāda*. A silver *māṣa* was one-sixteenth part of a *kārṣāpaṇa* and weighed 2 *rattīs* (3.6grains) as stated by Manu—*dve kṛṣṇale samadhṛto vijñeya raupya-māṣakaḥ* I (VIII.135).[77] The copper *māṣa* was a sub-multiple of copper *kārṣāpaṇa* and weighed 5 *rattīs,* i.e. one-sixteenth of a *tāmrika-paṇa* of 80 *rattīs*. Agrawala suggests that the *kārṣāpaṇa* was the standard unit of both silver and copper currencies similar to the *suvarṇa* of the gold currency.[78] Pāṇini refers to *adhyardha-māṣa* in *sūtra* (V.I.34), i.e. one-and-half *māṣa*—an actual coin called *ardha-māṣa,* was a copper coin.[79] The *aḍḍhamāsaka* coin is also mentioned to in the *Jātakas* (*Aḍḍhamāsaka Jātaka*).[80] Kauṭilya refers to the *ardha-māṣka, kākaṇi* and *ardha-kākaṇi* as the lower divisions in the copper series.[81]

Kātyāyana refers to *Kākaṇī* and *Ardha-kākaṇī* as current coins (*vārttika* on V.I. 33) *kākaṇyās-çopasaṁkhyānam; Bhāṣya – Adhyardha - kākaṇikaṁ, dvi-likākaṇikam; varttika – kevalāyāś ça* I - *kevalāyāś ça eti vakatavyam, kākaṇīkam,* i.e. an article purchased for one *kākaṇī* coin, or 1.1/2 *kākaṇī* or 2 *kākaṇī*.[82] *Arthaśāstra* too mentioned *kākaṇi* and *ardha-kākaṇi* (II.12) as copper pieces, – *kākaṇīka* being the charge per day for stamping weights and measures (II.19). Kauṭilya speaks of the minting of silver coins called *paṇa, ardha-paṇa, pāda-paṇa,* and *aṣṭa-bhāga – paṇa* as well as of copper coins called *māṣa, ardha-māṣa, pāda-māṣa,* i.e. *kākaṇī* and *aṣṭa-bhāga-māṣa-ardha-kākaṇī*.[83] *Çullaseṭṭhi Jātaka* states one *kākaṇi* as the price of a dead mouse (I.120) and *Sālittaka Jātaka* refers to village boys giving one *kākaṇī* coin to a cripple saying 'make an elephant' or 'make a horse' (I.419). *Kākaṇīs* are equal to one *māṣa*.[84] However, Pāṇini does not mention about *kākaṇī* and *ardha-kākaṇī*. Agrawala suggests, it is possible that *kākaṇī* came into use after Pāṇini's time.[85]

Pāṇini speaks of a heavy weight *kārṣāpaṇa* called *Viṁśatika* equivalent to 20 *māṣas* as against the standard *kārṣāpaṇa* of 16 *māṣas*. It is mentioned in the *sūtras* (V.I.27) – *śatamāna-viṁśatika-sahasra-vasanād-aṇ* I "that which is purchased for a *viṁśatika* coin" and (V.I.32) – *vimśatikāt khaḥ* I – '*viṁśatika* when preceded by the word *adhyardha-viṁśatikīnam, dvi-viṁśatikīnam* and *tri viṁśatikīnam,* purchased for 1.1/2, 2 and 3 *viṁśatika* coins.[86] Further, Pāṇini in *sūtra* (V.I.24) speaks about *viṁśatika* and *triṁśataka—viṁśati-trimśadbhyām ḍvunnasajñāyām*. The *viṁśatika* as it implies was a coin of twenty, and the *triṁśataka* of thirty parts, i.e. *māṣas*.[87] Pāṇini speaks of a specific coin, *triṁśataka* in a *sūtra* (V.I.24), which is not found elsewhere. *Triṁśataka* apparently stands for a coin of 30 *māṣas,* or 60 *rattīs*. *Viṁśatika* and *triṁśataka* coins also appear in copper, weighing – 20 X 5 = 100 and 30 X 5 = 150 *rattīs,* respectively. The *viṁśatika* coins seem to have their own sub-multiples of 1/2, 1/4, 1/8, 1/16, related to the weight standard of 40 *rattīs* in silver and 100 *rattīs* in copper.[88]

The *Samanta-Pāsādikā*, the commentary of Buddhaghoṣa on the *Vinaya-piṭaka*, shows that at the time of the king Bimbisāra in the city of Rajagriha, a *kārṣāpaṇa* was equal to twenty *māṣakas* and one *pāda* equaled five *māṣakas*—*Tadā Rājgahe vīsatimāsako kahāpaṇo hoti, tasmā pañçamāsako pādo.*[89] It is confirmed by *Sāratthadīpanī* of Sāriputta Thera, a commentary on the *Samanta-Pāsādikā*—*Iminā va sabba-janapadesu kahāpaṇassa visatimo bhāgo māsako ti.*[90] The *Gaṅgamāla Jātaka* (III.448), while referring the sub-divisions of a *kārṣāpaṇa*, speaks of a four-*māṣaka* piece as being lower in value than a *pāda*, if the *pāda* coin is equal to five *māṣakas*, being one-quarter of a *kārṣāpaṇa* of twenty *māṣakas.*[91] The *Yājñavalkyasmṛti* mentions *pala* weight equal to four or five *suvarṇas* (I.364) on the basis of which the *Mitākṣarā* notes: *Pañça-suvarṇa-pala-pakṣe viṁśatimāṣaḥ paṇo bhavati* (I.365), i.e. if a *pala* is equal to five *suvarṇas*, the *paṇa* should be twenty *māṣas* in weight.[92] The *Kātyāyanasmṛti* also preserved the tradition that *kārṣāpaṇa* is equal to twenty, and not sixteen *māṣas.*[93] Patañjali quotes another teacher (*apara*) – *aparastvāha* I *purākalpa etadāsīt ṣoḍaśamāṣāḥ kārṣāpaṇaṁ ṣoḍaṣpalāśç māṣaśambaṭyaḥ* I *tatra sañkhyāsāmānyātsiddham* I (I.2.64) stating that 'in times past sixteen *māṣās* made one *kārṣāpaṇa* and sixteen *palas* made one *māṣaśambaṭī*', implying that in his time the *kārṣāpaṇa* of 20 *māṣas* or *viṁśatika* was known in his locality.[94] R. Shamasastry suggests that *purākalpa kārṣāpaṇa* might be the same one mentioned in the *Arthaśāstra*. However, it cannot be concluded by these references that *kārṣāpaṇa* weighing 20 or 16 *māṣas* was not in circulation before or after the time of Kauṭilya. It appears that these were in use in different cities at the same time.[95] Agrawala suggests on the basis of these sources that *viṁśatika* (20 *māṣas*) was a current coin in certain localities, e.g. in Magadha and Panchala, as the *kārṣāpaṇa*, of 16 *māṣa*, was current in other localities.[96] The Pāli texts described it as *vīsati-māsaka kahāpaṇa*, whereas Pāṇini used the term *viṁśatika* as a specific name (*sañjñā*) in popular usage. He is referring to the *viṁśatika* and the *kārṣāpaṇas* as two varieties of coins of different values.[97]

Paṇa and *kārṣāpaṇa* were sometimes exclusively applied to the copper coin weighing one *kārṣa* or 80 *rattīs*. *Mitākṣarā* (on Yājñavalkya, I.365) refers to Manu and says: *Karṣa-sammītas = tāmra-vikāraḥ paṇa-sañjño bhavati kārṣāpaṇaś = ça.*[98] However, there are ample references in ancient literature to the name *kārṣāpaṇa* being applied to the coins of all these metals—gold, silver and copper. Though the name *paṇa* was generally used to indicate a copper coin but the authorities also speak of gold or silver *paṇa*. There is a difference of opinion in regard to the weight of the copper *paṇa*: 1 *kārṣa* or 80 *rattīs*. Nārada (*Pariśiṣṭa*, verse, 58) and some other authorities (*Mitākṣarā*, on Yājñavalkya, I.365) speak of the *paṇa* as weighing 20 *māṣas*: *māṣo viṁśatimo bhāgaḥ paṇasya parikīrtitaḥ* I[99] and hence, a *paṇa* is equal to 100 *rattīs*. According to *Agni Purāṇa* (ch. 227, verse, 2), *paṇa* weighing 120 *rattīs*: *kṛṣṇalānaṁ tathā ṣaṣṭyā karṣārdhaṁ Rāma kīrtitam*. Bhāskarāçārya's *Lilāvatī-* (I.3) makes 24 *rattīs* 1 *dharaṇa* and 48 *rattīs* = 2 *dharaṇa* = 1 Gadyāṇka. This *dharaṇa* was only 3/4 of the *dharaṇa* weighing 32 *rattīs*, which is known from Manu.[100]

The *Amarkoṣa* seems to take one *kārṣa* weight of gold and silver as *kārṣāpaṇa* and of copper as *paṇa*, while the commentator clearly says that *kārṣāpaṇa* is a silver coin weighing one *kārṣa* = 80 *rattīs* and the *paṇa* is a copper coin of same weight = *nena rūpya-rūpakeṇa kārṣāpaṇaḥ; kārṣaḥ pramāṇam=asya kārṣkaḥ; tāmramayaṁ kārṣa-pramāṇam tu rūpyaṁ paṇaḥ* II Kṣīrasvāmi applies the name *kārṣapaṇa* exclusively to the silver coin, which is also supported by the traditions,[101] equating 16 *paṇas* [of coweries] with one *kāhaṇa* (Prakrit—*kahāvaṇa*, Sanskrit—*kārṣāpaṇa*). The name *kārṣapaṇa*—a coin weighing one *kārṣa*, applied to the silver coin—also suggests that its original weight, even if theoretical weight, was 80 *rattīs.*[102]

Śatamāna signified the earliest coinage of India with its fractions—*pāda*—a quarter and *śāṇa*—one-eighth of *śatamāna*. However, the term *kārṣāpaṇa*, was not restricted to any particular metal. It applied to all the three metals—silver, gold and copper. It appears that the terms *niṣka, śatamāna, pāda,* and *kṛṣṇala* mentioned in different texts are believed to be the names of the various units of weight used as the currency of the contemporary period. Whether *niṣka* was a coin or an ornament or both, whether it was silver or gold is a matter of speculation; but if it was not a coin, in all likelihood, it was of gold. *Kṛṣṇala*, in all probability, was simply a weight. However, it may be postulated that *śatamāna* and *pāda* were definitely silver coins, which were in circulation in that period.[103] Conclusion is concurrent on the testimony of these references occurring in Brahmanical and Buddhist texts. The term *kārṣāpaṇa* appears to have acquired its name because in weight it conformed to one *kārṣa*.[104]

This was the currency in or about the time of Pāṇini (c. 5th century BCE). It continued in the subsequent period of Kauṭilya and remained in vogue at the time of compilation of the Buddhist texts. In fact, silver coins in various denominations have been mentioned in different ancient texts, which can logically be addressed as *kahāpaṇas* or *kārṣāpaṇas*.

Pāṇini	***Jātakas***	***Arthaśāstra***	**Division**
Kārṣāpaṇa and Paṇa	*Kahāpaṇa*	*Paṇa*	1/1
Ardha / Bhāga	*Aḍḍha*	*Ardha Paṇa*	1/2
Pāda	*Pāda; çattāro-Māsaka*	*Pāda*	1/4
Dvi-Māṣa	*Dve-Māsaka*	*Aṣṭabhāga*	1/8
Maṣa	*Eka-Māsaka*	*Māṣaka*	1/16
Ardha-Māṣa / Kākaṇī	*Aḍḍha-Māsaka / Kākaṇī*	*Ardha-Māṣaka Kākaṇi*	1/32
**Paṇamadharpaṇam pādamaṣṭabhāgamiti* I *pādājīvaṁ tāmrarūpaṁ māṣakamardhamāṣkaṁ kākiṇīmardhakākiṇīmiti* I *Arthaśāstra*, 2. 12.			
Tena hi pannāsa-sahassāni çattālīsa-tiṅsa-vīsati-dasa-pañça-çattāri-tayo dve eko kahāpaṇo, aḍḍho pādo çattāro māsakā, tayo dve eko māsako ti puçchi I *sabbaṁ paṭikhipitvā aḍḍhamāsako ti vutte āma deva ettakaṁ mahyaṁ dhanaṁ* I *Gaṅgamāla Jātaka*. 3. 448. **JNSI* (1953) 33.			
Gold and Silver			
1 *Niṣka or Śatamāna*	100 *Mānas*	560 grns / 36.288gms	
1/2 *Niṣka*	50 *Mānas*	280 grns / 18.144gms	
1/4 *Niṣka or Pāda*	25 *Mānas*	140 grns / 9.072gms	
1/10 *Niṣka or Dharaṇa* (*Purāṇa, salaka, kalañju*)	10 *Mānas*	56 grns / 3.6288gms	
1/20 *Niṣka* or *'Dharaṇa*	5 *Mānas*	28 grns / 1.8144gms	
1/100 *Niṣka* or *Māna* or *Fanam* (a variant of *Manam* or *panam* ?)	1 *Māna*	5.6 grns / 0.36288gm	

Silver Punch-marked Coins (*Śatamāna*)		
Śatamāna	100 *Rattīs*	180 grns / 11.66 gms
Ardha-Śatamāna	50 *Rattīs*	90 grns / 5.83 gms
Śāṇa	62.5 *Rattīs*	112.5 grns / 7.29 gms
Tri-Śāṇa	37.5 *Rattis*	67.5 grns / 4.37 gms
Pāda-Śatamāna or Dvi-Śāṇa	25 *Rattīs*	45 grns / 2.91 gms
Adhyardha-Śāṇa	18.75 *Rattīs*	33.75grns/2.18 gms
Pādārdha-Śatamāna or Śāṇa	12.5 *Rattīs*	22.5 grns / 1.45 gms
Aṣṭa-bhāga-Śatamāna or Ardha-Śāṇa	6.25 *Rattīs*	11.25 grns / 0.72 gm
***Kārṣāpaṇa* Series (silver)**		
Kārṣāpaṇa (=Prati)	32 *Rattīs*	57.6 grns / 3.73 gms
Ardha-kārṣāpaṇa (=Bhāga)	16 *Rattīs*	28.8 grns / 1.86 gms
Pāda-kārṣāpaṇa	8 *Rattīs*	14.4 grns / 0.93 gm
Aṣṭabhāga-kārṣāpaṇa	4 *Rattīs*	7.2 grns / 0.46 gm
Raupya Adhyārdha-Māṣaka	3 *Rattīs*	5.4 grns / 0.34 gm
Raupya Māṣaka	2 *Rattīs*	3.6 grns / 0.23 gm
***Viṁśatika* Series**		
Tri-Viṁśatika	120 *Rattīs*	216 grns / 14.00 gms
Dvi-Viṁśatikas	80 *Rattīs*	144 grns / 9.33 gms
Adhyardha-Viṁśatika or *Triṁśatika*	60 *Rattīs*	108 grns / 7.00 gms
Viṁśatika	40 *Rattīs*	72 grns / 4.66 gms
Ardha-Viṁśatika	20 *Rattīs*	36 grns / 2.33 gms
Pāda-Viṁśatika or *pañça-Māṣaka*	10 *Rattīs*	18 grns / 1.16 gms

JNSI (1953) XV (I) 39-40.

grains: grns
grams: gms
*Weight of *Rattī* is calculated as follows:
1 *Rattī* = 1.8 grains (0.11664 gram); 1 grain = 0.0648 gram; 1.8 grains = 0.11664 gram.
*Dilip Rajgor (2001), 7-8.

NOTES AND REFERENCES

1. *SB*, XI.4.1.1; 4.1.8; XIII.4.1.17; XXIII.4.1.17; *Gopatha Brhāhmaṇa*, I.3.6; 1.3.8; *Pañçaviṁśa Brāhmaṇa*; III.7.6.1.
2. *Chāndogya Upaniṣad*, IV. 7ff; *Bṛhadāraṇyaka Upaniṣad*, III.1.1-2.
3. A.S. Altekar (1953), "Early History of Coinage in Ancient India", *JNSI*, XV (I), 18.
4. *Ibid.*, 11.

5. *Ibid.*
6. *Ibid.*, 11-12.
7. *Ibid.*, 12-13
8. *Ibid.*, 14.
9. *Ibid.*
10. *Ibid.*
11. Altekar remarks that the silver was almost unknown to the Vedic Aryans. Silver (*rajata*) *niṣka*, mentioned in *Pañçaviṁśa Brāhmaṇa*, is in connection with the *Vrātyas*, who used to wear it as an ornament. *Vrātyas* were outlandish people. A.S. Altekar (1953), 10, 15.
12. *Ibid.*, 15-16.
13. V.S. Agrawala (1953), "Ancient Coins as known to Pāṇini", *JNSI*, XV (I), 27-28.
14. V.S. Agrawala (1969), *Pāṇini Kālīna Bhāratavarṣa*, 248.
15. *Pāli Jātaka*, VI. 546; *Juṇha Jātaka* (No. 456, IV. 97) referring to more than a 1,000 gold *niṣkas*, V.S. Agrawala (1953), 28, fn. 1; D.R. Bhandarkar (1921), *AIN*, 48-49. According to A.S. Altekar (1953), 18, probably something like gold currency had come into use in this period, and *niṣka*, *suvarṇa* and *śatamāna* were its main denominations. *Śatamāna* weighed 100 *rattīs* or 175 grains and in later times, while *suvarṇa* and *niṣka* followed the weight standard of 80 *rattīs* and 320 *rattīs*, respectively. *Pāda* was probably a quarter of the *suvarṇa* and *śatamāna*.
16. A.S. Altekar (1953), 16-17.
17. D.R. Bhandarkar (1921), *AIN*, 60.
18. *Ibid.*
19. V.S. Agrawala (1953), 28.
20. A.S. Altekar (1953), 17.
21. V.S. Agrawala (1953), 28.
22. *Ibid.*
23. *Ibid.*
24. *Ibid.*, 28.
25. A.S. Altekar (1953), 17.
26. V.S. Agrawala (1953), 29.
27. D.R. Bhandarkar (1921), *AIN*, 51.
28. V.S. Agrawala (1953), 29; *Pāṇini Kālīna Bhāratavarṣa* (1969), 250.
29. V.S. Agrawala (1953), 29.
30. *Ibid.*
31. *Ibid.*
32. D.R. Bhandarkar (1921), *AIN*, 52.
33. V.S. Agrawala (1953), 29.
34. A.S. Altekar (1953), 16.
35. V.S. Agrawala (1953), 30.
36. A.S. Altekar (1953), 21. "There are sufficient literary and archaeological evidence to show a silver currency called *śatamāna* existed from about the 6th century BCE; its subdivisions were also current in the Gangetic plain. Later on, this currency was apparently superseded by *kārṣāpaṇa* currency in c. 450 BC."
37. *Ibid.*, *ante*. 5, fn. 3. Thin and large coins found from Kosala. Weighing between 75 and 79 grains, the *ardha śatamāna*. (*JNSI*, III, 51). The coins of Paila hoard and the Kosala hoard, probably weighing 25 *rattīs* or 44 grains, probably would be the quarter *śatamānas* (*JNSI*, II, 27). Some conclusion can be drawn on the basis of a group of 13 coins, in the collection of State Museum Lucknow, weighing about 42 grains published by Durga Prasad, *NS*, XLV, 9-13. The Sonepur silver punch-marked coins, weighing 21 grains, would be *pādārdha-śatamānas*, or *śāṇas*, as eight of which constituted a *śatamāna* (*Mahābhārata*, III.134.14); E.H.C. Walsh, "Punch-marked Coins from Taxila", *MASI* (59), 1-2. Bhir mound hoard (1924) contained Bent-bar coins.
38. A.S. Altekar (1953), 22.

39. V.S. Agrawala (1953), 30.
40. A.S. Altekar (1953), 20.
41. V.S. Agrawala (1953), 30
42. *Ibid.*
43. D.C. Sircar (1968), *SIC*, 60.
44. S.K. Chakrabortty (1931), *A Study of Ancient Indian Numismatics*, 27, 243ff; D.C. Sircar (1968), 60. "The belief that the weight of the *Śatamāna* was 100 *Ratīs* is no doubt based on the name which literally means 'measuring 100' *i.e.* 'made up of 100 units of measurement', and on the conjecture that this unit of measurement is no other than the well known *Ratī*." Sircar quoted *Manusmṛiti* and *Yājñavalkyasmṛti* and suggested that "it is quite clear that the unit of measurement, one hundred of which made up the *Śatamāna* weighing 320 *Ratīs*, was not one *Ratī* but actually 3.1/5 *Ratī* or 5.8 grains". D.C. Sircar (1968), 54.
45. D.R. Bhandarkar (1921), *AIN*, 55 ff.
46. D.C. Sircar (1968), *SIC*, 49-50.
47. *Ibid.*, 49.
48. *Ibid.*
49. *Ibid.*
50. V.S. Agrawala (1953), 30-31.
51. A.M. Shastri (1966), "Literary Evidence Bearing on the Chronology of the Punch-marked Coins", *The Chronology of the Punch-marked Coins*, 116.
52. *Ibid.*
53. Maheshwari Prasad (1966), "Literary Evidence on the Chronology of the Punch-marked Coins", *The Chronology of the Punch-marked Coins*, 164.
54. *The Vedic Index*, 185.
55. A.S. Altekar (1953), 18.
56. *Ep. Ind.* VIII.82; *JNSI*, VII.32; V.S. Agrawala (1953), 32.
57. V.S. Agrawala (1953), 32; (1945), "Prati as the name of a coin", *JNSI*, VII, 37.
58. V.S. Agrawala (1953), 31.
59. V.S. Agrawala (1953), 33. *Tena hi pannāsa-sahassāni çattālīsa-tiṁsa-visati-dasa-pañça çattāro-māsakā, tayo, dve,eko māsako ti puçchi | sabbaṁ paṭikikhapitvā aḍḍhamāsako ti vutte, āma deva, ettakaṁ mahyaṁ dhanam | - Gaṅgamāla Jātaka* – 3|448; *Arthaśātra* – 2|12 - *paṇam, ardhapaṇam, pādam, aṣṭabhāgam iti | pādājīvaṁ tāmrarūpaṁ māṣkam, ardhamāṣakam, kākaṇīkam, ardhkākaṇīmiti | Pāṇini Kālīna Bhāratavarṣa* (1969) 255, fn. 1-2; V.S. Agrawala (1953), 32, fn. 2; *Mahābhāṣya* on Pāṇini, II. I. 69; V. 21; V. 2. 45.
60. V.S. Agrawala (1953), 27, 31-32; D.R. Bhandarkar (1921), 55.
61. V.S. Agrawala (1953), 33.
62. *Ibid.*, 34.
63. *Ibid.*, 33-34.
64. *Ibid.*, 31-32.
65. R.N. Mehta, *Pre-Buddhist India*, 235-36.
66. D.C. Sircar (1968), *SIC*, 74.
67. *Akkasavagga*, Vol. V. 83; A.S. Altekar (1953), 22, fn. 9.
68. V.S. Agrawala (1953), 32.
69. *Ibid.*
70. D.C. Sircar (1968), *SIC*, 77-78.
71. V.S. Agrawala (1953), 34. Cunningham opined that the silver coins were limited to three divisions, *kārṣāpaṇa*, with its half and its quarter. (1891), *CAI*, 46. Agrawala asserted that to this the name of one-eighth and one-sixteenth *kārṣāpaṇa* can be added.
72. A.S. Altekar (1953), 23, fn. 1.
73. *Ibid.*, 23. fn. 2; "We have also actually found the specimens of *kārshāpaṇas, ardha-kārshāpaṇas, pāda-kārshāpaṇas or chatur-māshakas, pādārdhha-kārshāpaṇas* or *dvimāshakas*, though their date is not possible to determine." fn. 3; *JNSI*, XIII, 144; XIV, 22.

74. V.S. Agrawala (1953), 34.
75. *Ibid.*
76. *Ibid.*, 31, "Pāṇini refers to certain taxes levied in east India (VI. 3. 10), on which the *Kāśikā* cites *Sūpe-Śāṇah* (VI. 2. 64 and VI. 3.10), a special cess at the rate of one *śāṇa* coin per kitchen (*sūpa*) or household"; (1952) "A new type of *Sāna* coin", *JNSI*, XIV (I), 22-26.
77. "Actual specimens of silver *māsha* coins (*raupya-māsha*) have now been found in a hoard at Bhir mound, Takshaśilā, and at Thaṭhārī in Central Province. They are minute coins with a single symbol stamped on one side, weighing 2 to 3 grains and with a diameter of .2 inches. (*J.N.S.I.*, VIII. 41; XIII, 168)"; V.S. Agrawala (1953), 34.
78. *Ibid.*, 34.
79. *Ibid.*, 34-35.
80. V.S. Agrawala (1953), 34-35; *Pāṇini Kālīna Bhāratavarṣa* (1969), 259.
81. V.S. Agrawala (1953), 34.
82. *Ibid.*, 35.
83. *Ibid.*
84. *Pāṇini Kālīna Bhāratavarṣa* (1969), 259.
85. *Ibid;* V.S. Agrawala (1953), 34.
86. V.S. Agrawala (1953), 35; *Trivimśatika - kāśikā-* V.1.32 – 120 *rattīs; dvivimśatika – kāśikā* – V.1.32 – 80 *rattīs; ardhyardha vimśatika sūtra* – V.1.84 – 60 *rattīs. Pāṇini Kālīna Bhāratavarṣa* (1969) 260-61.
87. *Pāṇini Kālīna Bhāratavarṣa* (1969) 261; Agrawala, V.S. (1953) 37. Quoted by V.S. Agrawala - Durga Prasad obtained from Bihar specimens of silver punch-marked coins, weighing 104 grains and 105-7 grains or about 53 *rattīs*, which should be identified as *trimśataka JUPHS*, (1939) 33.
88. V.S. Agrawala (1953) 37; *Pānini Kālīna Bhāratavarṣa* (1969) 261.
89. C.D. Chatterjee (1933), "Some New Terms in Pali Texts", *JUPHS* (VI) 157; D.R. Bhandarkar (1921), 111, 186; D.C. Sircar, *JNSI*, XIII, 187; V.S. Agrawala (1953), 35-36, fn.1.
90. C.D. Chatterjee (1933), 158; Agrawala (1953), 36, fn. 2.
91. D.R. Bhandarkar (1921), 112; V.S. Agrawala (1953), 36.
92. V.S. Agrawala (1953), 36.
93. D.R. Bhandarkar (1921), 186.
94. V.S. Agrawala (1969), *Pāṇini Kālīna Bhāratavarṣa*, 261; V.S. Agrawala (1953), 36.
95. V.S. Agrawala (1969), *Pāṇini Kālīna Bhāratavarṣa*, 261.
96. V.S. Agrawala (1953), 36. The actual specimens of *vimśatika* weight and their lower denominations have been found in the Panchala coinage. A. Cunningham (1891), *CAI*, 81.
97. V.S. Agrawala (1953) 36.
98. P.V. Kane, *History of Dharmaśāstra*, Vol. III. 120; D.C. Sircar (1968), *SIC*, 74.
99. *JNSI*, XIII, 187 ff.
100. D.C. Sircar (1968), *SIC*, 74-75.
101. *Ibid.*, 77; *JNSI*, VII, 83; XIII, 185.
102. D.C. Sircar (1968), *SIC*, 77.
103. P.L. Gupta (1963), *Am.* 142.
104. D.R. Bhandarkar (1921), *AIN*, 83-86.

3

Historical Background

There was no paramount power in north India in the beginning of 6th century BCE. The early political history of this region is complex, the main sources of information being the *Purāṇas,* supplemented by the epics, particularly, the *Mahābhārata,* and the early Jaina and Buddhist texts including certain classical Sanskrit literature. During the early 2nd or 3rd centuries, preceding the birth of Mahavira and the Buddha, the vast area of northern India was divided into sixteen principal city-states/*janapadas*, known in early Buddhist and Jain literature as the *solasa-mahājanapadas/soḍasamahājanpadas.* The account of these great *janapadas* is mentioned in Jaina *Bhagavati sūtra* and Buddhist *Aṅguttara Nikāya.*[1] Of these kingdoms, mention may be made of Magadha, Videha, Kasi, Kosala, Uttar Panchala and Kuru or Indraprastha. These *janapadas* included modern Bihar and the greater part of present Uttar Pradesh.[2]

The flourishing period of the *janapadas* ended in or about 6th-5th centuries BCE. History of the succeeding period records the growth of the Magadha kingdom. Kasi was a wealthy and prosperous city. The earliest known dynasty, which ruled in Varanasi, was Pururavas. Aila, a grandson of Manu and his grandson, Kshatravriddha was the first king of Varanasi.[3] The seventh king in the line was Kasha or Kashya, son of Suhotra and a grandson of Kshatravriddha, after whom the city, as also the kingdom, was named Kasi.[4]

The kingdom of Kasi was the most prominent in the period; it extended about 100 miles to the east and about 250 miles to the northwest of the city Varanasi, probably from Ballia in the east to Kanpur in the west, the kingdom of the Magadha to its east, that of Uttar Panchala to its north-west and Kosala to its north.[5] The city was fairly extensive, spreading over 12 leagues and probably bounded by the streams Varuṇā and Assi on north and south, respectively.[6] The combined extent of Kasi and Kosala is stated to be 300 *yojanas.*[7] In those days, the name of Kasi denoted the kingdom or *janapada* of which Varanasi was the capital.[8] The *Jātaka* speaks of a long rivalry between the two kingdoms of Kasi and Kosala for supremacy.[9] The strongest rivals of the kings of Kasi were the rulers of the neighbouring kingdom Kosala. These two kingdoms paired in early literature as Kasi-Kosala.[10] Kasi seems to have been successful at first but Kosala was gained in the end. Kosala began to grow in strength, contending first with Kasi and then with Magadha for a commanding position. Kamsa, the king of Kosala, addressed himself as *Bārānasiggaho*—the conqueror of Varanasi.[11]

Eventually, early in the 6th century BCE, the kingdom of Kasi completely collapsed in its struggle with Kosala and became one of its provinces. Thereafter, for some time Kasi was tossed between Kosala and Magadha.[12] There are also references in *Mahāvagga, Jātaka, Kosambi Jātaka, Mahāsilva Jātaka* and *Saṅyukta Nikāya* about the rivalry between Kasi and Anga and between Kasi and Magadha.[13]

The *Purāṇas* speak of the history of Magadha as the paramount power; there is a lot of uncertainty though about the political history of Magadha in the beginning. The first known king of Magadha was Bimbisāra. He extended his empire up to 800 leagues.[14] Kosala was a strong rival to Magadha. So, the latter made matrimonial alliance with the royal family of Kosala. However, this relationship was short-lived. His own son Ajātaśatru killed his father. Ajātaśatru extended the territories of Magadha by his conquest. He is said to have defeated nine Mallas (Mallaki), nine Lichchhavis, i.e. eighteen *Gaṇarājyas* of Kasi and Kosala.[15] Kosala, Kasi and Vaisali were ultimately annexed into the Magadha kingdom. Magadha was the most powerful state in the Gangetic plains about 400 BCE.

The successors of Ajātaśatru were not very significant. In about 414 BCE, the last king of the line of Bimbisāra was deposed and replaced by Śiśunāga.[16] He brought the greater part of north India under his sway. Despite continuous political intrigues, the empire remained powerful.[17] The Naṅdas followed the Śiśunāga dynasty in about c. 364 BCE. The founder of Naṅda dynasty was Mahāpadma.[18] Perhaps Śiśunāga had already conquered Avanti. The Naṅdas consolidated their control over this area and were supposed to have defeated the Ikshavakus, Panchalas, Kasis, Haihayas, Asamakas, Surasenas, Kurus, and some other states.[19] They also extended their empire to most of the subcontinent north of Vindhya Hills, except the North West, now Pakistan. The upward trend was continued and the wealth of Naṅda dynasty became legendary.[20]

The punch-marked coins struck by Magadha in the following centuries confirm its growing economic strength. The coins issued by the Naṅdas are found all over the country and continued to circulate during the succeeding Mauryan period, when the whole of the subcontinent of India was brought under one rule. History is not very clear about the successors of Mahāpadma Naṅda. This was the time when Alexander invaded the northern part of India. Çandragupta Maurya deposed the last Naṅda ruler, took over the Magadha realm and established the Maurya dynasty in c. 321 BCE, with the assistance of Çāṇkya, known as Kauṭilya, who authored *Arthaśāstra* and was also the chief minister of Çandragupta.[21] *Arthaśāstra* records the political and social conditions of the Mauryan Empire in detail and includes references to contemporary minting.

Çandragupta had strengthened the northern frontiers and his son Bindusāra (c. 297-272 BCE) campaigned in the Deccan and extended Mauryan control southward. The southern part included Kalinga, present-day Orissa, which was the only independent territory left in the subcontinent when his son Aśoka (c. 272-232 BCE) succeeded him.[22] After much bloodshed, Aśoka conquered Kalinga in the eighth year of his reign. This marked the turning point in Mauryan military policy. The Maurya dynasty lost its influence after the death of Aśoka (c. 232 BCE). The appearance of tribal copper coins (late 3rd or early 2nd centuries BCE) confirms that many tribes broke away from the Mauryan control. The Mauryas were succeeded by the Śuṅga dynasty (c. 184 BCE).[23] The realm of Puṣyamitra, the first king of the Śuṅga dynasty, was restricted to an area between the Indus and the Ganges delta. After the death of Puṣyamitra, the Śuṅgas were forced to abandon their capital at Pataliputra.[24]

Rulers	Period	Dynasty
Bimbisāra	c. 546-494 BCE / 52 years	Harayaṅka*
Ajātaśatru, son of Bimbisāra	c. 494-462 BCE / 32 years	Harayaṅka
Udayabhadra, son of Ajātaśatru	c. 462-446 BCE / 16 years	Harayaṅka
Anuruddha, son of Udayabhadra Muṇḍa, son of Anuruddha	c. 446.....) (..... 438 BCE / 8 years	Harayaṅka
Nāgādāśaka, son of Muṅḍa	c. 438-414 BCE / 24 years	Harayaṅka
Śiśunāga	c. 414-396 BCE / 18 years	Śaiśunāga
Kalāśoka-son of Śiśunāga	c. 396-368 BCE / 28 years	Śaiśunāga
Ten sons of Kālāśoka	c. 368-346 BCE / 22 years	Śaiśunāga
Mahāpadma Naṅda and nine sons in succession	c. 346-321 BCE / 22 years	Naṅda
Çandragupta	c. 321-297 BCE / 24 years	Maurya
Bindusāra, son of Çandragupta	c. 297-272 BCE / 28 years	Maurya
Aśoka, son of Bindusāra	c. 272-232 BCE / 40 years	Maurya
8 successors of Aśoka ruled in succession	c. 232-187 BCE / 45 years	Maurya
Puṣyamitra Śuṅga and his successors	c.187-151 BCE / 36 years c. 151-75 BCE / 75 years	Śuṅga

* Bimbisāra was a scion of *Harayaṅka-Kula* (Aśvaghoṣa's *Buddhaçarita*, XI. 2).

According to Ceylonese chronicles, Bimbisāra ruled for 52 years, his son Ajātaśatru for 32 years, Udaya for 16 years, Anuruddha and Muṅḍa for 8 years, Nāgadāśaka for 24 years, Śiśunāga for 18 years, Kālāśoka for 28 years and his sons for 22 years. Afterwards, nine Naṅdas ruled in sussession for 22 years. Çandragupta reigned for 24 years and his son Bindusāra ruled for 28 years. Aśoka, the son of Bindusāra, ruled for 40 years and the eight successors of Aśoka ruled in succession for 45 years. Puṣyamitra Śuṅga ruled for about 36 years and his succeccors for another 75 years. Gautam Buddha died when Ajātaśatru was on the throne for 8 years - 52 + 8 = 60 years after the accession of Bimbisāra. *Parinirvāṇa* took place in c. 486 BCE. Adding 60 to 486 BCE, we get the year c. 546 BCE as the date of accession of Bimbisāra.[25]

NOTES AND REFERENCES

1. Hemachandra Raychaudhuri (1923), *Political History of Ancient India* (*PHAI*) 46-47; *The Age of Imperial Unity* (1953) 1.
2. *The Age of Imperial Unity* (1953), 1; *Gazetteer of Uttar Pradesh* (1965), 29.
3. *The History and the Culture of the Indian People* (I), 273; *Gazetteer* (1965), 26.
4. A.S. Altekar (1937), *History of Benares*, 9; *Harivaṁśa Purāṅa*, 29, *The Kāśi Khaṅd of the Skaṅda Purāṇa*.
5. A.S. Altekar (1937), 12.
6. *Ibid.*, 14-15; *The Age of Imperial Unity* (1953), 329.
7. A.S. Altekar (1937), 12.
8. *Ibid.*, 14.
9. *The Age of Imperial Unity* (1953), 4; *Kosambi Jātaka*, No. 428; *Brahaçchatta Jātaka*, No. 336; *Sona Nanda Jātaka*, No. 532.

10. *Ibid.*, (I), 332.
11. *Seyya Jātaka*, No. 282; *Tesakuṇa Jātaka*, No. 521; *Buddhist India*, 25.
12. A.S. Altekar (1937), 13; *Gazetteer of Uttar Pradesh* (1965), 30.
13. *Mahāvagga Jātaka* (*SBE* (XVII) 294 - 99); *Kosambi Jātaka*, No. 248; *Mahāsilva Jātaka*, No. 51.
14. Hemachandra Raychaudhuri (1923), 97. Bimbisāra or Śrenika, the founder of Magadha dynasty, was also known as Seṇiya Bimbisāra, son of Bhaiyṭṭa; *ibid.*
15. *The Age of Imperial Unity* (1953), 29-30.
16. *Ibid.*, 23; *Bhagavati Sūttra*, 300. The first capital of Bimbisāra was at Rājgraha (Rājagṛha), the Girivraja of Magadha.
17. *Ibid.*, 20.
18. *Ibid.*, 31-32.
19. *Ibid.*, 32.
20. Hemachandra Raychaudhuri (1923), 139.
21. *Ibid.*, 140-41.
22. *Ibid.*, 161.
23. *Ibid.*, 197.
24. P.L. Gupta and T.R. Hardaker (1985), *AISPMC*, 2-3.
25. According to Sinhalese chronicles, Bimbisāra and Ajātaśatru ruled, repectively, for 52 and 32 years. The corresponding dates in the Purāṇas are 26 (or 28) and 25 (or 27) years. To Śiśunaga is assigned a reign of 18 years in the Sinhalese chronicles and 40 years in the Purāṇas. (*PHAI*, 198-99, *Mahāvaṁśa*, ch. 2; *The Age of Imperial Unity*, 37-38). The first Naṅda king, Mahāpadma Naṅda, ruled, according to the Purāṇas, for 88 years, but some scholars regard it is a mistake for 28, which is found in some manuscripts of the Purānas (*PHAI*, 189). The other kings are said to have ruled for 12 years. The Sinhalese chronicles assigned only 22 years to the nine Naṅdas. According to Ceylonese accounts, the Naṅdas ruled only for 22 years and 28 years according to the Purāṇas. (*PHAI*, 117). The Purāṇas give Chandragupta and Bindusāra a reign period of 24 and 25 years, respectively. According to Buddhist tradition, Bindusāra ruled for 27 or 28 years. Buddhist texts assign a reign of 37 years and Purāṇas 36 years to Aśoka. His coronation took place after 4 years of his accession. The date of accession may be provisionally fixed at 272 BCE to 232 BCE. Hemachandra Raychaudhuri (1923), 198-199. *The Age of Imperial Unity* (1953/1990), 19, 37-38, 88, 92.

4

Chronology

The chronology of India's ancient coinage has always been a subject of discussion. Even though the origin of coinage in ancient India is shrouded in considerable obscurity, the fact remains that these coins were in circulation for a long period covering several centuries. However, in the present state of our knowledge, it is still not possible to determine the exact date when these coins were first introduced and the period when they were driven out of circulation. The available evidences have been subjected to different interpretations, and hence, the scholars have drawn widely divergent conclusions upon the subject.

Wilson and Prinsep are of the opinion that coinage became prevalent in ancient India only after the advent of the Greeks in the subcontinent of India. According to Wilson, "It was likely that the currency of the country consisted chiefly, if not exclusively, of lumps of gold and silver not bearing any impression, until the Hindus had learnt the usefulness of money from their Bactrian neighbours and from their commerce, especially with Rome."[1] Prinsep is also of the same view. He argued, "Whether any native coins, properly so called, had circulation in India anterior to the invasion of Alexander the Great."[2] According to him, in none of the ancient books of Hindus, mention is made of coined money.[3] He reached the conclusion: "On the obvious resemblance between the Indo-Bactrian coins on one side and those of the Audumbaras on the other, altogether ignoring the punch-marked coins."[4] However, later on, he revised his opinion and admitted that the Hindus had an indigenous currency of precious metals, even before the advent of the Greeks. Nevertheless, he maintained, "The adoption of a die-device or of coined money, properly so called, by the Hindus has to be placed subsequent to their coming into contact with the Greeks."[5]

Allan held another opinion. He does not suggest any connection between the Greek currency and the earliest coinage of India—the *kārṣāpaṇas* or punch-marked coins. He, however, does not think that the antiquity of coinage of India can be pushed back to earlier than the c. 4th century BCE, while admitting that there is enough evidence to accept that the coins were known even before the Mauryan period. He adds,

> It is not impossible that the tradition of the great wealth of the Nandas owes its origin to their having been the first to issue coins on a large scale. In any case, there is no evidence that coinage in India is older than the Nanda period and the earliest finds from Paila, Set Mahet and Golakhpur, may

> indicate the region in which punch-marked coins originate. The similarity in the constitution of the usual finds indicates that punch-marked coinage did not exist over a very long period; the fact that it had not been established is indicated by the rapidity with which the new coins with type and inscription struck from a single die ousted the punch-marked coins from the second century BCE onwards. It is very possible that the idea of a coinage came to India in the late fifth or early fourth century BCE from Achaemenid territory, being suggested by Sigloi, although its character is entirely Indian.[6]

Decourdemanche suggested the theory of Achaemenian origin of Indian coinage. He argued that punch-marked coins, whether of silver or copper, constitute simply an Indian variety of the Achaemenian coinage.[7]

According to Kennedy, the punch-marked coins or the *kārṣāpaṇas,* considered to be the most ancient currency of India, were copied from Babylonian originals after the opening of the maritime trade with Western Asia in the 6th century BCE.[8] Smith more or less held the same opinion. He observed in his article on numismatics, contributed to the *Imperial Gazetteer*:

> The Introduction in India of the use of coins, that is to say, metallic pieces of definite weight authenticated as currency by marks recognized as guarnttee of value, may be ascribed with much probability to the seventh century BCE when foreign maritime trade seems to have begun. There is reason to believe that the necessities of commerce with foreign merchants were the immediate occasions for the adoption by the Indian people of a metallic currency as well as alphabetical writing.[9]

However, later on he modified his views and suggested that the earliest punch-marked coins, viz. the bent-bar pieces were not earlier than 5th or 6th century BCE.[10] However, Rapson believed that the punch-marked coins of India were developed independently of any foreign influence and he placed the *karṣāpaṇa* in c. 400 BCE.[11] Thomas also shared the same view. He observed,

> Designs, treatment and die-devices (of ancient Indian coins), evince independent thought. The Indian figures follow the ideal models of their own land and bear no trace of the conventionalities of the Greek art. The devices, though at times rising above mediocrity, affect only local associations and are as free from all symptoms of imitation of the favourite Greek subjects as their details are deficient in the boldness and freedom of classical dies.[12]

Cunningham holds the same view and does not believe in any foreign influence or origin. He assereted, "If the Hindus derived their knowledge of coinage from the Greeks, the types, shape and standard of all their money would have been Greek."[13] He further stated, "How old these punch-marked coins may be, it is difficult to say. They were certainly current in the time of the Buddha, i.e. in the 6th century B.C. But I see no difficulty in thinking that they might mount as high as 1000 B.C. They certainly belonged to infancy of coinage."[14] Chakrabortty agreed with the view of Cunningham, and concluded, "So it can be safely asserted that coinage in India was evolved at about 800 B.C. and if we fix the approximate date at 1000 B.C. and accept the view of Sir Alexander Cunningham, we are not likely to go wrong; at least the margin of error would be very small."[15]

Bhandarkar, however, places the origin of coinage in India much earlier. After considering both archaeological and literary evidence, he reached the conclusion that coined money was current in the Vedic period. He agreed with the view of Winternitz that the Vedic period in all probability extends from c. 2500 BCE to 800 BCE and observes, "If this is so, coined money must be considered to be existing in India as early as the middle of the third millennium before Christ."[16]

Bhandarkar believes that there are a number of references in Pāṇini's works that suggest the presence of currency during the period. He refers to at least seven kinds of coins and if seven different types of metallic currency were prevalent in India about 500 BCE, the beginning of the art of coin making in this country must be placed earlier than c. 700 BCE.[17] Altekar traced the origin of Indian coinage based on literary and archaeological studies, earlier than the time of the Buddha. He disagreed with the opinion of Cunningham that the silver punch-marked coins may be as old as 1000 BCE because of the absence of terms like *kārṣāpaṇas* or silver coins in the later Vedic literature, the Brāhmaṇas and the Upaniṣads. However, he suggests that the silver and copper currency of ancient India was well established in 600 BCE, and asserts that the antiquity of silver *kārṣāpaṇas* would go back to at least 500 BCE.[18]

Gupta and Hardaker placed these coins between c. 6th century BCE or earlier and 2nd century BCE. Their studies are based on literary and archaeological evidence and the nature of hoards.[19]

Cribb is of the opinion that "..... the Punch-marked coinage was developed as a response in the north-western corner of South Asia to the knowledge and use of Greek coins."[20] He further asserted that "... India's coinage tradition originated as an idea imported from the Greek world via Achamenid Afghanistan..." and reached the conclusion that the "Coinage in India was not an independent invention but was initially derived from the Graeco-Iranian world."[21] He proposes that India's earliest coins should be dated to early 4th century BCE.

Mitchiner suggests:

> The numismatic history of India begins with the rise of urbanised states in the Ganges valley and adjacent regions during the seventh century BCE. The introduction of widespread urbanization to the middle Ganges valley, a region where many of the new janapadas (early states) arose, slightly antedated the introduction of a new pottery form known as Northern Black Polished Ware. The inception of this pottery can be dated, with the help of radio carban analyses, to about the sixth century BC (1975).

He says (1973):

> The date when urbanisation commenced in this Ganges valley is important because it provides an approximation to the earliest date when centralised economic structures evolved and hence the earliest date at which is reasonable to infer that coinage could have commenced.

By taking into consideration all the factors concerning the economic condition of the four major areas – Magadha, Kosala, Avanti and Gandhara – he has come to the conclusion that one can place the commencement of the Taxila–Gandhara and the Avanti coinage, like that of the two major Ganges valley series, in the early sixth century BCE.[22]

Elliot (1886) suggested the date of the punch-marked coins to about 2500 BCE. He reported, how the punch-marked coins have been found among the ashes of men who introduced primitive tombs known as Paṇḍukuli in south India and are unearthed from the ruins of buried cities in excavating the head waters of the Ganges canal.[23] Altekar (1953) pointed out that we have no idea about the dates of buried cities and the punch-marked coins, if they were in circulation. These coins have not been found in any such tomb except in the solitary instance recorded by Elliot.[24] However, no archaeological observations have been reported about the stratification of the coins found, so it would not be safe to attach any value to that circumstances. Regarding the find of the punch-marked coins in the Paṇḍukuli graves reported by Elliot: "A large hoard of these coins was discovered in 1807 at opening of one of the ancient tombs known by Paṇḍukuli near the village Chavadi of Paleigm in Coimbatore, thus identifying the employment of this kind of money with aboriginal race, whose places of sepulchre are scattered over every part of southern India."[25]Altekar further remarked that if the punch-marked coins were in circulation among the original tribe, they would have been found in several of them, which have been opened by the archaeologists.[26]

In 1926, Dikshit recovered a silver casket from a wall of late period at Mohenjodaro. It contained jewellery along with twelve silver pieces. Of these, one square piece had a cuneiform inscription, showing that the piece was either imported from Assyria or inscribed in Sindh, by one who was acquainted with the script. Three were the silver ingots, weighing 34, 45 and 66.5 grains, respectively, following no regular weight system. Of the other remaining, four pieces, which weigh 45, 90, 91 and 94 grains, are different from the Indus Valley weight system, of which the unit is of 13 grains. Only two pieces weighing about 52 and 57 grains may be said to conform to the weight standard. These are the only pieces corresponding the size and shape of the coins. They bear no symbols and inscriptions and do not follow the recognised weight standard. Dikshit considered all the pieces, square or rectangular, as following Babylonian weight standard and as precursors of punch-marked coins.[27] Kosambi (1941) is inclined to stretch back the antiquity of coinage to the period of the Indus Valley civilization. He based his opinion on the few square and circular pieces, which were found with jewellery in a silver vase at Mohenjodaro.[28] He observed,

> There are two interpretations possible: that the pieces represent purchases of silver to an approximate weight, having had a little margin left and in fact as little margin as possible with fairly clumsy cutting tools. If the latter explanation is accepted, the conclusion must also be taken that we are already beginning to see bits of a precious metal trimmed to standard weight, hence the beginning of a coinage system. In any case the coinage that came later must have originated in some such way, if this be not its immediate origin.[29]

The archaeologists generally fix the relative chronology of the excavated materials with the help of P.G. Ware around 1000 BCE, N.B.P. roughly to 600 BCE to 2000 BCE and with the help of C-14 dating applied to organic materials contained in the strata. Ray (1959) suggested that since the punch-marked coins occur in association with Nothern Black Polished Ware, the beginning of coinage in India should also be assigned to the fifth century BCE, for at no site in the subcontinent have coins so far been reported from a still earlier level. On the other hand, at several sites they appear somewhat later and have therefore, been assigned to the fourth century BCE.[30] In 1966, in his article 'Archaeological Evidence on the Date of Punch-Marked Coins', Ray has summed up the archaeological evidence on the antiquity of punch-marked coins.

> It is true that these coins do not contain any internal evidence about their dates, at least which can be interpreted as such uptil now. The interpretation of symbols is as a matter of mere guesswork. The analysis of weights and measures may be helpful, at times to fix the comparative chronological relation within a group, but cannot be applied to decide positive dating. It is the external evidence to which one has to turn to and this consists mainly of the position of these monetary issues in stratigraphic sequence of closely observed excavation.[31]

The time from c. 600 BCE to 300 CE is indeed an enormous period to which punch-marked coins have been ascribed. A critical analysis of punch-marked coins in the context of the levels of their find and comparative study of the associated materials are likely to yield further results contracting the assigned period of circulation. While broadly speaking the N.B.P. is contemporary to punch-marked coins, stratigraphic evidence nowhere shows that the punch-marked coins are anterior to N.B.P. Rather, it is slightly later in date than the beginning of the N.B.P. So if the origin of the N.B.P. is considered to be c. 600 BCE, the possibility of punch-marked coins being pushed onwards up to c. 500 BCE or so cannot be excluded. It has also to be remembered that punch-marked coins have many distinctive classes, based on symbols, weights, sizes, nature of metal used and mode of manufacture. A detailed analysis of all these factors, with reference to stratigraphic evidence, is likely to produce results by which individual punch-marked coins can be fitted to particular geographical and chronological context, and even the chronological interrelation of various types within the group can be determined with reasonable accuracy. With such detailed evidence at disposal, even solitary find will speak for itself.[32]

Dhavalikar (1975) suggests,

> In the Indian subcontinent the bent bar coins are found only in the Gandhara region, whereas the punch-marked coins, which are usually rectangular or oval pieces of silver punched with symbols, are widely found. The bent bars are the earliest coins, but the punch-marked coins begin slightly later, in any case not later than the fifth or fourth century BCE, as evidence from excavations demonstrates. The bent bars (*śatamāna*) are the earliest coins of India dated to the end of the sixth century or late fifth century BCE, appear to have been inspired by the similar currency of the Achamenian empire.[33] The bar currency must have been found to be not only cumbersome to handle but also difficult for smaller transactions. In India, therefore, the authorities may have issued pieces of silver cut off from such bars. It is these pieces of silver, either rectangular or oval or irregular in shape, which were stamped with symbols, and they are the true punch-marked coins of India. It appears that bent bars were current only for a very brief period some time in the first half of the fifth century BC or even earlier, for they have been identified as the silver *śatamānas* of 100 *rattīs* referred to in the later Vedic literature.
>
> Soon after, in the fifth century, only the punch-marked coins appear and in a very short time they become current over almost all over north India, more particularly in the Ganges valley, as the evidence from several excavated sites shows. Thereafter the punch-marked coins begin to occur in eastern and central India and slightly later in western India as well.[34]

The recent discovery of the bar currency without symbols in Iran (Nush-i-jan, near Malayir) and with symbols in Afghanistan is of great significance. The bent-bars are the earliest coins of India, dated to the end of the 6th century BCE, as is attested by the finds of silver punch-marked coins in Indian excavations, particularly in northern sites. This dating is further corroborated by radiocarbon dates.[35]

Dhavalikar also suggests the impact of Iran in the word *kārṣāpaṇa.* According to him, the same idea is expressed twice, using two different words in reduplicated form. The *kārṣa* was a Persian weight standard and *paṇa* the Indian weight standard. The early Indian copper coins, which have been identified as of the *paṇa* class, weigh 80 *rattīs* or 146.4 grains. They, however, were current in those areas where silver currency was not in use.[36]

The above reading gives us the framework of diverse terms by which the various coins were known. Beyond the terms and names, for coins, we have not touched upon the very fact that such a coinage indeed existed. Local or imperial, silver or any other metal, this coinage was above all the very first coinage of ancient India. The maiden coinage was of course a local/ imperial issue and preponderantly in silver. However a hoary antiquity may have been suggested by us on the strength of the Vedic and later references cited above, it is necessary to find out whether such an antiquity is also borne out by archaeological and numismatic evidence. We surely have reports of punch-marked coins having been found as chance finds and accidental discovery of hoards, in addition, we have punch-marked coins found in proper contexts in archaeological excavations. In the beginning, say in the later part of the 19th century, there were too inadequate numbers of the punch-marked coins discovered to make any distinct impression on the scholars. However, as the number of stray finds as well as coin hoards grew in course of years, there came a realization that we had stumbled upon the earliest coinage of India.

This monograph deals with silver punch-marked coins of Imperial Series, by which name these coins are known today. All these coins invariably bear a group of five symbols on one face of the coin, having the weight standard of 3.5 grams or 56 grains or 32 *rattīs*. Such coins are found in abundance all over the subcontinent of India. This suggests that these were the official coinage of a central authority, who had control over most parts of the country. Historical and numismatic evidence indicate that during the period, when these coins were in circulation between c. 5th and 2nd centuries BCE, Magadha was the most powerful kingdom and hence, these coins could be ascribed as the coinage of the Magadha Empire.

To come back to the classification of silver punch-marked coin series, these coins are classified into two main groups: (i) those coins issued by the states/*janapadas* (most of them maintained their independent status until up to c. 4th century BCE) are of different fabric, weight and in style, and (ii) the coins issued by the imperial authority, between c. 4th century BCE and c. 2nd century BCE, are of some defined weight. These vary in shape like round, square, rectangular, elliptical and irregular size and fabric. The coins distinguished into first category are termed as 'Local Series' and the coins of second category are called 'Imperial Series'. The largest numbers of coins are those that bear five official symbols.

During the reign of Bimbisāra, the coinage of the Magadhan kingdom was reformed in both weight and design. The coins were replaced by broad thin *karṣāpaṇa* of 3.5 grams. Single punch coin design was replaced by five separate punches. The coins of Magadha issued during the period of Bimbisāra bear two main symbols—sun and six-armed, which are the constant symbols on later coins of five-symbol series. These coins are known as *paṇa* in earlier literature and as *kārṣāpaṇa*, later identified as Magadha issues. This was the main silver coinage circulating in the subcontinent for the next hundred to two hundred years and it is by far the commonest kind of punch-marked coins known. It appears that the four-symbol coin series of Magadha *mahājanapada* was replaced by the five-symbol series, sometime during the period. It is more likely that Series I coins were struck in the period of Ajātaśatru and his successors would have issued some of the later varieties of Series I and most of the varieties of Series II and III.

Silver punch-marked coins of the Imperial Series have been classified as Series I–VII by Gupta and Hardaker.[37] Coins of Series I are assigned to the period of Bimbisāra and Ajātaśatru; Series II and III to the successors of Ajātaśatru; Series IV (IVa-IVc) to Śiśunāga and his successors, Śiśunāga dynasty; and Series IVd to the Naṅda dynasty; Series Va and Vb to Çandragupta and Bindusāra – Maurya dynasty; Series VIa and VIb to Aśoka and his successors – Maurya dynasty and Śuṅga dynasty; and the coins of Series VII to the successors of the Maurya. As already mentioned, the classification of the coins is followed as proposed by Gupta and Hardaker and the chronology adopted here is based on the date of the Buddha's *mahāparinirvāṇa* (c. 486 century BCE). It can be proposed that the five-symbol series or Series I would have started sometime in the period of Bimbisāra and Ajātaśatru, and Series II, as suggested by Gupta and Hardaker, may be contemporary with the latest issues of Series I and may have been struck by the successors of Ajātaśatru. Having thus established the chronology of the *kārṣāpaṇa* coinage between c. 4th century BCE and c. 2nd century BCE, the coins of the hoard under study can conveniently be proposed in the chronological time span between c. 3rd century BCE and 2nd century BCE. It is to be mentioned here that the earliest coins present in this hoard belong to Series II. However, the coins belonging to Series II and Series III are less in number (only 19 coins). The coins classified under Series IVa by Gupta and Hardaker are not present in this hoard. Even the coins of Series IVb and IVc are only 4 in number.[38]

NOTES AND REFERENCES

1. *Ariana Antiqua*, 484; A.S. Altekar (1953), "Origin and Early History of Coinage in Ancient India", *JNSI*, XV (I) 1.
2. *JASB*, (I), 394; Edward Thomas (1971-Reprint), *Essays on Indian Antiquities* (I), 53-4.
3. Edward Thomas (1971), *Prinsep's Essays* (I) 54; A.S. Altekar (1953), 1.
4. *JASB* (I) 394.
5. *JASB* (IV) 626.
6. J. Allan (1936), *BMC*, Introduction, Ixxi.
7. J.A. Decourdemanched (1912), "Note sur les anciennes monnaies de l'inde – dities Punch-marked coins et sur le Manou", *Journal Asiatique*, 19:117-32; D.R. Bhandarkar (1921), *AIN*, 118-20.
8. J. Kennedy (1898), "The Early Commerce of Babylon with India", *JRAS*, 279 ff.
9. V.A. Smith, *Imperial Gazetteer* (II), 183.
10. V.A. Smith (1906), *IMC*, (I), 183.
11. E.J. Rapson (1898), *Indian Coins*, 2; *JRAS* (1895), 869.
12. Thomas Edward (1971), 211; A.S. Altekar (1953), *JNSI*, (XV), 2-3.
13. *NC* (1873), XIII, 212.
14. A. Cunningham (1891), *CAI* 43.
15. S.K. Chakrabortty (1973), *Ancient Indian Numismatics*, 33.
16. D.R. Bhandarkar (1921), *AIN*, 70-71.
17. *Ibid.*, 25.
18. A.S. Altekar (1953), 23-26.
19. P.L. Gupta & T.R. Hardaker (1985), *AISPMC*, 29.
20. J. Cribb (2005), *The Indian Coinage Tradition: Origins Continuity and Changes*, 62.
21. *Ibid.*, 19-20, 69.
22. M. Mitchiner (1975), *Ancient and Classical World*, 499; (1973), The Origin of Indian Coinage, London.
23. Sir Walter Elliot (1886), *Coins of Southern India*, 45; *JASB*, III, 44.
24. A.S. Altekar (1953), 24-25.
25. *Ibid.*, 24; fn. 2; Sir Walter Elliot (1858), *Madras Journal of Literature and Science*, 227.
26. A.S. Altekar (1953), 24.
27. *JRAS* (1937), 7-26; A.S. Altekar (1953), 14-15.
28. D.D. Kosambi (1941), "On the Origin and Development of Silver Coinage in India", *Current Science*, 10 (9) 395-400; M.K. Dhavalikar (1975), "The Beginning of Coinage in India", *World Archaeology*, VI, No. 3, 332.
29. D.D. Kosambi (1941), 398-99.
30. S.C. Ray (1959), *Stratigraphic Evidence of Coins in Indian Excavations and Some Allied Issues*, 13-14.
31. S.C. Ray (1966), "Archaeological Evidence on the Date of Punch-marked Coins", *The Chronology of the Punch-marked Coins*, 26-27.
32. *Ibid.*, 37-38.
33. M.K. Dhavalikar (1975), 334-35.
34. *Ibid.*, 336.
35. *Ibid.*, 338.
36. *Ibid.*, 335-37.
37. P.L. Gupta & T.R. Hardaker (1985), *AISPMC*, 31-32, Table (I) 9.
38. *Ibid.*, 62-63.

5

Metallurgy

Before discussing the hoard proper (Section 2), we intended to scan through the work already done on the earliest phase of Indian numismatics. The preceding paragraphs were penned in that direction. With regard to future studies, pertinent issues vis-à-vis source of metals will be on the following lines:

a) of all the metals, why was silver selected as the commonest metal for the purpose of coinage?
b) did smelting of silver bear any particular advantage in this selection?
c) which areas in the north were known for silver smelting?
d) what type of silver ores are found in different areas? and,
e) was silver, used for minting punch-marked coins, selected from any particular smelting area?

> Coins will not carry much meaning for economic history unless we identify the ancient sources of gold, silver and other metals, explain the abundance and paucity of coins, determine the area and period of circulation, and above all calculate the volume of coins in the context of time and place. At the moment all our ideas about the quantities of coins are impressionistic and subjective.[1]

Thousands of silver punch-marked coins—have been reported—hoards and stray finds – and yet more to be recovered in future. These serve as an indicator of the abundance of coins that were struck. The metallurgical studies of these coins from different hoards also reveal a high percentage of silver. These coins also seem to imply that during the period that these coins were minted, there was no paucity of silver; on the contrary, silver was abundantly available.

SILVER: SCARCE OR PLENTIFUL

> Silver is one of the five noble metals. It has white brilliant colour, malleability and resistance to atmospheric oxidation. Hence, it is in use since last 6000 years. In India, there are no known native silver deposits except the small and unique Bharak deposit of silver in Rajasthan. It occurs generally with lead, zinc, copper and gold ores and is extracted as a by-product from electrolysis or chemical methods. Silver was recovered in the past as a co-product in gold refining at KGF Complex and Hutti

> Gold Mines in Karnataka, as a by-product in smelting and refining of lead, zinc and copper concentrates at Chanderiya and Debari smelters in Rajasthan, Tundoo and Moubandar (Ghatsila) smelters in Jharkhand and at Visakhapatnam smelter in Andhra Pradesh. The present production of silver comes from Ghatsila copper smelter of HCL, Chanderiya lead-zinc smelter of HZL and from gold refinery of HGML. In addition, Hindalco extracts silver as by-product during smelting of imported copper concentrates, at Dahej in Gujarat.[2]

Gopal has tried to find plausible answers to some of these questions – citing J.C. Brown and A.K. Dey (*India's Mineral Wealth*) and John Marshall (*Mohenjodaro and the Indus Valley Civilisation*): India's present poverty in respect of silver is well known.[3] At present silver in very small quantity is recovered in association with gold from the Kolar mines in Mysore and from Anantpur in Madras.[4] At some other places silver is to be found as an impurity of lead. Argentiferous lead from Zawar (Udaipur, Rajasthan) and Bawdwin (or Dawdwin) (Shan States, Burma) alone is generally considered.[5] But it may be pointed out that Bhagalpur, Manbhum, Monghyr and Singhbhum in Bihar, Rewa, Durg, Hoshangabad and Jabalpur in Madhya Pradesh, Cuddapah and Karnul in Madras and the Kulu valley in Punjab also have argentiferous lead, though the quantity of silver extracted from them is not adequate enough for the extraction of silver from this source to be of much consequence.[6] The doubt has been expressed if, in the context of the primitive ways of extraction in antiquity, the process of extracting silver from such ores could have been better paying.[7] Of course, one would not be justified to expect the modern technological advancement in any period of antiquity but we may note that in removing the impurities of silver ore and in extracting silver from lead, India had made considerable advancements in the ancient period.[8] Moreover, in ancient times when labour was cheap, it may have been worthwhile to extract even small percentage of silver from such ores.[9]

There are no references to silver ores in ancient India. Most of the silver was imported product of smelting of local ores. It is quite likely that silver ores also came from Baluchistan, Afghanistan and Iran. A small amount of silver could have come from the gold mines of South India, where this metal was found naturally alloyed with gold and believed to have been used since the Harappan times.[10] According to Smith, India was never known for production of silver and the paucity of metal as compared with gold and copper in excavations of the Indus Valley would clearly indicate that silver was at best mainly secured from foreign lands and was not in common use; and the argument that the silver coins are extremely old would not put out of the court the claim of copper to be of higher quantity. Smith asserted, "In some part of the country the use of silver preceded that of copper."[11] Cunningham is also of the opinion that silver was mainly imported from abroad: "India, in fact, produced little or no silver, while gold was abundant,"[12] therefore, its paucity stood in the way of its use for the manufacturing of coins. Some of the states in ancient India like Vidisa and Malava retained only copper coins even though silver had come in use in the neighbouring states.[13] India was never noted for the production of silver and had always to depend mainly on foreign countries for supply of silver metal.[14]

It is obvious that in the earlier period, when the geographical horizon was limited in character, the source of silver must have been within the reach of their contact. In this context, any contact with the regions to the south of the Vindhyas and to the east of Bengal and Bihar are not established before the 4th century BCE. Not much evidence is available to work on a probability of any sizable import of silver from Burma and Mysore. Thus, it is likely that in the earlier period silver was mostly extracted out of argentiferous lead ores that were available in India. Hence, it was silver from these indigenous sources that was used for minting coins in the earlier period. A chemical analysis of the metallic contents of the coins can thus be helpful in determining the source of the silver used. However, the opposite view may support the possibility that India imported silver in abundance.[15]

SILVER IN PERSIA AND AFGHANISTAN

The studies reveal that Taxila and Pushakalavati became significant commercial centres of trade with Mesopotamia in about 6th century BCE.[16] The silver mines of Persia and Afghanistan were within approach and not far from the borders of India. Famous silver mines near Herat and the head of the Panjshir valley in Hindukush were rich in argentiferous lead deposits.[17] It is significant that in earlier periods, whenever an appreciable use of silver is noticeable, contacts with Afghanistan were close. Thus, silver objects are first found in the Harappan context,[18] which is known to have maintained brisk commercial relations with the regions situated even to the west of Afghanistan. Another important discovery of silver objects is from Sirkap (Taxila).[19] At this time the city was under the Parthian rulers, who also controlled a large part of Afghanistan.[20] It is possible that in the case of punch-marked coins also, contact with Persia and Afghanistan can be demonstrated. It has been suggested that in some quarters punch-marked coins were the currency struck by the Achaemenid rulers for their Indian provinces.[21] This opinion that punch-marked coins were minted by Achaemenid kings was strongly refuted. It is to be mentioned that the Bent-bar coins, which form the earliest series among the punch-marked coins, circulated in areas that were originally parts of the Achaemenid Empire. *kārṣāpaṇa*, the term used for punch-marked coins, is based on the weight of *kārṣa*, though differing from *Karsa in*, a weight unit in Achaemenid records has close resemblance in the form of its name.[22]

It is about c. 500-600 BCE that silver became abundantly available. Most of it came from Afghanistan and Persia as a result of international trade. Silver for coins was available in three types, namely *Tuthatat* of Tutha Mountain, *Gandika* from Burma, and *Kambu* from Afghanistan's Kamboja. Kambu silver was used for earlier coins more than the other two types. Certain small ingot of silver, whose mark is three circular dots, often known as pulley, represent probably the earliest form. The heavy bent-bars of silver and copper with heptha-radiated symbol stamped on the two ends of concave surface seem to be the next in order. These two categories are believed to have been in circulation as coins at least as early as 600 BCE.[23]

SILVER IN ANTIQUITY

The earliest appearance of silver is in the form of the Harappan antiquities. However, to the best of our knowledge, it has not been reported from any site in association with the Painted Grey Ware, Northern Black Polished Ware or any other early ware. It is also noticed from Sirkap (Taxila) about the first century CE. Its absence from the intervening period could be accidental, but may also be interpreted to show the paucity of silver for not being in much use during the period.[24] The reports of Rupar excavations also support the suggestion. The silver objects first reported from Period IV (three silver utensils of ritual use – a ladle, a spoon and a pedestalled cup) are described as the product of Gupta craftsmanship.[25]

SOURCE AND PURITY

Bhardwaj has suggested that –

> ... the impurity patterns of Mohenjodaro silver (the chemical analysis of, silver from Lothal is not available) and punch-marked coins in general show that their source was argentiferous galena rather than electrum. However, silver plates reported from GUNGERIA show 3.70% gold and punch-marked coins in the Lucknow Museum have also been reported to contain 10.53% gold. This could imply that a method of separation of Silver from Gold was worked out during the Copper Hoard period (4, 11). The production of both lead and silver was from the same Ore - argentiferous galena (basically an ore of Lead in which silver occurs as an impurity) and smelting of this one as an extraction of lead from it is one of the simplest metallurgical operations. In ancient times metallic Lead could have been obtained by simply heaping the ore on top of the field placed on the grounds or in a pit. Fused metal, which melts at 327° C, could have run out at the bottom of the heap and was collected - (Reduction temperature of the lead Oxide is well within 800° C and so smelting could be done easily in domestic fire using Charcoal). Crude Lead (base bullion) as obtained above was repeatedly melted and crystallized and Lead crystals were removed. This resulted in the concentration of silver as in the modern Pattinson's process. Metallurgical studies of punch-marked coins reveal that despite primitive techniques in application by 600 BCE, Indians could obtain silver of high purity (0.1 to 0.5% Lead was the main impurity). It indicates that cupellation was carried out with great perfection. Alloying of silver with copper was deliberate and in correct proportion, giving ease in coding, providing optimum strength and wear resistance. It also economized the metal.[26]

NAMES OF SILVER

Literary evidence provides more information. It would seem from the absence of any common term signifying silver in the Indo-European languages that silver was not known to Indo-Europeans before their dispersal.[27] In some of their languages, the term for 'bright' or 'whitish' is found later on to have been used for silver. However, it cannot be inferred definitely that the term actually signified silver from the very beginning. In some non-Indo-European languages also, the term for silver originally meant 'white-shining.'[28] In the *Ṛgveda,* the Sanskrit term *Rajata* was used for silver in the adjective sense 'white.'[29] In *Taittirīya*[30], *Kathaka Saṁhitās*[31] and *Śatapatha Brāhmaṇa,*[32] "Silver is named as *rajata-hiraṇyam* or *rajata hiraṇyam.*"[33] The descriptive term would suggest that acquaintance of the Vedic Aryans with this metal was of recent origin.[34] It is to be noted that the *Vājasaneyi Saṁhitā*[35] mentions *hiraṇya* (gold), *ayas, śyāma* (iron), *lohā* (copper), *sīsā* (lead) and *trapu* (tin), but silver is absent from this list of metals. Subsequently, the term *rajata* is used as a substantive and denoting silver.[36] Objects made of silver—ornaments and dishes—are mentioned in the *Brāhmaṇa* literature.[37] The term *rajata* has been referred to in the *Jātakas* along with other metals known in the period.[38] The *Arthaśāstra* refers to regular use of silver.[39] It also describes the good, bad, pure and impure silver metal in reference with the description of the methods employed by goldsmiths for adulteration of gold by substituting base metals such as silver and copper.[40] The text further gives the ratio in which silver is to be used along with other metals for jewellery and other articles.[41] In Greek and Roman accounts also, there are occasional references to the use of silver objects.[42] References of regular use of silver are found in Indian literature.[43] In the list of other metals—gold, copper, lead, tin and iron, silver is also mentioned with slight variations in nomenclature in reference to the works on medicines and alchemy.[44] The *dhātukriyā* gives a number of synonyms of silver and adds that there are hundreds of others.[45]

INTERNATIONAL TRADE IN METALS

In the Old Testaments, the products mentioned in the account of the Ophir trade are gold, sandalwood, precious stones, ivory, silver, apes and peacocks.[46] The name Ophir resembles Abhira, but Lassen has referred to the Indian city Sophir (Suppara).[47] Another Indian name which resembles Ophir is Sauvira.[48] However, the northern end of India's west coast, where Ophir is located, is purely an agricultural country and does not have products mentioned here. Some scholars locate Ophir on the Arabian coast of the Persian Gulf, a trading centre dealing with India. It is to be noted that most of the commodities are of Indian origin. However, the words like ape, ivory, sandalwood, almug and peacock are derived from Sanskrit words.[49] Gopal stated, "Unless the list is suggested to include commodities of other countries also, the reference would imply that India was in a position to export silver in the early period."[50] Another reference in the Old Testament is that King Solomon's (933-923 BCE) 'navy of Tharshish' brought him every three years ivory, gold, silver, apes and peacocks.[51] If on the basis of the inclusion of ivory, apes and peacocks the source of articles is taken to be India, it will also support the case for India having silver.[52]

REFERENCES TO INDIAN SILVER

A more direct and authentic testimony to Indian silver is to be found in *Indika* of Megasthenes.[53] The passage reads: 'And while the soils bear on its surface all kinds of fruits which are known to cultivation, it has also underground numerous veins of all sorts of metals, for it contains much gold and silver, and copper and iron in no small quantity, and even tin and other metals, which are employed in making articles of use of ornament, as well as the implements and accoutrements of war.' It is worth mentioning that Ball has also quoted the observation of Megasthenes with approval as being absolutely true.[54] Strabo says on the testimony of Gorgos' the mining, that good mines of gold and silver existed in other mountains not far from the Salt Range in the Punjab.[55] Hiuen Tsang also speaks of gold and silver as natural products of India.[56] He mentions specifically silver along with gold as being available from Śatadru[57] (Śatadru or river Satluj seems to have been used for the kingdom through which it passed and of which Sarhind was the chief town). Bolor[58] and Takka,[59] Sulaiman[60] and Al Masudi[61] refer to the reports of gold and silver mines in the Gurjara-Pratihara kingdom of Kanauj. They further speak of gold and silver to be found in the kingdom of Rahma,[62] generally identified with Pala Kingdom.[63] However, Bengal is not known to have either gold or silver. It is to be mentioned that besides the testimony of the *Arthaśāstra* and *Vaijayantī*, small quantities of silver have been found in Manbhum and Deogurh (Santhāla Parganā).[64] Probably, Arab accounts of Rahma have mixed up Bengal with lower Burma and Pegu, where these metals are found.[65] Chau Ju Kua[66] included silver in his list of exports of Tien Chu, which generally refers to India, but all the commodities in the list cannot be said to have originated from eastern India only.[67] It is worth mentioning that *Ain-i-Akbari*, the 16th-century text, speaks of silver mines near Agra and in Kashmir.[68]

Before going through the native supply of silver, there is also evidence that speaks of India receiving or importing silver from outside. *Periplus* speaks of expensive silver vessels being imported into Barygaza for the king's use.[69] A more specific reference in favour of the argument is that silver and gold plates were imported into Barbaricum.[70] Chinese sources also speak about receiving silver from China.[71] The Chinese accounts significantly remark that in return for the native produce which the Chola embassy of 1077 offered, the Chinese emperor gave strings of cash and tales of silver.[72] Marco Polo refers to a ship that came from east and brought silver along with other articles to the kingdom of Melibar (Malabar).[73] Likewise, he describes foreign merchants coming to Cambay and bringing with them silver also.[74] Tavernier says that China sent silver in exchange for silk and gold from Assam and northern Burma.[75] The Zomorin of Calicut, in a letter to the king of Portugal sent through Vasco-da-Gama, refers to his own kingdom expecting silver along with other things in return for her own export.[76] The medieval texts of alchemy, however, make no mention about silver while referring to mines of other metals.

On the other hand, Kauṭilya speaks of many varieties of silver and gives the impression that there was no scarcity of silver during the period.[77] There is no conceivable reason as to why all of a sudden the supply of indigenous silver should dry up immediately after Kauṭilya. It was exactly the period that the foreign supply increased as the trade with the West must have been accelerated by Greek invasion under Alexander. Foreign trade was an important feature in the period of Çandragupta Maurya.[78]

Arthaśāstra gives a definite impression that there were silver mines in the country. The features described in the text provide some clues for identification of silver ores.[79] The text specifically names five regions, which were yielding silver—*Tutthodagataṁ gauḍikam kāmbukaṁ çakravālikaṁ çarūpyam.*[80] Of these, Gauḍa (Bengal) is clear but the remaining sources (Tutthodgata, Kambuka and Çakravā-lika) are difficult to identify.[81] According to the commentators, Tuttha, Kambu and Çakravāla are the names of mountains whereas Gauḍa is Kāmarūpa region.[82]According to Ray, these silver ores which were till then not known to occur in India suggested their importation from neighbouring countries.[83] However, Gopal is of the opinion that the specific enumeration of the mines and description of silver ores leave no doubt that most of the mines listed in the passage were in India.[84] The commentary quoted by R. Shamasastry describes the specific colour of the silver from these five mines.[85] Varāhamihira[86] and Vaijayantī[87] (early medieval) mention *baṅga-jivanam* as one of the names of silver and thus associates it with Bengal. The *Rasaratnasmuççaya* does not name any specific mine of silver but mentions silver as being of three kinds: that of mythical origin (*sahajam*), begotten of mines *(khani-sañjātam)*, and artificial (*kṛtrimam*).[88]

These references indicate that there appears to be a sizeable number of mines in the northern part of India, in some parts of Punjab, Rajasthan and northwestern frontier provinces and with another concentration in Bengal or to its east. The paucity of silver is noticed from the first century but it seems to have been felt in some areas, which possibly could not utilise the native sources. From the combined testimony of Megasthenes and Kauṭilya, it appears that the native supply of silver was by no means scarce. It must have been the western mines, which supplied silver for the punch-marked coins. It is, therefore, not necessary to connect the source of silver with foreign trade with Afghanistan and Persia or to date the beginning of punch-marked coins only after the beginning of such trade contacts.[89]

MORE REFERENCES TO TRADE IN SILVER

Silver in India, as mentioned above, is generally extracted from argentiferous lead. The presence of lead suggests the indigenous origin of silver. India's mercantile contacts with the ancient West are not known with certainty. The evidences of the contact are liable to be interpreted in different ways. However, trade contact has been suggested by scholars through the Phoenicians during the golden age of their history (1200-900 BCE).[90] The Phoenicians mostly supplied Indian spices and perfume to the western markets, as can be guessed from the available evidences, among goods of a definite Indian nature.[91] However, later on, as is shown by the Old Testament, the Phoenicians built a fleet and Hiram (969-936 BCE) of tyre, for Solomon (963-923 BCE).[92] This fleet, possibly under the Phoenician navigators,[93] made successful triennial trips to Ophir and brought back home frankincense, silver, ivory, apes and peacocks,[94] probably also algum or almug trees and gold.[95] The location of Ophir is not certain. According to Josephus, the golden land was located in India[96] somewhere around the mouth of the Indus, in Abhira territory.[97]

The Hebrews under Solomon brought silver from Tarshish. "The imports of Tarshish were silver beaten into plates (Jeremiah, 10:9) and iron, tin and lead (Ezek, 27:12). It is believed that Tarshish was Tartessues, in South Spain, near Gibraltar (Herod, IV.152). The mineral wealth of the region attracted the Phoenicians, who established a colony there. Spain has long been noted for its mineral wealth."[98]

The Jews knew India as Hoddu[99] in Hebrew, which apparently seems to be derived from *hindav*.[100] Hoddu was the eastern limit of the Eastern Empire. The western trade advanced in the early centuries of the 1st millennium BCE. In the 7th–6th century BCE, much of the trade was dominated by the Babylonians.[101] With the rise of Persian rulers as the paramount power in Western Asia, Indian trade must have increased. As also in later period that merchants brought gold and silver to exchange with other commodities or Indian goods,[102] so also in early times. All the trade of India with the West must have brought considerable quantity of silver in the country by 6th century BCE. It has been suggested that India in ancient times received much of its silver from the mines of both Spain and Asia Minor. The discovery of some silver pieces from the Indus cities – one of which at least is a West Asian piece as it contains a cuneiform inscription – shows that they knew this metal. But Aryans came to know of it rather late and hence referred it as 'white gold'. Later Vedic references to silver conclusively indicate of its knowledge. In all probability, during much of the later Vedic period, silver remained an item of luxury and used only by the nobility. The precious metals, especially silver, thus received in exchange of Indian goods suggested the necessity of a common media of exchange, acceptable to all.[103]

The opinion that India produced no silver cannot be accepted, though the quantity produced was small indeed.[104] "Small quantities have been found though associated with lead in Kullu and Manbhum and at Deogurh in the Santhāla Parganā."[105] However, it is noticeable that silver was not so abundant as gold during the period.[106] This view is further strengthened by the statement of Jeremiah, who points to the East as the source of gold, and to the West as that of silver, when he speaks of "silver beaten into plates brought from Tarshish, and gold from Uphaz (or Ophir)".[107] There also exists a strong belief that silver as a metal was rarely available in Vedic India. The question then arises as to how it becomes abundantly available by the 6th century BCE? Commercial interaction with other countries may be the answer. It has been suggested that most of the silver came from Afghanistan and Persia as a result of international commerce.[108] Importation of silver was a regular feature in the ancient commerce of India. The relative cheapness of gold would facilitate the flow of silver coins to this country, where they would remain in active circulation.[109]

MORE RESEARCH INDICATED

To sum up, the chronology of punch-marked coins, on the basis of intrinsic evidence and that evidence derived from archaeological excavations, is more or less agreed to be between 6th century BCE and 1st century CE. In many seminars and colloquia, numismatists and archaeologists have tried to push its antiquity, taking into account the gamut of literary evidence, by a couple of centuries but could not evolve a consensus. Metallurgical studies leading to any firm hypotheses, let alone clear theories on the provenance of silver, are conspicuous by its absence save some contribution on the subject. In the present state of knowledge, chemical composition of the punch-marked coins also does not conclusively provide any firm indicator in this direction. A holistic approach of research and study into various aspects of coins—location of the hoard, physical features of its geographical area, metallurgical studies consisting of chemical composition, metallographic structure of coins, measurement, weight, thickness, specific gravity, authentication of minting of coins and availability of metal from other areas—may alone define its antiquity in unambiguous terms.[110]

NOTES AND REFERENCES

1. R.S. Sharma (1976), "Coins and Problems of Early Indian Economic History" (Seminar on Coins as a Source of Economic History of Ancient India, 1969, Patna), *Memoirs Series*, No. 6, The Numismatic Society of India, 7.
2. Ibm.nic.in/silver.pdf
3. J.C. Brown and A.K. Dey (1955), *India's Mineral Wealth*, 142; Wadia, *Geology in India*, 479; O.H.K. Spate (1964), *India and Pakistan*, London, 266; J. Marshall (1951), *Taxila*, 607, 4; A. Cunningham (1891), *CAI*, 5. Quoted by L. Gopal (1966), 'Source of Silver for the Punch-marked Coins', *The Chronology of the Punch-marked Coins*, No. 1, 65.
4. J.C. Brown and A.K. Dey (1955), 140; J. Marshall (1931), *Mohenjodaro and the Indus Valley Civilisation* (II), 675.
5. C.J. Brown and A.K. Dey (1955), 137-40; Wadia, *Geology in India*, 479; P. Ray (1956), *History of Chemistry*, 28-29.
6. J. Marshall (1931), (II), 675; (1951) *Taxila*, 607; O.H.K. Spate (1964), *India and Pakistan*, 266; Sir Walter Elliot (1886), *Coins of Southern India*, 51, fn. 1. Of these, only Bawdwin is of any economic importance: "It should not be forgotten that the Chinese mined this ore deposit for its silver content alone for centuries, and the vast quantities of cupellation slag which they left behind were some measure of the large amounts of the metal which they recovered. Though primarily a lead-zinc-copper sulphide ore body, it is easy to understand how it obtained its Burmese name of Bawdwin (Dawdwin) or 'silver mine'" - J.C. Brown and, A.K. Dey (1955), 140.
7. J. Marshall (1931), (II), 675.
8. P. Ray (1956), *History of Chemistry—Arthaśāstra*, II. 13. 13, 49 (53-54); Ray observes that the procedure given in the *Arthaśāstra* resembles the modern process of cupellation; *Rasarainākara* of Nāgārjuna, I. 13 (Ray, 312); *Sarveśvarasāyana*, 11 (Ray, 142); *Rasaratnasamuççaya*, V.32. - 41 (Ray, 387); *Dhāturatnamālā* (Ray, 409). L. Gopal (1966), 66, fn. 1.
9. L. Gopal (1966), 66.
10. H.C. Bhardwaj (1968), "Aspects of Ancient Indian Technology" (Ph.D. Thesis), Vol. I & II; Bhardwaj & Mishra, *JNSI*, 30, 241-51; For Silver Coins, 1971.
11. V.A. Smith (1906), *IMC*, 136.
12. A. Cunningham (1891), *CAI*, 5.
13. D.R. Bhandarkar (1921), *Lectures on Ancient Indian Numismatics*, 190.
14. *The Cambridge History of India* (I) 343.
15. L. Gopal (1966), 66.
16. "Commercial intercourse with Mesopotamia was developed, both along the overland route through Iran-Afghanistan and Taxila and also maritime trade, which passed through the port of Broach in Avanti. Development of these two separate commercial milieux led to the introduction of two distinct

metrological standards for tariffing silver, one based on a silver unit weighing about 11 grammes and the other based on a lighter unit of 31/2 grammes. The heavy standard was essentially the tariff used along the overland trade route. The heavy unit of silver [c.11 gm] was related to the Babylonian shekel of 10.9 grammes and its later Persic derivative (Shekel 11.2 gms) in the west and to the Indian Satamana weighing 100 rattis (c.11 gm: one ratti was the average weight of the Gunja creeper seed: Abrus precatoris: this weighed in the range 0.104 to 0.117 gm) in the east. The Satamana standard was used in northern Pakistan and in several early states of the upper and middle Ganges valley. The lighter weight standard, essentially the tariff used along the maritime trade route, was linked in the west with the lighter Babylonian shekel of 7.27 grammes and in the east with the Indian Karsapana of 32 rattis (c. 31.2 gm). Use of the Karshapana standard commenced in Avanti and spread across the Ganges valley." M. Mitchiner (1975), *Ancient and Classical World*, 499.

17. J. Marshall (1931) (II), 677.
18. *Ibid.*
19. J. Marshall (1951), ch. 29-30 - Silver Ware and Jewellery – c.1st century CE, Silver vessels and ornaments, 204-06.
20. *Ibid.*, 607.
21. J.A. Decourdemanches (1912), *Journal Asiatique*, 117-32; D.R. Bhandarkar (1921), *AIN*, 118-20 and A.S. Altekar (1953), *JNSI*, (XV), 6-7.
22. A.K. Narain (1957), *JNSI*, (XIX), 181-83; K.de B. Codrington, *Bulletin of the Institute of Archaeology*, No. 4, 1-24.
23. http://prabhu.50g.com/earliest/punch.mark.html
24. P. Mitra (1923), *Pre-Historic India*, 189, reported 102 silver objects from Gungeria in 1870 along with 400 copper axes; V.A. Smith (1905), *IA*, IXXXI, 233 ff. Copper hoards of Gangetic Valley are generally taken to be of pre-Painted Grey Ware period; B.B. Lal (1951), *AI*, No. 7, 20 ff.
25. Y.D. Sharma, *Lalita Kalā* (1955-56) Nos. 1-9, 127.
26. H.C. Bhardwaj, "Aspects of Ancient Indian Technology" (Ph.D. Thesis), Vol. I & II. (Materials.iisc.ernet.in/~wootz/heritage.htm); Bhardwaj & Mishra (1968), *JNSI*, (XXX), 241-51.
27. O. Schrader, *Prehistoric Antiquities of the Aryan People*, 180-86, 119, 126; C.D. Buck, *A Dictionary of Selected Synonyms in the Principal Indo-European Languages*, 610-11. Silver and its parallels in some languages were loans from some common source perhaps somewhere in Asia Minor. L. Gopal (1966), 70, fn. 1.
28. O. Schrader, *op. cit.*, 181.
29. In the Vedic literature, the word *hiraṇya*, sometimes, was used to indicate 'silver'. "Gold is described sometimes as '*harit*' "yellowish" (*KS*, X. 4; *SB*, XII. 4. 4. 6; *Śadviṁśa Brāhmaṇa*, II. 9; Sometimes as '*Rajata*' "*Whitish*" (*TS*, I. 5. 1.2; *SB*, XII. 4. 4. 7; XIII, 4. 2. 10; XIV. I. 3. 4) when probably 'Silver' is alluded to. *The Vedic Index* (II) 505. It is further said - '*Rajata*' as an adjective with '*hiraṇya*' (*TS*, I.5. 1.2; *KS*, X. 4; *SB*, XII. 4. 4. 7; XIII. 2. 10; XIV. I. 3. 4) designate 'silver' ornaments (*rukma*) *SB*, 8. 3. 11); dishes (*pātra*) *TB*, II. 2. 9. 7; III. 9. 6. 5) and coins (*niṣka*) *Pañçaviṁśa Brāhmaṇa*. XVII. 1. 14 - made of silver". D.C. Sircar (1968), *SIC*, 59.
30. *TS*, I. 5. 1. 2.
31. *KS*, X. 4.
32. *SB*, XXII. 4.4.7; XIII. 4.2. 10; XIV. 1. 3. 4.
33. "The term *rajatahiraṇyam* very well suits electrum. It is interesting to note that in the mines of Kolar (Mysore) silver is found associated with gold ores. But it is difficult to believe that this source, beyond the geographical horizon of the Vedic period, was actually in use in those times." L. Gopal (1966), 70, fn. 6.
34. *Ibid.*, 70, fn. 7. "Silver is rare and harder to get than gold. Gold is found in the sands of river but silver occurs only in mountains. In the history of mankind, oriental countries in particular, silver, for this very reason, appears later than gold."
35. *Vājasaneyisaṁhitā*, XVII. 2.1.

36. *Maitrāyaṇīsaṁhitā*, II. 2. 2; *Atharvaveda*, V. 28. 1; XIII. 4. 51; *Aitareya Brāhmaṇa*, VII. 12. 2; *Ṣaḍviṁśa Brāhmaṇa*, VI. 6.
37. *SB*, XII. 8. 3. 11. – *Athasuvaraṇarajatau rukmau vyupāsyati; TB*, II. 2. 9. 7; III. 9. 6. 5.
38. II. 296 - G. 16-17; I. 351; IV. 60 – G. 101, 85 – G. 142; V, 416; VI, 119 and also II. 6, 67; IV 102 - G. 31, 256; VI, 279 - G. 1224. Quoted by L. Gopal (1966), 71, fn. 3.
39. IV, 107; *Nāyādhmmakahā Tīkā* I, 26, 42 a.
40. II. 13, 42, 51, 54.
41. II. 13. 45. 46.
42. McCrindle, *The Invasion of India by Alexander the Great*, 188-189; As referred by Curtius, when the king made a public appearance, the royal attendants carried in their hands silver censers (VIII. 9). He further, in describing the royal palace, refers to silver images of those birds, which most charm the eye (XV.1.69). *Ancient India as Described in Classical Literature*, 189. Strabo speaks of elephants adorned with gold and silver being included in the processions at festivals. Philotratus (c. 230 CE) refers to the use of silver in pictures on copper tablets hung in a shrine in Taxila. *Ibid.*, 192; L. Gopal (1966), 71, fn. 7-10.
43. *Milindapañho*, 331.
44. P. Ray (1956), *History of Chemistry* (Medicine - for Çaraka and Śuśuruta) 61, 65. (Alchemy - *Rasārṇava*, VII. 89-90; *Dhāturatnamālā*, V. 3. (Ray, 409); Some texts differentiate these six metals called *lohas* (also described as *akṛtrima*) from alloys (*miśra or kṛtrima*), which include bell-metal, brass and *vartaloha-Rasakalpa*, II.1; *Rasaratnasamuççaya*, V. I; X. 70 (Ray, 366, 386, 401). In some texts, lead and tin are described as *pūtis* (emitting a foetid odour) and gold and silver as noble or pure metals—*Rasaratnasamuççaya*, V. 1; *Rasahṛdaya*, IX (Ray, 386, 340). L. Gopal (1966), 72, fn.1-2.
45. L. Gopal (1966), 72, fn. 3, VV, 43-46; P. Ray (1956), 419-20-*Rajatam ça tathā rūpyam çandraśçandrasya dīpakam. āubhrajyotiḥkaram savarṇeṣadbījam tārakaṁ tathā. Anantā varttate taṣāṁ kathā vṛddhikarāśça ye. Sthāpitam laukikaṁ çaiva yenāgranthasamūhanaṁ. Śītavīryyaṁ laghuvīryyaṁ viṣaghnaṁ vātanāśanam. Rasapuñjikaraṁ śrīdaṁ dhātupuñjanakārakam. Ratidaṁ bahuvīryyaṁ ça śubhadhāma ça saṁkṣyam. Etāni rajatanāmāni śatānyanyāni santi vai.* "Among seventeen names of silver mentioned in the *Rajanighantu* (ed. R. Garbe) 35, we find *Çandralohaka Çandrabhuti* and *Çandrahala*, which are derived from the moon.
46. I. Kings, IX, 26-28; I Kings, X, 114; II, Chronicles, VIII, 17, and IX, 10. For almugs – Chronicles X, II; L. Gopal (1966), 73, fn. 1.
47. L. Gopal (1966), 73, fn. 2. *Indische Allerthumskunde*, I, 538-39.
48. L. Gopal (1966), 73, fn. 3—for Ophir being in India—Rufus Learsi, *Israel: A History of the Jewish People*, 61.
49. W.H. Schoff (1912), *The Periplus of the Erythraean Sea*, New York, 175; R.C. Majumdar and A.D. Pusalkar, *The Age of Imperial Unity*, 612.
50. L. Gopal (1966), 73.
51. *Ibid.*, I Kings, X, 18-22.
52. *Ibid.*, 73.
53. *Ibid.*, fn. 6. Fragment I Diodorus II. 36; McCrindle, *Ancient India as described by Megasthenes and Arrian*, 30.
54. V. Ball (1882), *Economic Geology of India*, Introduction, xv; *Journal of the Society of Arts*, 582.
55. XV. 1. 30; McCrindle, *Ancient India as Described in Classical Literature*, 38.
56. Beal, I, 89; L. Gopal (1966), 73.
57. *Ibid.*, 178.
58. *Ibid.*, 135.
59. *Ibid.*, 165 f.
60. Elliot and Dowson, I. 4.
61. *Ibid.*
62. Ferrand, *Textes*, 44, 105.
63. *IHQ* (XVI), 232 ff. R.C. Majumadar (ed.), *History of Bengal* (I) 122.
64. *Coedes, Histoire Ancienne des Etats Hindouises d'Extreme-Orient*, 135; Sir Walter Elliot (1886), 51, fn. 1; L. Gopal (1966), 74.
65. *Ibid.*

66. *Ibid.*, 111.
67. L. Gopal, *Economic Life of Northern India*, 158.
68. Quoted by B.K. Sarkar, *Positive Background of Hindu Sociology*, 97; L. Gopal (1966), 74.
69. W.H. Schoff (1912), 42, 49.
70. *Ibid.*, 37, 39.
71. In 1296, the Chinese government had to prohibit the export of gold and silver and to limit value of trade with Ma'bar, Kulam and Fandaraina. *T'oung Pao*, XV. 425-26; L. Gopal (1966), 76.
72. Chau Ja Kua, 101, n. 12.
73. II. 390.
74. II. 395, 398.
75. III. 16. Quoted by W.H. Schoff (1912), 259.
76. W.H. Schoff (1912), 237.
77. S.K. Chakrabortty (2004), *Indian Numismatics*, 46-47.
78. *Ibid.*; V.A. Smith (1919), *The Oxford History of India*, 87; S.K. Chakrabortty (2004), 47.
79. II.12.6 - *Śaṅkha-karpūra-sphaṭika-navanīta-kapota pārāvata-vimalaka-mayūra-grīvā-varṇāḥ sasyaka-gomedaka-guḍamatsyaṇ-ḍikā-varṇāḥ-kovidāra-padma-pāmalīkalāya-kaṣaumātasī-puṣpa-varṇāḥ sasīsāḥ sāñjanāḥ visrābhinnāḥ śvetābhāḥ kṛṣṇāḥ kṛṣṇābhāḥ śvetāḥ sarve vā lekhābinduçitrā mṛdavo dhmāyamānā na sphumanti bahuphenadhūmāśça rūpyadhātavaḥ*. L. Gopal (1966), 75, fn. 1.
80. *Arthaśāstra*, II.13.10.
81. R.P. Kangle, *Kauṭilya Arthaśāstra*, II, 127, n. 10.
82. *Ibid.*
83. P. Ray (1956), 57-58.
84. L. Gopal (1966), 75, fn. 2.
85. *Ibid.*
86. *Bṛhatasamhita*, XVI. 26.
87. 43. 1. 47; L. Gopal (1966), 75.
88. P. Ray (1956), 387; V.22. - *sahajaṁ khanisañjātaṁ kṛtrimaṁ ça tridhā matam*.
89. L. Gopal (1966), 76.
90. Jai Prakash (1966), "The Bearing of Trade & Commerce on the Chronology of Punch-marked Coins", *The Chronology of the Punch-marked Coins*, No. 1, 82.
91. P.K. Hitti, *Lebanon in History*, 98.
92. *Ibid.*, 106.
93. *Ibid.*
94. I. Kings 9: 28; 10: 11-12; 22; Chronicle 9:10, 21; 22:48; CF. Rufus Israel Learsi; *A History of Jewish People*, 61 (Cleveland, 1949); Adolphe Lods, *Israel*, 370 (1932, London); Jai Prakash (1966), 82, fn. 4.
95. Chronicle, 10: 11.
96. *JOS. Antiq.*, (VIII), 6. 4. Cf. Also for location of Ophir in India – Israel Rufus: *A History of the Jews People*, 61; H.R. Hall (1954), *The Ancient History of the Near East*, London, 434; Rhys-David (1903), *Buddhist India*, 19-20; Jai Prakash (1966), 82, fn. 6.
97. Jai Prakash (1961- 62), "Parallel Accounts of the Origin of Kingship in Judea and India", *Bharati*, Dept. of A.I.H.C. and Archaeology, BHU, Varanasi, No. 5 (I) 60; *The Age of Imperial Unity*, 612.
98. *The Westminster Dictionary of Bible*, 592.
99. I *Book of Easther*, 1:1; 8:9.
100. *The Westminster Dictionary of Bible*, 265.
101. Jai Prakash (1966), 83.
102. K.V.R. Aiyangar, *Aspects of Ancient Indian Economic Thought*, 98-99. "Silver though known and prized in ancient India was comparatively scarcer than gold, since silver had to be imported. It came in usually in exchange (along with gold) for the export of silk, spices and gems, and during the early centuries of the Christian era, this trade resulted in a drain of the precious metals from the West to the East and caused anxiety to Roman statesman and economists like Pliny." Jai Prakash (1966), 84, fn.1.

103. Jai Prakash (1966), 84.
104. A. Cunningham (1891), *CAI*, 5.
105. Sir Walter Elliot (1886), 51, fn. 1; S.K. Chakrabortty (2004), 60. "In the Gungeria 400 flat axes of various lengths all in copper and 102 objects in silver were discovered in 1870 and these must date from the copper age." P. Mitra (1923), 189. Silver ornaments and utensils have been found in the excavations at Mohenjodaro and Harappa.
106. A. Cunningham (1891), *CAI*, 5.
107. *Ibid.*, 6.
108. *The Cambridge History of India* (I), 343.
109. *Ibid.*
110. H.C. Bhardwaj (1966), "Bearing of Chemical Composition & Metallography on the Chronology of the Punch-marked Coins", 60; *Arthaśāstra of Kauṭilya* records the composition of silver coins—that the Superintendent of mint is enjoyed the composition of silver coins—"The Superintendent of mint (*Lakshanadhyaksha*) shall carry on the manufacture of silver coins (*rupya-rupa*) made up of four parts of copper and one sixteenth part (*masha*) of any one of the metals, *Tikshana* (iron), *trapu* (tin), *sisa* (lead) and *anjana* (antimony)." *Kauṭilya's Arthaśāstra*, R. Samasastry's translation (1929), 86; Satya Prakasha and N.S. Rawat (1965), *Chemical Study of Some Indian Archaeological Antiquities*, 70 – Sr. No. 2.

Part II

CATALOGUE

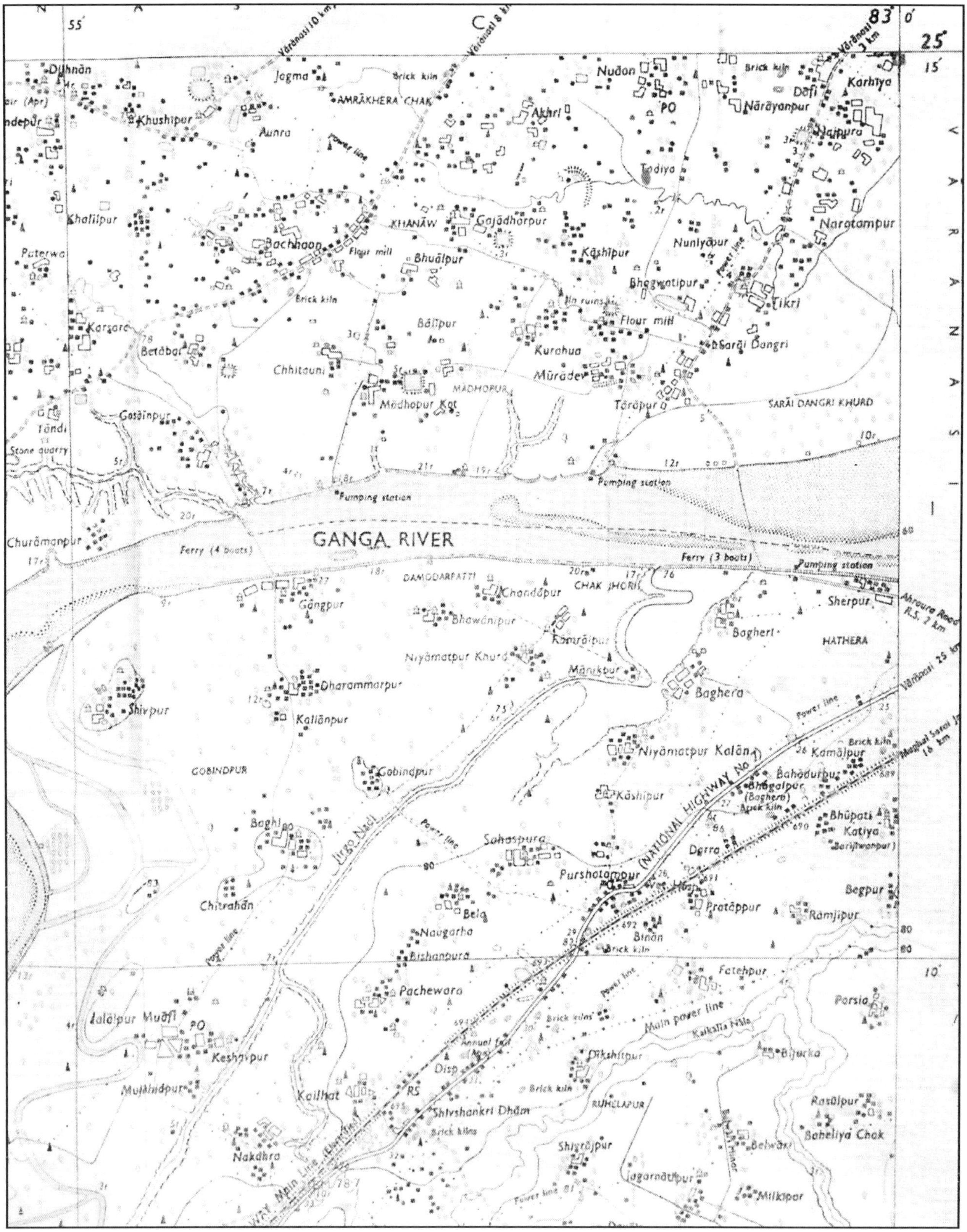

Location Map-Sarāi Dangri, Varanasi.

6

Find-Spot of the Hoard

The find-spot of the hoard under study lies in the holy city of Varanasi, formerly known as Benares or Beneras. It is picturesquely situated on the crescent-shaped left bank of the river Gaṅgā. According to the *Purāṇas*, the kingdom and the city were named Kasi after Kashya or Kasha, the ancient king of this region, whereas according to another legend the name Kasi is derived from the shining *Liṅgam* created by Viṣṇu in this place.[1] According to the *Atharva Veda*, Varanasi, the chief city of Kasi, was connected with the river Varanāvatī, but the name Varanasi is probably derived from a combination of the names of *Varuṇā* and *Assi*, an affluent of the Gaṅgā between which the city is situated, having been thus described in the *Purāṇas*.[2] Varanasi is also known by the names of *Surundhana*, *Sudassana*, *Brahmavaddhana*, *Pupphavati*, *Ramma* and *Molini*.[3]

Varanasi is one of the easternmost districts of the state of Uttar Pradesh, and lies between the parallels of 24°43′ and 25°35′ N. Lat. and 82°11 and 83°34 E. Long., with the length of 82 miles from north to south. Towards the west is the northern boundary of Jaunpur district for about 65 miles and the remaining part of northern boundary towards east is contiguous with the southwestern boundary of the district of Ghazipur. The river Gaṅgā flows between the two districts for the greater part of the distance. On the south lies the district Mirzapur and to the west the district touches the eastern boundary of Allahabad district and on the east lies the district of Ghazipur and that of Shahabad in the state of Bihar.[4]

Varanasi is one of the most ancient cities in the world. For centuries, it was the political capital of Kasi *Janapada*. Even in the *Mahābhārata* and *Rāmāyaṇa*, Varanasi is mentioned as being the capital of the Kasi.[5] At present the city forms a part of Pargana Dehat Amanat, in Varanasi the southern part of the District.

The discovery of a hoard of silver punch-marked coins of the Imperial Series was made in July 1997 from Sarāi Dangri village. An earthen pot containing coins was unearthed whilst digging for the foundation of a primary school. It was brought to notice through the local newspapers shortly thereafter. The possession of coins was taken over by the district administration and subsequently the coins were given to the Bharat Kala Bhavan on 14th December 1998.

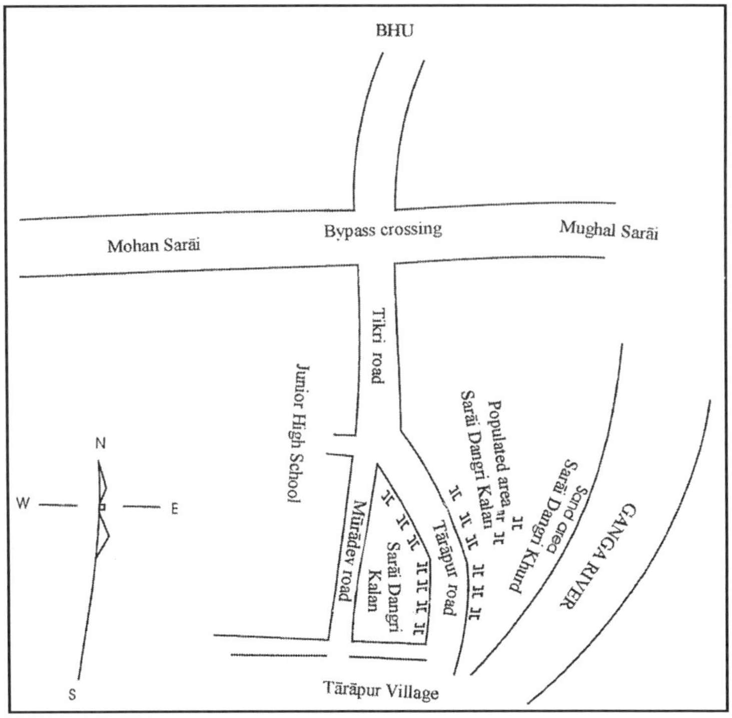

Location Map-Sarāi Dangri, Varanasi (Line Drawing).

The village Sarāi Dangri, Pargana Dehat Amanat, Tehsil Varanasi Sadar, is about 5½ km away to the south of Lanka police station and is approachable by road. This large village is divided by a metal road into two sectors—Sarāi Dangri Kalan and Sarāi Dangri Khurd. Sarāi Dangri Khurd sector, demarcated as a sand area, and is next to the river Gaṅgā, about one kilometer towards the south, the area known as Sarāi Dangri Kalan on the left hand side of Tikri–Tārāpur road. Sarāi Dangri Kalan, from where the treasure was found about 500 meters away from the main road, lies between Mūrādev and Tārāpur roads merging into Tikri road, which finally joins the highway connecting Mughal Sarāi and Mohan Sarāi. A small mound littered with Red and Black and Grey slipped ware sherds is situated at the western side of the mound, from where the treasure-trove was found at a depth of about 1 ft. There is a big pond to the west of the mound. The villagers ascribed the antiquity of this place in terms of large number of seemingly Black and Red and Northern Black Polished ware sherds, often found from the fields. They drew attention to the amplitude to these pottery pieces, thereby substantiating the antiquity of the village.

The earthen pot contained silver punch-marked coins, reported 333 in number. As per local newspapers, the coins were immediately deposited with the village Pradhan, Shri Ram Asare Pal and subsequently, the district administration of Varanasi took these into safe custody. Due to the prompt action of the district administration, the hoard was recovered intact. The earthen pot, containing the treasure, however, was broken and appears to have been discarded into the nearby village well.

These coins form the subject matter of the present monograph. This hoard now constitutes part of the numismatic colletion of the Bharat Kala Bhavan, a museum of national repute, in the premises of the Banaras Hindu University. The accession numbers allocated to these coins are 2002.1 to 2002.333.

NOTES AND REFERENCES

1. A.S. Altekar (1937), 28; *Harivaṁśa Purāṇa*, 29. (*Kāśi Khaṅda of Skanda Purāṇa*).
2. S.B. Chaudhuri, "Ethnic Settlements in Ancient India", 60.
3. *Gazetteers of India* (1965), Uttar Pradesh, 428.
4. The name Benaras was officially in use until May 24, 1956, when by order of the State Government it was changed to Varanasi. The appellation Varanasi seems to have been corrupted to Benaras in the medieval period. Aurangzeb, the Mughal Emperor, is said to have bestowed Muhammadabad. Though it apparently did not come in use except as the mint name, it was found on Muslim coins along with the name of Benaras. *Gazetteers of India* (1965) 429.

7

About the Hoard

This hoard was found in Varanasi region. It contained 333 silver punch-marked coins of *kārṣāpaṇa* Imperial Series, spread over from Series II to Series VI (a and b). The intact nature and the definite provenance of the hoard does provide a clue to the chronological sequence of these coins. The largest number of coins, one hundred thirty-three, belong to the Series VI (a and b) and form 14 groups of varieties. The next largest number, one hundred sixteen coins, constituting 25 groups of varieties, belongs to Series V (a and b). Further, sixty-five coins belonging to Series IV (b, c and d), forms 29 groups of varieties. Coins of Series IVa are conspicuously absent in this hoard and seventeen coins assignable to Series III present five groups of varieties. Only two coins belong to Series II, and form two groups of varieties. The contents of the hoard show a chronological sequence spread between Series II to Series VI (a and b).

It has already been established by the scholars working in this field that the abundance of coins of any variety, group or class, suggests that those coins were current at the time of the deposition of the hoard. The paucity of the coins of any variety, group or class in a hoard, indicates that these coins were in currency long before the deposit of the hoard and over a passage time the number of coins was reduced, or those were issued shortly before the deposition of the hoard. Fabric of coins also suggests the period of their circulation; the earliest issues would be relatively in worn condition and accordingly their weight affected. However, the coins which appear fresh in look, their approximate full weight remains intact. To be more precise, the weight of coins would be in proportion to their period and duration of currency. Where the coins of any class are conspicuous by their absence, it would suggest that these coins disappeared from circulation either long before the hoard was deposited or these were not in vogue when the hoard was buried.

The largest numbers of coins found in this hoard belong to Series VI (a and b) and Series V (a and b), which apparently indicates that these were the main coins current in the region at the time of its deposition. Likewise, the coins less in number suggest that these were in circulation long before the hoard was deposited.

However, no firm conclusion can be drawn because of the numbers of varieties of coins and their marks impressed upon them on the reverse. Nevertheless, it may be postulated, as the nature of the hoard indicates, leaving no doubt that it is an assembled hoard. It may be emphasized further that it was not a depository of one time. These coins could have been minted in different regions and at different mints. The ancient holy city of Kasi was not only a great trade centre but also a pilgrimage centre frequently visited by devotees from the earliest times. This implies that the coins were constantly moving from one region to another.

8

Classification of Coins

A. KEY TO CLASSIFICATION

The classification of the present hoard reveals that all the coins are found scattered between Series II to Series VI. Within each series is placed a number of class and within each class one or more groups constituting varieties.

The series is placed first and indicated by Roman figures. For instance, this series starts from Series II and up to the coins of later period, which fall into Series VI, and are indicated accordingly Series II to Series VI. The next step highlights the 'Class' marked by another Roman numeral followed by alphabet letters—A, B, C, D—and so on, indicating the 'Group' and the classification of the 'Varieties' is indicated by Arabic numerals—1, 2, 3, 4, etc. Thus, each variety is codified indicating its constituents.

II. I. A1 - Variety 1 of Group A of Class I belongs to Series II.

A serial number is given to each variety—S. No. 1 to S. No. 76—as is given to each variety, represented in the hoard, which follows the codified classification of the varieties, based entirely on the classic system, then weight and size of the coin, illustrated in the catalogue (Figs. 1-19) and then the number of coins represented in the hoard and, lastly, the museum accession number of the respective coin illustrated in the catalogue. The remaining coins of particular variations are placed in the Plates (I-XXIII) starting with S. No. 2 onwards, as the selected one is illustrated in the catalogue. In case of the single coin in the hoard, it is illustrated in the catalogue only. The accession numbers along with their weight, size and thickness of each coin are being listed separately according to their arrangements in the catalogue and plates.

Most of the symbols have been drawn directly from the coins, but where the symbol is seen partly or is not clear, it has been made complete and the series is confirmed on the guidelines of Gupta and Hardaker's work (*AISPMC*, 1985). The obverse as well as the reverse marks along with their associate marks are duly arranged in tabular form. The number of identical coins present in other hoards and the cross-references are incorporated in this monograph based on the methodology of the *Amaravati Hoard* (*Am*) and *Ancient Indian Silver Punch-marked Coins (AISPMC)* publications.

References are given only of those coins which belong to the published hoards. All the photographs of the coins in black and white are enlarged approximately up to 1.5 times of the actual size of the coin for better visibility and study point of view.

S. No.	:	Serial Number.
Sr.	:	Series.
Cl.	:	Class.
Gr.	:	Group.
Vr.	:	Variety.
Wt. (gms)	:	Weight in grams.
Sz. (cms)	:	Size in cms.
Acc. No.	:	Accession Number.

1. II. I. A or A1.

S. No.	:	indicates varieties of coins in classification of present hoard.
Roman II	:	indicates the series—the chronological distribution of coins.
Roman I	:	indicates the class.
Alphabet-A	:	indicates the group within the class.
Arabic numeral	:	indicates the variety within the group. Numeral not used where the coin belongs to one variety only.

i. *Am*	:	*The Amaravati Hoard of Silver Punch-Marked Coins*, P.L. Gupta.
ii. *Taxila*	:	*Punch-marked Coins from Taxila* (*MASI* No. 59) by E.H.C. Walsh, Archaeological Survey of India, New Delhi.
iii. *Patraha*	:	*A Hoard of Silver Punch-marked Coins from Purnea (Patraha)* (*MASI* No. 62) by P.N. Bhattacharya, Archaeological Survey of India, New Delhi.
iv. *Hyderabad*	:	*Punch-marked Coins in the Andhra Pradesh Government Museum* by P.L. Gupta, Hyderabad, 1961.
v. *Rairh*	:	*Excavations at Rairh* by K.N. Puri.
vi. *Barwani*	:	"Barwani Hoard of Silver Punch-marked Coins in National Museum", by P.L. Gupta in *Numismatic Digest*, New Delhi.
vii. *AISPMC*	:	*Ancient Indian Silver Punch-marked Coins of the Magadha-Maurya Kārshāpana Series,* P.L. Gupta and T.R. Hardaker.

B. FIGURES

Fig. 1

S.No. Sr/cl/gr/vr Wt.(gm)/Sz.(cm) No. of Coins Acc. No.	Symbols	Illustrations Obv. Rev.	Select Publication Remarks
1. **II.I.A** 3.2383 / 2.10 × 1.40 (1) 2002.1	Obv. 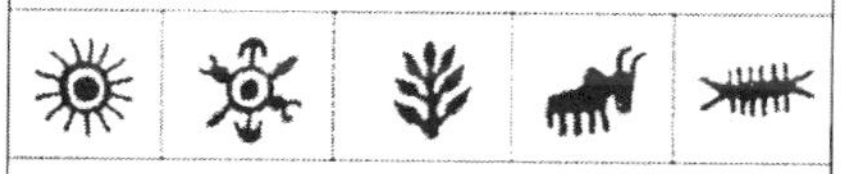 Rev. 		*AISPMC*, II (II I A 3) 265. *Am*, II. II. A. 1. **Rare**
2. **II.II.A** 3.2815 / 2.23 (1) 2002.2	Obv.  Rev. 		*AISPMC*, II (II X A 1) 283. *Am*, II. XI. 1. Taxila, B (d) 2. **Scarce**
3. **III.I.A** 3.1705 / 2.30 × 1.70 (1) 2002.3	Obv.  Rev. 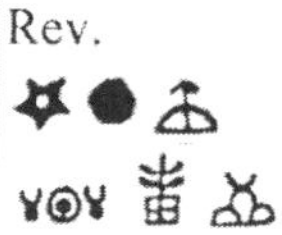		*AISPMC*, III (III I A 1) 291. *Am*, II. XIII. 1. Taxila, Q 9. Rairth (V). Barwani, *ND*, 16. 1. **Rare** **Restruck**
4. **III.II.A** 3.0863 / 2.50 × 1.90 (7) 2002.5	Obv.  Rev. 		*AISPMC*, III (III IV A 1) 305. *Am*, III. I. 4. Patraha, III. VII. a. Taxila, B (b) 1. Hyderabad (Raichur), I.D.1. Rairh (V). Barwani, *ND*, 16. 7. **Very Common** **Restruck** **Extra sixth-mark on obverse in addition.**

Fig. 2

S.No. Sr/cl/gr/vr Wt.(gm)/Sz.(cm) No. of Coins Acc. No.	Symbols	Illustrations Obv. Rev.	Select Publication Remarks
5. **III.III.A** 3.2145 / 2.23 × 1.36 (1) 2002.11	Obv.  Rev. 		*AISPMC*, III (III X A 1) 319. *Am*, III. II. 6 a. Barwani, *ND*, 16. 12. **Scarce**
6. **III.III.A1** 3.2114 / 2.05 × 1.40 (6) 2002.14	Obv.  Rev.  Vr. 321- III.X.A1b 2nd symbol - 		*AISPMC*, III (III X A Ia) 320 or 321. *Am*, III. II. 6 b & c. Patraha, III. I. a. Taxila, M 1. Hyderabad (Karimanagar, Gulbarga), I. E .1. Big Bhir mound, III.II.6. Barwani, *ND*, 16.12. 2nd symbol seen partly, variety indeterminable, may be 320 or 321 **Extremely Common**
7. **III.III.A2** 3.2547 / 1.45 × 1.90 (2) 2002.19	Obv.  Rev.  Vr. 327- III.X.A10. - 5th symbol - 		*AISPMC*, III (III X A 6 or A 10) 326-327. *Am*, (III. II. 3). Ramna H. (Patna M) Mathura H (M) or Rairah (V). Patraha (III. I. b). Barwani, 71.548/358, 91 tail of 5th symbol out of flan, two varieties clubbed together, may be 326/327 **Rare**
8. **IVb.I.A** 3.3130 / 1.90 × 1.40 (1) 2002.20	Obv.  Rev. 		*AISPMC*, IV b (IV X A 10) 362. *Am*, III. IV. A. 1. Patraha, III.VI. f. Taxila, B (a) 1. Rairh (V). **Rare**

Fig. 3

S.No. Sr/cl/gr/vr Wt.(gm)/Sz.(cm) No. of Coins Acc. No.	Symbols	Illustrations Obv. Rev.	Select Publication Remarks
9. **IVb.I.A1** 3.3329/ 1.92 × 1.95 (1) 2002.21	Obv.  Rev. 		*AISPMC*, IV b (IV X A 11) 363. *Am*, III. IV. A. 2. Taxila, B (1) 1a **Scarce**
10. **IVc.I.A** 3.4189 / 1.76 × 1.20 (1) 2002.22	Obv.  Rev. 		*AISPMC*, IVc (IV XXVI B 9) 386. *Am*, IV. V. C. 2. Patraha, III.VIII. b. Taxila, 13. Rairh (V). **Rare**
11. **IVc.II.A** 3.3047 / 1.60 (1) 2002.23	Obv.  Rev. 		*AISPMC*, IV c (IV XXVII A 1) 390. *Am*, IV. IV. 1. **Extremely Rare**
12. **IVd.I.A** 3.4673 / 1.30 (1) 2002.24	Obv.  Rev. 		*AISPMC*, IV d (IV XXXI A 1) 398. Taxila hoard (BHU). Mambalam hoard (Madras, M). **Very Rare**

Fig. 4

S.No. Sr/cl/gr/vr Wt.(gm)/Sz.(cm) No. of Coins Acc. No.	Symbols	Illustrations Obv. Rev.	Select Publication Remarks
13. **IVd.I.A1** 3.4346 / 1.60 × 1.50 (2) 2002.26	Obv.  Rev. 		*AISPMC*, IV d (IV XXXI A 15) 402. *Am*, IV. III. A. 1. Patraha, III.V. a-b. Taxila, A19. Hyderabad (Gulbarga, Raichur), II. H (b). 3. Barwani, *ND*, 17. 25. **Common**
14. **IVd.I.B** 3.3373 / 2.20 × 1.40 (1) 2002.27	Obv. 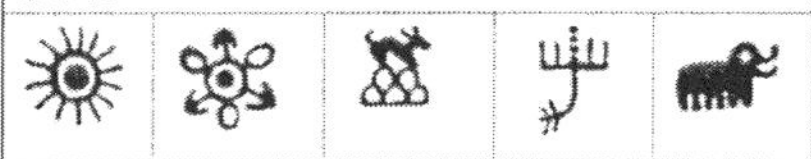 Rev. 		*AISPMC*, IV d (IV XXVI C 1) 405. *Am*, IV. VIII. B. 1. Patraha, III.VIII. c. Taxila, A31. Hyderabad (Raichur), II. H (e).1. Rairh (I & V). Barwani, *ND*, 17. 26. **Normal**
15. **IVd.I.C** 3.3186 / 2.10 × 1.20 (1) 2002.28	Obv.  Rev. 		*AISPMC*, IV d (IV XXXI D 1) 406. *Am*, IV. VIII. C. 1. Patraha, III. III. a. Taxila, A23 Barwani, *ND*, 17. 27. **Scarce**
16. **IVd.I.C1** 3.3530 / 1.80 × 1.40 (1) 2002.29	Obv.  Rev. 		2nd symbol forms a New variety. **Rare**

Fig. 5

S.No. Sr/cl/gr/vr Wt.(gm)/Sz.(cm) No. of Coins Acc. No.	Symbols	Illustrations Obv. Rev.	Select Publication Remarks
17. **IVd.I.D** 3.3093 / 1.86 (16) 2002.36	Obv.  Rev. 	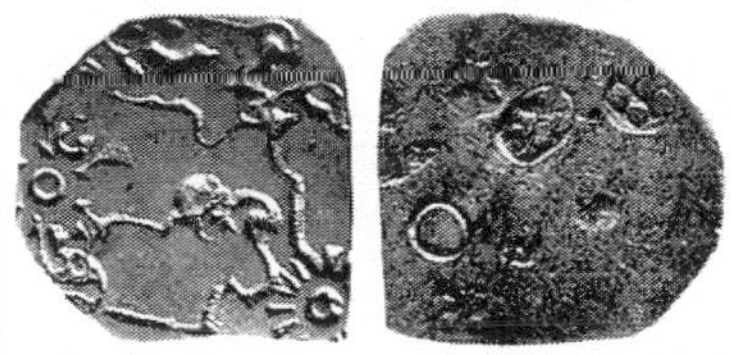	*AISPMC*, IV d (IV XXXI G 1) 416. *Am*, IV. VIII. F. 2. Patraha, III. IV. b. Taxila, A 1. Hyderabad (Karimnagar, Gulbarga, Raichur), II. H (a) 2. Barwani, *ND*, 17. 31. **Extremely Common**
18. **IVd.I.D1** 3.4350 / 1.75 × 1.46 (1) 2002.46	Obv.  Rev. 		*AISPMC*, IV d (IV XXXI G 5) 419. *Am*, IV. VIII. F. 8. Patraha, VIII. V. a. Taxila, A3. Hyderabad (Karimnagar, Raichur), II. H (a) 1. Barwani, *ND*, 17. 33. **Very Common**
19. **IVd.I.D2** 3.4229 / 1.73 × 1.40 (1) 2002.47	Obv.  Rev. 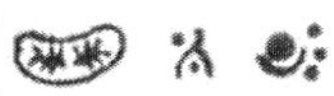		*AISPMC*, IV d (IV XXXI G 9) 422. *Am*, IV. VIII. F. 10. Patraha, III. IV. b. Taxila, A 9. Hyderabad (Raichur), II. H (a) 5. Barwani, *ND*, 17. 34. **Common**
20. **IVd.I.D3** 3.2347 / 2.10 × 1.80 (2) 2002.49	Obv.  Rev. 		*AISPMC*, IV d (IV XXXI G 12) 424. *Am*, IV. VIII. F. 6. Patraha, III. IV. f. Taxila, A5. Rairh (I & V). Barwani, *ND*, 17. 35. **Common**

Fig. 6

S.No. Sr/cl/gr/vr Wt.(gm)/Sz.(cm) No. of Coins Acc. No.	Symbols	Illustrations Obv. Rev.	Select Publication Remarks
21. **IVd.I.D4** 3.2772/ 2.30 × 1.20 (3) 2002.51	Obv.  Rev. 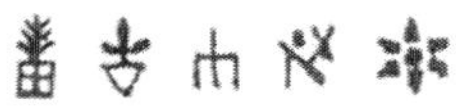		*AISPMC*, IV d (IV XXXI G 13) 425. *Am*, IV. VIII. F. 7. Patraha, VIII. V. h - i. Taxila, A4. Hyderabad (Karimnagar, Gulbarga, Raichur). II. H. (a). 7. Barwani, *ND*, 17. 36. **Very Common**
22. **IVd.I.D5** 3.3908 / 1.95 × 1.42 (2) 2002.53	Obv.  Rev. 		*AISPMC*, IV d (IV XXXI G 14) 426. *Am*, IV. VIII. F. 9. Patraha, III. IV. K. Taxila, A8. Hyderabad (Karimnagar), II. H (a). 6. Rairh (IV & V). Barwani, *ND*, 17. 37. **Common**
23. **IVd.I.D6** 3.3833 / 1.90 (6) 2002.56	Obv.  Rev. 	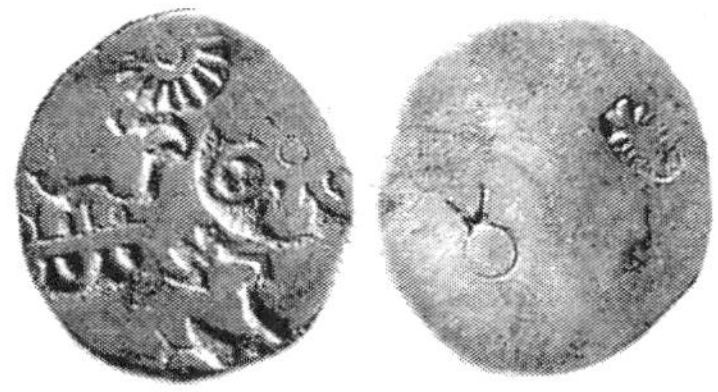	*AISPMC*, IV d (IV XXXI G 15) 427. *Am*, IV. VIII. F. 4. Patraha, III. IV. j. Taxila, A2. Hyderabad (Karimnagar, Gulbarga, Raichur), II.H (a). 8. Rairh (I, IV & V). Barwani, *ND*, 17. 38. **Extremely Common**
24. **IVd.I.D7** 3.4068 / 1.75 × 1.34 (2) 2002.62	Obv.  Rev. 		*AISPMC*, IV d (IV XXXI G 90) 428. *Am*, IV. VIII. F. 3. Patraha, III. IV. e. Taxila, A6 Hyderabad (Raichur), II. H (a). 4. Rairh (V). Barwani, *ND*, 17. 38. **Common**

Fig. 7

S.No. **Sr/cl/gr/vr** **Wt.(gm)/Sz.(cm)** **No. of Coins** **Acc. No.**	**Symbols**	**Illustrations** **Obv. Rev.**	**Select Publication Remarks**
25. **IVd.I.D8** 3.4031/ 1.70 (1) 2002.63	Obv.  Rev. 		*AISPMC*, IV d (IV XXXI G 5) 432. *Am*, IV. VIII. F. 1. **Rare**
26. **IVd.II.A** 3.3689 / 2.10 × 1.20 (5) 2002.67	Obv.  Rev. 		*AISPMC*, IV d (IV XXVI A 1) 442. *Am*, IV. IX. A. 3. Patraha, III. VIII. a. Taxila, L1. Hyderabad (Karimnagar, Gulbarga, Raichur), II. G (a). 1. Barwani, *ND*, 18. 47. **Extremely Common**
27. **IVd.II.A1** 3.2193 / 1.23 × 2.05 (1) 2002.331	Obv. 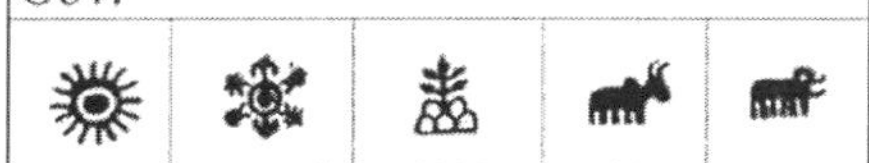 Rev. 		2nd symbol forms a new variety. **Restruck** Extra sixth-mark on obverse in addition
28. **IVd.II.A2** 3.3899 / 2.25 × 1.35 (1) 2002.69	Obv.  Rev. 		*AISPMC*, IV d (IV XXXII A 2) 443. *Am*, IV. IX. A. 4. Patraha, III. VIII. b. Taxila, L2. Rairh (V). Barwani, *ND*, 18. 48. **Common**

Fig. 8

S.No. Sr/cl/gr/vr Wt.(gm)/Sz.(cm) No. of Coins Acc. No.	Symbols	Illustrations Obv. Rev.	Select Publication Remarks
29. **IVd.III.A** 3.2320 / 2.10 × 1.60 (3) 2002.70	Obv.  Rev. 		*AISPMC*, IV d (IV XXXIII A 1) 450. *Am*, IV. X. 2. Patraha, III. II. b. Taxila, C1. Hyderabad (Karimnagar, Gulbarga, Raichur), II.F.1. Rairh (I, IV & V). Barwani, *ND*, 18. 50. **Extremely Common**
30. **IVd.III.A1** 3.3345 / 1.75 (1) 2002.73	Obv.  Rev. 		*AISPMC*, IV d (IV XXXIII A 2) 451. *Am*, IV. X. 4. Patraha, III. II. d. Taxila, C 3. Hyderabad (Gulbarga) II. F. 2. Rairh (V). Barwani, *ND*, 18. 51. **Normal**
31. **IVd.III.A2** 3.3206 / 2.25 × 1.25 (1) 2002.74	Obv.  Rev. 		*AISPMC*, IV d (IV XXXI G 12) 456. *Am*, III. X. 5. Patraha, III. II. C. Taxila, C2. Hyderabad (Karimnagar, Gulbarga, Raichur), II. F. 3. Rairh (II, IV & V). Barwani, *ND*, 18. 53. **Common**
32. **IVd.IV.A** 3.3015 / 1.73 × 1.36 (4) 2002.77	Obv.  Rev. 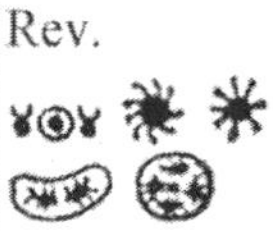		*AISPMC*, IV d (IV XXXIV A 1) 464. *Am*, IV. XI. 2. Patraha, III. I. h. Taxila, J 1. Hyderabad (Karimnagar, Gulbarga), II. E. 1. Rairh (IV). Barwani, *ND*, 18. 55. **Common**

Fig. 9

S.No. Sr/cl/gr/vr Wt.(gm)/Sz.(cm) No. of Coins Acc. No.	Symbols	Illustrations Obv. Rev.	Select Publication Remarks
33. **IVd.IV.A1** 3.2276 / 1.85 (1) 2002.79	Obv.  Rev. 		*AISPMC*, IV d (IV XXXIV A 6) 465. *Am*, IV. XI. 1. Patraha, III. I. g. Taxila, C1. Hyderabad (Raichur), II. E. 2. Rairh (I). **Rare**
34. **IVd.V.A** 3.4347 / 1.80 × 1.40 (1) 2002.80	Obv.  Rev. 		*AISPMC*, IV d (IV XXXV A 1) 467. *Am*, IV. XII. I. Patraha, II. XII. C. Taxila, D1. Hyderabad (Karimnagar, Gulbarga), II. C. 3. Rairh (I & II). Barwani, *ND*, 18. 56. **Normal**
35. **IVd.V.A1** 3.3916 / 1.76 (1) 2002.81	Obv.  Rev. 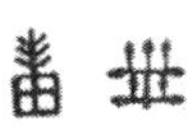		*AISPMC*, IV d (IV XXXV A 17) 471. *Am*, IV. XII. 4. Taxila, D2. Patraha, II. XIII. b. Hyderabad (Karimnagar, Gulbarga), II. C. 3. Rairh (I, II, IV & V). Barwani, *ND*, 18. 59. **Very Common**
36. **IVd.VI.A** 3.5271 / 1.20 × 1.02 (1) 2002.82	Obv.  Rev. 	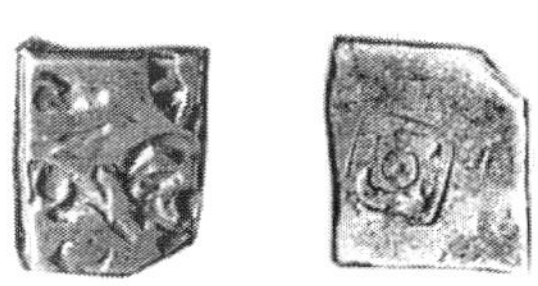	*AISPMC*, IV d (IV XXXVII A 6) 473. *Am*, IV. XIV. 1. **Extremely Rare**

Fig. 10

S.No. Sr/cl/gr/vr Wt.(gm)/Sz.(cm) No. of Coins Acc. No.	Symbols	Illustrations Obv. Rev.	Select Publication Remarks
37. **IVd.VII.A** 3.4750 / 1.50 × 1.25 (1) 2002.83	Obv.  Rev. 		*AISPMC*, IV d (IV XXXIX A 13) 475. *Am*, IV. XVI. 1. Patraha, II. X. 1. Hyderabad (Gulbarga, Raichur), II. I. 1. Rairh (I). Barwani, *ND*, 18. 60 **Normal**
38. **Va.I.A** 3.4189 / 1.80 × 1.20 (7) 2002.90	Obv.  Rev. 		*AISPMC*, V a (V I A 1) 477. *Am*, V. I. 1. Patraha, II. XI. h. Taxila, B (e) 1. Hyderabad (Karimnagar, Raichur), II. K. 1. Rairh (I, IV & V). Barwani, *ND*, 18. 63. **Very Common**
39. **Va.I.A1** 3.4301 / 1.62 (2) 2002.92	Obv.  Rev. 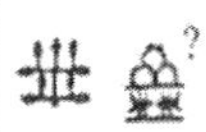	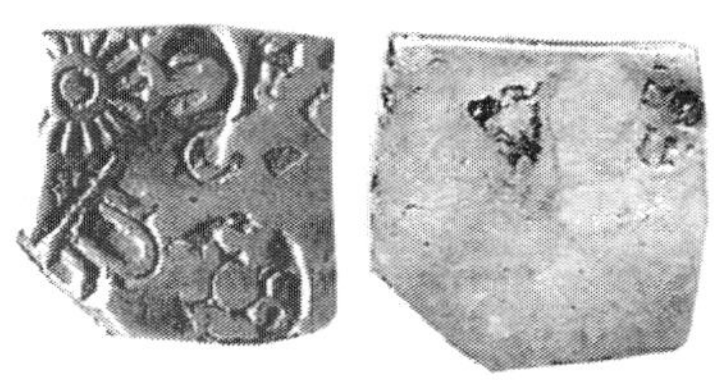	*AISPMC*, V a (V I A 14) 479. *Am*, V. I. 5. Patraha, II. XI. d. Hyderabad (Karimnagar), II. K. 3. Rairh (I, IV & V). Barwani, *ND*, 18. 63. **Very Common**
40. **Va.I.A2** 3.4382 / 1.80 × 1.42 (8) 2002.98	Obv.  Rev. 		*AISPMC*, V a (V I A 15) 480. *Am*, V. I. 6. Patraha, II. XI. C.. Hyderabad (Karimnagar, Gulbarga, Raichur), II. K. 4. Barwani, *ND*, 19. 64. **Very Common**

Fig. 11

S.No. Sr/cl/gr/vr Wt.(gm)/Sz.(cm) No. of Coins Acc. No.	Symbols	Illustrations Obv. Rev.	Select Publication Remarks
41. **Va.I.A.3** 3.4357 / 1.66 (2) 2002.101	Obv.  Rev. 		*AISPMC*, V d (V I A 17) 481. *Am*, V. I. 3. Patraha, II. XI. f. Taxila, B (e) 2. Hyderabad (Karimnagar), II. K. 2. Rairh (II & V). Barwani, *ND*, 19.65. **Common**
42. **Va.I.A4** 3.4038 / 1.73 × 1.43 (20) 2002.103	Obv.  Rev. 		*AISPMC*, V a (V I A 18) 482. *Am*, V. I. 2. Patraha, II. XI. b. Hyderabad (Karimnagar, Gulbarga, Kondapur find), II. K. 7. Rairh (I, II, IV & V) Barwani, *ND*, 19. 66. **Extremely Common**
43. **Va.I.A5** 3.3894 / 1.82 (5) 2002.127	Obv.  Rev. 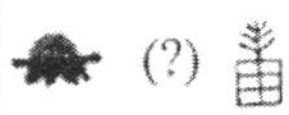	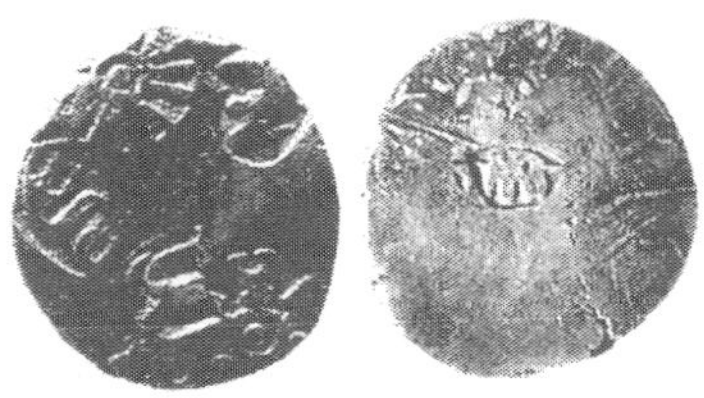	*AISPMC*, V a (V I A 103) 484. *Am*, V. I. 7. Patraha, II. XI. e. Hyderabad (Karimnagar, Raichur) II. K. 6. Rairh (I, II, IV & V). Barwani, *ND*, 19. 67. **Extremely Common**
44. **Va.II.A** 3.4342 / 1.56 × 1.24 (3) 2002.128	Obv.  Rev. 		*AISPMC*, V a (V II A 17) 486. *Am*, V. II. A. 1. Patraha, II. XII. F. Hyderabad (Karimnagar, Gulbarga, Raichur), II. J. 6. Rairh (I, II & IV). Barwani, *ND*, 19. 69. **Very Common**

Fig. 12

S.No. Sr/cl/gr/vr Wt.(gm)/Sz.(cm) No. of Coins Acc. No.	Symbols	Illustrations Obv.	 Rev.	Select Publication Remarks
45. **Va.III.A** 3.4114 / 1.50 × 1.30 (8) 2002.136	Obv. Rev.			*AISPMC*, V d (V III A 13) 488. *Am*, V. III. 1. Patraha, II. X. h. Taxila, B (e) 2. Hyderabad (Karimnagar, Gulbarga), III. E. 1. Rairh (I, IV & V). Barwani, *ND*, 19. 70. **Extremely Common**
46. **Va.IV.A** 3.4055 / 1.80 (1) 2002.332	Obv. Rev.			*AISPMC*, V a (V VIII B 16) 499. *Am*, V. XIX. 2. Patraha, II. XI. b. Hyderabad (Karimnagar), III. G. 1. Rairh (IV & V). Barwani, *ND*, 19. 77. **Common**
47. **Va.V.A** 3.4707 / 1.40 × 1.15 (1) 2002.139	Obv. Rev.			*AISPMC*, V a (V X A 1) 501. *Am*, V. VI. 1. Patraha, II. VII. a. Hyderabad (Karimnagar), IV. E. 1. Barwani, *ND*, 19. 78. **Normal**
48. **Va.V.A1** 3.4846 / 1.36 × 1.25 (2) 2002.140	Obv. Rev. (?)			*AISPMC*, V a (V X A 102) 503. *Am*, V. VI. 2. Patraha, II. VII. b. Rairh (I. IV. & V). Barwani, *ND*, 19. 79. **Normal**

Fig. 13

S.No. Sr/cl/gr/vr Wt.(gm)/Sz.(cm) No. of Coins Acc. No.	Symbols	Illustrations Obv. Rev.	Select Publication Remarks
49. **Va.VI.A** 3.4569 / 1.35 (5) 2002.143	Obv.  Rev. 		*AISPMC*, V a (V XI B 109) 505. *Am*, V. V. A. 2. Patraha, II. X. h. Hyderabad (Karimnagar, Gulbarga), IV. C. 1. Rairh (V). **Common**
50. **Va.VII.A** 3.2749 / 1.96 × 1.30 (3) 2002.148	Obv.  Rev. 		*AISPMC*, V a (V XII A 20) 506. *Am*, V. IV. A. 1. Patraha, II. V. b. Hyderabad (Karimnagar, Gulbarga, Raichur), IV. A. 1. Rairh (I & V). Barwani, *ND*, 19. 84. **Very Common**
51. **Va.VIII.A** 3.4997 / 1.64 (4) 2002.152	Obv.  Rev. 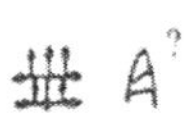		*AISPMC*, V a (V XII A 110) 509. *Am*, V. IV. B. 2. Patraha, II. V. i. Hyderabad (Karimnagar, Gulbarga), IV. B. 2. Rairh (I, II, IV & V). Barwani, *ND*, 19. 85. **Extremely Common**
52. **Vb.I.A** 3.4188 / 1.40 × 1.30 (9) 2002.164	Obv. 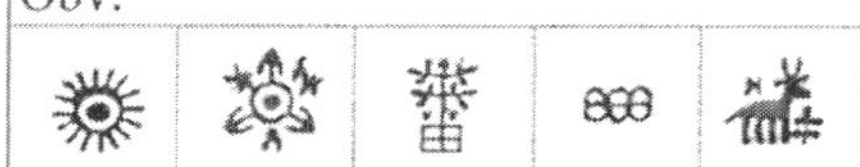 Rev. 		*AISPMC*, V b (V XIV A 21) 510. *Am*, V. IV. B. 1a. Patraha, II. V. a-h. (Karimnagar, Gulbarga, Raichur, Kondapur Find), IV. B. 1 Rairh (I, II, IV & V). Barwani, *ND*, 19. 86. **Extremely Common**

Fig. 14

S.No. Sr/cl/gr/vr Wt.(gm)/Sz.(cm) No. of Coins Acc. No.	Symbols	Illustrations Obv. Rev.	Select Publication Remarks
53. **Vb.I.A1** 3.4137 / 1.43 × 1.15 (7) 2002.176	Obv. Rev.		*AISPMS*, V b (V XIV A 21b) 512. *Am*, V. IV. B. 1b. Barwani, *ND*, 20. 88. **Normal**
54. **Vb.I.A2** 3.3944 / 1.40 (3) 2002.185	Obv. Rev.	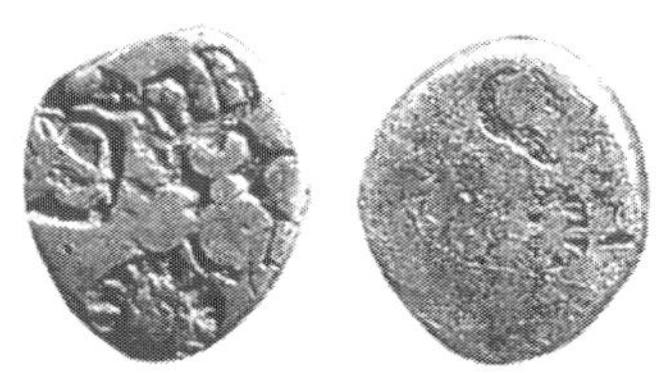	*AISPMS*, V b (V XIV A 21c) 513. *Am*, V. IV. B. 1c. **Scarce**
55. **Vb.I.A3** 3.5255 / 1.32 × 1.16 (14) 2002.156	Obv. Rev.		On these coins, the 5th Symbol i.e. the object on the back of the stag is either out of flan or seen partly, hence the group of these coins can not be determined. These coins are grouped and mentioned as unattributed. Numbers of such coins are more in other hoards also, e.g. Barwani hoard contains 76 such coins.
56. **Vb.II.A** 3.4192 / 1.35 (1) 2002.186	Obv. Rev.		*AISPMC*, V b (V XV A 21) 516. *Am*, V. V. A. 1a. Patraha, II. VI. 1 a. Rairh (I & IV). **Very Common**

Fig. 15

S.No. Sr/cl/gr/vr Wt.(gm)/Sz.(cm) No. of Coins Acc. No.	Symbols	Illustrations Obv. Rev.	Select Publication Remarks
57. **Vb.II.A1** 3.5071 / 1.60 (1) 2002.187	Obv.  Rev. 		*AISPMC*, V b (V XV A 21b) 517. *Am*, V V A. 1.b. **Scarce**
58. **Vb.II.B** 3.4959 / 1.50 (3) 2002.190	Obv.  Rev. 		*AISPMC*, V b (V XV B 107) 518. *Am*, V. V. B. 2. Patraha, II. VI. d. Hyderabad (Karimnagar, Gulbarga, Maski Find), IV. D. 2. Rairh (I, IV & V). **Common**
59. **Vb.II.B1** 3.4518 / 1.52 (2) 2002.191	Obv.  Rev. 	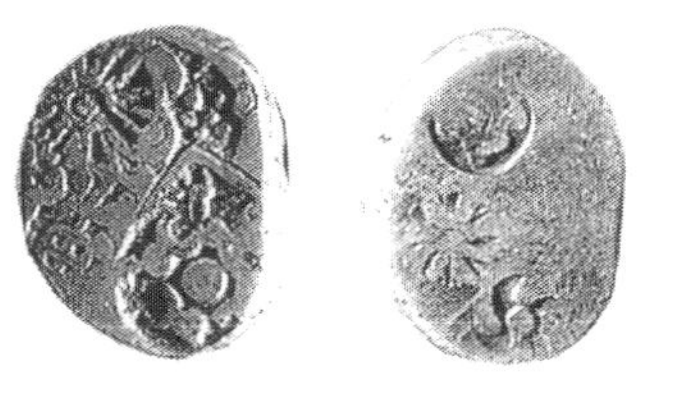	*AISPMC*, V b (V XV B 109) 519. *Am*, V. V. B. 1. Hyderabad (Karimnagar, Gulbarga, Maski Find). IV. D. 1. Patraha, II. VI c. Rairh (I, II, IV & V). **Very Common**
60. **Vb.III.A** 3.3952 / 1.35 (2) 2002.194	Obv.  Rev. 	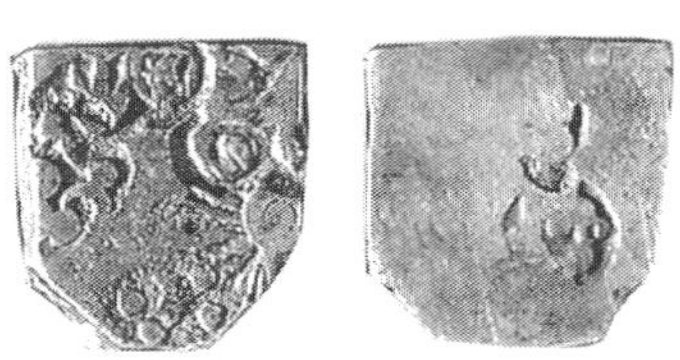	*AISPMC*, V b (V XVI B 112) 522. *Am*, V. VIII. 2. Barwani, *ND*, 20. 89. **Normal**

Fig. 16

S.No. Sr/cl/gr/vr Wt.(gm)/Sz.(cm) No. of Coins Acc. No.	Symbols	Illustrations Obv. Rev.	Select Publication Remarks
61. **Vb.IV.A** 3.3224/ 1.50 × 1.30 (1) 2002.195	Obv.  Rev. 	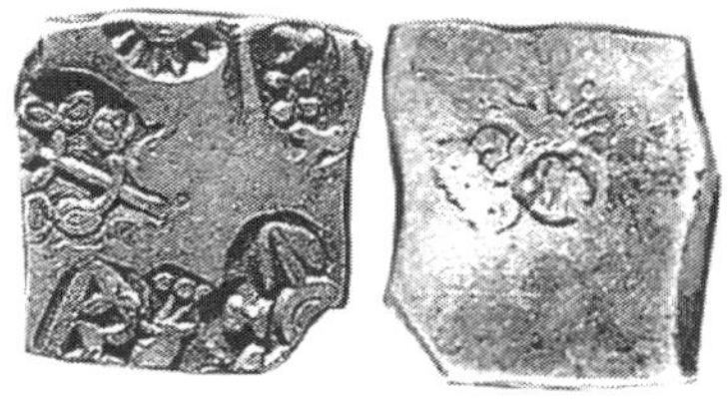	*AISPMC*, V b (V VII A 114) 525. *Am*, V. XIV. 2. Barwani, *ND*, 20. 92. **Very Rare**
62. **Vb.V.A** 3.4159 / 1.36 (2) 2002.196	Obv.  Rev. 		*AISPMC*, V b (V XVIII A 16) 526. *Am*, V. XVIII. 1. **Rare**
63. **VIa.I.A** 3.5750 / 1.40 × 1.10 (1) 2002.198	Obv.  Rev. 		*AISPMC*, VI a (VI I A 115) 527. *Am*, VI. II. A. 1. Patraha, II. X. a.b. Hyderabad (Karimnagar), III. F. 1. **Rare**
64. **VIa.II.A** 3.4742 / 1.35 × 1.05 (9) 2002.199	Obv.  Rev. 		*AISPMC*, VI b (VI II D 115) 534. *Am*, VI. III. G. 2. Patraha, II. X. a-b. Hyderabad (Karimnagar), III. A (b). Rairh (V). **Very Common**

Fig. 17

S.No. Sr/cl/gr/vr Wt.(gm)/Sz.(cm) No. of Coins Acc. No.	Symbols	Illustrations Obv. Rev.	Select Publication Remarks
65. **VIa.II.A1** 3.4682 / 1.17 × 1.10 (2) 2002.208	Obv.  Rev. 	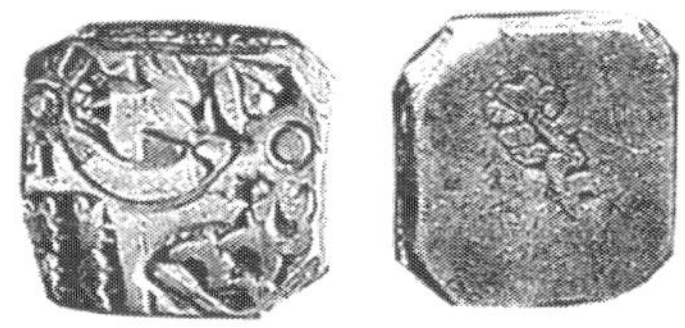	*AISPMC*, VI a (VI II D 118) 537. *Am*, VI. III. G. 1. Patraha, II. X. c. Hyderabad (Karimnagar) III. A (b) 2. **Very Common**
66. **VIa.II.A2** 3.4493/ 1.5 × 1.14 (4) 2002.210	Obv.  Rev. 		*AISPMC*, VI a (VI II D 119) 538. *Am*, VI. III. G. 4. Barwani, *ND*, 20. 100. **Common**
67. **VIb.I.A** 3.4441/ 1.45 × 1.23 (19) 2002.219	Obv. 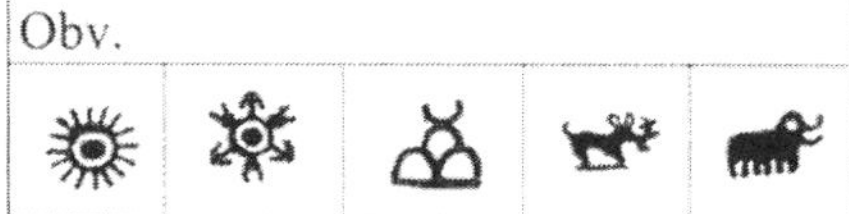 Rev. 		*AISPMC*, VI b (VI IV A 1) 542. Am, VI. III. A. 1. Patraha, II. XI. i. Hyderabad (Karimnagar, Gulbarga, Raichur), IV. 1 (a) 1. Rairh (I, III, IV & V). Barwani, *ND*, 20. 102. **Extremely Common**
68. **VIb.I.A1** 3.4386 / 1.55 × 1.13 (43) 2002.248	Obv.  Rev. 		*AISPMC*, VI b (VI IV A 18) 543. *Am*, VI. III. A. 2. Patraha, II. XI. a-b. Hyderabad (Karimnagar, Gulbarga, Raichur Maski find), III. A (a). Rairh (I, II, IV & V). Barwani, *ND*, 21. 103. **Extremely Common**

Fig. 18

S.No. Sr/cl/gr/vr Wt.(gm)/Sz.(cm) No. of Coins Acc. No.	Symbols	Illustrations Obv. Rev.	Select Publication Remarks
69. **VIb.I.B** 3.4883 / 1.20 (18) 2002.282	Obv. 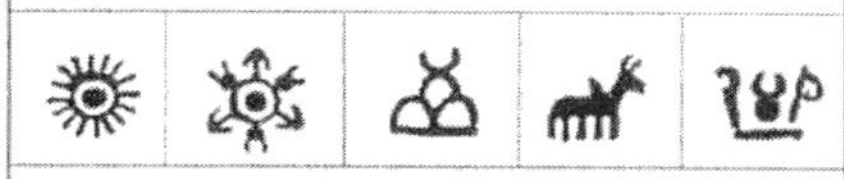 Rev. 		*AISPMC*, VI b (VI IV B 129) 546. *Am*, VI. III. C. 2. Barwani, *ND*, 21. 104 **Very Common**
70. **VIb.I.C** 3.5262 / 1.33 (4) 2002.294	Obv.  Rev. 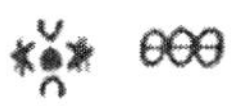		*AISPMC*, VI b (VI IV C 21) 548. *Am*, VI. III. I. 2a. Patraha, II. IV. j. Hyderabad (Karimnagar, Gulbarga), III. A (h) 7. Rairh (I & V). Barwani, *ND*, 21.105. **Common**
71. **VIb.I.C1** 3.4337 / 1.30 (6) 2002.298	Obv. 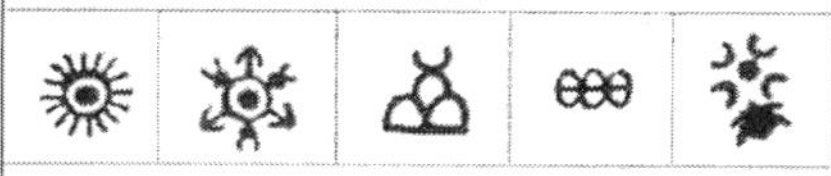 Rev. 		*AISPMC*, VI b (VI IV C 130) 552. *Am*, VI. III. I. 1a, c, e. Patraha, II. IV. .i. Hyderabad (Karimnagar, Gulbarga), III. A (b). 2. Rairh (I, II, IV & V). Barwani, *ND*, 21.108. **Extremely Common**
72. **VIb.I.C2** 3.5346 / 1.86 × 1.14 (5) 2002.306	Obv. 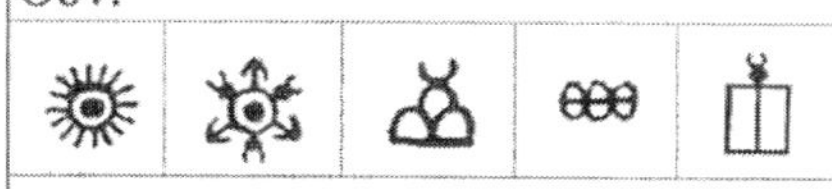 Rev.  (?)		*AISPMC*, VI b (VI IV C 133) 555. *Am*, VI. III. I. 3. Patraha, II. IV. C. Hyderabad (Gulbarga), III. A (b). 6. Rairh (I, II, IV & V). Barwani, *ND*, 21.109. **Very Common**

Fig. 19

S.No. Sr/cl/gr/vr Wt.(gm)/Sz.(cm) No. of Coins Acc. No.	Symbols	Illustrations Obv.	Illustrations Rev.	Select Publication Remarks
73. **VIb.I.C3** 3.3999 / 1.30 × 1.10 (1) 2002.309	Obv.  Rev. 		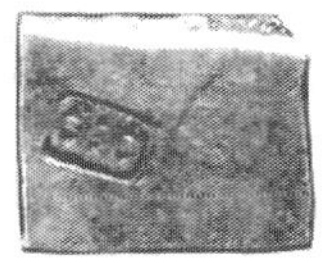	*AISPMC*, VI b (VI IV C 135) 557. *Am*, VI. III. I. 5. Barwani, *ND*, 21.110. **Common**
74. **VIb.I.D** 3.4059 / 1.30 (9) 2002.313	Obv.  Rev. 		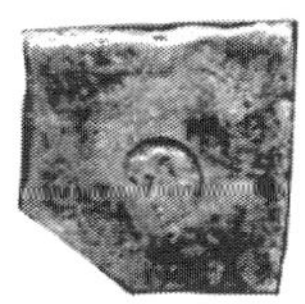	*AISPMC*, VI b (VI IV E 27) 571. *Am*, VI. III. H. 1a,1b,1c Patraha, II. VIII. b. Hyderabad (Karimnagar, Gulbarga, Raichur, Maski find), III. A (e) 1. Rairh (I, II & V). Barwani, *ND*, 22. 116. **Extremely Common**
75. **VIb.I.E** 3.4874 / 1.60 × 1.00 (10) 2002.324	Obv. 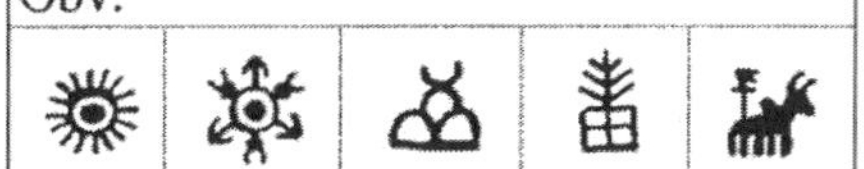 Rev. 			*AISPMC*, VI b (VI IV G 122) 576. *Am*, VI. III. B. 1. Patraha, II. IX. b. Rairh (I). Barwani, *ND*, 22.119. **Common**
76. **VIb.I.E1** 3.4333 / 1.20 (2) 2002.329	Obv.  Rev. 			*AISPMC*, VI b (VI IV G 123) 577. *Am*, VI. III. B. 2. Patraha, II. IX. a. Barwani, *ND*, 22.120. **Normal**

C. PLATES

Pl. I – 2002.8, 4, 6, 7, 9, 10. - Sr. III.II.A.
Pl. I – 2002.12, 13, 18, 17, 16. - Sr. III.III.A1.
Pl. II – 2002.15. - Sr. III.III.A2.
Pl. II – 2002.25. - Sr. IVd.I.A1.
Pl. II & III - 2002.31, 34, 32, 33, 35, 37, 45, 38, 39, 30, 42, 44, 41, 40, 43. - Sr. IVd.I.D.
Pl. III – 2002.48. - Sr. IVd.I.D3.
Pl. III – 2002.52, 50. - Sr. IVd.I.D4.
Pl. III – 2002.54. - Sr. IVd.I.D5.
Pl. IV – 2002.55, 57, 60, 58, 59. - Sr. IVd.I.D6.
Pl. IV - 2002.61. - Sr. IVd.I.D7.
Pl. IV – 2002.68, 64, 65, 66. - Sr. IVd.II.A.
Pl. IV - 2002.71, 72. - Sr. IVd.III.A.
Pl. V - 2002.75, 76, 78. - Sr. IVd.IV.A.
Pl. V - 2002.85, 89, 87, 84, 88, 86. - Sr. Va.I.A.
Pl. V - 2002.91. - Sr. Va.I.A1.
Pl. V & VI – 2002.93, 94, 95, 96, 97, 99, 100. - Sr. Va.I.A2.
Pl. VI - 2002.102. - Sr. Va.I.A3.
Pl. VI & VII - 2002.111, 106, 113, 108, 109, 107, 114, 104, 112, 110, 105, 116, 121,122, 115, 117, 118, 120, 119. - Sr. IVd.I.A4.
Pl. VIII - 2002.126, 123, 124, 125. - Sr. Va.I.A5.
Pl. VIII - 2002.129, 130. - Sr. Va.II.A.
Pl. VIII & IX - 2002.137, 133, 132, 134, 135, 138, 131. - Sr. Va.III.A.
Pl. IX - 2002.333. - Sr. Va.V.A1.
Pl. IX - 2002.144, 142, 141, 145. - Sr. Va.VI.A.
Pl. IX – 2002.147, 146. - Sr. Va.VII.A.
Pl. IX – 2002.150, 151, 149 - Sr. Va.VIII.A.
Pl. X - 2002.161, 167, 153, 166, 163, 171, 172, 169. - Sr. Vb.I.A.
Pl. X & XI – 2002.179,177,178,181,180,182. – Sr. Vb.I.A1.
Pl. XI – 2002.184, 183. - Sr. Vb.I.A2.
Pl. XI & XII – 2002.162, 158, 157, 155, 168, 165, 159, 160, 154, 175, 173, 174, 170. - Sr. Vb.I.A3.
Pl. XII - 2002.188, 189. - Sr. Vb.II.B.
Pl. XII – 2002.192. - Sr. Vb.II.B1.
Pl. XII – 2002.193. - Sr. Vb.III.A.
Pl. XII - 2002.197. - Sr. Vb.V.A.
Pl. XIII - 2002.203, 204, 205, 206, 202, 207, 201, 200. - Sr. VIa.II.A.
Pl. XIII – 2002.209. - Sr. VIa.II.A1.
Pl. XIII - 2002.211, 213, 212. - Sr. VIa.II.A2.
Pl. XIV & XV - 2002.224, 225, 227, 216, 215, 214, 229, 217, 223, 221, 218, 222, 228, 226, 230, 220, 232, 231. - Sr. VIb.I.A.
Pl. XV - XVIII - 2002.238, 233, 267, 243, 249, 268, 271, 275, 240, 241, 262, 254, 253, 264, 265, 266, 260, 259,258, 274, 257, 250, 247, 261, 242, 252, 239, 251, 237, 255, 236, 272, 273, 244, 234, 245, 235, 246, 256, 269, 263, 270. - Sr.VIb.I.A1.
Pl. XIX & XX – 2002.277, 292, 293, 281, 280, 284, 287, 278, 286, 276, 285, 283, 279, 288, 290, 289, 291. - Sr. VIb.I.B.
Pl. XX – 2002.296, 297, 295. - Sr. VIb.I.C.
Pl. XX & XXI. – 2002.299, 300, 301, 302, 303. - Sr. VIb.I.CI.
Pl. XXI - 2002.308, 307, 304, 305. - Sr.VIb.I.C2.
Pl. XXI. & XXII - 2002.311,315,314,317,318,316,312,310. - Sr. VIb.I.D.
Pl. XXII & XXIII - 2002.327, 328, 323, 322, 326, 321, 325, 320, 319. - Sr. VIb.I.E.
Pl. XXIII – 2002.330. - Sr. VIb.I.E1.

PL. I

III.II.A - (2-7)

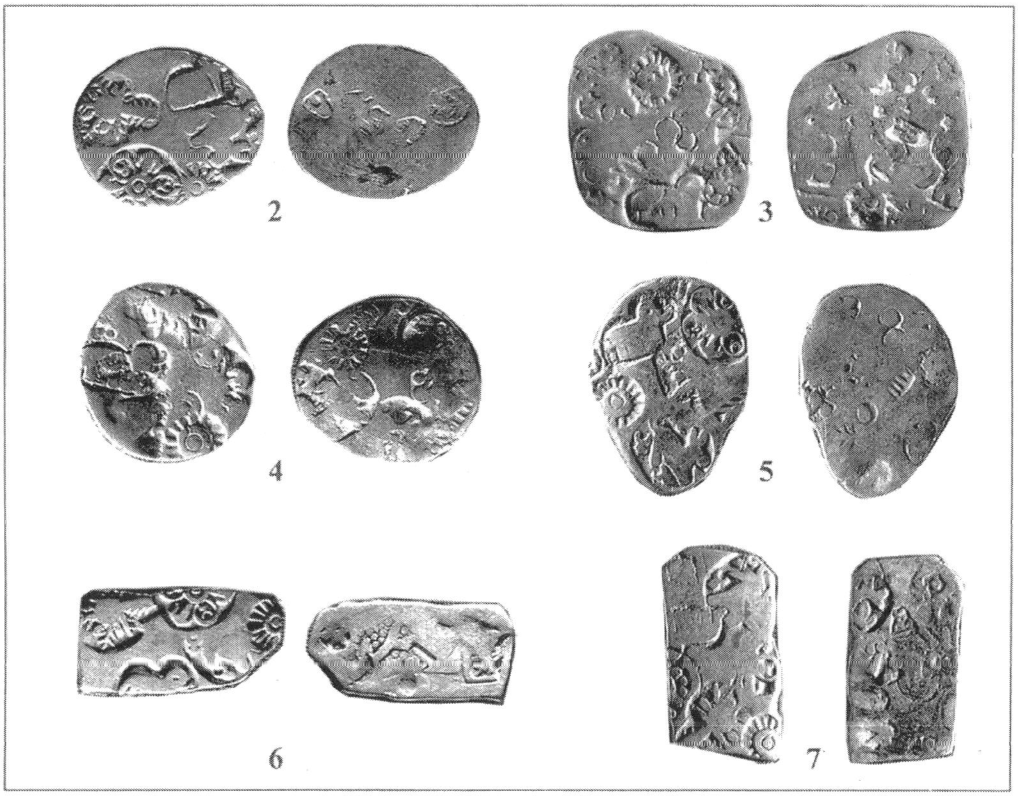

III.III.A1 - (2-6)

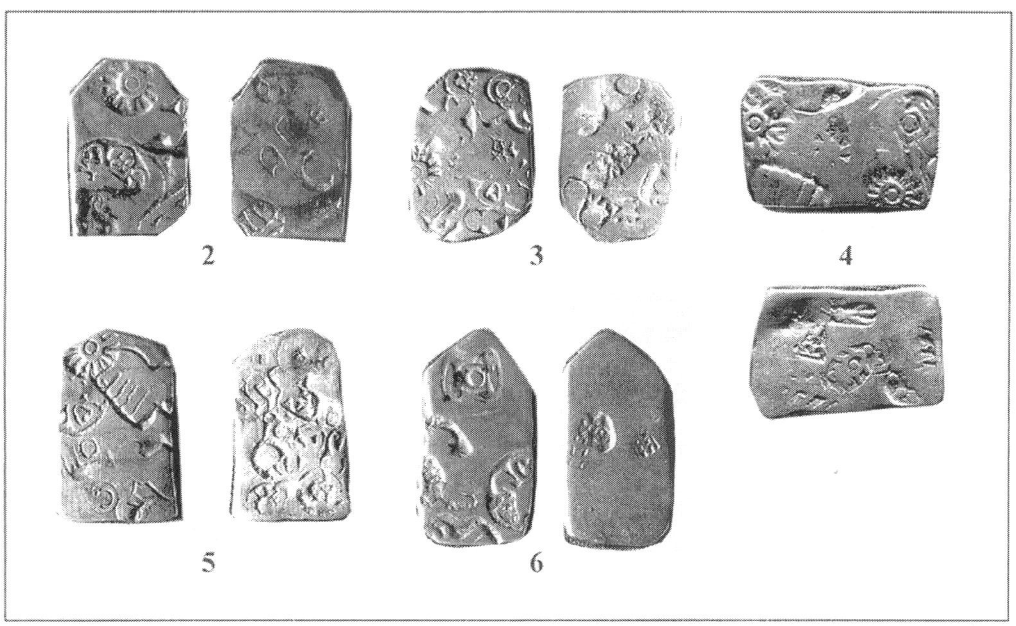

PL. II

III.III.A2 - (2)

2

IVd.I.A1 - (2)

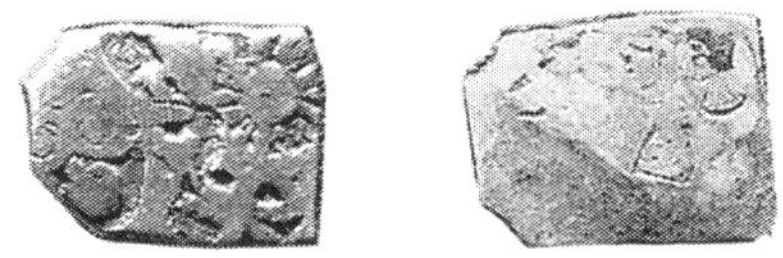

2

IVd.I.D - (2-9)

2

3

4

5

6

7

8

9

PL. III

IV.I.D - (10-16)

10

11

12

13

14

15

16

IVd.I.D3 - (2)

2

IVdI.D4 - (2-3)

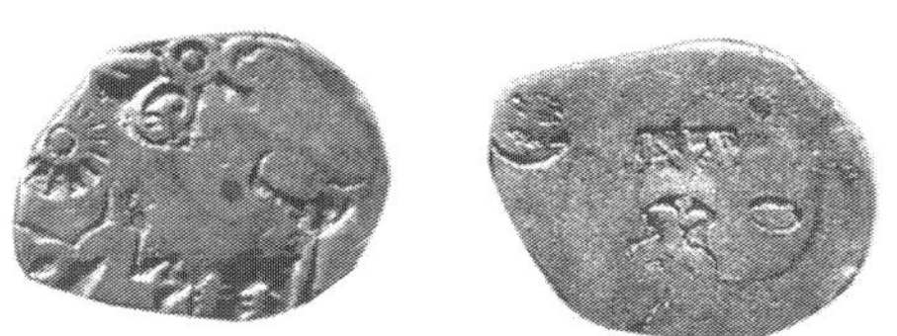

2

3

IVd.I.D5 - (2)

2

PL. IV

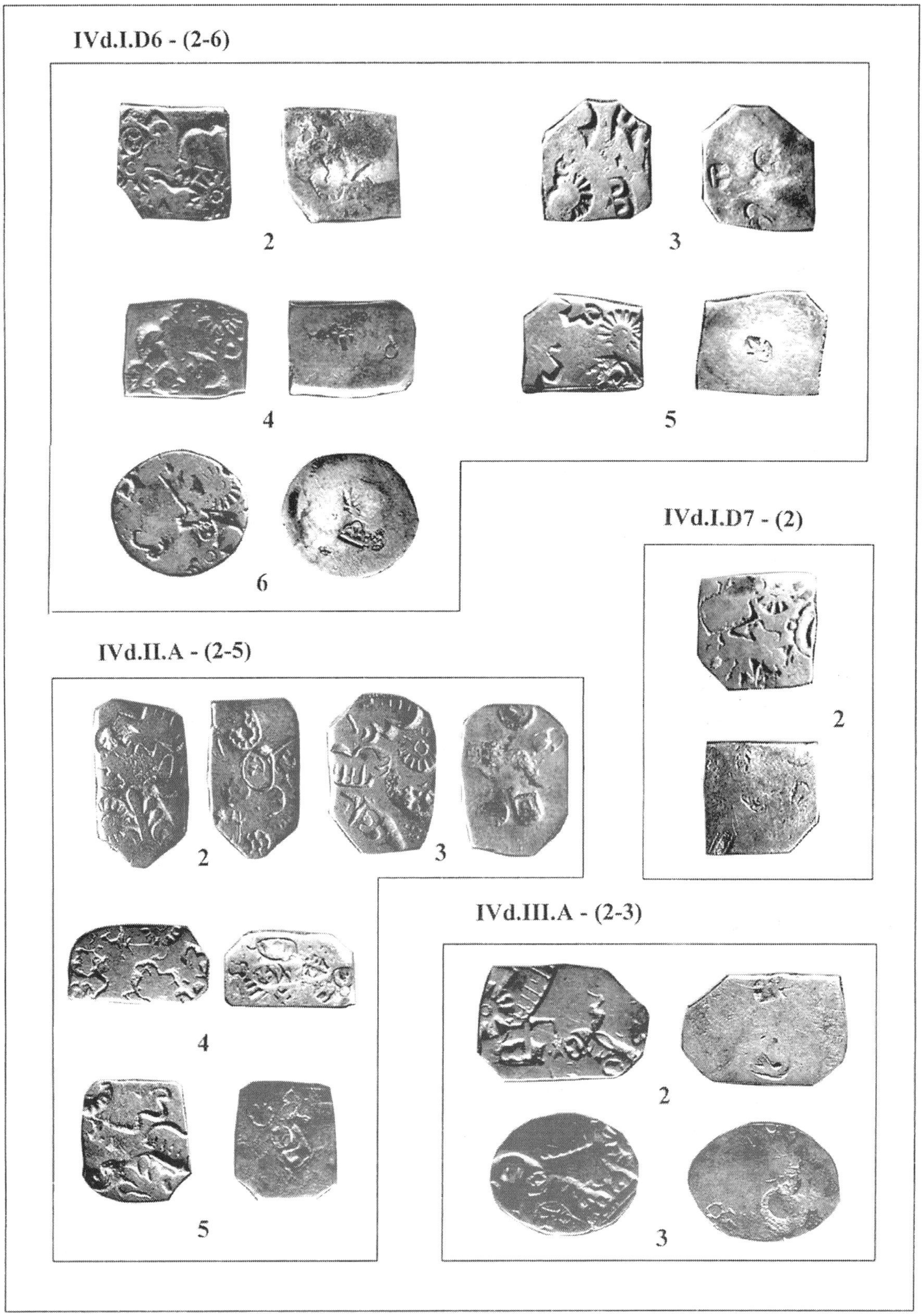

PL. V

IVd.IV.A - (2-4)

Va.I.A - (2-7)

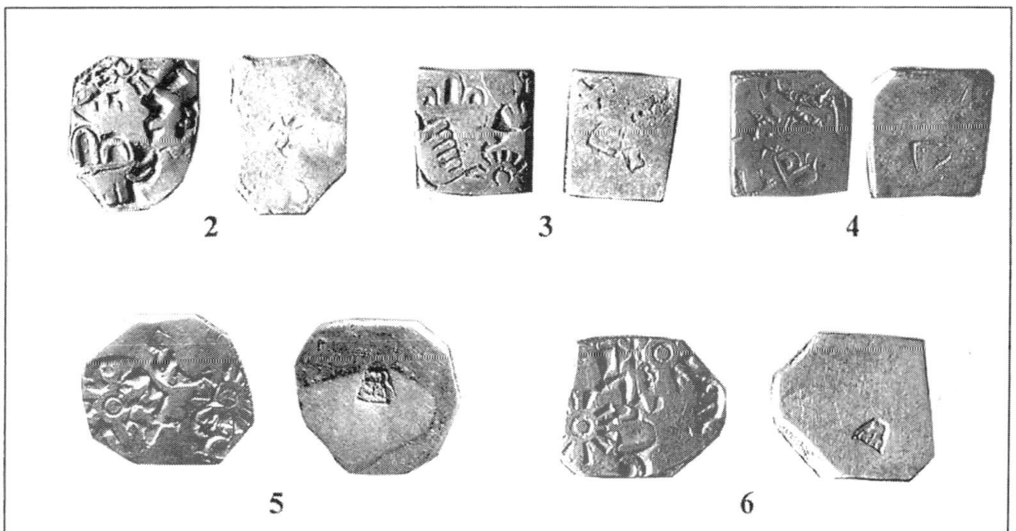

Va.I.A1 - (2)

Va.I.A2 - (2-3)

PL. VI

Va.I.A2 - (4-8)

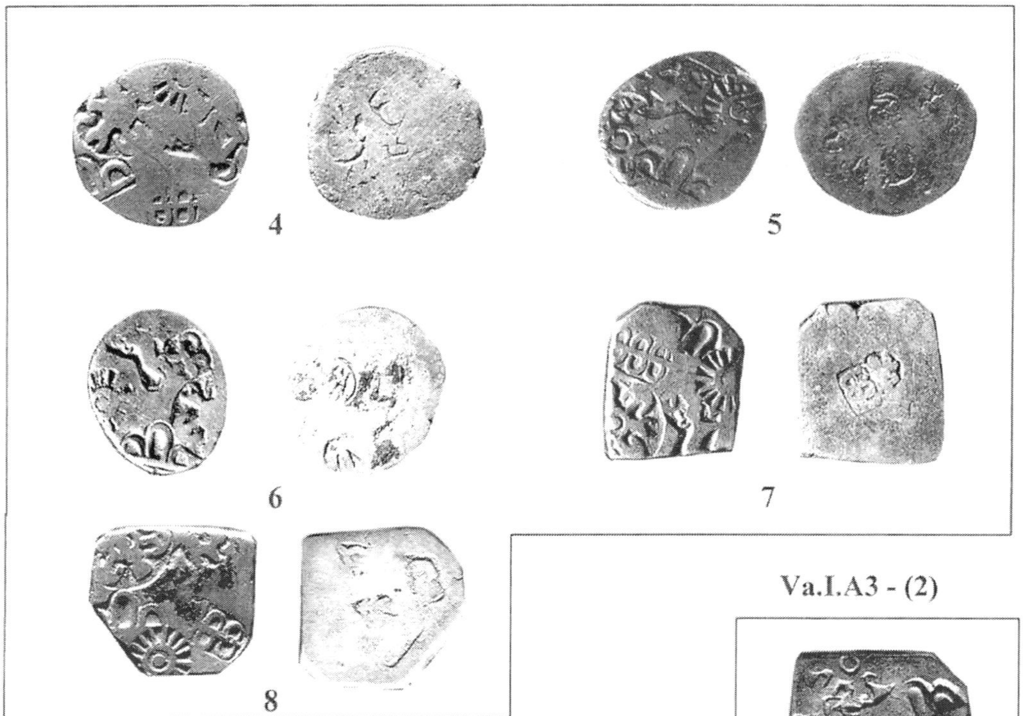

4 5 6 7 8

Va.I.A3 - (2)

2

Va.I.A4 - (2-6)

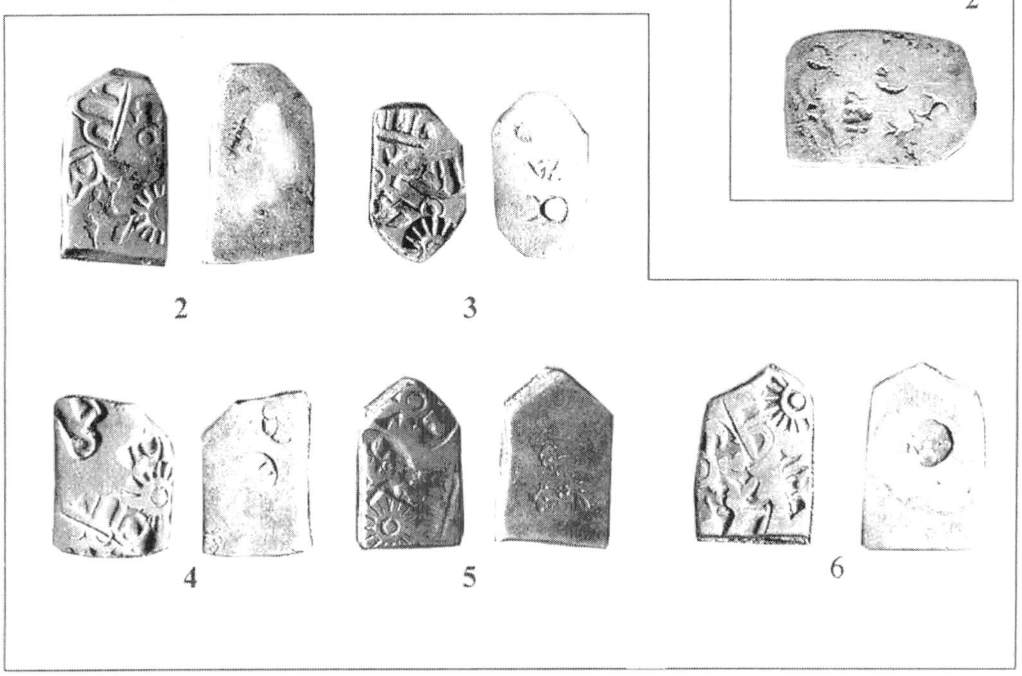

2 3 4 5 6

PL. VII

Va.I.A4 - (7-20)

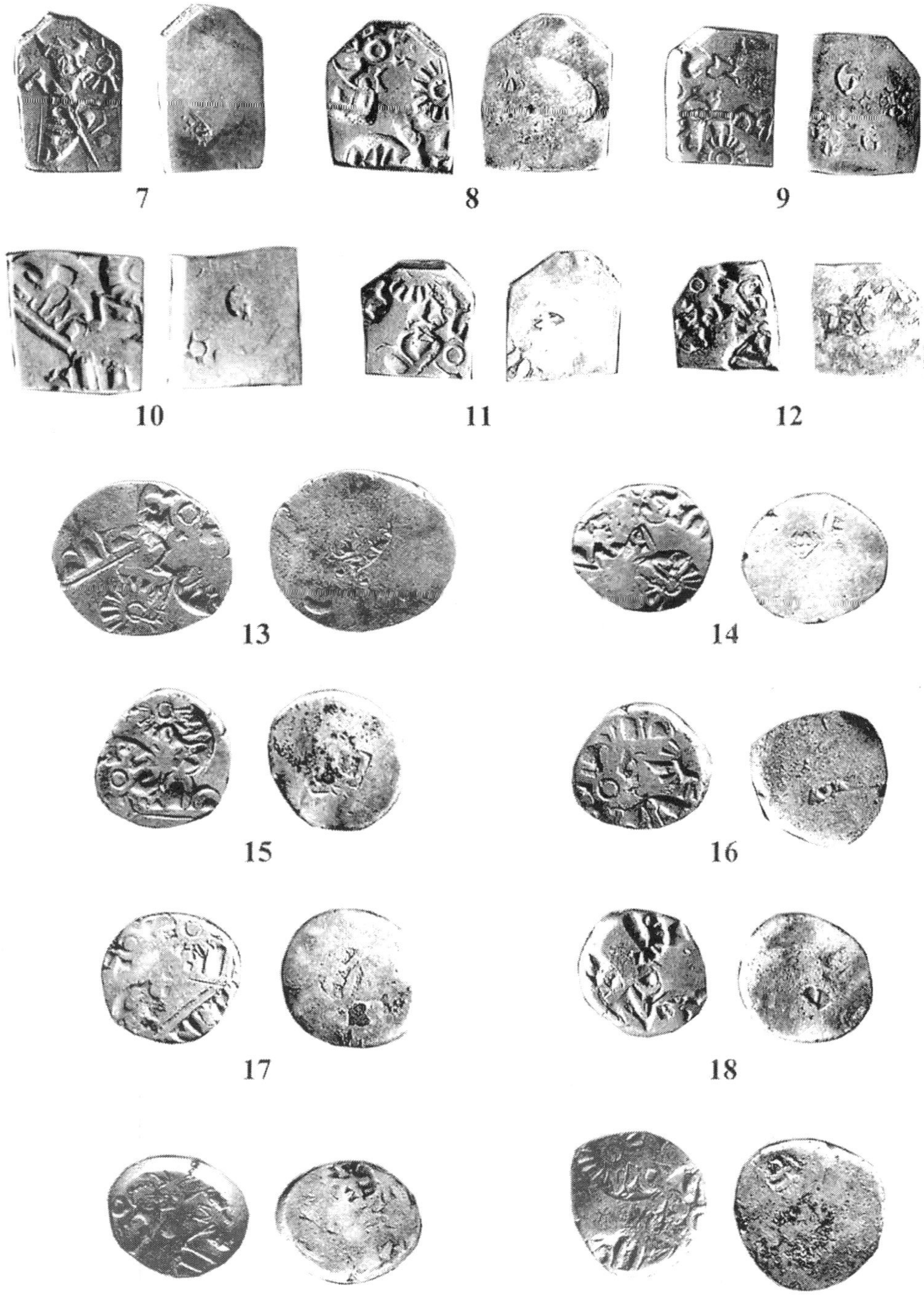

7 8 9 10 11 12 13 14 15 16 17 18 19 20

PL. VIII

Va.I.A5 - (2-5)

Va.II.A - (2-3)

Va.III.A - (2-5)

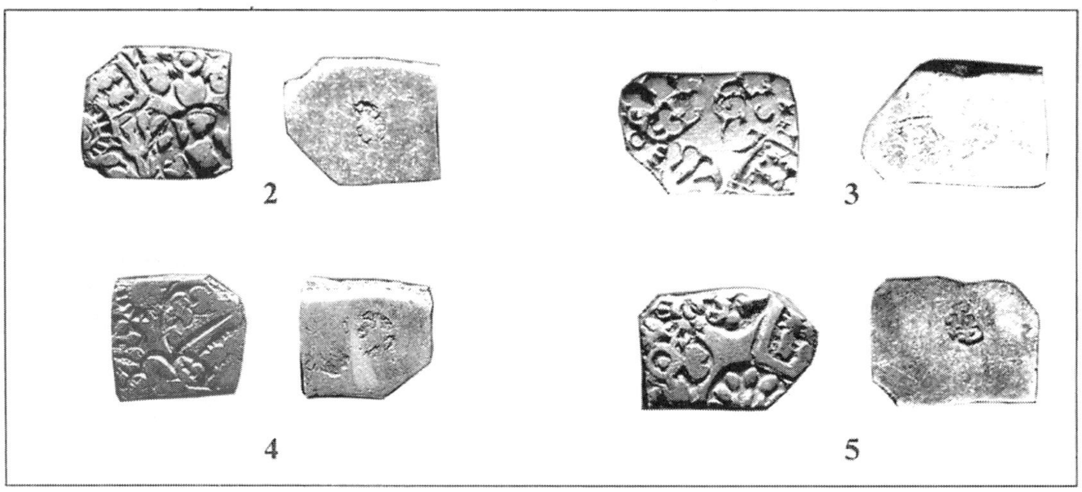

PL. IX

Va.III.A - (6-8)

6 7 8

Va.V.A1 - (2)

2

Va.VI.A - (2-5)

2

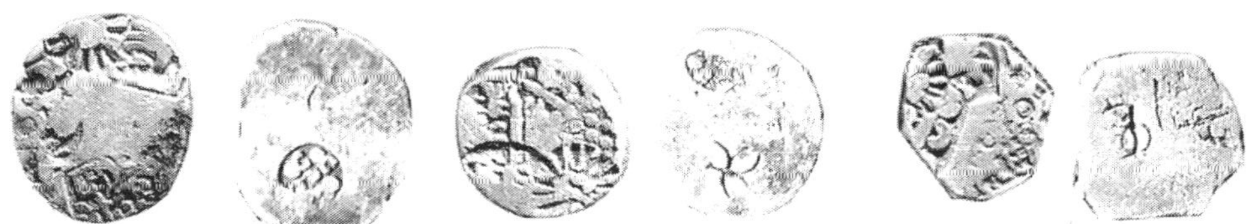

3 4 5

Va.VII.A - (2-3)

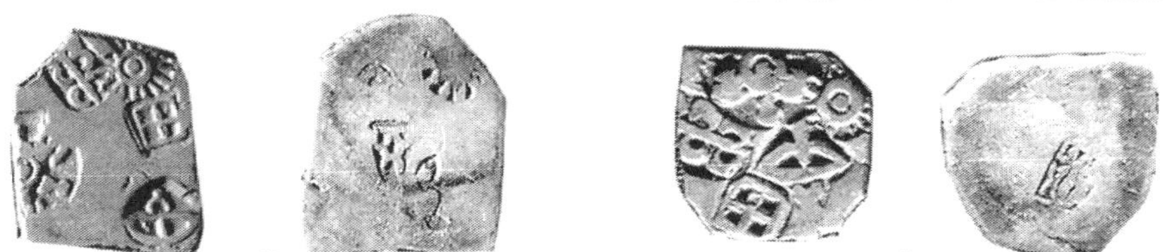

2 3

Va.VIII.A - (2-4)

2 3 4

PL. X

Vb.I.A - (2-9)

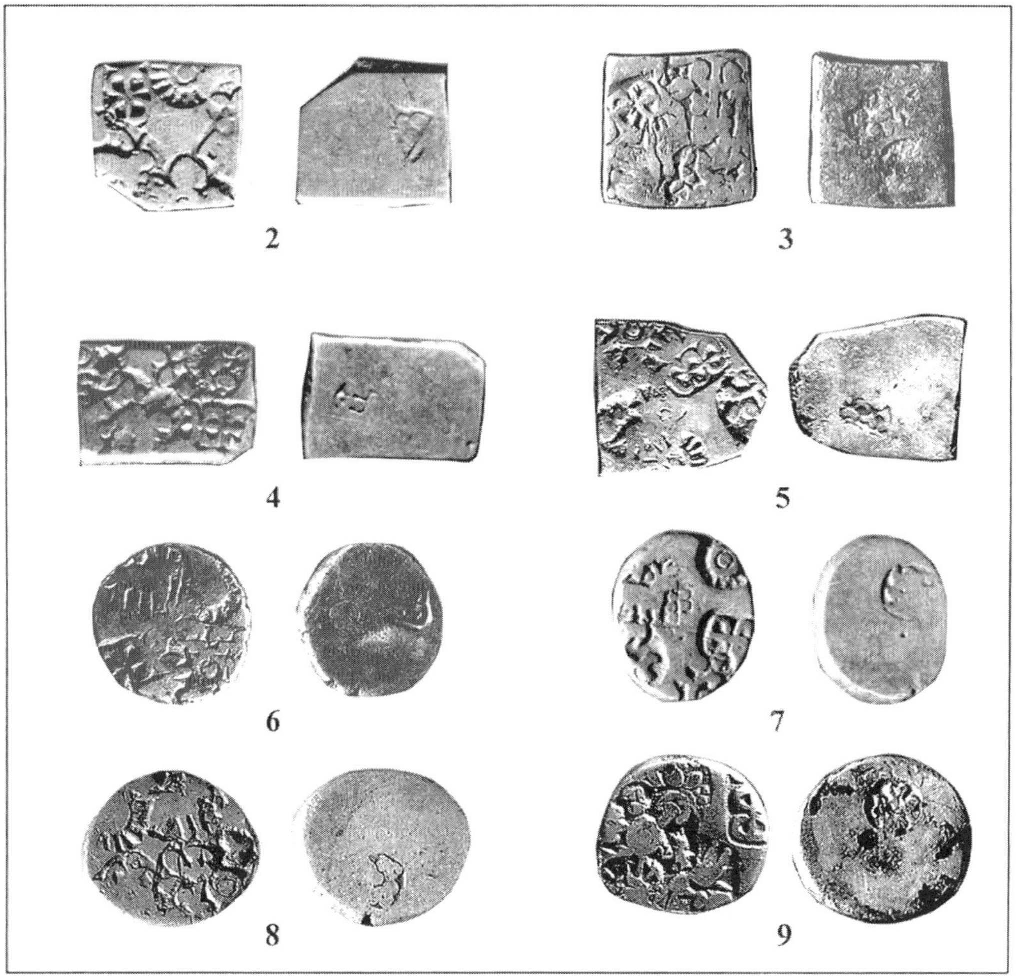

Vb.I.A1 - (2-4)

PL. XI

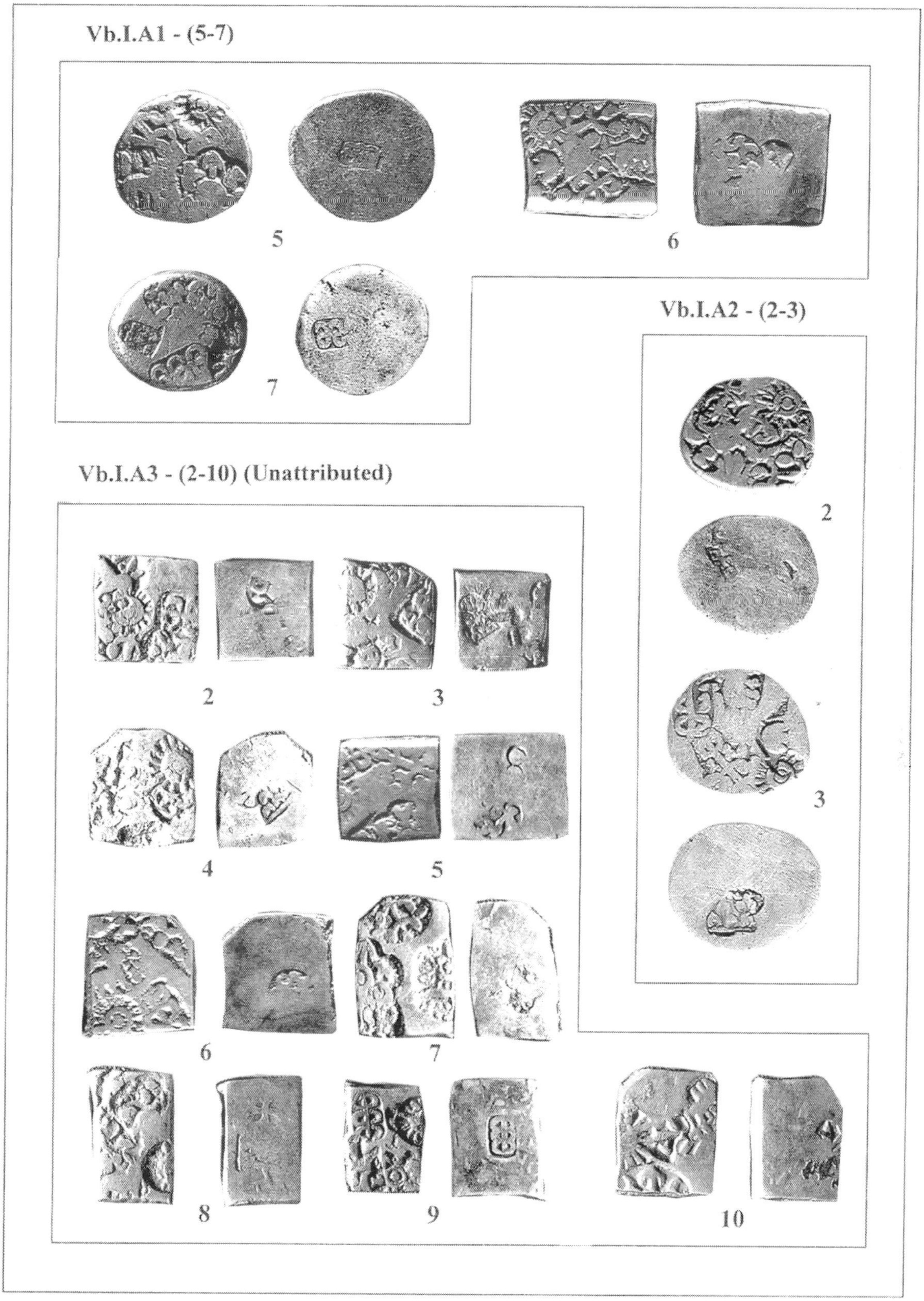

PL. XII

Vb.I.A3 - (11-14) (Unattributed)

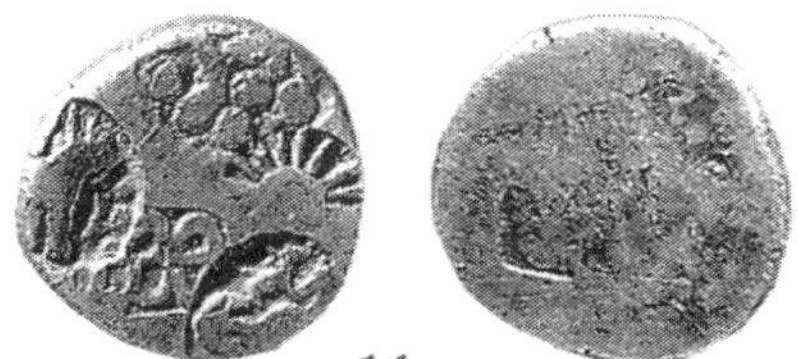

11

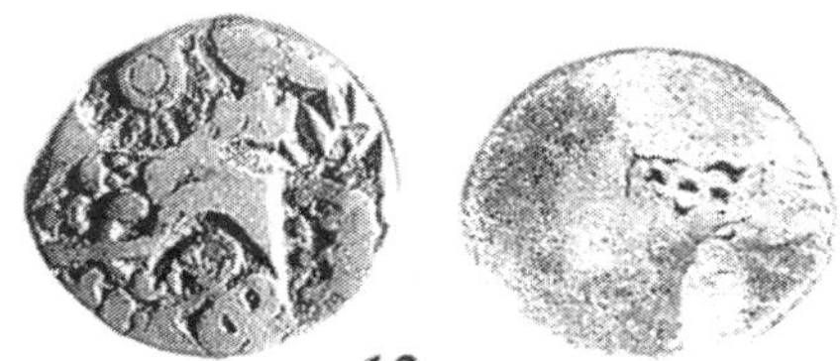

12

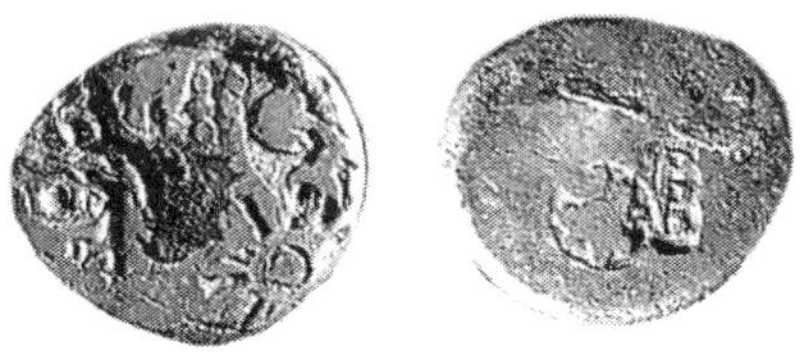

13

14

Vb.II.B - (2-3)

2

3

Vb.II.B1 - (2)

2

Vb.V.A - (2)

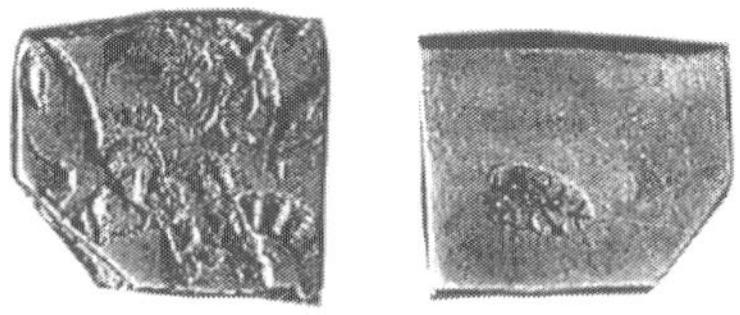

2

Vb.III.A - (2)

2

PL. XIII

VIa.II.A - (2-9)

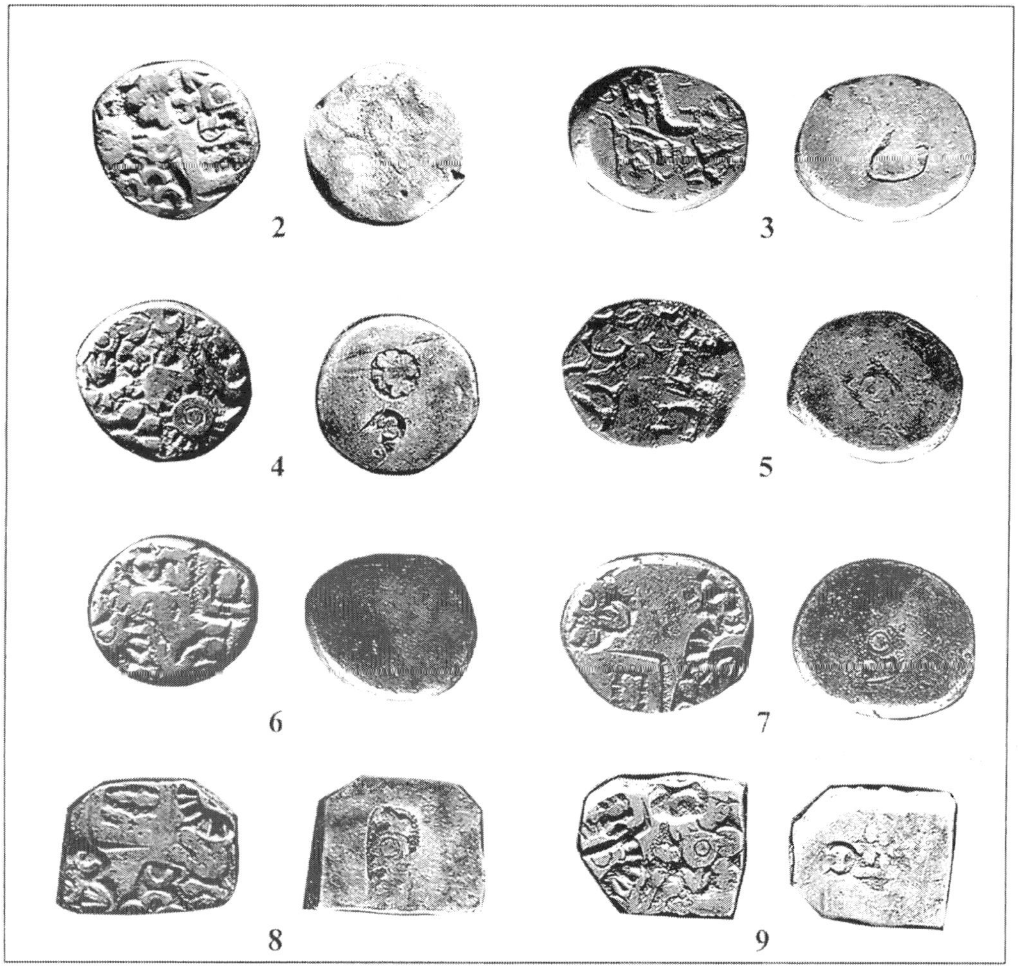

VIa.II.A1 - (2)

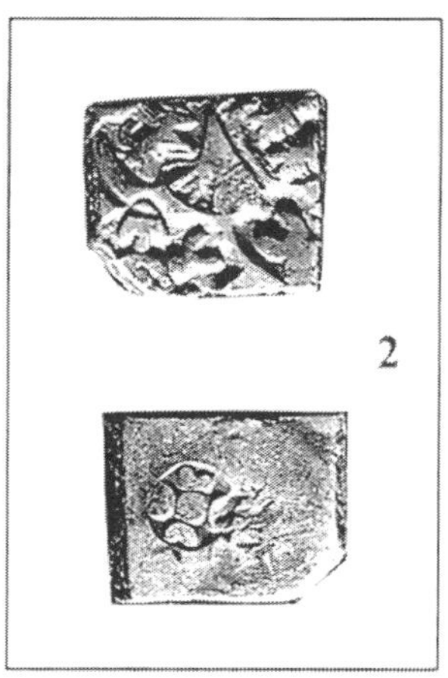

VIa.II.A2 - (2-4)

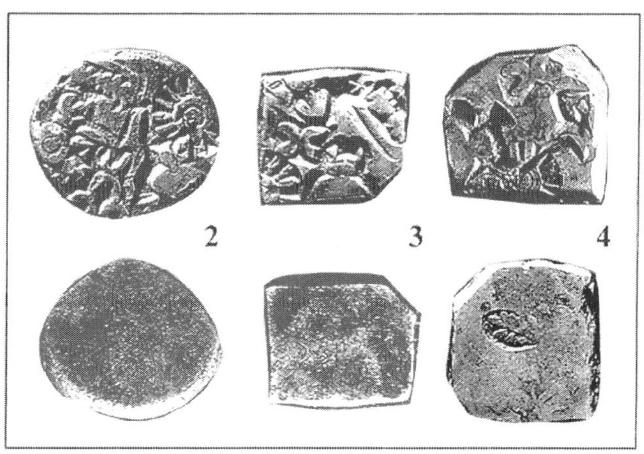

PL. XIV

VIb.I.A - (2-13)

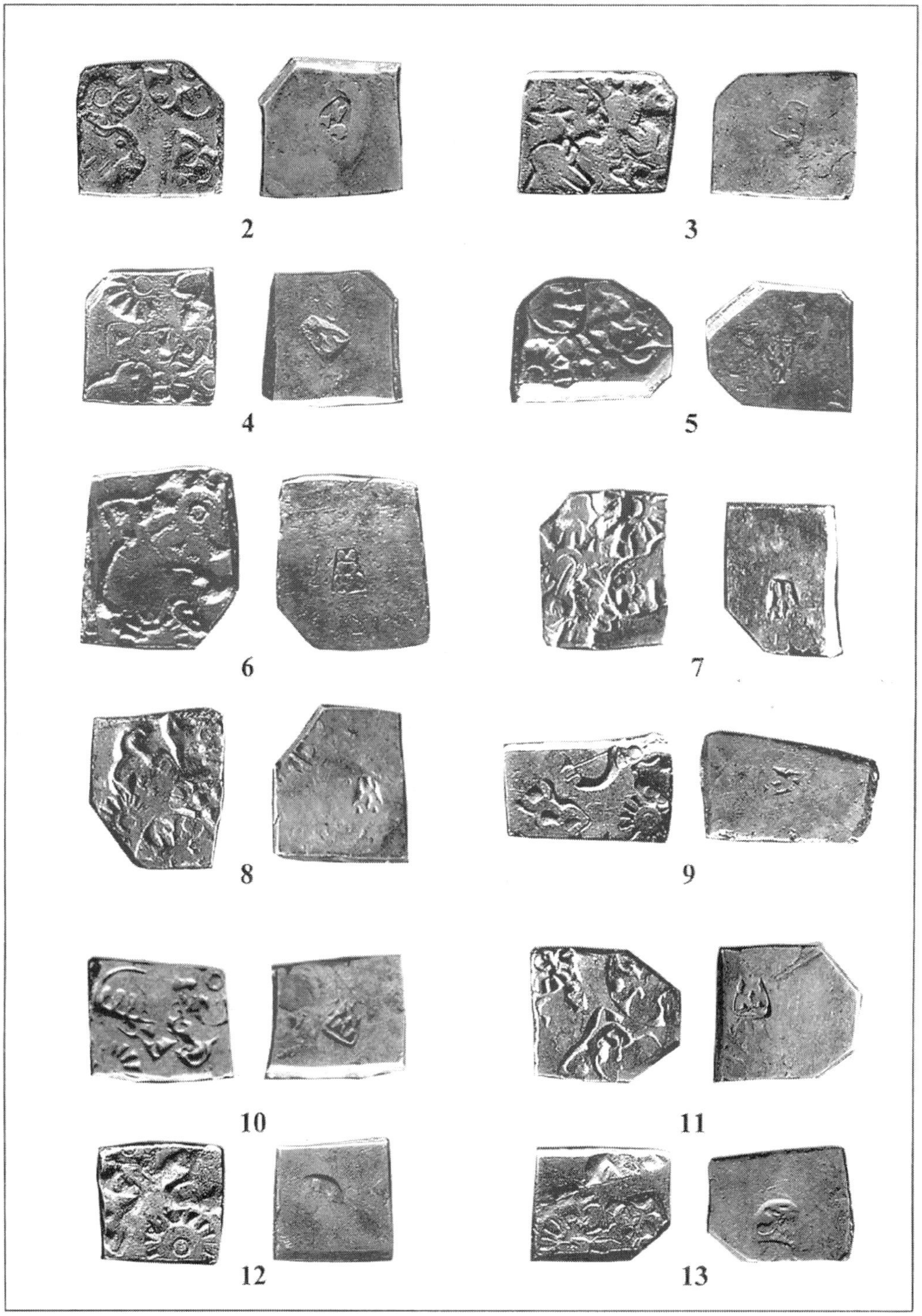

PL. XV

VIb.I.A - (14-19)

14 15 16 17 18 19

VIb.I.A1 - (2-9)

2 3 4 5 6 7 8 9

PL. XVI

VIb.I.A1 - (10-21)

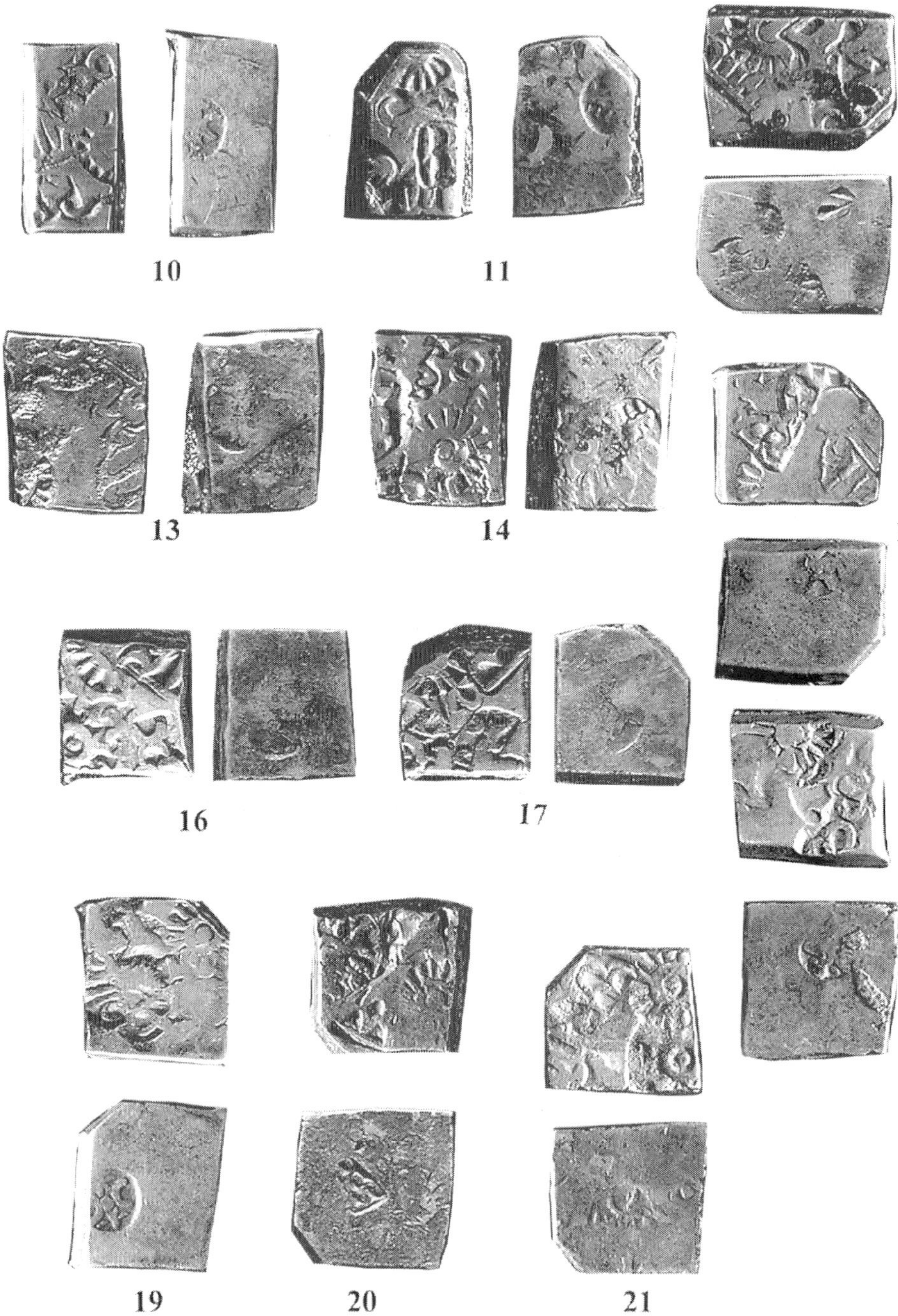

10 11 12 13 14 15 16 17 18 19 20 21

PL. XIX

VIb.I.B - (2-15)

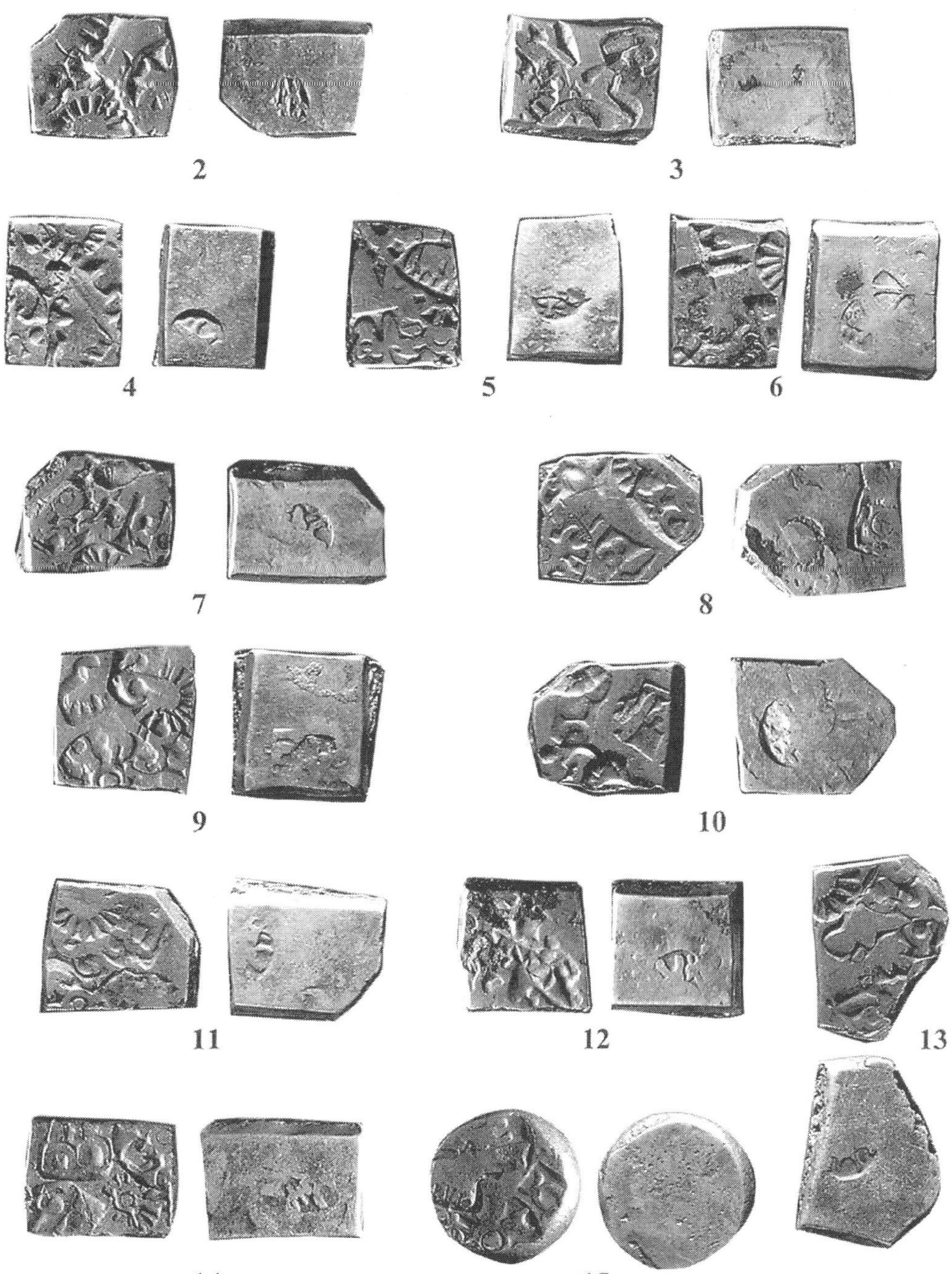

2 3 4 5 6 7 8 9 10 11 12 13 14 15

PL. XX

VIb.I.B - (16-18)

16 **17** **18**

VIb.I.C - (2-4)

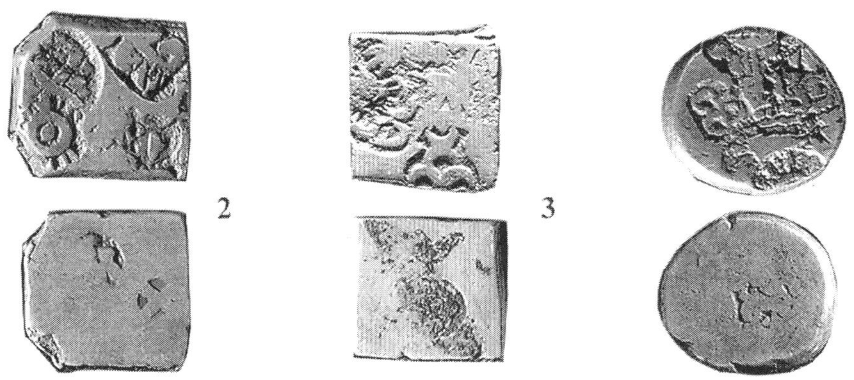

2 3 4

VIb.I.C1 - (2-4)

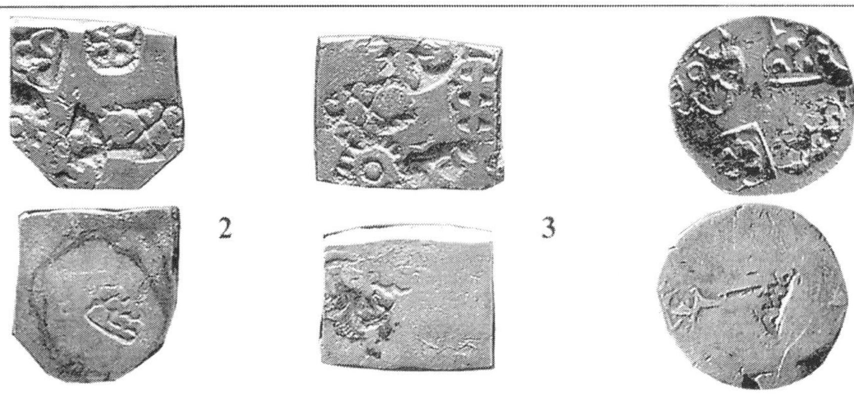

2 3 4

PL. XXI

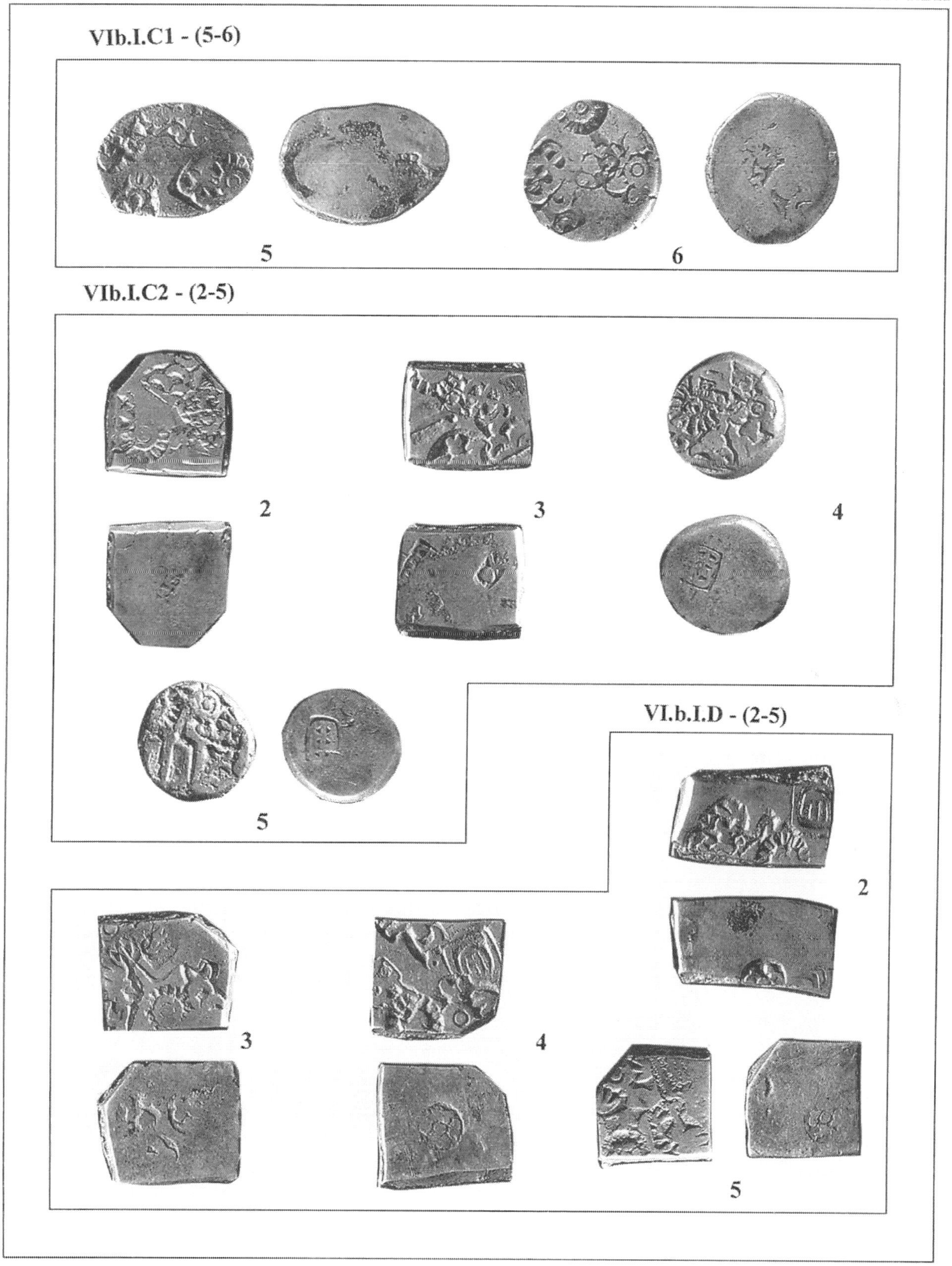

PL. XXII

VIb.I.D - (6-9)

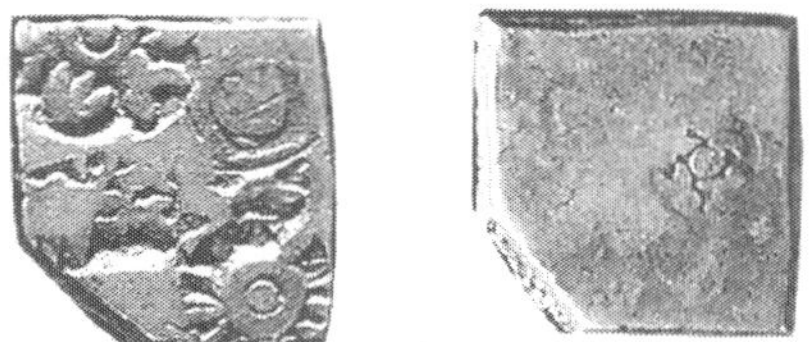

6

7

8

9

VIb.I.E - (2-8)

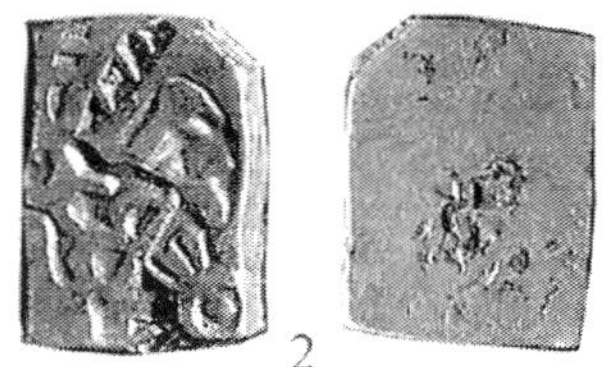

2

3

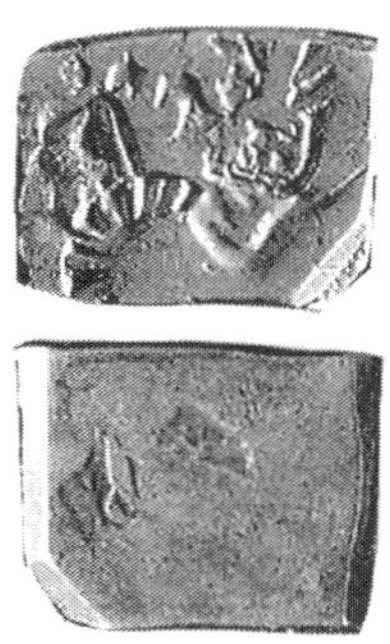

4

5

6

7

8

PL. XXIII

VIb.I.E - (9-10)

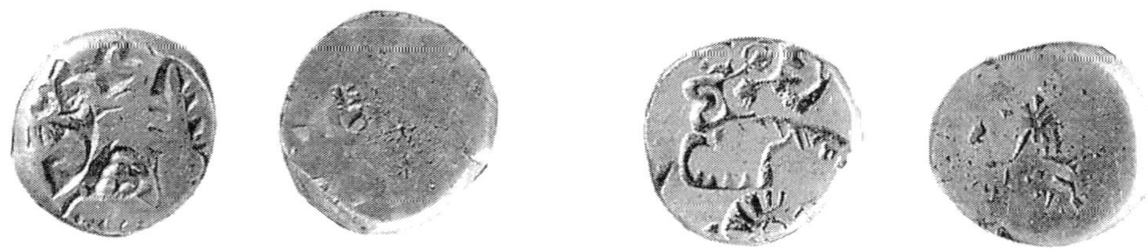

9 10

VIb.I.E1 - (2)

2

Part III

DISCUSSION

9

Observations

Kārṣāpaṇa, the earliest emergence of punch-marked coins in ancient India by purely indigenous methodology of impressing symbols with individual punches and with predetermined weights, irregular shapes and sizes, has been termed as 'Punch-marked coins' by James Prinsep, by which name these coins are known today. Such coins cover a wide range of period. The largest number of these coins bears five bold symbols on the obverse and is considered to conform to 32 *rattīs*/ 56 grains/3.6 grams (between 3.3 and 3.6 grams)/weight standard. These metal pieces of a particular weight were stamped with the impression from individual dies engraved with a mark at the end, which was struck with hammer to mark an impression from one to five separate punches. No order or system has been followed in the orientation or sequence to impress symbols. These symbols appear in varying sequence on various pieces and impression of each symbol varies in depth and direction. On some of the coins, the group of five symbols also appears on both sides, suggestive of a restruck/double obverse type of coins.

These coins were produced by two different processes. In the present hoard, 245 coins are made by the cut sheet process and 88 coins are made by a different technique, known as droplet or globule method. Out of these 88 coins, 73 coins are thick and small while 15 coins are given a flattened shape. The coins produced by globuler technique are round or elliptical—polygonal. The cracked edges of such coins indicate that they were fabricated from globules, poured out of molten metal. However, it is not certain as to what technique was used to prepare these globules. Probably, the coin blanks were prepared by dropping the molten metal of required weight on flat surface *(Am,* 144). Coins minted by this technique are found in the later series. The fabric of coins also provides a linkage to the successive series one after the other. The coins issued by different fabrics suggest that they have been issued at different periods and at the same time denotes their transition from one series to another. The earliest coins issued in the early series are thin and of broad flan, whereas the later coins are thick and small in size, though of the same weight standard. The thin and broad pieces represent the coins of Series I and Series II. A few coins of Series II are also found minted of thick fabric, which is the exclusive fabric of Series III. However, a few coins of Series III are also found fabricated in thin and broad flan. The coins of medium thickness exclusively belong to the coins of Series III and Series IV. However, a few coins of medium fabric and of a broad flan are found in Series III and that of thick in Series IV. The coins of Series V are produced in both medium as well as in thick fabric. This indicates a transition from one series to the following series.

However, the coins in the present hoard, attributed to Series II and III, are of medium fabric. This confirms the coins belonging to Series II have been either issued just before the beginning of the coins belonging to Series III or issued simultaneously, with Series III. Further, the coins of Series IV are also fabricated in medium fabric, which shows their continuity with Series III. Likewise, some coins belonging to Series IV are found minted of thick fabric showing their transition between Series IV and V. The coins of Series V are fabricated both in medium and thick fabric while the coins belonging to Series VI and Series VII are issued only in thick fabric. The transition of fabric from one series to another suggests the continuous sequence and chronological relationship between them.

Further, the reverse marks also offer some indications as to chronological sequence. The coins of Series I to Series IV are found either blank or having a number of minute marks. Such marks are also noticed on some of the coins of Series V. The reverse side of the coins reveals some small and conspicuous marks distinguished from the marks that occur on the obverse. Certain obverse marks are also employed on the reverse of some of the coins of Series V, but these marks are smaller than the corresponding mark on the obverse. Some bold marks are also seen on the reverse of this series, which in fact is the exclusive characteristic feature of most of the coins of Series VI. The use of these marks shows an intermediatory link between the series throughout.

The different types of reverse marks on the coins are also indicative of different series. The marks on the reverse of the later coins are entirely different from those found on the earlier coins. The earlier coins bear a number of minute marks both on the reverse and on the obverse. The numbers of marks are less on the coins belonging to the later series. These minute marks appeared in a haphazard way on the coins belonging to early series, but in case of the latter, they are employed as a fixed mark, either single or a fixed group of marks of two or three. These appear to be stamped by authority on a definite system.

The weight of the coins to some extent could also be a helpful indicating factor in fixing up the chronology of these coins. It is believed that the coins less in weight would be the earliest coins and the ones heavy in weight would be the later coins in the present hoard under study. However, the study of this hoard reveals inconsistency in weight. Coins with heavy and lesser weight are found almost in every series. Coins of lesser weight indicate their longer circulation. In the present hoard, the earliest coins belong to Series II—only 2 in number and 17 coins attributed to Series III. Out of these 17 coins, 4 coins are found restruck on the coins originally belonging to Series II. They are all compartively light in weight and bear the largest number of minute/banker marks. These may well be accepted as the oldest among the coins present in this hoard.

Minimum and Maximum Weight of Coins

Series	Minimum	Maximum	No. of Coins
II	3. 2815 gms	3. 2383 gms	2
III	3. 1083 gms	3. 2885 gms	17
IVb	3. 3130 gms	3. 3329 gms	2
IVc	3. 3047 gms	3. 4189 gms	2
IVd	3. 1891 gms	3.5271 gms	61
Va	3. 2447 gms	3. 5947 gms	71
Vb	3. 2128 gms	3. 3900 gms	45
VIa	3. 3197 gms	3. 5723 gms	16
VIb	3. 2391 gms	3. 5723 gms	117

Four coins attributed to Series III are restruck on Series II—3. 1075 gms, 3. 0863 gms, 3. 2120 gms and 3. 2427 gms. One coin belongs to Series IVd (2002. 333) it is a half coin, weight 1. 6796 gms.

10

Restruck/Double Obverse coins

A number of silver punch-marked coins are found to bear the obverse group of symbols on both sides of the coin. Faint traces of reverse marks can also be noticed on the face of each coin. The symbols on one side are found more worn and sometimes blurred more than that of the other side, suggesting that originally these coins were first issued with a set of obverse symbols, which now appears worn, and after some time these were struck with another set of obverse marks. It appears that the coins were re-issued by the authorities having the later set of obverse marks as the mark of their power and supremacy.[1] These coins are technically termed as 'restruck' or 'double' obverse coins.

It appears that such coins were originally issued with the blank reverse, on which successive reverse marks are impressed in course of time. It is believed that after a period of long circulation, the coins became worn and hence, these were reissued. The set of new obverse symbols of second issue are being over struck on the original reverse, and the reverse marks subsequently stamped on the original obverse side of the coins. Such coins positively show the sign of being restruck. The coins with older and new obverse can be judged apart by their relatively worn condition. Thus, the obverse of the coin became the reverse and the original reverse became the new obverse. Simultaneously, the reverse marks of the later issues are stamped on the former obverse.

In the present hoard, four coins (2002.3-6) are found restruck. These coins, originally belonging to Series II, were restruck by the group of symbols of Series III. The symbols on all the coins of the old obverse are clear enough to enable their varieties and series and thus could be identified. One coin in this hoard (Fig. 1, S.No. 3, III.I.A, 2002.3) is found restruck on the variety, classified in Amaravati hoard as II.I.1 (*AISPMC*, II.XII.A2, 286) and three coins (Fig. 1, S.No. 4, III.II.A1, 2002.5 and 2002.6 & 2002.4, pl. I, 3-4) are restruck on the varieties (Series II), classified in Amaravati hoard as II.VI.1 (*AISPMC*, II.III.B3, 269) and II.IX.B1 & II.XVI.1 (*AISPMC*, II.VIII. A3, 278 & II.XII.A1, 285), respectively.

A good number of coins of Series II are generally found restruck by the devices of Series III and Series IV, whereas the coins belonging to Series I are rarely found restruck. Only thirteen specimens have been reported so far.[2] However, eight more coins have been noticed by Mitchiner.[3] Recently, we noticed one more such coin originating from Jaunpur in trade. Walsh first noticed

Table (1): Restruck/Double Obverse Coin

S.No. Acc. No.	Symbols	Illustration	Reference
1. New Obv III.I.A. 2002.3	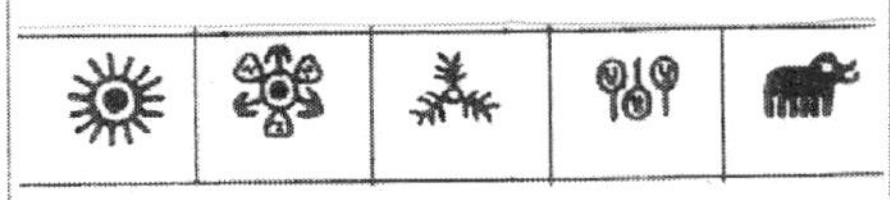		Series III *AISPMC*, 291 *Am*, II.XIII.1. Wt. 3.1705 gm Size. 2.10 × 1.40 cm
Old Obv.			Series II *Am*, II.I.1. *AISPMC*, II.XIII A2, 286
2. New Obv III.II.A1. 2002.5	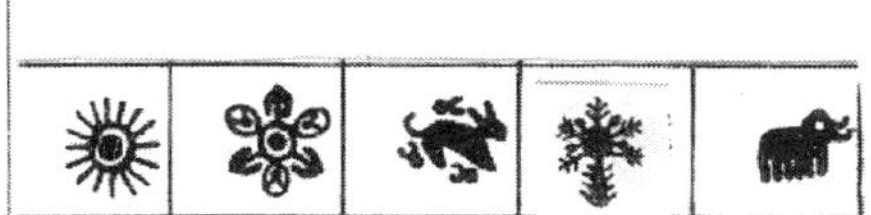		Series II *Am*, III.I.4 *AISPMC*, 305 Wt. 3.0865 gm Size. 2.05 × 1.90 cm Bold obverse mark
Old Obv.	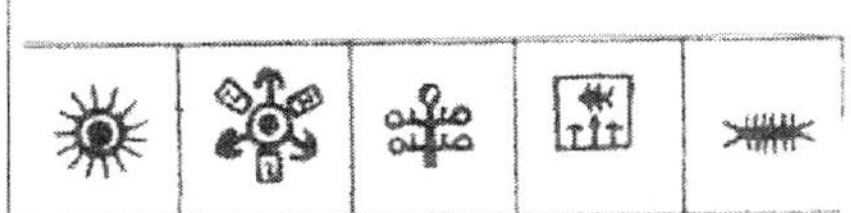		Series II *Am*, II.VI.1. *AISPMC*, II, III B.3, 269 Badly Punched reverse marks
3. New Obv III.II.A1 2002.6			Series III *Am*, III.I .4 *AISPMC*, 305 Wt. 3.2427 gm Size. 2.10 cm
Old Obv.	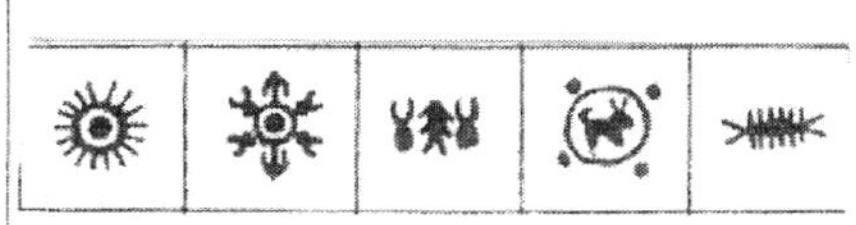		Series II *Am*, II.IX.B1 *AISPMC*, 278
4. New Obv III.II.A1 2002.4			Series III *Am*, III.I.4 *AISPMC*, 305 Wt. 3.2120 gm Size. 2.30 × 2.14 cm
Old Obv.	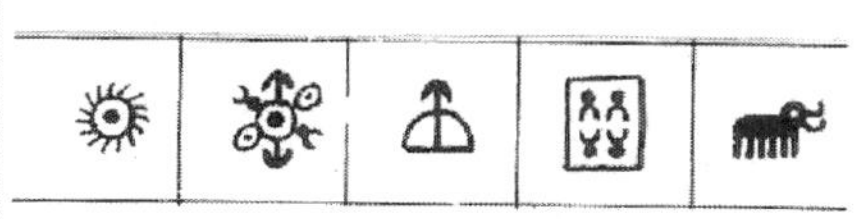		Series II *Am*, II.XVI.1 *AISPMC*, II.XII AI, 285 Badly punched with reverse marks

such coins in Paila hoard.[4] He also reported sixty-five such coins from Bhir mound hoard.[5] Gupta has reported ninety-six coins of this type in Amaravati hoard[6] and two coins in Raichur hoard.[7]

It has been observed that most of the coins of Series II of different varieties are found restruck by the group of symbols, classified as Series III.IV.A. 305.[8] In the present hoard also, out of four, three coins are found restruck of the same variety. In Amaravati hoard itself, fifty-one coins of Series II of different varieties are found restruck exclusively by the devices III.I.4 *(AISPMC,* III.IV.A 1, 305).[9]

It is believed that these restruck coins might have been the result of political turmoil. However, the more appropriate logic behind restriking of the coins may be the changing policies and the rapid expansion of the Magadha state. Probably, the authority responsible for coins restruck the earlier coins to validate them for further circulation.[10] These restruck or double obverse coins with many marks impressed on them provide valuable information regarding the chronology between the two series and indicate their different periods of production. Further, the numbers of these marks on coins are also a useful indicator of their continuous circulation, probably indicating the reuse of the coins and the chronology between the two series.

Series II, coin (2002.1) escaped restriking is exceedingly rare.

Later bold mark (Mauryan symbol). Three-arched hill with crescent, stamped on the reverse of Series II coin (2002.2) indicated its circulation in the period.

NOTES AND REFERENCES

1. P.L. Gupta (1963), *Am*, 112.
2. P.L. Gupta and T.R. Hardaker (1985), *AISPMC*, 9.
3. M. Mitchiner (2004), *Ancient Trade and Early Coinage*, Vol. 2, London, 827; *ND*, 31, 36-37.
4. E.H.C. Walsh (1940), *JNSI*, II, 15-78; P.L. Gupta and T.R. Hardaker (1985), *AISPMC*, 9.
5. E.H.C. Walsh in J. Marshall (1951), *Taxila*, ch. 40, 849.
6. P.L. Gupta (1963), *Am*, 112.
7. P.L. Gupta (1960-61), "Punch-marked Coins in A.P.G. Museum", 24.
8. P.L. Gupta and T.R. Hardaker (1985), *AISPMC*, 9.
9. P.L. Gupta, (1963), *Am*, 114-16.
10. P.L. Gupta and T.R. Hardaker (1985), *AISPMC*, 9.

11

Half-Coin

One coin (Va.V. A1, Pl. IX, 2002.333) present in this hoard appears to be a half-coin. It weighs 1.6790 gms and measures 1.00 x 0.86 cms. There is another coin in this hoard (Fig. 12, S. No. 48, Va.V.A1, 2002.140), wt. 3.4846 gms / size 1.36 x1.25 cms, which belongs to the same variety. The former coin is almost half the weight of the later coin. Further, a cut mark impression can also be seen on both sides of the coin under study. We do not find such impression on any other coin in this hoard. It appears that the coin has been cut deliberately into two pieces. This was earlier noticed by Gupta during the time of his study of Amaravati hoard (1963).[1]

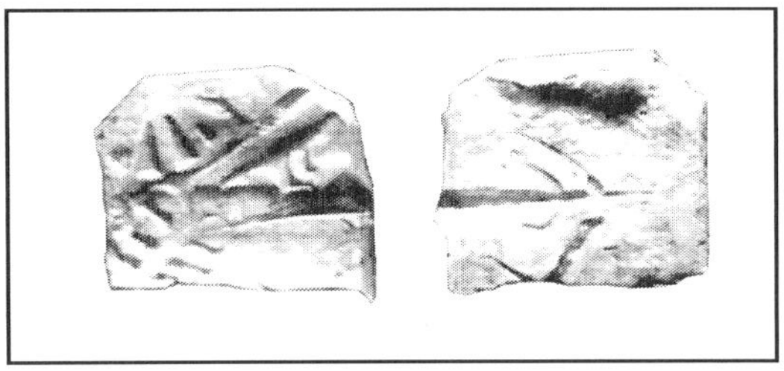

(Acc. no. 2002. 333)

Gupta has noticed about twelve such coins (7655-7667) in Amaravati hoard. He observed that some of the coins (7658, 7660, 7662, 7665 and 7667) appear to be accidentally broken pieces, while the other half pieces (7656, 7657, 7659, 7661, 7663, 7664 and 7667) in all likelihood appeared to be cut deliberately into two pieces. Of these, 7663 and 7664 are the pieces of the same coin, while the others are only the half pieces of different coins.[2] He also noticed such pieces from other hoards, such as Tregna and Vembvour hoards (Patna Museum, Patna, 4273 and 6222, respectively); Bahal hoard (Prince of Wales Museum, Bombay, 21682-86); Sialkot hoard, Bhandara hoard, Bilaspur hoard, Karchulha hoard (Nagpur Museum Nos. -1737, 1648, 1672, 1673, 1675, 1676, 1677, 1679, 1680, 1681 and 1681a, 1690 and 1909, respectively) and 20 coins in Taxila hoard (BHU- No. 1)[3] and Bahal hoard.[4]

During the course of his study of the Amaravati hoard, he noticed that the weights of such coins are approximately half of the full weight. The weight of the full coins are nearly double (little less or little heavier) when compared with the half pieces. As Gupta suggests that in all probability, the half pieces were half denominations of the full coins.[5] He suggested that full coins were cut into approximately two halves and were used for the value of the half coin and they were accepted as legal tender. This type of dichotomy seems to have been practiced in the country even in later times.[6] The Kura coins found in a hoard from Brahmpuri in Kolhapur district revealed a number of halves, quarters and one-third, which were cut from the full coins of the Kura kings.[7]

NOTES AND REFERENCES

1. *JNSI*, VIII (I), 63.
2. P.L. Gupta (1963), *Am*, 141.
3. *JNSI*, III (I) 64-65, pl. III, 12, 13 & 16.
4. *JNSI*, XIII, 64-65.
5. P.L. Gupta (1963), *Am*, 141.
6. *JNSI*, XIII (I), 65.
7. *Bulletin of the Prince of Wales Museum* (1955 - 57), No. 5, 71, pl. 26.

12

Extra Sixth-Mark

The extra sixth-mark is an additional mark seen punched on the obverse of some of the coins besides the group of five symbols, which is generally noticed on some of the Pre-Mauryan coins. However, this was not noticed on any Mauryan coin.[1] It is either in the form of four adjacent circles inside a frame or four adjacent circles with a central pellet inside a frame always punched near the edge of the coin. It is believed to be a counter-mark, perhaps added later. These extra marks are not exclusive to any variety.

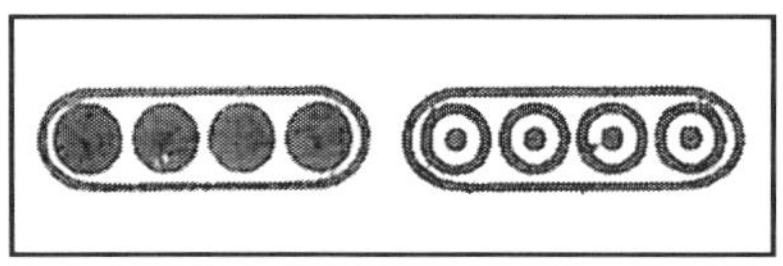

There are five such coins present in the hoard, bearing these marks: two coins having the mark of earlier type, i.e. four adjacent circles inside a frame (Fig. 1, S.No. 4, III.II.A, 2002.5, III.III.A1,18), and three coins bearing the later mark, four adjacent circles with a pellet in the centre inside a frame (III.III.A1, pl. I, 2002.13,17 and fig. S. No. 27, IVd.II.A1, 2002.331). These marks are generally noticed on Series II, III and IVd. The exact nature and purpose of these extra marks are not known. It appears that these marks were punched on the coins at one time on some definite occasions, when the coins of these varieties on which they are found were current. The mark is seen only on a set of certain class and the mark on the coins of another set of classes. According to Gupta and Hardaker, these marks were stamped on the coins pertaining to the middle of the Magadha period, but ceased very early in the Naṅda times.[1] It appears that these marks form an intervening issue between early Naṅda coins and the later Naṅda coins, confirming the chronology already determined by other sources.[2] Coins having these marks may have been issued earlier while those not carrying these marks may be latter coinage. Gupta has suggested that the mark is earlier than this mark and these were punched at different times.[3]

This mark has been noticed in Amaravati hoard on twenty coins and on one coin from the Rairh hoard. This mark has also been noticed on forty-six coins in Amaravati hoard, on two coins in the Gulbarga hoard, on one coin in Patraha hoard, on two coins in the

Bhir mound hoard, Taxila (1924)[4] and on six coins in Barwani hoard.[5] Four coins from Bhimalipatan and Palanpur hoards, preserved in British Museum, London, also have this mark.[6]

Table 2. Extra Sixth-Mark.

III.II.A, 2002.5

III.III.A1, 2002.18

III.III.A1, 2002.13

III.III.A1, 2002.17

IVd.II.A1, 2002.331

NOTES AND REFERENCES

1. P.L. Gupta and T.R. Hardaker (1985), *AISPMC*, 6. It has been observed that these extra marks are noticed only on pre-Mauryan coins. However, a few extra marks are also noticed on Mauryan coins but they are of different ones. *JNSI*, VIII (I) 66; Rairh hoard, *JNSI*, XXVI, 131-56; *JNSI*, III (I), 120; *NC*, 72-73.
2. P.L. Gupta and T.R. Hardaker (1985), *AISPMC*, 6.
3. P.L. Gupta (1963), *Am*, 118.
4. *Ibid*., 116-18.
5. Barwani hoard, 71.548/2879, 2888, 2892, 2827, 3268 and 3270.
6. P.L. Gupta (1963), *Am*, 118; J. Allan (1936) *BMC*, pl. VII, variety d; (*AISPMC*, Series III, 305; Series IVd, 416, 450 and 442); the reverse of these coins have various punches.

13

Numismatic Findings

The dating of the earliest Indian coinage is mainly focused on the date of the *Parinirvāṇa* of Gautama Buddha. The Buddha is believed to have lived from c. 565 BCE to c. 486 BCE.[1] The dated coins found in some important hoards—Chaman Hazouri hoard, Kabul; Mirzakah hoards, I and II, Afghanistan; Bhir mound hoards, Taxila. Chaman Hazouri hoard[2]—included the coins of different Greek states - c. 5th- 4th centuries BCE, Achaemenid Siglos of Darius I - c. 521-486 BCE, imitation of the Athenian owl coin type, struck in Afghanistan and Punch-marked coins of earliest phase, the Bent-bar, issued in north-west subcontinent, particularly in Gandhara area. The presence of Athenian owl coin type in the haord suggests that this hoard would not have been deposited until after c. 360 BCE, when the Athenian type coin was first issued.[3] Besides the Greek and Achaemenid coins, this hoard contains a number of punch-marked coins, but none of these belong to *kārṣāpaṇa* Series, which clearly indicates that these coins had not come in vogue during the period, when the hoard was deposited. In all probability, the hoard was deposited not later than c. 400 BCE.[4]

The discovery of two important hoards of silver punch-marked coins of *kārṣāpaṇa* Series from Bhir mound, Taxila (1912-13) - 167 coins and (1924) - 1167 coins, from stratum III, provides some definite link to the chronology of punch-marked coins.[5] Both the hoards contained Greek coins along with the ancient Indian silver punch-marked coins belonging to local as well as the Imperial Series, providing statistical evidence to the time of the deposit of the hoards. Hoard (1924) contained two coins of Alexander the Great and one coin of Philip Arideaus (died c. 317 BCE) and an old worn Persian Siglos (c. 4th century BCE).[6] The presence of 1055 coins in this hoard, all bearing five symbols and confining only up to Series V, indicate the approximate date of the deposit of the hoard to c. 3rd century BCE.[7] Coins attributed to Series I to Series V are present in this hoard. Coins belong to Series V are assigned, exclusively to class I, varieties 1 and 3, Walsh, varieties B (e) 1 and 2.[8] These are the latest coins in this hoard—21 out of 1055 coins. These coins are comparatively in fresh condition and slightly heavy in weight. Almost all the coins are having blank reverse except one coin, bearing only one mark on the reverse. This suggests that the coins attributed to Series V had come in circulation about the time when the hoard was interred. However, the hoard contains coins belonging to Series I (six coins) and

Series II (sixteen coins). They are almost worn out and comparatively light in weight. They also bear the largest number of minute marks. Thus, these coins may well be considered the oldest among the coins present in the hoard. The coins belonging to Series V are the latest.[9] On the other hand, the hoard (1912-13) only contains punch-marked coins of the later phase with crescent three-arched hill symbol as a class-mark and a coin of Diodotus II (c. 250 BCE).[10] The absence of local series coins in the hoard (1912-13) indicates that these were no longer in use by the second half of the third century BCE, while the presence of these coins in Taxila hoard (1924) suggests their circulation in the region after the middle of c. 4th century BCE.

Another hoard of later punch-marked coins of Imperial Series has been found during the excavation of the site of Greek city Al Khanum. This hoard contained six coins of Agathoclese (c. 180 BCE). In all probability, the hoard was deposited after c. 180 BCE but before c. 140 BCE.[11]

However, Cribb is of the opinion that the contents of the hoards do not provide any definite clue for the dating of the coins. According to him,

> coins in the hoards in fresh condition, probably kept unused as curiosities or good luck pieces. It can therefore be concluded that the Chaman Hazouri hoard and the earlier Taxila deposit seem that at least one issue of the local Series of punch-marked coins was still in use in the Gandharan area after the middle of the 4th century BC and at least as late as the end of it. The later Taxila hoard appears to indicate that the locally issued coins were no longer in use by the second half of the third century BC. These termini post quos are complemented with a terminus ante quem provided by another hoard from Afghanistan.[12]

He reached his conclusion that "the Local Series of Punch-marked coins was in circulation in the 4th century BC and the national Series (Imperial Series) was issued during the 3rd-2nd centuries BC (beginning before 350 BC and ending c. 140 BC). He disagrees with the views of Gupta that these coins were issued between c. 6th century BC to c. 2nd century BC."[13]

A number of hoards of silver punch-marked coins of *kārṣāpaṇa* Series are found from various parts of the country. The chronological evidence furnished from some hoards established their existence in c. 5th-6th century BCE. This remains as a continuous currency up to c. 1st-2nd century CE, though the minting of the coins of *kārṣāpaṇa* Series had ceased in c. 2nd century BCE. Punch-marked coins of *kārṣāpaṇa* Series have also been reported in several hoards containing Greek, Indo-Greek, Indo-Scythian, Indo-Parthian, Kuṣāṇa and Roman coins from several parts of the subcontinent of India.[14]

Besides these two hoards from Bhir mound, Taxila, 1912-13 and 1924, yielded 245 other coins—63 punch-marked coins, 179 local Taxila coins and one each of Demetrius, Azes I and Vasudeva.[15] The stratigraphical finding of these coins corroborate the evidence as supplied by these two hoards. Long bars and round concave coins were found in the 3rd and 4th stratum makes it clear that these two classes must date back to the 4th or possibly the 5th century BCE. The punch-marked coins of later series were found within 5 feet of the surface, datable to the 3rd or early 2nd century BCE.[16]

The composition of the hoards may be taken as supporting evidence in fixing up the dating of early coins of India. The datable Greek coins in Chaman Hazouri hoard do not suggest that the punch-marked coins in the hoard are of the same period as the datable coins. Probably, these coins may have come into circulation much earlier. The contents of Mirzakah hoards I and II contained Greek, Bactrian, Indo-Greek, Parthian and Kuṣāṇa coins together with Mauryan punch-marked coins. Such hoards, in all probability, would not have formed at one time. However, the literary information and the composition of the hoards give no proof of the later beginning of the coinage of India. The contents of the hoards itself provide some links for the internal chronology and hence, the composition of the hoard may be used as an argument for an earlier dating.

However, the work proposed the beginning of the earliest coinage of India sometimes in c. 6th century BCE, i.e. *Janapada* Series and the date of silver punch-marked coins of five-symbol series to Imperial Series from late c. 5th century BCE or early 4th century BCE. As suggested, the minting of punch-marked coins ceased in about 2nd century BCE; therefore, it can be proposed that the punch-marked coins in this hoard must be the issues of c. 3rd-2nd century BCE.

NOTES AND REFERENCES

1. *Ajātasattuno vasse, atthame muni nibbuto, Mahāvaṁsatika*, II. 52.20.
2. R. Curiel and D. Schlumberger (1953), *Tresors Monetaires D' Afghanistan, MDAF* (XIV) Paris, 4-5; P.L. Gupta (1963), *Am*, 143; J. Cribb (2005), *The Indian Coinage Tradition Origins Continuity and Changes*, 62.
3. J. Cribb (2005), 62.
4. P.L. Gupta (1963), *Am*, 143; Babelon, Les Presee Achemenides (1893) xi-xviii.
5. E.H.C. Walsh (1939), "Punch-marked coins from Taxila", *MASI* (No. 59); J. Marshall (1951), *Taxila*, "Two hoards of silver punch-marked coins found in the Bhir mound at Taxila", ch. 40, 843-52.
6. J. Marshall (1951), *Taxila*, 843.
7. P.L. Gupta (1963), *Am*, 146; J. Marshall, (1951) *Taxila*, 845.
8. J. Marshall (1951), *Taxila*, 845.
9. *Ibid.*
10. J. Cribb (2005), 63.
11. *Ibid.* (R. Audouin and P. Bernard, Tresor de monnaies iniennes et Indogrecques d'Ai Khanoum [Afghanistan]. Revue numismatique [XV] 238-89; [XVI] 6 - 41, Paris).
12. J. Cribb (2005), 62-63. "However the hoard does not necessarily provide any information about how or why the coins it contained were drawn together. Hoards can consist of coins taken directly from circulation at the time of their deposit or coins accumulated over a lifetime. The coin hoard could also represent a selection of coins taken out of circulation as substandard for melting down or as above standard and therefore best coins to save. They could even have been assembled for use as non-monetary objects—to make jewellery or as votive offering. The only definitive statement made by a hoard that the coins is contained were available for accumulation at a date subsequent to the date of issue of the most recently made coin it contains. This evidence can be enhanced in two ways. The first is by analyzing the contents of hoards and comparing different hoards with each other, as statistical evidence can make it clearer why a particular range of coins was selected. The second is the probability that most accumulations of coins have been made for economic reasons."

    "With this mind the hoards of punch-marked coins containing Greek coins do provide some evidence of their absolute chronology, but of a limited nature. It has been presumed by most scholars using this evidence that the latest Greek coin in each of these hoards is its actual latest coin, but in reality, the date of the latest coins in these hoards cannot be correctly determined until the date of issue of the punch-marked coins is known. It can only be shown that the hoards must have been deposited later than the latest datable coin, but how much later cannot be determined. The proportion of the punch-marked coins to Greek or Iranian coins in the Chaman Hazouri hoard provides statistical evidence that they both could have been in circulation at the time of the deposit of the hoard, and it could therefore be suggested that the date of issue of both is comparable. However, in the case of the two hoards from Taxila, the Greek or Iranian coins are so few in number that such a statement cannot be made. The Greek or Iranian coins could in that context be derived from a source other than circulation—they could have been good luck pieces or even recently found coins found from an earlier hoard. These hoards can only be dated on the basis of the Greek and Iranian coins to a period after their issue."
13. *Ibid.*

14. P.L. Gupta (1963), *Am*, 143-44.
15. J. Marshall (1951), *Taxila*, 752.
16. Punch-marked coins were found associated with Bactrian, Indo-Greek, Indo-Scythian, Indo-Parthian and Kuṣāṇa coins in several hoards. These coins have been found with the coins of Kuṣāṇa-Kujula Kadphises, Vima Kadphises, Kanishka I and Vasudeva and the Sassanian coins of the 3rd to 4th century CE, in a monastery of Taxila (*ASIAR* (1923-24), 26). They were found along with the Indo-Greek coins of Appolodotus, Philoxenos, Indo-Scythian and Parthian coins of Maues, Azes, Gonophores and Kuṣāṇa coins of (Soter Megas), Kujula Kadphises and Vima Kadphises in the lower city of Taxila (*BMC* (1936) Introduction, xliv). Further, more than 4000 coins were found at Mirzakah along with Bactrian, Indo-Greek, Indo-Scythian and Kuṣāṇa coins (*Tresore Monetaires D'Afghanistan*, 67- 69). Three *kārṣāpaṇa* coins were found in the deposit at the foot of *Vajrāsana*, in the *Mahābodhi* temple at Gaya, placed during the reign of Huvishka (*CASR*, XVI, 4). *Kārṣāpaṇa* coins were also discovered in a number of hoards with Indo-Greek coins (Kangra hoard, 1853), Antimachus II, Philoxenos, Lysias, Antialkidas and Menander (P.L. Gupta, (1963), *Am*, 144; *BHPCAI*, 2, entry no. 7; *Numismatic chronicle* (1873) 209); Thatta hoard (Distt. Attock), a coin of Philoxenos along with a *kārṣāpaṇa* coins (*ASIAR* (1926-1927) 229); Bairat hoard (Distt. Jaipur, Rajasthan) had 8 *kārṣāpaṇa* coins along with 25 Indo-Greek coins of Heliokles, Appolodotus, Menander, Antialkidas and Hermaeus ("Archaeological Remains at Excavations at Bairat", *JNSI* (VIII) 24). The presence *kārṣāpaṇa* coins in the hoards suggests that these were the currency along with Indo-Greek coins in c. 2nd-1st century BCE. *Kārṣāpaṇa* coins of the same variety found along with the Roman coins of c.1st century CE, and also in the hoards deposited in the Kuṣāṇa period suggest that undoubtedly, these coins remained in circulation along with Indo-Greek coins i.e., c. 2nd century BCE, although their minting had ceased and they continued to be current in later period also i.e., 1st-2nd century CE. Thus, it can be concluded that the punch-marked coins of *kārṣāpaṇa* Series, may conveniently be placed in c. 2nd century BC." These coins have also been found associated with Roman coins in South India. Mamblam hoard (Madras) contains 270 punch-marked coins along with the coins of Augustus (*BHPCAI*, 17, entry 116). *Kārṣāpaṇa* punch-marked coins were found at Eyyal (Cochin), along with 12 gold and 50 Roman silver coins (*ibid.*, entry 112; *AI* (No.2) 120). Nasthulpur, Distt. Karimnagar (Andhra Pradesh) contains 39 Roman silver and 8 *kārṣāpaṇa* coins (*punch-marked coins in A.P.G. Museum*, 27-28). Besides these hoards, a number of *kārṣāpaṇa* coins were found along with Roman coins at several places in South India in Tumulis (*Transactions of the International Congress of Pre-historic Archaeology* (1868) 255, *Numismatic Gleanings*, 10). P.L. Gupta (1963), *Am*, 144.

14

Symbols

Symbols appearing on the coins form an integral part of the punch-marked coins. A large number of symbols in variation have been noticed on this series. These include animate and inanimate objects like birds, trees, flora, hills, human figures, planet signs, geometrical and religious symbols. The symbols used on coins also reveal a rich configuration of everyday life in contemporary times. With our limited knowledge, it is not possible to ascertain the precise significance and meaning of all these symbols and to determine the system according to which they were employed. Generally, their religious significance have been upheld. However, it is not true in case of the coins. It can be said that symbols employed on the coins have some possibility of being heraldic in nature and used as a particular mark of a person or a place without any reference to their own religious merit and significance. May be, they were accepted as religious symbols but it appears that they were also used as a mark of trade and commerce on the coins, which were selected because of their familiarity with the populace.

Scholars have put forward different interpretations of the symbols from Buddhist, *Tāntrika* and Brahmanical point of view. However, comparative study of coin symbols with those found on the seals and sealings of Mohenjodaro and Harappa makes one believe that some of the primitive religious beliefs formed an impetus towards the gradual development of the symbols. The symbols are recognized as a definite and important stage in the development of Indian iconography. Therefore, it would be unreasonable to associate them always with a particular cult or religion, especially in the context of the coins. Theobald has enumerated more than three hundred symbols occurring on the punch-marked coins. He has suggested that most of the symbols, noticeable on the punch-marked coins, also occurred in such diverse lands as Assyriya, Egypt and Scotland.[1] Bhandarkar also shared his views regarding some of the coins.[2] He has further suggested that some of the symbols can be explained as the seven jewels, the possession of which, according to Pali literature, represents permanent sovereignty.[3] Rapson opines that the symbols on punch-marked coins were used simply as the mark of localities and individuals without any special religious significance.[4] Kosambi has suggested that some of the names of the kings given in the Puranic and Buddhist literatures lend themselves very readily to direct representations by symbolism of punch-marked coins.[5] Cunningham considers these symbols as Buddhist in nature. He has tried to identify some of the symbols as representing the localities and states.[6] Spooner at first suggested that many of the symbols were particularly Buddhist in character. However, later on he revised his opinion and held that many of the symbols were Zoroastrian in nature.[7]

Chakravartti is of the opinion that from the group of four constant symbols out of the five, the two most common ones probably has religious significance and of the other two, one may be of the locality mark where it was struck and the other of the mint masters.[8] Durga Prasad has suggested their *tāntrika* affliations,[9] but this explanation is rather doubtful as he is ignoring the presence of first two symbols and suggested that the third symbol most probably stood for the king and the fourth and fifth ones for the year and the place of the issue.[10] Kosambi opines that the sun symbol is universal as to be devoid of any particular significance. The six-armed symbol is the particular mark of the dynasty. Of the three other remaining marks, the third mark signified descent being a clan or totem symbol; the fourth one is the seal of the ruler under whose authority the coin was issued; and the fifth mark is probably the issuing authority or a mint master.[11] Allan holds that the symbols may represent a series of officials of diminishing area of jurisdiction. The last and most frequently changing symbol would represent the actual issuer of the coin. The constant Sun symbol would represent the highest official, perhaps the king himself; and the next commonest, six-armed symbol in the various forms, the highest official next under him.[12] Walsh is of the opinion that one mark might represent the state, one of the king or the local government, one the place where the coin was struck and perhaps one a religious mark recognising the presiding deity, also the mint master might have had his on mark, which would fix the responsibility for the coin and the additional varying mark might have been those of *Saṅghas*, village communities or *Janapadas* or *naigamas* in which the coin was current.[13] In short, the first symbol, sun, represents the political jurisdiction; the second symbol, six-armed, may be the sign of imperial expansion; the fourth and fifth symbols stand for the sign of mint master, feudal authority and place of origin. However, no definite opinion has yet been made. Based on the study of the punch-marked coins, it can be said that the symbols and the group of the symbols on various series mostly differ from each other. As such, not much can be made out of the symbols or the group of the symbols. This long series of the coins shows the absence of old symbols and adoption of new symbols. The coins with double obverse and many symbols stamped on them indicate valuable information. It indicates the re-use of the coins and the chronology between two series. The reverse marks are indicative of different periods and their numbers on the coins are useful in determining their chronology.

The symbols appearing on Indian coinage are far from being arbitrary as each must have had some significance and meaning. A passage of *Viśuddhimagga* of Buddhaghoṣa (c. 5th century CE) clearly states in the context of *kārṣāpaṇa* coins that by means of symbols—*rūpa* stamped on coins any experienced banker would be able to tell the source of their issue, such as village, borough, mountain or river bank, and by the mint master.[14] Thus, regarding the meaning of these symbols at present, it can only be said that either some of these symbols may be used as private or differenciated marks of the king or may be concerned with different authorities, responsible for the minting of these pieces. On the other hand, the reverse marks may have been considered as the counter marks of the moneyers. It appears that these symbols confined to a particular area, representing a locality mark.

As rightly pointed out by Gupta and Hardaker: "Distinction must first be made between recognition of the objects depicted (in many cases simple but in others utterly baffling) and recognition of the meaning they had to the main authority." The said analysis is based on three criteria: "(i) position of the symbols in the five marks sequence and interchangeability in this respect, (ii) duration of individual symbol and its reocurrence in more than one Series and (iii) the objects and form of the symbols and their relation to historical records."[15]

The main characterstics of punch-marked coins are their symbols, each portraying some special significance. The symbol punched on these silver pieces have their fixed place in the sequence of five and each symbols has a separate function. All those coins that have five symbols in a group constitute one variety. The sun and the six-armed symbols are uniformly seen throughout the *kārṣāpaṇa* Series, except the Series VII and are placed at first and second place respectively, in the group of five symbols without any specific meaning. Only the other remaining three symbols have their major role in this classification system. In all the varieties, which have one of their symbols as common and other two vary, are clubed together. They constitute one class and this common symbol is given third place in the sequence and termed as 'class-mark'. Then, within the varieties, constituting a class, coins have another common symbol, which forms a distinct group within a class. This common symbol indicating the group is placed as the fourth mark, after the 'class-mark' and is termed as 'group-mark'. The remaining fifth symbols noticed exclusive to its variety. It is called a 'Variety mark' and placed as fifth mark. Thus, in short, the first two symbols—Sun and Six-armed—are common to the series and placed at first and second place respectively; the third symbol is a 'Class-mark'; the fourth symbol is a 'Group mark'; and the fifth one is a 'Variety mark'.

It is clear that each symbol in the group of five symbols has a nominated place with its own meaning and function. It can be said that the first mark 'Sun', in the group of five symbols on the obverse, represents the state authority—the king; the second symbol 'Six-armed', probably connected either with the mint or series as it employed in different forms on the coins; the third symbol 'Class-mark'; and the fourth mark—'Group-mark', possibly representing the government or mint officials; and the fifth mark—'Variety-mark', may represent the mint. In all probability, bankers' marks or the minute marks may be the marks of a moneyer, who guaranteed the purity of metal and weights.[16]

A. OBVERSE SYMBOLS

The obverse employed in a fixed group of four symbols while the fifth symbol varies. The symbol representing the class is found confined almost in themselves and hardly seen repeated in any subsequent series. The symbols, representing the group, are generally confined to a class, often seen associated on the coins of more than one class, but remain confined to the same series, except in a few cases. Presumably, it may be a continued link, which may proffer some clue to their chronology. The symbols, classified as variety marks are found repeating on the coins of different groups within a class and on the coins of different series. It has been observed that not all the symbols have been used on more than one series. However, it is noticed that some of the symbols employed on the earlier series are also found in the subsequent series, while the remaining few disappeared. Some new symbols also crop up, which are being used in every series. This shows a trend of adoption of new symbols and dropping the older symbols. However, the second symbol is found associated with the third and fourth symbols on the coins belonging to a different class and different series.[1]

The study of these symbols reveals that the present hoard possessed 120 varieties of obverse symbols (Table 5). According to the classifications, these symbols constitute 76 varieties of groups

Table 3. Six-armed Symbol.

S.No.	Illustration	Symbol	Line drawing	Reference
1.	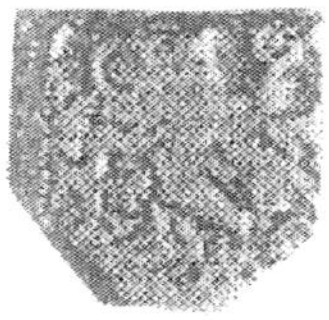	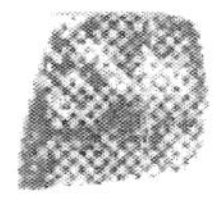	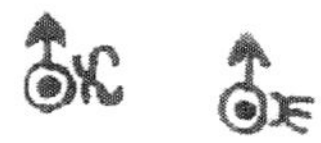	Amaravati Hoard 3958-3964 AISPMC, V.XVIII A.16, 526
2.	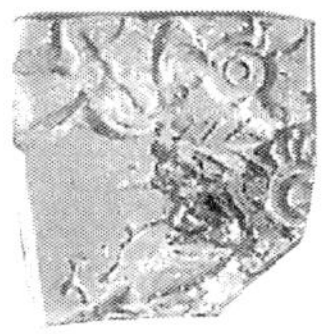			Sarai Denguri Hoard 2002.196 Vb
3.		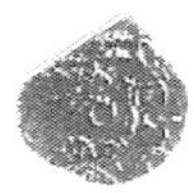		Sarai Denguri Hoard 2002.197 Vb
4.	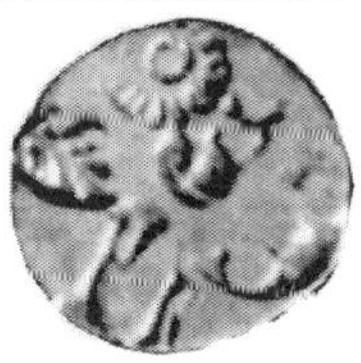	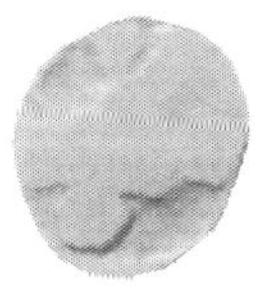		Barwani Hoard 71.548/3277
5.				Barwani Hoard 71.548/3268
6.	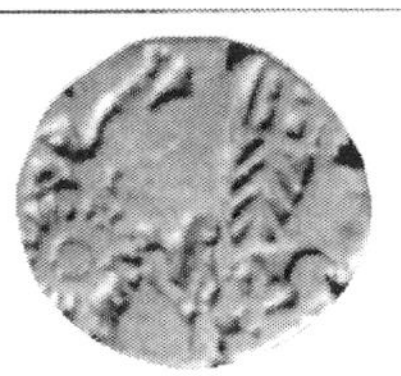			Barwani Hoard 71.548/3276
7.		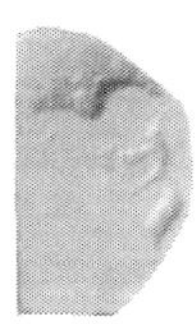		Barwani Hoard 71.548/3269
8.	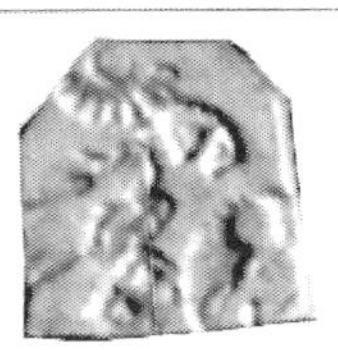			Barwani Hoard 71.548/3270

(Figs. 1-19). All the varieties are charaterised by the sun, as the first symbol and the six-armed, as the second symbol. The six-armed symbol is common to all varieties with the exception of those that do not have the sun symbol. The first symbol is constant while the second symbol is found on these coins in variations. Except for the fact that the coins belong to Series VI (a and b), the symbol does not change its form. However, this variety is also seen on some of the coins belonging to the Series IVd, 2002.82 and Series Va, 2002.332 (GH, Series I, 227-242; Series IVb, 372; Series IVd, 447, 473 and Series Va, 497-500). The six-armed symbol in the present hoard exhibits 31 varieties. Series II - 2 varieties; Series III - 5 varieties; Series IVb - 2 varieties; Series IVc - 2 varieties; Series IVd - 7 varieties; Series Va - 8 varieties; Series Vb - 5 varieties; Series VIa and Series VIb have only one form of six-armed symbol.

In course of study of the present hoard and one another hoard, discovered at Barwani (Madhya Pradesh, 1945), now preserved in National Museum, New Delhi, the form of a six-armed symbol, which was left out incomplete, could be restored .[2] The complete form of this symbol could not be determined as on all the coins, which belong to this variety, is generally found punched out of the flan (Amaravati hoard - 3958-3965). Two coins attributed to this variety, in the present hoard, (Fig. 16, S.No. 62, Vb.V.A, 2002.196 and pl.XII.197) and five coins of the same variety are noticed in Barwani hoard (71.548/3268-3270 and 3277-3278). It is interesting to note that all the seven coins in these two hoards present a curious form of the symbol under discussion. It has been observed that in all the cases one or the other space has been left blank and only five arms of the said symbol are seen , which can be noticed from the coins itself. Nevertheless, nothing can be proposed at this stage, whether it has been done deliberately or is a mistake of a die-cutter. However, an attempt has been made to restore the form of the symbol as seen on these coins, as far as it is possible (Table 3).

Again, another coin belonging to Series IVd (Fig. 4, S.No.16, IVd.I.C1, 2002.29), bearing the symbol, which is different from another coin, is attributed to the same variety in this hoard (Fig. 4, S.No.15, IVd.I.C, 2002.28). Except the second symbol, the remaining symbols are the same on both the coins. Generally, the fish is seen as one of its lower arm .[3] However, in case of the coin present in the hoard, a fish can clearly be noticed inside an oval , constitute another form of the symbol, is classified in separate variety, and marked as unnoticed so far listed as 406a.

Another coin (2002.331) also presents a new form of six-armed symbol, and mentioned as unnoticed in the catalogue (Fig. 7, S.No.27, IVd.II.A1). There are five coins (Fig. 7, S. No. 26, IVd. II. A) present in this hoard, belonging to the same group of variety except the second symbol. However, in case of the said coin, the second symbol appears in its new form. Here two inverted 'taurines' can be seen clearly attached across the central circle as its two arms .

Two marks, bull and elephant, find frequent occurrence on the punch-marked coins. Bull is employed in all the series as a 'group-mark'—the fourth mark, where it is always seen standing to right on the coins, and rarely standing to left.[4] As a 'class-mark' (Series IVb) bull is depicted either standing over the six-arches, standing to left, or inside a frame along with taurines and fishes. In some cases, bull is employed standing to left as 'class-mark'.[5] Some of the varieties belonging to Series IVb, bull is also used as a fifth variety mark along with the combination of other symbols. However, on Series I, it is shown standing both on right and left as variety mark.

Elephant is noticed on a large number of coins as a fifth mark or variety mark. Both bull and elephant are being employed together as fourth and fifth marks, respectively (Series IVd).

Symbols used on these coins of each variety are illustrated with corresponding series and the place of the symbols in the groups of five symbols.

Table 4. Number of obverse symbols occurring in different series.

S.No.	**Series**	**No. of coins**	**Varieties**	**First mark**	**Second mark**	**Class mark**	**Group mark**	**Variety mark**
1	II	2	2	Sun	2	2	2	2
2	III	17	5	Sun	5	3	3	2
3	IVb	2	2	Sun	1	1	1	2
4	IVc	2	2	Sun	2	2	2	2
5	IVd	61	26	Sun	9	7	7	12
6	Va	71	14	Sun	8	8	6	12
7	Vb	45	11	Sun	6	5	4	7
8	VIa	16	4	Sun	1	2	1	3
9	VIb	117	10	Sun	1	1	5	10
	II-VI	333	76	_	**35**	**31**	**31**	**52**

Table (5) - Obverse Symbols

SN	Symbols	Series in which symbols appear									Position of symbols in different series
		II	III	IVb	IVc	IVd	Va	Vb	VIa	VIb	
1.		●	●	●	●	●	●	●	●	●	First symbol
2.		●									Second symbol
3.		●									
4.			●								
5.			●			●					
6.			●								
7.			●								
8.			●								
9.				●		●					
10.					●						
11.					●						
12.						●					
13.	 *					●					
14.	 **					●					

* = 2 coins in this hoard are classified – * (S.No.15, IVd.I.C. – (406), on one coin the symbol is seen partly, following the classification of GPL & HRD. On the other coin of the same group – ** (S.No. 16, IVd.I.C1), the symbol is seen as produced above.

SN	Symbols	Series in which symbols appear									Position of symbols in different series·
		II	III	IVb	IVc	IVd	Va	Vb	VIa	VIb	
15.						●					
16.						●					
17.						●	●		●	●	
18.						●					
19.							●				
20.							●				
21.							●				
22.							●				
23.							●	●			
24.							●				
25.							●				
26.								●			
27.								●			
28.								●			
29.								●			

SN	Symbols	Series in which symbols appear									Position of symbols in different series
		II	III	IVb	IVc	IVd	Va	Vb	VIa	VIb	
30.								●			
31.						●					unnoticed
32.		●									Third symbol
33.		●									
34.			●								
35.			●								
36.			●								
37.				●							
38.					●						
39.					●						
40.						●					
41.						●					
42.						●					
43.						●					
44.						●					

SN	Symbols	Series in which symbols appear									Position of symbols in different series .
		II	III	IVb	IVc	IVd	Va	Vb	VIa	VIb	
45.						●					
46.						●					
47.							●				
48.							●				
49.							●				
50.							●				
51.							●				
52.							●	●			
53.							●				
54.							●	●			
55.								●			
56.								●			
57.								●			
58.									●		
59.									●	●	

SN	Symbols	Series in which symbols appear									Position of symbols in different series .
		II	III	IVb	IVc	IVd	Va	Vb	VIa	VIb	
60.		●				●					Fourth symbol
61.		●									
62.			●								
63.			●								
64.			●								
65.					●						
66.					●						
67.						●					
68.						●					
69.						●					
70.						●					
71.						●					
72.						●					
73.							●			●	
74.							●				

SN	Symbols	Series in which symbols appear									Position of symbols in different series
		II	III	IVb	IVc	IVd	Va	Vb	VIa	VIb	
75.							●		●		
76.							●				
77.	 or 						●	●		●	
78.								●			
79.								●			
80.								●			
81.										●	
82.										●	
83.		●									Fifth symbol
84.		●	●		●	●	●			●	
85.			●	●		●					
86.			●	●		●					
87.				●							
88				●	●						
89					●						

SN	Symbol	Series in which symbols appear									Position of symbols in different series
		II	III	IVb	IVc	IVd	Va	Vb	VIa	VIb	
90						●					
91						●	●				
92						●	●	●			
93						●					
94						●					
95						●					
96						●	●				
97						●					
98							●				
99							●			●	
100							●		●		
101							●				
102							●				
103							●				
104								●		●	
105							●				

SN	Symbol	Series in which symbols appear									Position of symbols in different series
		II	III	IVb	IVc	IVd	Va	Vb	VIa	VIb	
106								●			
107								●			
108							●	●			
109								●			
110								●			
111									●		
112									●		
113								●			
114										●	
115										●	
116										●	
117										●	
118										●	
119										●	
120										●	

B. REVERSE SYMBOLS – MINUTE/BANKER'S MARK

The minute marks generally found stamped on the reverse side of the coins are known as the 'reverse marks', also termed as 'banker's marks' or 'testing marks'. The reverse sides of the coins were treated differently in different periods but it is not certain under which system these marks were stamped on the coins. There is no uniformity in the number of marks. These marks are known in a number of varieties and are entirely different from those found on the obverse. They are much smaller and are punched deeply on the face of the coin.

It appears that during the minting, one side of the coin was left blank and sometime later, some minute marks were impressed upon them. Some of these marks look blurred and worn out but some of them appear distinct. It indicates that these marks were not struck on the coins at one time but at intervals, while the coins were in circulation. Possibly, coins with more marks may have remained in circulation for a longer period, but those with fewer marks were driven out earlier. Occurrences of these marks on such a large number of coins also suggest that these were individual marks (*Rūpataraka or Rūpadarśaka*), signifying control on the authenticity of both weight and purity.[6]

Marks used on the reverse on the earlier coins are quite different than those found on the reverse of the coins belonging to later period. On the earlier coins, these marks appeared in a haphazard way but in the case of the later series, these were employed either as a fixed mark, singly or in fixed group of marks of two or three, which appears to be stamped by some recognised authority following some definite system.

The reverse marks are found to bear a relation to a particular group of obverse symbols on the later coins. According to Gupta, they appear to have some territorial or periodical cosideration. The different marks found on the reverse of one and the same variety were stamped in different periods. Some of the coins having two symbols together suggest the latter possibility.[7] Like two coins (2002.236 and 282) present in this hoard, having a Taxila symbol ocurred twice, probably stamped in different periods.

Besides these minute marks, some miniature forms of certain obverse symbols are also used on the reverse, particularly on later coins. It has been observed that with the appearance of these miniature marks, the number of minute marks decreased and in many cases, they were found absent from both the sides of the coin. This shows a process of change, which finally took the form of a single bold mark on the reverse, which can be distinguished in a sequence like number of minute marks; miniature marks of the symbols found on the obverse; single miniature marks; and bold reverse marks. It appears that the associate marks were not punched along with the bold marks, but were stamped later on and each mark appears to be independent.

It has also been noticed that these coins have a specific symbol that is found on the reverse of all the coins reported from a particular region. This constantly appearing symbol with minor variations can thus be designated as a 'state' symbol, suggesting that the state is the issuing authority. Similarly, the symbols may stand for mints and minting authority.

The classification shows that the coins of one and the same variety, having the same group of symbols on the obverse, are found punched on the reverse with more than one variety of the obverse symbols. Generally, one obverse symbol in its miniature form is found stamped on the reverse of the coins and rarely two symbols are found punched together. It clearly shows that these are not the marks of the *Rūpataraka*/the money testers. In all likelihood, these different marks occurred on the reverse of one and the same variety, and were impressed in different areas in one and the same period or they were punched during different periods.[8]

In brief, it is believed that the minute marks were the private marks of the bankers or money-changers, as their numbers and diversity is great. Probably on early series, these denote the persons or the bankers through whose hands the coins passed, as a mark of their having tested its weight and fineness. However, the miniature marks on the later series are probably the marks of the issuing authority. Each hoard brings out a large number of these minute marks on their coins. In our hoard, 171 reverse marks have been noticed (Table 6). Some of the marks are so indistinct and blurred that it is difficult to identify or draw them, hence, have been left out. It has been observed that the numbers of reverse marks were also used as obverse marks on various coins.

Table (6) : Reverse - marks

S.No.	Acc.No. Series	Marks on Reverse									Marks on Obverse
1	2002.1 **II.I.A**					?					
2	2002.2 **II.II.A**										
3	2002.3 **III.I.A**				or						restruck
4	2002.4 **III.II.A**										restruck
5	2002.5 **III.II.A**										restruck
6	2002.6 **III.II.A**										restruck
7	2002.7 **III.II.A**										
8	2002.8 **III.II.A**										
9	2002.9 **III.II.A**										
10	2002.10 **III.II.A**										
11	2002.11 **III.III.A**										
12	2002.12 **III.III.A1**										
13	2002.13 **III.III.A1**										
14	2002.14 **III.III.A1**										
15	2002.16 **III.III.A1**										
16	2002.17 **III.III.A1**										

S.No.	Acc.No. Series	Marks on Reverse	Marks on Obverse
17	2002.18 **III.III.A1**		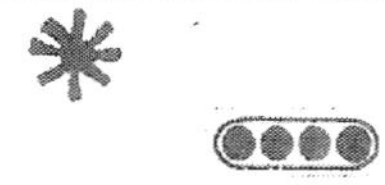
18	2002.15 **III.III.A2**		
19	2002.19 **III.III.A2**	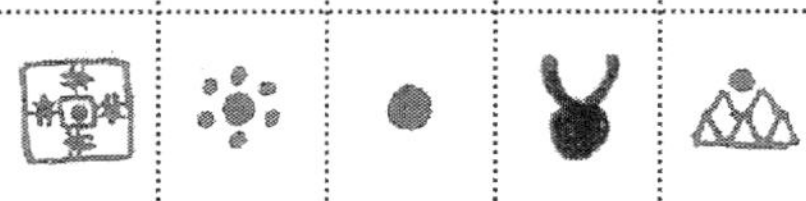	
20	2002.20 **IVb.I.A**		
21	2002.21 **IVb.I.A1**		
22	2002.22 **IVc.I.A**		
23	2002.23 **IVc.II.A**		
24	2002.24 **IVd.I.A**		
25	2002.25 **IVd.I.A1**		
26	2002.26 **IVd.I.A1**		
27	2002.27 **IVd.I.B**		
28	2002.28 **IVd.I.C**		
29	2002.29 **IVd.I.C1**		
30	2002.30 **IVd.I.D**		
31	2002.31 **IVd.I.D**		
32	2002.32 **IVd.I.D**	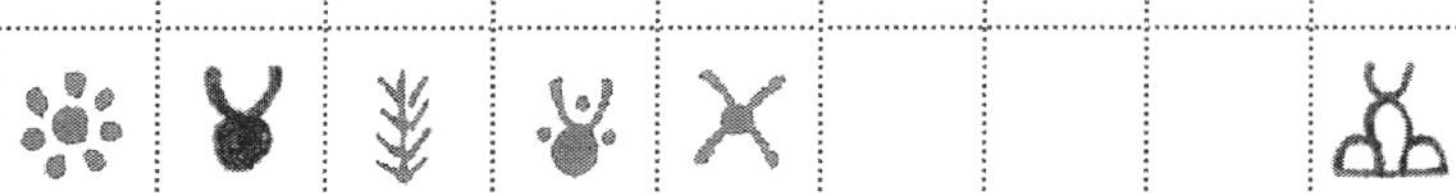	

S.No.	Acc.No. Series	Marks on Reverse	Marks on Obverse
33	2002.33 **IVd.I.D**		
34	2002.34 **IVd.I.D**		
35	2002.35 **IVd.I.D**		
36	2002.36 **IVd.I.D**		
37	2002.37 **IVd.I.D**		
38	2002.38 **IVd.I.D**		
39	2002.39 **IVd.I.D**		
40	2002.40 **IVd.I.D**		
41	2002.41 **IVd.I.D**	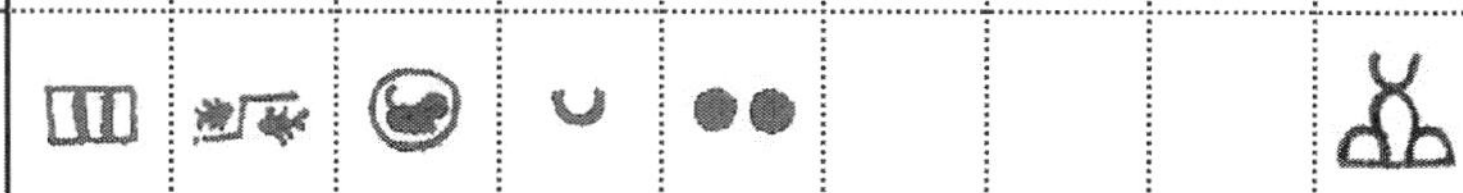	
42	2002.42 **IVd.I.D**	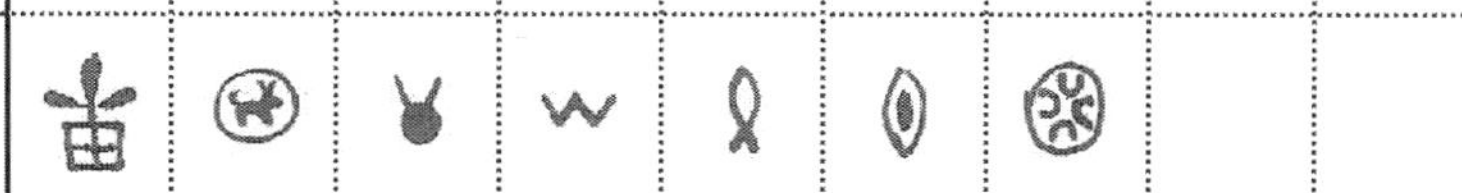	
43	2002.43 **IVd.I.D**		
44	2002.44 **IVd.I.D**		
45	2002.45 **IVd.I.D**		
46	2002.46 **IVd.I.D1**		
47	2002.47 **IVd.I.D2**		
48	2002.48 **IVd.I.D3**	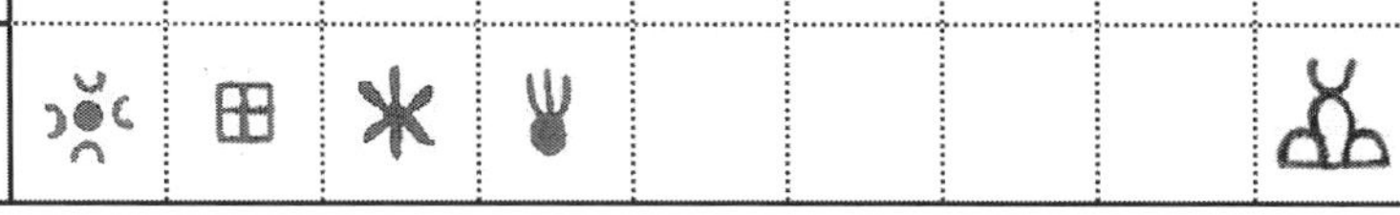	

S.No.	Acc.No. Series	Marks on Reverse	Marks on Obverse
49	2002.49 **IVd.I.D3**		
50	2002.50 **IVd.I.D4**		
51	2002.51 **IVd.I.D4**	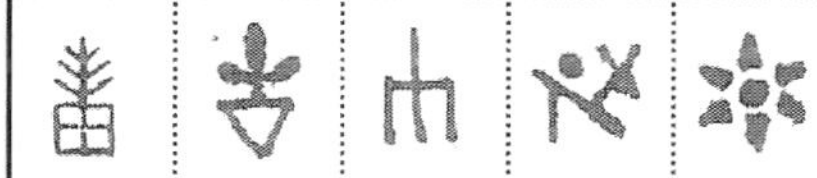	
52	2002.52 **IVd.I.D4**	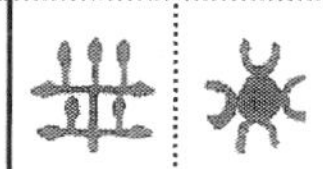	
53	2002.53 **IVd.I.D5**		
54	2002.54 **IVd.I.D5**		
55	2002.55 **IVd.I.D6**	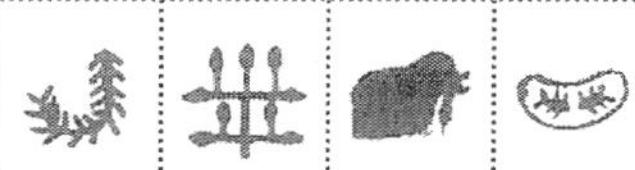	
56	2002.56 **IVd.I.D6**	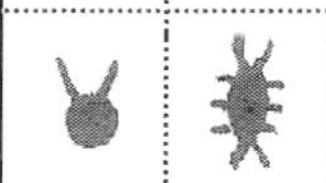	
57	2002.57 **IVd.I.D6**	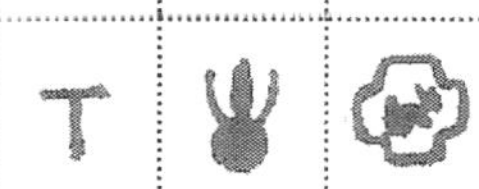	
58	2002.58 **IVd.I.D6**		
59	2002.59 **IVd.I.D6**		
60	2002.60 **IVd.I.D6**	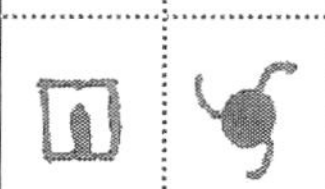	
61	2002.61 **IVd.I.D7**		
62	2002.62 **IVd.I.D7**	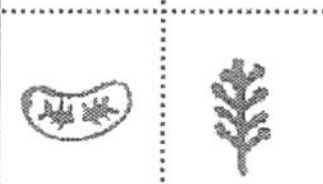	
63	2002.63 **IVd.I.D8**		
64	2002.64 **IVd.II.A**		

S.No.	Acc.No. Series	Marks on Reverse	Marks on Obverse
65	2002.65 **IVd.II.A**		
66	2002.66 **IVd.II.A**	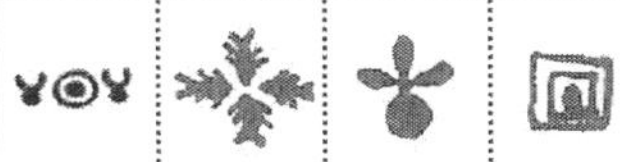	
67	2002.67 **IVd.II.A**		
68	2002.68 **IVd.II.A**	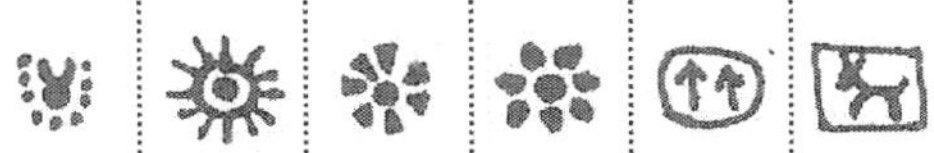	
69	2002.331 **IVd.II.A1**		
70	2002.69 **IVd.II.A2**	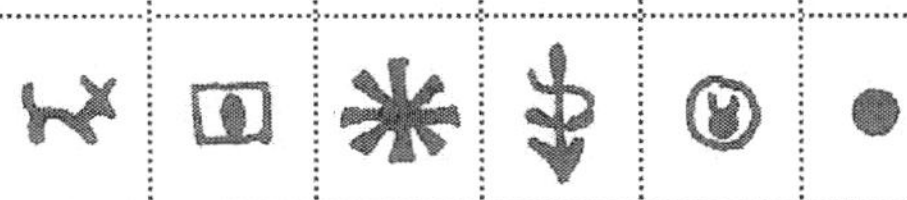	
71	2002.70 **IVd.III.A**	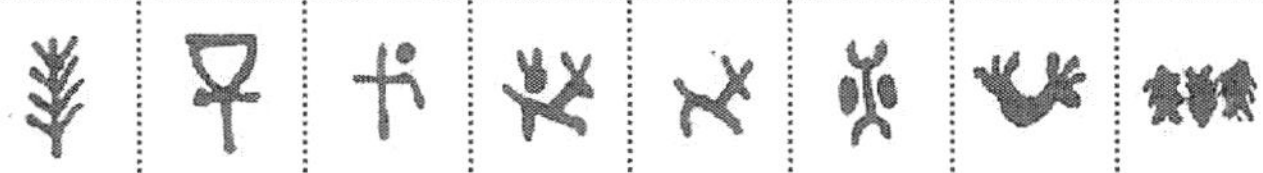	
72	2002.71 **IVd.III.A**		
73	2002.72 **IVd.III.A**		
74	2002.73 **IVd.III.A1**		
75	2002.74 **IVd.III.A2**		
76	2002.75 **IVd.IV.A**		
77	2002.76 **IVd.IV.A**		
78	2002.77 **IVd.IV.A**		
79	2002.78 **IVd.IV.A**	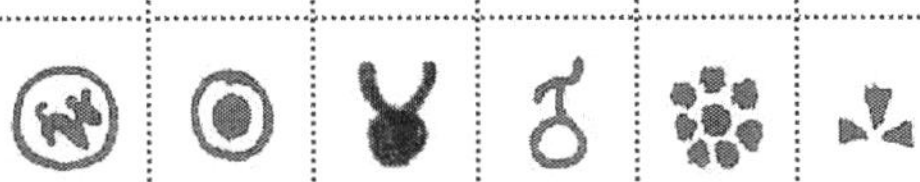	
80	2002.79 **IVd.IV.A1**		

S.No.	Acc.No. Series	Marks on Reverse	Marks on Obverse
81	2002.80 **IVd.V.A**		
82	2002.66 **IVd.V.A1**	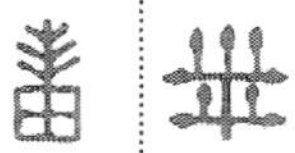	
83	2002.67 **IVd.VI.A**		
84	2002.68 **IVd.VII.A**		
85	2002.331 **Va.1.A**		
86	2002.69 **Va.1.A**		
87	2002.70 **Va.1.A**		
88	2002.71 **Va.1.A**		
89	2002.72 **Va.1.A**		
90	2002.73 **Va.1.A**		
91	2002.74 **Va.1.A**	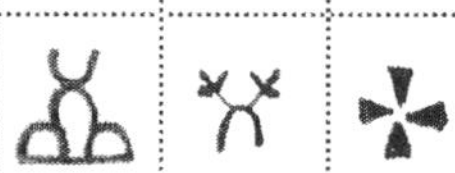	
92	2002.75 **Va.1.A1**		
93	2002.76 **Va.1.A1**	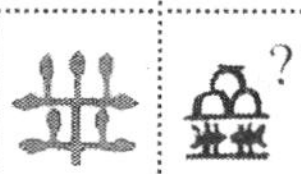	
94	2002.77 **Va.1.A2**		
95	2002.78 **Va.1.A2**		
96	2002.79 **Va.1.A2**	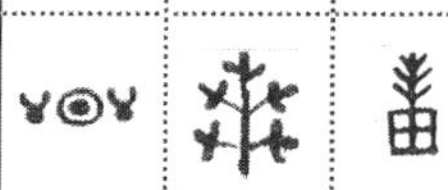	

S.No.	Acc.No. Series	Marks on Reverse
97	2002.96 **Va.I.A1**	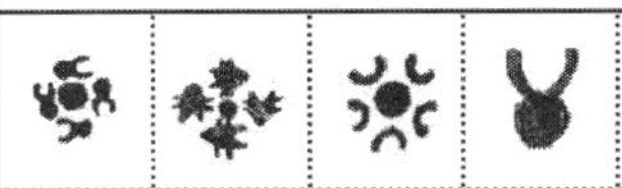
98	2002.97 **Va.I.A2**	
99	2002.98 **Va.I.A2**	
100	2002.99 **Va.I.A2**	
101	2002.100 **Va.I.A2**	
102	2002.101 **Va.I.A3**	
103	2002.102 **Va.I.A3**	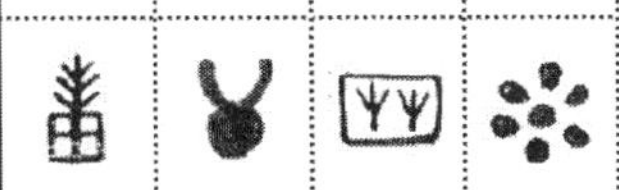
104	2002.103 **Va.I.A4**	
105	2002.104 **Va.I.A4**	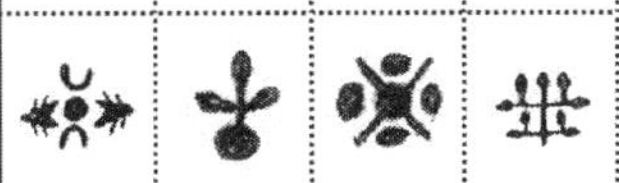
106	2002.105 **Va.I.A4**	
107	2002.106 **Va.I.A4**	
108	2002.107 **Va.I.A4**	
109	2002.108 **Va.I.A4**	
110	2002.109 **Va.I.A4**	
111	2002.110 **Va.I.A4**	
112	2002.111 **Va.I.A4**	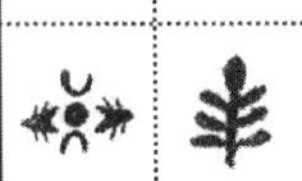
113	2002.112 **Va.I.A4**	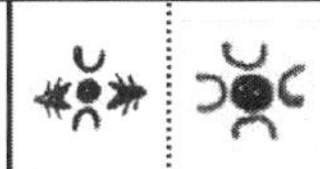
114	2002.113 **Va.I.A4**	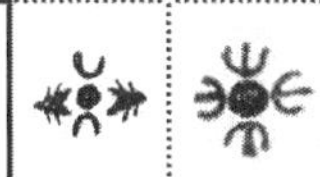
115	2002.114 **Va.I.A4**	
116	2002.115 **Va.I.A4**	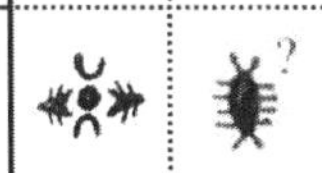
117	2002.116 **Va.I.A4**	
118	2002.117 **Va.I.A3**	
119	2002.118 **Va.I.A4**	
120	2002.119 **Va.I.A4**	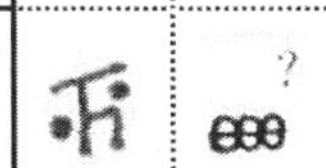
121	2002.120 **Va.I.A4**	
122	2002.121 **Va.I.A4**	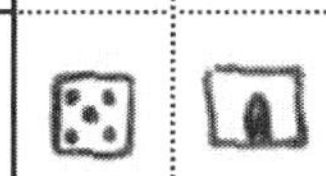
123	2002.122 **Va.I.A4**	
124	2002.123 **Va.I.A5**	
125	2002.124 **Va.I.A5**	
126	2002.125 **Va.I.A5**	
127	2002.126 **Va.I.A5**	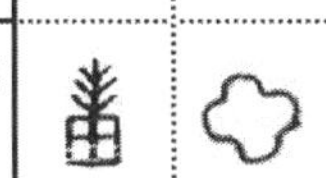
128	2002.127 **Va.I.A5**	

S.No.	Acc.No. Series	Marks on Reverse				
129	2002.128 **Va.II.A**					
130	2002.129 **Va.II.A**					
131	2002.130 **Va.II.A**					
132	2002.131 **Va.III.A**					
133	2002.132 **Va.III.A**					
134	2002.133 **Va.III.A**					
135	2002.134 **Va.III.A**					
136	2002.135 **Va.III.A**					
137	2002.136 **Va.III.A**					
138	2002.137 **Va.III.A**					
139	2002.138 **Va.III.A**					
140	2002.332 **Va.IV.A**					
141	2002.139 **Va.V.A**					
142	2002.140 **Va.V.A1**					
143	2002.333 **Va.V.A1**					
144	2002.141 **Va.VI.A**	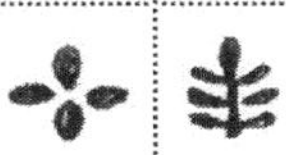				

S.No.	Acc.No. Series	Marks on Reverse				
145	2002.142 **Va.VI.A**					
146	2002.143 **Va.VI.A**					
147	2002.144 **Va.VI.A**	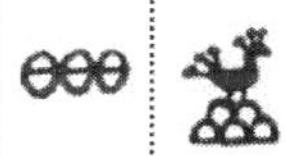				
148	2002.145 **Va.VI.A**	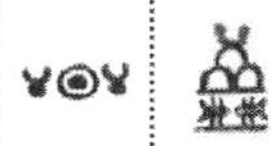				
149	2002.146 **Va.VII.A**					
150	2002.147 **Va.VII.A**	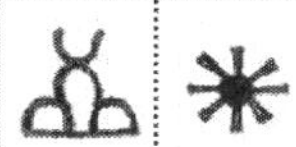			?	
151	2002.148 **Va.VII.A**	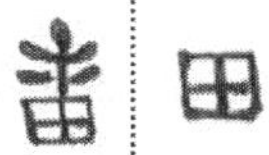				
152	2002.149 **Va.VIII.A**	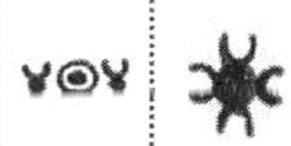				
153	2002.150 **Va.VIII.A**					
154	2002.151 **Va.VIII.A**		?			
155	2002.152 **Va.VIII.A**	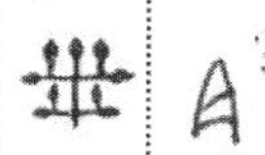				
156	2002.153 **Vb.I.A**	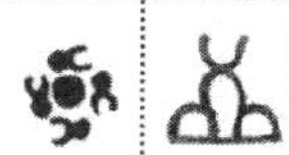				
157	2002.161 **Vb.I.A**					
158	2002.163 **Vb.I.A**	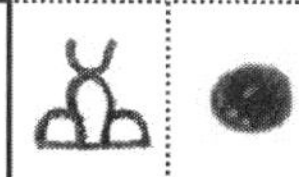				
159	2002.164 **Vb.I.A**					
160	2002.166 **Vb.I.A**					

S.No.	Acc.No. Series	Marks on Reverse				
161	2002.167 **Vb.I.A**					
162	2002.168 **Vb.I.A**					
163	2002.171 **Vb.I.A**					
164	2002.172 **Vb.I.A**					
165	2002.176 **Vb.I.A1**					
166	2002.177 **Vb.I.A1**					
167	2002.178 **Vb.I.A1**					
168	2002.179 **Vb.I.A1**					
169	2002.180 **Vb.I.A1**					
170	2002.181 **Vb.I.A1**					
171	2002.182 **Vb.I.A1**					
172	2002.183 **Vb.I.A2**		?			
173	2002.184 **Vb.I.A2**					
174	2002.185 **Vb.I.A2**					
175	2002.154 **Vb.I.A3**					
176	2002.155 **Vb.I.A3**					

S.No.	Acc.No. Series	Marks on Reverse				
177	2002.156 **Vb.I.A3**					
178	2002.157 **Vb.I.A3**					
179	2002.158 **Vb.I.A3**					
180	2002.159 **Vb.I.A3**					
181	2002.160 **Vb.I.A3**					
182	2002.162 **Vb.I.A3**					
183	2002.165 **Vb.I.A3**					
184	2002.168 **Vb.I.A3**					
185	2002.170 **Vb.I.A3**					
186	2002.173 **Vb.I.A3**					
187	2002.174 **Vb.I.A3**					
188	2002.175 **Vb.I.A3**					
189	2002.186 **Vb.II.A**					
190	2002.187 **Vb.II.A1**					
191	2002.188 **Vb.II.B**					
192	2002.189 **Vb.II.B**					

S.No.	Acc.No. Series	Marks on Reverse				
193	2002.190 **Vb.II.B**					
194	2002.191 **Vb.II.B1**					
195	2002.192 **Vb.II.B1**					
196	2002.193 **Vb.III.A1**					
197	2002.194 **Vb.IV.A**					
198	2002.195 **Vb.V.A**					
199	2002.196 **Vb.V.A**					
200	2002.197 **Vb.V.A**					
201	2002.198 **VIa.II.A**					
202	2002.199 **VIa.II.A**					
203	2002.200 **VIa.II.A**	 ?				
204	2002.201 **VIa.II.A**					
205	2002.202 **VIa.II.A**	blank				
206	2002.203 **Vb.II.A**	blank				
207	2002.204 **VIa.II.A**					
208	2002.205 **VIa.II.A**					
209	2002.206 **VIa.II.A**					
210	2002.207 **VIa.II.A**					
211	2002.208 **VIa.II.A1**					
212	2002.209 **VIa.II.A1**					
213	2002.210 **VIa.II.A2**					
214	2002.211 **VIa.II.A2**	blank				
215	2002.212 **VIa.II.A2**					
216	2002.213 **VIb.I.A2**	blank				
217	2002.214 **VIb.I.A**	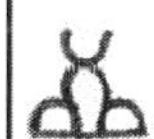				
218	2002.215 **VIb.I.A**	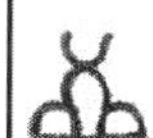				
219	2002.216 **VIb.I.A**	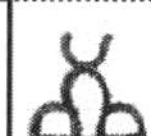				
220	2002.217 **VIb.I.A**					
221	2002.218 **VIb.I.A**					
222	2002.219 **VIb.I.A**	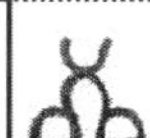				
223	2002.220 **VIb.I.A**	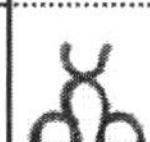				
224	2002.221 **VIb.I.A**	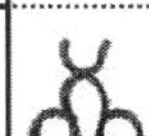				

S.No.	Acc.No. Series	Marks on Reverse				
225	2002.222 **VIb.I.A**					
226	2002.223 **VIb.I.A**					
227	2002.224 **VIb.I.A**					
228	2002.225 **VIb.I.A**					
229	2002.226 **VIb.I.A**					
230	2002.227 **VIb.I.A**					
231	2002.228 **VIb.I.A**					
232	2002.229 **VIb.I.A**		?			
233	2002.230 **VIb.I.A**					
234	2002.231 **VIb.I.A**					
235	2002.232 **VIb.I.A**					
236	2002.233 **VIb.I.A1**					
237	2002.234 **VIb.I.A1**		?			
238	2002.235 **VIb.I.A1**		?			
239	2002.236 **VIb.I.A1**					
240	2002.237 **VIb.I.A1**					

S.No.	Acc.No. Series	Marks on Reverse				
241	2002.238 **VIb.I.A1**					
242	2002.239 **VIb.I.A1**					
243	2002.240 **VIb.I.A1**					
244	2002.241 **VIb.I.A1**				?	
245	2002.242 **VIb.I.A1**					
246	2002.243 **VIb.I.A1**					
247	2002.244 **VIb.I.A1**					
248	2002.245 **VIb.I.A1**		?			
249	2002.246 **VIb.I.A1**		?			
250	2002.247 **VIb.I.A1**		?			
251	2002.248 **VIb.I.A1**		?			
252	2002.249 **VIb.I.A1**					
253	2002.250 **VIb.I.A1**		?			
254	2002.251 **VIb.I.A1**					
255	2002.252 **VIb.I.A1**					
256	2002.253 **VIb.I.A1**					

S.No.	Acc.No. Series	Marks on Reverse
257	2002.254 **VIb.I.A1**	
258	2002.255 **VIb.I.A1**	
259	2002.256 **VIb.I.A1**	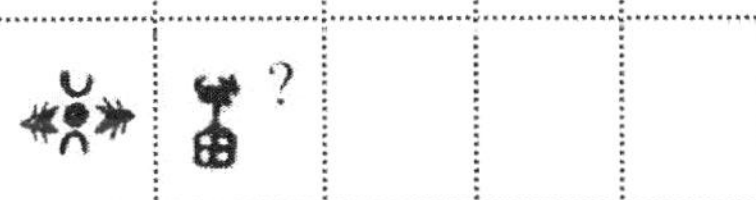 ?
260	2002.257 **VIb.I.A1**	
261	2002.258 **VIb.I.A1**	 ?
262	2002.259 **VIb.I.A1**	
263	2002.260 **VIb.I.A1**	
264	2002.261 **VIb.I.A1**	
265	2002.262 **VIb.I.A1**	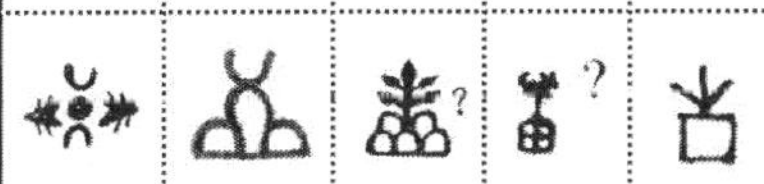
266	2002.263 **VIb.I.A1**	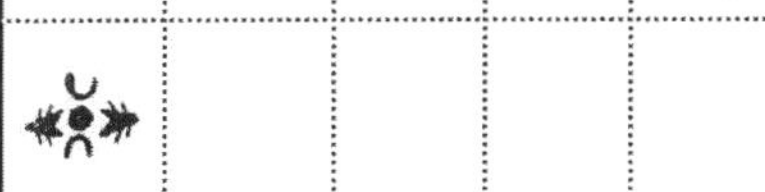
267	2002.264 **VIb.I.A1**	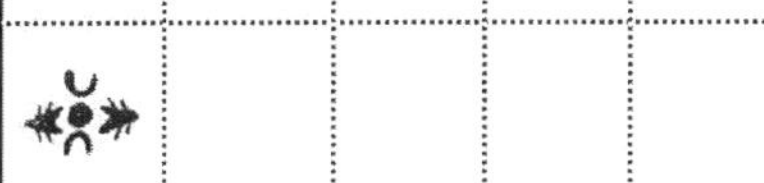
268	2002.265 **VIb.I.A1**	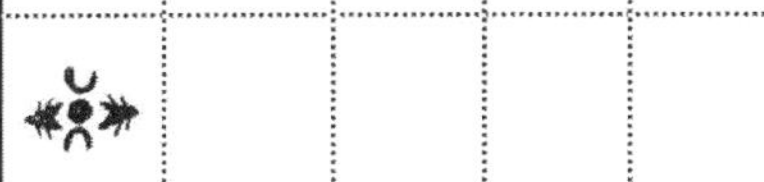
269	2002.266 **VIb.I.A1**	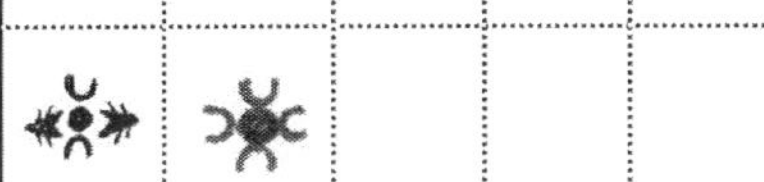
270	2002.267 **VIb.I.A1**	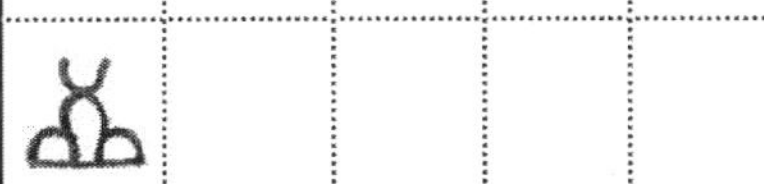
271	2002.268 **VIb.I.A1**	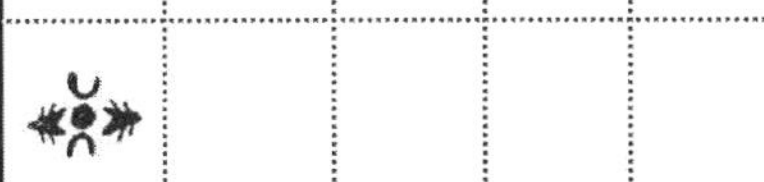
272	2002.269 **VIb.I.A1**	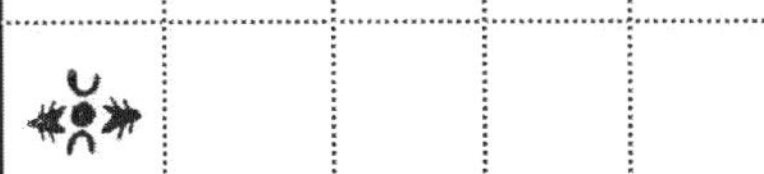

S.No.	Acc.No. Series	Marks on Reverse
273	2002.270 **VIb.I.A1**	
274	2002.271 **VIb.I.A1**	
275	2002.272 **VIb.I.A1**	
276	2002.273 **VIb.I.A1**	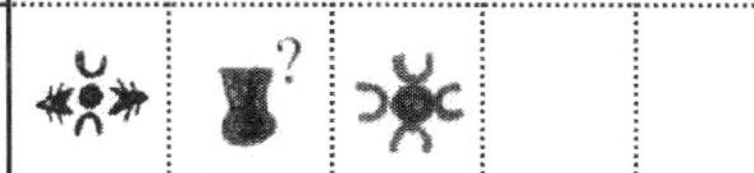
277	2002.274 **VIb.I.A1**	
278	2002.275 **VIb.I.A1**	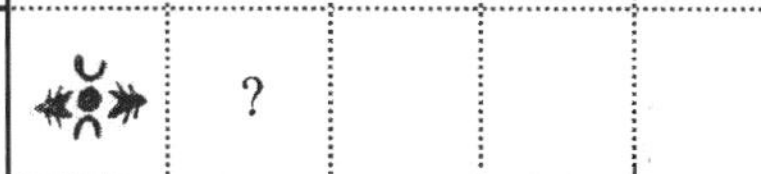 ?
279	2002.276 **VIb.I.A1**	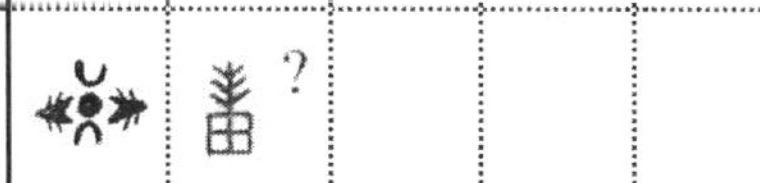
280	2002.277 **VIb.I.A1**	
281	2002.278 **VIb.I.A1**	
282	2002.279 **VIb.I.A1**	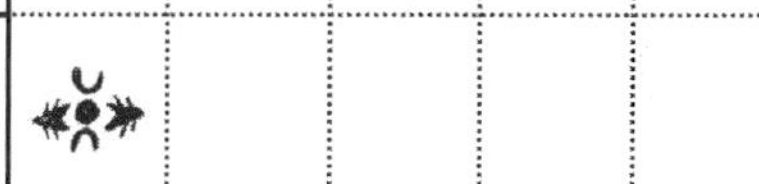
283	2002.280 **VIb.I.A1**	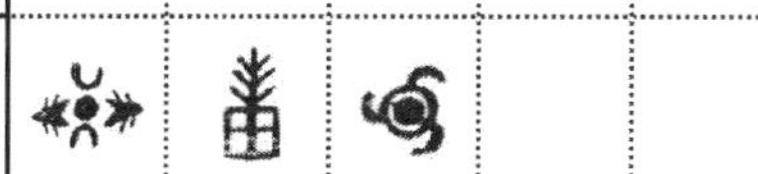
284	2002.281 **VIb.I.A1**	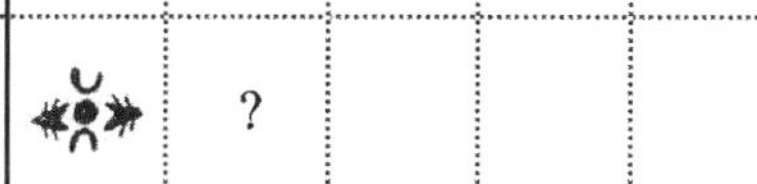 ?
285	2002.282 **VIb.I.A1**	
286	2002.283 **VIb.I.A1**	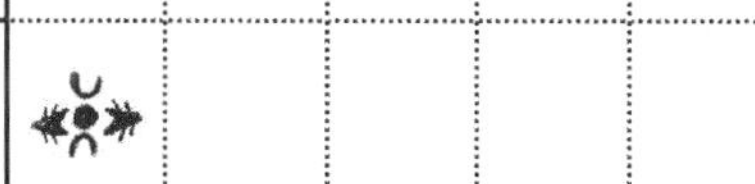
287	2002.284 **VIb.I.A1**	
288	2002.285 **VIb.I.A1**	

S.No.	Acc.No. Series	Marks on Reverse				
289	2002.286 **VIb.I.B**		?			
290	2002.287 **VIb.I.B**			?		
291	2002.288 **VIb.I.B**					
292	2002.289 **VIb.I.B**					
293	2002.290 **VIb.I.B**					
294	2002.291 **VIb.I.B**					
295	2002.292 **VIb.I.B**					
296	2002.293 **VIb.I.B**					
297	2002.294 **VIb.I.C**					
298	2002.295 **VIb.I.C**					
299	2002.296 **VIb.I.C**					
300	2002.297 **VIb.I.C**					
301	2002.298 **VIb.I.C1**					
302	2002.299 **VIb.I.C1**					
303	2002.300 **VIb.I.C1**					
304	2002.301 **VIb.I.C1**		?			
305	2002.302 **VIb.I.C1**					
306	2002.303 **VIb.I.C1**		?			
307	2002.304 **VIb.I.C2**					
308	2002.305 **VIb.I.C2**					
309	2002.306 **VIb.I.C2**					
310	2002.307 **VIb.I.C2**					
311	2002.308 **VIb.I.C2**					
312	2002.309 **VIb.I.C3**					
313	2002.310 **VIb.I.D**					
314	2002.311 **VIb.I.D**					
315	2002.312 **VIb.I.D**					
316	2002.313 **VIb.I.D**					
317	2002.314 **VIb.I.D**					
318	2002.315 **VIb.I.D**					
319	2002.316 **VIb.I.D**					
320	2002.317 **VIb.I.D**					

S.No.	Acc.No. Series	Marks on Reverse				
321	2002.318 **VIb.I.D**		?			
322	2002.319 **VIb.I.E**					
323	2002.320 **VIb.I.E**		 ?			
324	2002.321 **VIb.I.E**					
325	2002.322 **VIb.I.E**		?			
326	2002.323 **VIb.I.E**		?			
327	2002.324 **VIb.I.E**					
328	2002.325 **VIb.I.E**					
329	2002.326 **VIb.I.E**			?		
330	2002.327 **VIb.I.E**		 ?			
331	2002.328 **VIb.I.E**					
332	2002.329 **VIb.I.E**					
333	2002.330 **VIb.I.E**					

Table (7) – Associate reverse marks

Reverse marks	Associate marks	Series	No. of coins
	As 3rd mark on obverse on series VIa & VIb; symbol used as counter mark on series II onwards. 2002.24,25,83,84,87,84,128,139,199,214-217,219-221,223-225,227-230,232,267,276,288		On **69** coins / **33** coins single
		IVd.III.A1, 2002.73	
		Vb.I.A, 2002.163	
		Va.I.A4, 2002.117	
		VIb.I.A1, 2002.326; VIb.I.A8, 2002.327	
		Va.III.A, 2002.136	
		Va.VII.A, 2002.147	
		IVd.III.A, 2002.72	
		Va.I.A4, 2002.106	
		Vb.I.A3, 2002.159	
		Va.I.A, 2002.89	
	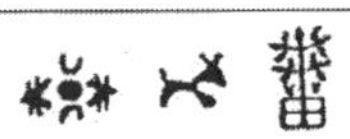	Va.I.A, 2002.86	
		VIb.I.A1, 2002.262	
	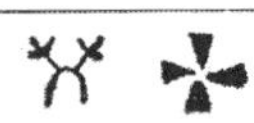	Va.I.A, 2002.90	
	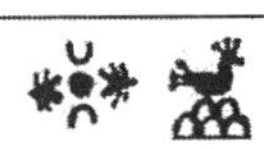	Va.I.A4, 2002.114	
	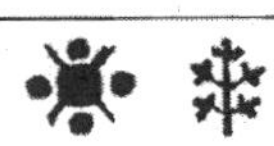	Va.I.A4 2002.116	
		Va.I.A, 2002.85	
		IVd.I.A12, 2002.63	
	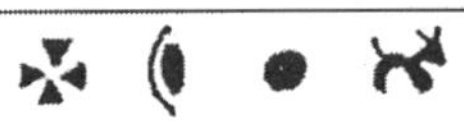	IVd.III.A2, 2002.74	

Reverse marks	Associate marks	Series	No. of coins
	As 5th mark on obverse, series I to V. 2002.38,135,332,201,206,207		On **19** coins / **6** coins single
		VIa.I.A, 2002.198	
		IVd.I.D, 2002.39	
		IVd.I.D, 2002.37	
		Va.VIII.A, 2002.149	
		IVd.I.A10, 2002.35	
		Va.I.A2 2002.95	
		Va.V I.A, 2002.145	
		Vd.I.A8, 2002.49	
	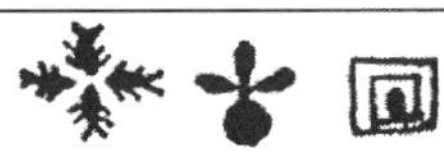	IVd.II.A, 2002.66	
		IVd.IV.A, 2002.77	
		Vb.II.A1, 2002.187	
	As 4th and 5th mark on series IV & V. 2002,142,153,164,171,172,177, 162, 168, 188,193,196,297,310-314,316-318		On **28** coins / **18** coins single
		Vb.III.A, 2002.194	
		Vb.I.A, 2002.155	
	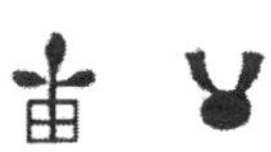	VIb.I.D, 2002.315	
		VIb.I.A1, 2002.296	
		Vb.I.A2, 2002.189	

Reverse marks	Associate marks	Series	No. of coins
		Vb.I.A1, 2002.180	
		Va.I.A6, 2002.97	
		Va.I.A5, 2002.96	
	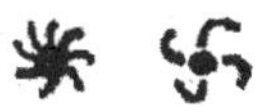	Vb.II.A3, 2002.191	
		Vb.II.A2, 2002.190	
	As 4th mark on obverse on series Vb. (2002.161,166,167,176,183,156,157, 165, 295,298-300,302,301)		On **20** coins / **15** coins single
		Vb.I.A3, 2002.169	
		Va.I.A4, 2002.122	
		Va I.A4, 2002.120 Va.III.A, 2002.132	
		Va.I.A5, 2002.124	
		VIb.IV.A, 2002..195	
		IVd.IV.A, 2002.76	
		Va VI.A,2002.144 Vb.I.A3, 2002.175	
	As 4th mark on obverse on series Va, VIb & VII. 2002.134,178,181,182, 154,173,186,294,304, 305,308,309		On **18** coins / **12** coins single
		Va.I.A2, 2002.99	
		Vb.I.A3, 2002.174	
		VIb.I.A5, 2002.307	
	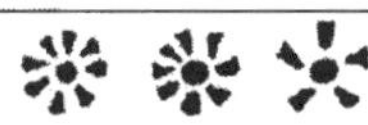	VIb.I.A5, 2002.306	
		Va.I.A4, 2002.119	

Reverse marks	Associate marks	Series	No. of coins
	As 5th mark on obverse on series, IVd, Va & Vb and 4th mark on series VIb & VII. 2002.107,321,322,328-330		On **22** coins / **8** coins single
		IVd.V.A1, 2002.81	
	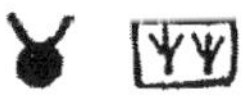	Va.I.A.4, 2002.102	
		Va.I.A.5, 2002.126	
	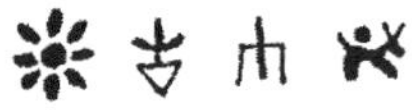	IVd.I.D5, 2002.53	
		IVd.I.A4, 2002.51	
		IVd.II.A, 2002.331	
	As 3rd mark on obverse on series II, IVd, 2002.28,29,36,40,55,62; Va, 2002.97,100, 129,		On **9**coins / **1** coin single
		IVd.I.C, 2002.28	
		IVd.I.C1, 2002.29	
		IVd.I.D, 2002.36	
		IVd.I.D, 2002.40	
		IVd.I.D7, 2002.61	
		IVd.I.D7, 2002.62	
		Va.I.A2, 2002.100	
	As 4th mark on series III, 2002.82, & 133		On **6** coins /**2** coins single
		III.III.A2,2002.19	
		IVd.II.A, 2002.67	
		VIb.I.A, 2002.226	

Reverse marks	Associate marks	Series	No. of coins
		VIb.I.B, 2002.287	
	As 5th mark on obverse on series III, VIb, c, d, Va,b & VIb. (2002, 131)		On 8 coins / 1 coin single
		IVb.I.A1, 2002.21	
		IVd.I.D6, 2002.55	
	 ?	Va.I.A, 2002.92	
		IVd.ID4, 2002.52	
		IVd.V.A1, 2002.81	
	 ?	Va.III.A, 2002.152.	
	2002.105, 109, 111, 210, 218, 222,231, 233-240, 246,247, 249, 252-254, 256 ,257, 259-261, 263-266, 268-270, 272,274-275, 279, 281-286, 289-293, 243 ,246,2 47, 249 ,252-254,		On75coins / 42 coins single. Only on reverse.
		Va.I.A4, 2002.110	
		VIa.II.A, 2002.209 VIb.I.A1, 2002.270	
		VIb.I.A1, 2002.242; 250; 255	
		VIb.I.A1, 2002.241	
	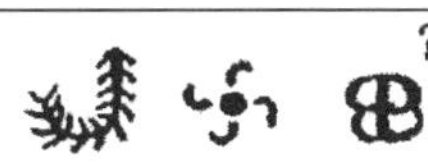 ?	Va.I.A4, 2002.103	
		Va.I.A4, 2002.104	
		Va.I.A4, 2002.112	
		Va.I.A4, 2002.113	
		Va.I.A4, 2002.115	

Reverse marks	Associate marks	Series	No. of coins
		Va.I.A4, 2002.118	
		VIb.I.A1, 2002.248	
		VIb.I.B, 2002.278	
		VIb.I.B, 2002.280	
		VIb.I.A1, 2002.273	
		VI.b.I.A1, 2002.236 VIb.I.B, 2002.282	Stamped twice
	As 5th mark, Va.I.A2, 2002.94. Never seen on obverse.		On 2 coins, only, on reverse
		Va.III.A, 2002.138	

NOTES AND REFERENCES

Symbols

1. *JASB* (1890), LIX, 183-85.
2. D.R. Bhandarkar (1984), *AIN* 103-07.
3. *Ibid.*, 106-07.
4. *JRAS* (1915), 411-13.
5. *JBBRAS*, XXIV-XXV, 35; *NIA* (IV) 164-65.
6. A. Cunningham (1891), *CAI*, 50-57.
7. *ASIAR* (1904-05), 15; *JRAS* (1915) 411-13.
8. *JBBRAS*, XX, 84.
9. *JNSI*, XII, 18-22.
10. *NS*, XLV, 80.
11. *NIA*, IV, 167.
12. J. Allan (1936), *BMC*, Introduction, Lxii.
13. *JBORS* (1919) V (I) 5.
14. *ASIAR* (1913-14), 226; *Viśuddimagga*, 14th *pariçcheda*, cf.
15. P.L. Gupta and T.R. Hardaker (1985), *AISPMC*, 16.
16. *Ibid.*

A - Obverse Symbols

1. P.L. Gupta (1963), *Am*, 32-33 and 148-149.
2. *Ibid.*, V. XVIII. 1; P.L. Gupta and T.R. Hardaker (1985), *AISPMC*, V. XVIII. A. 16.
3. P.L. Gupta (1963) *Am*, IV.VIII. C 1; P.L. Gupta and T.R. Hardaker (1985), *AISPMC*, IV. XXXI. D 1.
4. P.L. Gupta and T.R. Hardaker (1985), *AISPMC*, I. 70, 77; 196-204; IVc, 385, IVd, 438.
5. *Ibid.*, I. 15-17; IVb, 376-378.

B - Reverse Symbols

1. P.L. Gupta (1963), *Am*, 119.
2. *Ibid.*, 128.
3. *Ibid.*

15

Dispersal of Coins

The present hoard containing 333 *kārṣāpaṇa* coins, covering Series II to VI, constitutes 76 varieties. Not a single coin in the present hoard belongs to Series I. Only 19 coins fall into Series II and Series III (Series II – 2 coins and Series III – 17 coins); of these, 4 coins found restruck on the coins originally belong to Series II. The remaining 314 coins are scattered into Series IV to Series VI. Sixty-five coins belong to Series IV. Out of these, only 4 coins (2 coins to each Series) are assignable to Series IVb and IVc, and 61 coins belonging to Series IVd, constituting 19 varieties. However, no coin in our hoard belongs to Series IVa. 116 coins fall into Series V, 71 coins are assignable to Series Va, constituting 14 varieties and 45 coins to Series Vb constituting 11 varieties. 133 coins belong to Series VI of which, only 16 coins belong to Series VIa, constitute 4 varieties and 117 coins to Series VIb, constituting 10 varieties, and are the latest coins present in the hoard.

The largest numbers of coins are limited only to two series in this hoard—Series V and Series VI. This apparently indicates that these were the main coins current during the period when the hoard was buried. However, it is less likely that they were the local issues. They could be the issues of the neighbouring regions of the same period, and probably reached the region, through trade. Again, the absence of the coins belonging to Series VII suggests that these coins would not have come to vogue when the hoard was deposited.

According to the present classification, these coins constitute 76 varieties of groups (Figs. 1–19). All the varieties are known from the other hoards also. The six-armed symbol presents two new forms and mentioned in the catalogue as unnoticed and as a sub-variety of the main symbol.

Series II: (2 coins)
Only 2 coins belong to this series in the present hoard, constituting 2 varieties.

(i) II. I. A. (S. no.1, Fig. 1, 2002.1)
This variety is also seen in Amaravati hoard on 1 coin and also as an older obverse on 2 coins—198 and 362. Coin 198 is re-struck by Series III. I. 4 and 362 by Series IV. V. E. 2, respectively (*Am*, 113-114).

(ii) II. II. A. (S. no. 2, Fig. 1, 2002.2)
Four coins of this variety are noticed in Big Bhir mound hoard (Bhir mound hoard, 1924) (832, 844, 894 and 1148), classified as variety B (d)2. Three coins (27, 117 and 228) of this variety are reported as restruck coins in Amaravati hoard. Coin no. 27 re-struck by the variety II.XV.1 and other 2 coins were re-struck by the Series III.I.4, respectively (*Am*, 39).

Series III: (17 coins) constitute 5 varieties.

(i) III. I. A. (S. no. 3, Fig. 1, 2002.3) – Restruck.
Only 1 coin belongs to this variety, which is re-struck on the coin, originally belonging to Series II. Walsh has noticed this variety on a coin (708) in Big Bhir mound hoard (Taxila hoard - 1924) (Q9). However, Gupta has noticed another coin (906a) of this variety in the same hoard. This variety is noticed on 9 coins (37- 45) in Amaravati hoard (II. XIII. 1). Out of these 9 coins, 2 coins (39 and 44) are found re-struck on the coins belonging to Series II – II. I. I and II. III. I, respectively. This variety is also seen in Mambalam hoard (Madras) on 1 coin; Machuatoli hoard (Patna) – 2 coins; Patraha hoard (Purnea, Bihar) – 1 coin; Thathari hoard (Bilaspur, Madhya Pradesh) – 1 coin; Barwani hoard (Madhya Pradesh) – 4 coins (71.548/77- 80); Bahal hoard (East Khand desh, Maharashtra) – 1 coin; Palanpur hoard (Gujarat) – 1 coin and Rairh hoard (Rajsthan) (V) – 4 coins. Gupta has remarked, "no coin of this variety is so far known in any hoard from Uttar Pradesh, Bengal and Orrisa" (*Am*, 40). However, in the hoard, this variety is present, which is found re-struck on the coin originally belonging to Series II (*Am*, II. I. 1; *AISPMC, 286*).

(ii) III. II. A: (7 coins) (S. no. 4, Fig. 1, 2002.5; Pl. I (2 7) 2002.4, 6-10).
Three coins of this variety (2002.4- 6) found re-struck on the coins originally belong to Series II. Ninety-nine coins (179-152; 154 278) belong to this variety in Amaravati hoard (III. I. 4). Of these, 35 coins are found restruck on different varieties of Series II (*Am*, 46). This variety is also known from Raichur hoard (Hyderabad) – 1 coin; Mambalam hoard – 18 coins; Vembavur hoard (Trichnapally) (No. 1) – 3 coins; Vizagapatam hoard (Hyderabad) – 1 coin; Veersigamani hoard (Tinnevelly) – 2 coins; Bhimalipatan hoard (Vizagapatam) – 5 coins; Dharapuram hoard (Distt. Koimbatore, Tamil Nadu) – 1 coin; Palanpur hoard – 3 coins; Rairh hoards (II) – 1 coin, (IV) – 2 coins, (V) – 47 coins; Big Bhir mound hoard – 46 coins (22 coins are re-struck on Series II coins); Taxila hoard (BHU-No. 2) – 2 coins; Mathura hoard (Uttar Pradesh) – 1, 1, 3 coins; Machuatoli hoard – 14 coins; Chandraketugarh (Bengal) – 2 coins; Mayurbhanj hoard (Orissa) – 2 coins; Barwani hoard – 23 coins (71.548/93, 2873–2894); and Raichur hoard (Hyderabad) – 1 coin, re-struck on a coin, originally belonging to Series II.

(iii) III. III. A: (1 coin) (S. no. 5, Fig. 2, 2002.11).
Only 1 coin is attributed to this variety in this hoard.
This variety is also noticed on 1 coin (1149) in Big Bhir mound hoard; Amaravati hoard – 5 coins (117-120, 253) and Barwani hoard – 2 coins (71.548/3382 and 3397).

(iv) III. III. A1: (6 coins) (S. no. 6, Fig. 2, 2002.13; Pl. II (2-6) 2002.12, 14-18).
This variety is seen on 6 coins. However, the second symbol—six-armed symbol is seen partly on all the coins and hence, the coins attributed to this variety are clubbed together in one variety. This variety is classified into two varieties by Gupta as III. II. 6b, 6c (*Am*, 45-50) and in his latest work with Hardaker as III. X. A1a, 320 and III. X. A. 1b, 321 (*AISPMC*, 60-61), as the said symbol forms two varieties. However, in this hoard, the symbol is seen partly on all the coins. Therefore, its form could not be determined, and hence, it could not be attributed to any specific variety.

This variety (III. II. 6b) is seen in Amaravati hoard on 68 coins (48-115). Coin (116) is attributed to its sub-variety (III. II. 6c). Gupta notices that the 'Taurine' is missing from one of its arms of the symbol. He further explains whether this constitutes a new variety or the symbol is a die-cutter's mistake, belonging to variety III. II. 6b and hence, cannot be determined. However, a coin (1024) in the Big Bhir mound hoard, of the same variety (III. II. 6) is reported where one of its arms with *mandap* is off the flan. Of the other two-*mandap* arms of the symbol, one has taurine inside the oval and the other appears to have a dot inside. It is possible that the coin may also be of the present sub-variety, and the dot in our coin might not be clear (*Am*, 49-50).

This variety is also noticed in Karimnagar hoard (Hyderabad) on 6 coins; Gulbarga hoard (Hyderabad) – 2 coins; Mambalam hoard – 13 coins; Vembavur hoards (No. 1) – 2 coins, (No. 2) – 1 coin; Vizagapatam hoard – 2 coins; Dharapuram hoard (Distt. Koimbatore, Tamil Nadu) – 1 coin; Venne hoard (Vizagapatam) – 1 coin; Bahal hoard – 2 coins; Bhandara hoard (Madhya Pradesh) – 1 coin; Palanpur hoard – 2 coins; Rairh hoards (II) – 1 coin, (IV) – 2 coins and (V) – 35 coins; Big Bhir mound hoard – 35 coins; Taxila hoard (BHU- No. 1) – 2 coins and (No. 2) – 1 coin; Sialkot hoard (Punjab) – 1 coin; Lalganj hoard (Azamgarh, Uttar Pradesh) – 3 coins; Gorakhpur hoard (Uttar Pradesh) – 4 coins; Allahabad hoard (Uttar Pradesh) – 1 coin; Kausambi hoard (Uttar Pradesh) – 1 coin; Hathuma hoard (Kanpur, Uttar Pradesh) – 1 coin; Mathura hoards (Uttar Pradesh) – 3, 1, 1 coins; U. P. T. T. R. No. 28/1916-hoard – 4 coins; Patraha hoard – 10 coins; Machuatoli hoard – 33 coins; Mayurbhanj hoard – 1 coin and Barwani hoard – 16 coins (71.548/ 3379-3381, 3383-3394, 3396). Ten coins of this variety from a hoard of unknown location are in the collection of Lucknow museum.

(v) III. III. A2: (2 coins) (S. no. 7, Fig. 2, 2002.15; Pl. II (2) 2002.19).
This variety is seen on two coins. However, the fifth symbol on both the coins is seen partly. This variety is also noticed on the coins in Ramna hoard (Bihar), Patna Museum and Mathura museum (*AISPMC*, 326) and Barwani hoard – 2 coins (71.548/3258, 91). It is worth mentioning here that if the tail of fifth symbol is turning to right, then this variety belongs to another variety (*AISPMC, 327*) as seen on the coins in Amaravati hoard (III. II. 3).

Series IV: (65 coins).

Series IVb – (2 coins) constitute 2 varieties.

(i) IVb. I. A. (1 coin) (S. no. 8, Fig. 2, 2002.20).
Amaravati hoard contains 2 coins (325 – 326) of this variety; Veersigmani hoard – 1 coin; Rairh hoard (V) – 1 coin; Big Bhir mound hoard – 2 coins; and Gorakhpur hoard – 1 coin.

(ii) IVb. I. A1. (1 coin) (S. no. 9, fig. 3, 2002.21).
This variety is seen on 5 coins (320 - 324) in Amaravati hoard; Big Bhir mound hoard – 3 coins; Allahabad hoard – 1 coin; Patraha hoard – 2 coins; Machuatoli hoard – 1 coin; and Bhalna hoard (Distt. Gaya) – 1 coin. This variety is not seen in any hoard found from south India and western India (*Am*, 52-53).

Series IVc: (2 coins) constitute 2 varieties.

(i) IVc. I. A. (1 coin) (S. no. 10, Fig. 3, 2002.22).
This variety is noticed in Amaravati hoard on 7 coins (393-399); Big Bhir mound hoard – 2 coins; Tregna hoard (Bihar) – 1 coin; Rairh hoard (V) – 1 coin; Patraha hoard – 1 coin;

Bhimalipatan hoard – 1 coin; and purchased hoard of unknown provenance, Lucknow museum – 1 coin.

On both the coins from Big Bhir mound hoard, the fourth symbol is seen partly. In Tregna hoard coin, published by Durga Prasad, the fifth symbol is recorded as tree-in-railing. Even in Amaravati hoard, the fifth symbol is shown of a different variety (IV.V. C2) (*Am*, 59).

(ii) IVc. II. A. (1 coin) (S. no. 11, Fig. 3, 2002.23).
Only 1 coin (402) is known of this variety from Amaravati hoard (*Am*, 58).

Series IVd: (61 coins) constitute 26 varieties.

(i) IVd. I. A. (1 coin) (S. no. 12, Fig. 3, 2002.24).
This variety is also reported from Taxila hoard (BHU) and Mambalam hoard (number of coins are not mentioned) (*AISPMC*, 398).

(ii) IVd. I. A1. (2 coins) (S. no. 13, Fig. 3, 2002.26; Pl. II (2) 2002.25).
This variety is seen in Amaravati hoard on 32 coins (411- 442 and 462?); Gulbarga hoard – 1 coin; Raichur hoard (Hyderabad) – 1 coin; Mambalam hoard – 3 coins; Vizagapatam hoard – 1 coin; Veersigamani hoard – 1 coin; Bahal hoard – 5 coins; Thathari hoard (Bilaspur) – 1 coin; Rairh hoards (I) – 2 coins, (II) – 1 coin and (V) – 4 coins; Big Bhir mound hoard – 25 coins; Taxila hoard (BHU-No. 2) – 1 coin; Lalganj hoard – 1 coin; Gorakhpur hoard – 1 coin; Gorhoghat hoard (Bihar) – 1 coin; Chandraketugarh hoard – 1 coin; Mayurbhanj hoard – 3 coins; and Barwani hoard – 10 coins (71.548/2859-2868).

(iii) IVd. I. B. (1 coin) (S. no. 14, Fig. 4, 2002.27).
Amaravati hoard contains 6 coins (463-468); Raichur hoard – 1 coin; Mambalam hoard – 4 coins; Veersigamani hoard – 1 coin; Bahal hoard – 2 coins; Rairh hoards (I) – 1 coin and (V) – 1 coin; Big Bhir mound hoard – 2 coins; Lalganj hoard – 2 coins; Gorakhpur hoard – 1 coin; Kausambi hoard – 1 coin; Patraha hoard – 3 coins; Machuatoli hoard – 3 coins; Ramna hoard (Patna city) – 1 coin and Barwani hoard – 2 coins (71.548/2787-2788).

(iv-v) IVd. I. C. and **IVd. I. C1.** (2 coins) (S. nos. 15 & 16, Fig. 4, 2002.28; 2002.29).
Two coins in this hoard belong to this variety and are classified into two separate varieties – IVd. I. C. and IVd. I. C1.

IVd. I. C. (2002.28) variety is noticed on 9 coins (470-478) in Amaravati hoard; Mambalam hoard – 2 coins; Big Bhir mound hoard – 6 coins; Patraha hoard – 5 coins; Hardoi hoard (Uttar Pradesh) – 3 coins; and Barwani hoard – 1 coin (71.548/2833).

Not a single coin in these hoards represents the complete form of second symbol—the six-armed symbol, which is always found out of the flan and does not provide any indication of the exact form of this symbol. The lower arm of the symbol on Amaravati hoard coins (IV. VIII. C.1, 470-478) is not clearly visible. However, Gupta and Hardaker referred the same variety (IV. XXXI. D2, 406, *AISPMC*) where a fish is shown as its lower arm, but here also, the symbol is seen partly and the fish is not visible on the coin given in the plate. A coin (2002.29) classified as variety (S. no. 16, IVd. I. C1), present in our hoard, clearly shows the sixth arm of the second symbol, which helps in restoring the complete form of the said symbol. In its lower arm, a fish can be noticed clearly inside an oval, which completes the form of symbol as shown in the catalogue and remarked as unnoticed so far.

(vi) IVd. I. D. (16 coins) (S. no. 17, Fig. 4, 2002.36; Pl. II (2-9) and Pl. III (10-16), 2002.35 and 37-45).
This variety is seen on 298 coins (510 - 807) in Amaravati hoard; Karimnagar hoard – 18 coins; Gulbarga hoard – 9 coins; Raichur hoard – 7 coins; Kondapur find (Hyderabad) – 1 coin; Maski find (Hyderabad) – 1 coin; Mambalam hoard – 68 coins; Vembavur hoards (No. 1) – 21 coins and (No. 2) – 2 coins; Vizagapatam hoard – 5 coins; Bahal hoard – 68 coins; Bhandara hoard (Madhya Pradesh) – 1 coin; Umrer hoard (Nagpur) – 2 coins; Bilaspur hoard (Madhya Pradesh) – 1 coin; Palanpur hoard – 5 coins; Rairh hoards (I) – 17 coins, (II) – 1 coin, (IV) – 4 coins and (V) – 37 coins; Big Bhir mound hoard – 220 coins; Lalganj hoard – 18 coins; Gorakhpur hoard – 16 coins; Allahabad hoards (No. 1) – 3 coins and (No. 2) – 12 coins; Kausambi hoard – 9 coins; Harha hoard (Uttar Pradesh) – 4 coins; Hardoi hoard (Uttar Pradesh) – 8 coins; Mathura hoards – 17, 3, 1, 2, 3 coins; U. P. T. T. R. No. 28/1916 hoard – 9 coins; Patraha hoard – 106 coins; Gorhoghat hoard – 2 coins; Mayurbhanj hoard – 23 coins; and Barwani hoard – 70 coins (71.548/2711- 2778, 2831-2832).

(vii) IVd. I. D1. (1 coin) (S. no. 18, Fig. 5, 2002.46).
Forty-two coins (1050-1091) belong to this variety in Amaravati hoard; Karimnagar hoard – 1 coin; Raichur hoard – 3 coins; Mambalam hoard – 6 coins; Vembavur hoards (No. 1) – 3 coins and (No. 2) – 1 coin; Veersigmani hoard – 1 coin; Bhimalipatan hoard – 1 coin; Dharapuram hoard – 2 coins; Bahal hoard – 16 coins; Rairh hoards (IV) – 2 coins and (V) – 4 coins; Big Bhir mound hoard – 34 coins; Taxila hoard (BHU-No. 1) – 1 coin; Peshawar hoard (Modern Pakistan) – 1 coin; Gorakhpur hoard – 3 coins; Allahabad hoard – 1 coin; Kausambi hoard – 1 coin; Harha hoard – 1 coin; Mathura hoards – 1, 3, 1 coins; Patraha hoard – 12 coins; Machuatoli hoard – 17 coins; Mayurbhanj hoard – 7; and Barwani hoard – 8 coins (71.548/2790-2797).

(viii) IVd. I. D2. (1 coin) (S. no. 19, Fig. 5, 2002.47).
This variety is seen on 13 coins (1096-1108) in Amaravati hoard; Raichur hoard – 1 coin; Mambalam hoard – 4 coins; Vembavur hoard – 3 coins; Bahal hoard – 2 coins; Rairh hoard (V) – 4 coins; Big Bhir mound hoard – 8 coins; Lalganj hoard – 2 coins; Mathura hoards – 1, 1 coins; Patraha hoard – 6 coins; Machuatoli hoard – 10 coins; Ramna hoard – 1 coin; and Barwani hoard – 6 coins (71.548/2779-2784).

(ix) IVd. I. D3. (2 coins) (S. no. 20, Fig. 5, 2002.49; Pl. III (2) 2002.48).
Amaravati hoard contains 29 coins (955-983); Mambalam hoard – 10 coins; Bahal hoard – 5 coins; Rairh hoards (I) – 1 coin and (V) – 1 coin; Big Bhir mound hoard – 18 coins; Taxila hoards (BHU-No. 1) 1 coin and (BHU-No. 2) – 1 coin; Lalganj hoard – 1 coin; Mathura hoards – 1, 1 coins; Patraha hoard – 6 coins; Machuatoli hoard – 7 coins; Chandraketugarh hoard – 1 coin; and Barwani hoard – 3 coins (71.548/2821-2823).

(x) IVd. I. D4. (3 coins) (S. no. 21, Fig. 5, 2002.51; Pl. IV (2-3) 2002.50 and 2002. 52).
This variety is noticed on 41 coins (984-1024) in Amaravati hoard; Karimnagar hoard – 1 coin; Gulbarga hoard – 1 coin; Raichur hoard – 2 coins; Mambalam hoard – 6 coins; Vembavur hoard – 1 coin; Vizagapatam hoard – 1 coin; Veersigmani hoard – 2 coins; Bhimlipatan hoard – 1 coin; Venne hoard – 1 coin; Bahal hoard – 13 coins; Thathari hoard – 2 coins; Rairh hoards (I) – 1 coin, (IV) – 3 coins and (V) – 3 coins; Big Bhir mound hoard – 21 coins; Peshawar hoard – 1 coin; Gorakhpur hoard – 3 coins; Allahabad hoards (No. 1) – 1 coin and (No. 2) – 1 coin; Harha hoard – 1 coin; Mathura hoards – 1, 3, 1 coins; Patraha hoard – 14 coins; Machuatoli hoard – 13 coins; Ramna hoard – 1 coin; Mayurbhanj hoard – 1 coin; and Barwani hoard – 10 coins (71.548/2798-2807).

(xi) IVd. I. D5. (2 coins) (S. no. 22, Fig. 6, 2002.53; Pl. IV (2) 2002.54).
25 coins (1025-1049) belong to this variety in Amaravati hoard; Karimnagar hoard – 3 coins; Vembavur hoard – 1 coin; Veersigmani hoard – 2 coins; Bhimlipatan hoard – 3 coins; Venne hoard – 1 coin; Bahal hoard – 4 coins; Rairh hoards (IV) – 1 coin and (V) – 7 coins; Big Bhir mound hoard – 11 coins; Allahabad hoard – 1 coin; Hathuma hoard – 1 coin; Machuatoli hoard – 16 coins; U. P. T. T. R. No. 28/1916 hoard – 1 coin; Patraha hoard – 1 coin; Mathura hoards – 1, 1 coins; Bhalna hoard – 1 coin; and Ramna hoard – 2 coins; and Barwani hoard – 3 coins (71.548/2827-2829).

(xii) IVd. I. D6. (6 coins) (S. no. 23, Fig. 6, 2002.56; Pl. IV (2-6) 2002.55 and 57-60).
Amaravati hoard contains 100 coins (808-907) of this variety; Karimnagar hoard – 2 coins; Gulbarga hoard – 6 coins; Raichur hoard – 4 coins; Mambalam hoard – 18 coins; Vembavur hoard – 2 coins; Vizagapatam hoard – 2 coins; Bhimlipatan hoard – 5 coins; Dharapuram hoard – 3 coins; Venne hoard – 3 coins; Bahal hoard – 23 coins; Bhandara hoard – 2 coins; Rairh hoards (I) – 2 coins, (IV) – 1 coin and (V) – 12 coins; Big Bhir mound hoard – 42 coins; Taxila hoards (BHU- No. 1) – 1 coin and (BHU- No. 2) – 4 coins; Peshawar hoard – 1 coin; Lalganj hoard – 5 coins; Gorakhpur hoard – 8 coins; Allahabad hoards (No. 1) – 2 coins and (No. 2) – 2 coins; Kausambi hoard – 1 coin; Harha hoard – 1 coin; Mathura hoards – 7, 2, 3 coins; U. P. T. T. R. No. 28 /1916 hoard – 1 coin; Patraha hoard – 23 coins; Machuatoli hoard – 24 coins; Bhalna hoard – 2 coins; Ramna hoard – 2 coins; Mayurbhanj hoard – 7 coins; and Barwani hoard – 20 coins (71.548/2839-2858).

(xiii) IVd. I. D7. (2 coins) (S. no. 24, Fig. 6, 2002.62 and Pl. IV (2) 2002. 61).
This variety is noticed on 23 coins (908-930) in Amaravati hoard; Raichur hoard – 2 coins; Mambalam hoard – 3 coins; Vembavur hoard – 4 coins; Vizagapatam hoard – 1 coin; Bhimlipatan hoard – 1 coin; Dharapuram hoard – 1 coin; Bahal hoard – 3 coins; Bhandara hoard – 2 coins; Thathari hoard – 2 coins; Rairh hoard (V) – 3 coins; Big Bhir mound hoard – 15 coins; Taxila hoard (BHU-No. 2) – 2 coins; Lalganj hoard – 1 coin; Gorakhpur hoard – 2 coins; Gokulvan hoard (Sitapur, Uttar Pradesh) – 1 coin; Harha hoard – 1 coin; Mathura hoards – 2, 1, 1 coins; U. P. T. T. R. No. 28/1916 hoard – 1 coin; Patraha hoard – 4 coins; Machuatoli hoard – 6 coins; and Barwani hoard – 7 coins (71.548/2808-2814).

(xiv) IVd. I. D8. (1 coin) (S.no. 25, Fig. 6, 2002.63).
This variety is seen on 3 coins (507-509) in Amaravati hoard; Machuatoli hoard – 2 coins; and Bahal hoard – 1 coin.

(xv) IVd. II. A. (5 coins) (S. no. 26, Fig.7, 2002.67; Pl.V (2-5) 2002.64-66 and 2002.68).
Eighty-nine coins (1155-1242 and 6075) of this variety are reported in Amaravati hoard; Karimnagar hoard – 3 coins; Gulbarga hoard – 8 coins; Raichur hoard – 1 coin; Mambalam hoard – 13 coins; Vembavur hoard – 4 coins; Vizagapatam hoard – 1 coin; Veersigmani hoard – 1 coin; Bahal hoard – 2 coins; Rairh hoards (I) – 4 coins, (II) – 1 coin, (IV) – 4 coins and (V) – 16 coins; Big Bhir mound hoard – 22 coins; Taxila hoard (BHU-No. 2) – 1 coin; Lalganj hoard – 4 coins; Gorakhpur hoard – 2 coins; Kausambi hoard – 1 coin; Mathura hoards – 7, 1, 1, 1 coins; U. P. T. T. R. No. 28/1916 hoard – 1 coin; Patraha hoard – 15 coins; Machuatoli hoard – 31 coins; Ramna hoard – 2 coins; Chandraketugarh hoard – 1 coin; Mayurbhanj hoard – 3 coins; and Barwani hoard – 14 coins (71.548/83, 2026-2032, 2034-2038, 2955).

(xvi) IVd. II. A1. (1 coin), (S. no. 27, Fig. 7, 2002.331).
The second symbol – six-armed – forms a new variety, unnoticed so far.

(xvii) IVd. II. A2. (1 coin) (S. no. 28, Fig. 7, 2002.69).
This variety is seen on 21 coins (1243-1263) in Amaravati hoard; Mamblam hoard – 1 coin; Vizagapatam hoard – 2 coins; Veersigmani hoard – 1 coin; Vembavur hoard (No. 2) – 1 coin; Bhimlipatan hoard – 1 coin; Dharapuram hoard – 1 coin; Venne hoard – 1 coin; Bahal hoard – 1 coin; Bhandara hoard – 1 coin; Rairh hoard (V) – 8 coins; Mathura hoards – 1, 1 coins; Patraha hoard – 6 coins; Machuatoli hoard – 8 coins; Chandraketugarh hoard – 2 coins; Mayurbhanj hoard – 3 coins and Barwani hoard – 6 coins (71.548/84, 2955, 3190-3193).

(xviii) IVd. III. A. (3 coins) (S. no. 29, Fig. 7, 2 002.70; Pl. V (2-3) 2002.71-72).
This variety occurs on 95 coins (1282-1377) from Amaravati hoard; Karimnagar hoard – 8 coins; Gulbarga hoard – 2 coins; Raichur hoard – 4 coins; Maski find – 1 coin; Mamblam hoard – 20 coins; Vizagapatam hoard – 2 coins; Vembavur hoards (No. 1) – 8 coins and (No. 2) – 3 coins; Bhimalipatan hoard – 4 coins; Dharapuram hoard – 4 coins; Venne hoard – 1 coin; Bahal hoard – 27 coins; Dharwar hoard (Karnataka) – 2 coins; Umrer hoard – 1 coin; Thathari hoard –1 coin; Palanpur hoard – 1 coin; Rairh hoards (I) – 5 coins, (IV) – 2 coins and (V) – 14 coins; Big Bhir mound hoard – 72 coins; Taxila hoard (BHU- No. 2) – 2 coins; Peshawar hoard – 1 coin; Lalganj hoard – 4 coins; Gorakhpur hoard – 5 coins; Allahabad hoard – 1 coin; Kausambi hoard – 5 coins; Harha hoard – 1 coin; Hardoi hoard – 1 coin; Mathura hoards – 5, 3, 1, 1 coins; U. P. T. T. R. No. 28/1916 hoard – 2 coins; Patraha hoard – 21 coins; Machuatoli hoard – 34 coins; Ramna hoard – 2 coins; Chandraketugarh hoard – 2 coins; Mayurbhanj hoard – 4 coins; and Barwani hoard – 25 coins (71.548/ 3281-3305).

(xix) IVd. III. A1. (1 coin) (S. no. 30, Fig. 7, 2002.73).
This variety is seen in Amaravati hoard on 7 coins (1396-1402); Gulbarga hoard – 1 coin; Mambalam hoard – 1 coin; Vembavur hoards (No. 1) – 1 coin and (No. 2) – 1 coin; Vizagapatam hoard – 1 coin; Bahal hoard – 1 coin; Rairh hoard (V) – 1 coin; Big Bhir mound hoard – 6 coins; Mathura hoard – 1 coin; Patraha hoard – 4 coins; Machuatoli hoard – 4 coins; Gorhoghat hoard – 3 coins; and Barwani hoard – 2 coins (71.548/2362-2363).

(xx) IVd. III. A2. (1 coin) (S. no. 31, Fig. 8, 2002.74).
This variety is noticed on 18 coins (1378-1395) from Amaravati hoard; Karimnagar hoard – 2 coins; Gulbarga hoard – 1 coin; Raichur hoard – 1 coin; Mambalam hoard – 3 coins; Vizagapatam hoard – 2 coins; Bahal hoard – 3 coins; Dharwar hoard – 1 coin; Thathari hoard – 1 coin; Palanpur hoard – 3 coins; Rairh hoards (II) – 1 coin, (IV) – 1 coin and (V) – 2 coins; Big Bhir mound hoard – 13 coins; Taxila hoard (BHU- No. 2) – 1 coin; Gorakhpur hoard – 2 coins; Kausambi hoard – 1 coin; Mathura hoards – 1, 1 coins; Patraha hoard – 5 coins; Machuatoli hoard – 1 coin; and Barwani hoard – 4 coins (71.548/86-89).

(xxi) IVd. IV. A. (4 coins) (S. no. 32, Fig. 8, 2002.77; Pl. V (2-4) 2002.75-76, 78).
This variety is seen on 16 coins (1416-1431) in Amaravati hoard; Karimnagar hoard – 3 coins; Gulbarga hoard – 1 coin; Mambalam hoard – 4 coins; Bhimalipatan hoard – 1 coin; Dharapuram hoard – 1 coin; Bahal hoard – 2 coins; Kasarawad hoard (Indore, Madhya Pradesh) – 1 coin; Rairh hoard (IV) – 2 coins; Big Bhir mound hoard – 10 coins; Lalganj hoard – 6 coins; Allahabad hoard – 1 coin; Mathura hoard – 1 coin; U. P. T. T. R. No. 28/1916 hoard – 1 coin; Patraha

hoard – 9 coins; Machuatoli hoard – 10 coins; and Barwani hoard – 7 coins (71.548/3364-3370).

(xxii) IVd. IV. A1. (1 coin) (S. no. 33, Fig. 8, 2002.79).
This variety is noticed in Amaravati hoard on 4 coins (1432-1435); Raichur hoard – 1 coin; Bahal hoard – 1 coin; Rairh hoard (I) – 1 coin; Big Bhir mound hoard – 2 coins; Mathura hoard – 1 coin; Kausambi hoard – 1 coin; and Patraha hoard – 2 coins.

(xxiii) IVd.V.A. (1 coin) (S. no. 34, Fig. 8, 2002.80).
This variety is noticed in Amaravati hoard on 17 coins (1436-1452); Karimnagar hoard – 1 coin; Gulbarga hoard – 1 coin; Mambalam hoard – 1 coin; Bahal hoard – 1 coin; Rairh hoards (I) – 1 coin and (II) – 4 coins; Big Bhir mound hoard – 21 coins; Taxila hoard (BHU- No. 1) – 1 coin; Lalganj hoard – 1 coin; Kausambi hoard – 1 coin; Mayurbhanj hoard – 1 coin; and Barwani hoard – 2 coins (71.548/2162-2163).

(xxiv) IVd. V. A1. (1 coin) (S. no. 35, Fig. 9, 2002.81).
Fifty-five coins (1503-1557) belong to this variety in Amaravati hoard; Karimnagar hoard – 2 coins; Gulbarga hoard – 1 coin; Mambalam hoard – 8 coins; Vembavur hoard – 6 coins; Vizagapatam hoard – 3 coins; Veersigmani hoard – 1 coin; Bhimalipatan hoard – 1 coin; Dharapuram hoard – 1 coin; Bahal hoard – 9 coins; Thathari hoard – 1 coin; Palanpur hoard – 1 coin; Rairh hoards (I) – 6 coins, (II) – 1 coin, (IV) – 3 coins and (V) – 13 coins; Big Bhir mound hoard – 78 coins; Lalganj hoard – 2 coins; Gorakhpur hoard – 2 coins; Kausambi hoard – 3 coins; Mathura hoards 5, 1 coins; U. P. T. T. R. No. 28/1916 hoard – 1 coin; Mayurbhanj hoard – 1 coin; and Barwani hoard – 16 coins (71.548/ 2173-2188).

(xxv) IVd. VI. A. (1 coin) (S. no. 36, Fig. 9, 2002.82).
This variety is noticed in Amaravati hoard on 2 coins (1153–1154).

(xxvi) IVd. VII. A. (1 coin) (S. no. 37, fig. 9, 2002.83).
Twenty-four coins (1573-1596) of this variety are present in Amaravati hoard; Gulbarga hoard – 1 coin; Raichur hoard – 1 coin; Mambalam hoard – 3 coins; Vembavur hoard – 2 coins; Baroda hoard (Gujrat) – 1 coin; Rairh hoard (I) – 1 coin; Taxila hoard (BHU-No. 2) – 2 coins; Patraha hoard – 6 coins; Machuatoli hoard – 4 coins; and Barwani hoard – 6 coins (71.548/ 3102-3107).

Series V (116 coins).

Series Va: (71 coins) constitute 14 varieties.

(i) Va. I. A. (7 coins) (S. no. 38, Fig. 9, 2002.90; Pl.V (2-7) 2002.84-89).
This variety is noticed in Amaravati hoard on 111 coins (1607-1717); Karimanagar hoard – 3 coins; Raichur hoard – 1 coin; Mambalam hoard – 6 coins; Vembavur hoards (No. 1) – 1 coin and (No. 2) – 1 coin; Vizagapatam hoard – 1 coin; Bhimalipatan hoard – 2 coins; Gudivada hoard (Distt. Krishna) – 1 coin; Bahal hoard – 8 coins; Umrer hoard – 1 coin; Thathari hoard – 1 coin; Palanpur hoard – 1 coin; Baroda hoard – 1 coin; Rairh hoards (I) – 4 coins, (IV) – 2 coins and (V) – 3 coins; Big Bhir mound hoard – 2 coins; Taxila hoards (BHU-No. 1) – 3 coins and (BHU-No. 2) – 2 coins; Peshawar hoard – 3 coins; Lalganj hoard – 1 coin; Gorakhpur hoard – 1 coin; Kausambi hoard – 1 coin; Gokulvan hoard – 4 coins; Mathura hoards – 6, 4, 3 coins; Mayurbhanj hoard – 4 coins; and Barwani hoard – 35 coins (71.548/109-18, 125-49).

(ii) Va. I. A1. (2 coins) (S. no. 39, Fig. 10, 2002.92; Pl.V (2) 2002.91).
Amaravati hoard contains 47 coins (1729-1775) of this variety; Karimanagar hoard – 1 coin; Mambalam hoard – 5 coins; Vembavur hoard – 4 coins; Veersigmani hoard – 1 coin; Bhimalipatan hoard – 1 coin; Dharapuram hoard – 1 coin; Venne hoard – 1 coin; Bahal hoard – 1 coin; Bhandara hoard – 1 coin; Umrer hoard – 1 coin; Rairh hoards (I) – 3 coins, (IV) – 1 coin, (V) – 1 coin; Taxila hoard (BHU-No. 2) – 2 coins; Peshawar hoard – 1 coin; Lalganj hoard – 1 coin; Gorakhpur hoard – 1 coin; Kausambi hoard – 1 coin; Gokulvan hoard – 1 coin; Mathura hoards – 5, 2, 2,1 coins; U. P. T. T. R. No. 28/1916 hoard – 1 coin; Patraha hoard – 20 coins; Machuatoli hoard – 17 coins; Gorhoghat hoard – 1 coin; Bhalna hoard – 1 coin; Mayurbhanj hoard – 3 coins; and Barwani hoard – 9 coins (71.548/23-31).

(iii) Va. I. A2. (8 coins) (S. no. 40, Fig. 10, 2002.98; Pl. V (2-4) and Pl.VI (5-8) 2002.93-97, 99-100). This variety is noticed in Amaravati hoard on 85 coins (1776-1860); Karimanagar hoard – 8 coins; Gulbarga hoard – 4 coins; Raichur hoard – 1 coin; Mambalam hoard – 4 coins; Vembavur hoard – 2 coins; Veersigmani hoard – 1 coin; Dharapuram hoard – 1 coin; Bahal hoard – 17 coins; Palanpur hoard – 1 coin; Baroda hoard – 2 coins; Umrer hoard – 1 coin; Rairh hoards (I) – 2 coins, (II) – 2 coins, (IV) – 4 coins and (V) – 3 coins; Taxila hoard (BHU-No. 1) – 1 coin; Lalganj hoard – 6 coins; Allahabad hoard – 1 coin; Kausambi hoard – 1 coin; Gokulvan hoard (Uttar Pradesh) – 1 coin; Mathura hoards – 8, 2, 1 coins; Patraha hoard – 20 coins; Machuatoli hoard – 24 coins; Mayurbhanj hoard – 6 coins; and Barwani hoard – 15 coins (71.548/1-15).

(iv) Va. I. A3. (2 coins) (S. no. 41, Fig. 10, 2002.101; Pl. VI (2) 2002.102).
This variety is noticed from Amaravati hoard on 9 coins (1718-1726); Karimanagar hoard – 5 coins; Mambalam hoard – 3 coins; Vizagapatam hoard – 1 coin; Bhimalipatan hoard – 1 coin; Vembavur hoard (No. 2) – 1 coin; Bahal hoard – 3 coins; Bhandara hoard – 1 coin; Umrer hoard – 1 coin; Big Bhir mound hoard – 20 coins; Taxila hoard (BHU-No. 1) – 1 coin; Lalganj hoard – 3 coins; Rairh hoards (II) – 1 coin and (V) – 1 coin; Gokulvan hoard – 1 coin; Mathura hoards – 1, 1, 1 coins; U. P. T. T. R. No. 28/1916 hoard – 1 coin; Patraha hoard – 7 coins; Machuatoli hoard – 5 coins; Mayurbhanj hoard – 1 coin; and Barwani hoard – 4 coins (71.548/2153-2156).

(v) Va. I. A4. (20 coins) (S. no. 42, Fig. 10, 2002.103; Pl.VI (2-6) and Pl.VII (7-20) 2002.104-122). This variety is seen in Amaravati hoard on 392 coins (1985-2376); Gulbarga hoard – 4 coins; Karimnagar hoard – 11 coins; Kondapur find – 1 coin; Mambalam hoard – 11 coins; Vizagapatam hoard – 1 coin; Veersigmani hoard – 1 coin; Kauniankuttai hoard (Distt. Salem) – 2 coins; Bhimalipatan hoard – 5 coins; Vembavur hoard (No. 2) – 1 coin; Venne hoard – 2 coins; Gudivada hoard – 1 coin; Bahal hoard – 48 coins; Bhandara hoard – 4 coins; Umrer hoard – 1 coin; Baroda hoard – 9 coins; Palanpur hoard – 2 coins; Rairh hoards (I) – 16 coins, (II) – 1 coin, (IV) – 3 coins, (V) – 16 coins; Taxila hoards (BHU- No. 1) – 23 coins and (BHU-No. 2) – 2 coins; lalganj hoard – 4 coins; Gorakhpur hoard – 1 coin; Allahabad hoard – 2 coins; Hathuma hoard – 1 coin; Gokulvan hoard – 21 coins; Harha hoard – 2 coins; Mathura hoards – 12, 1, 4 coins; Patraha hoard – 50 coins; Machuatoli hoard – 128 coins; Gorhoghat hoard – 1 coin; Mayurbhanj hoard – 9 coins; and Barwani hoard – 156 coins (71.548/1456-1607 and 1609-1612).

(vi) Va. I. A5. (5 coins) (S. no. 43, Fig. 11, 2002.127; Pl.VIII (2-5) 2002.126, 123-125).
One hundred and twenty coins (1860-1979) of this variety are noticed in Amaravati hoard; Karimnagar hoard – 6 coins; Raichur hoard – 1 coin; Mambalam hoard – 14 coins; Vembavur hoard (No. 1) – 2 coins and (No. 2) – 1 coin; Vizagapatam hoard – 1 coin; Bahal hoard – 7 coins;

Thathari hoard – 1 coin; Baroda hoard – 1 coin; Palanpur hoard – 2 coins; Taxila hoard (BHU-No. 2) – 1 coin; Lalganj hoard – 5 coins; Gorakhpur hoard – 5 coins; Rairh hoards (I) – 3 coins, (II) – 1 coin, (IV) – 1 coin and (V) 15 coins; Kausambi hoard – 1 coin; Harha hoard – 1 coin; Mathura hoards – 6, 1, 1 coins; Patraha hoard – 33 coins; Machuatoli hoard – 21 coins; Gohada hoard (Monghyr, Bihar)– 1 coin; Mayurbhanj hoard – 3 coins; and Barwani hoard – 16 coins (71.548/32- 42, 97-101).

(vii) Va. II. A. (3 coins) (S. no. 44, Fig. 11, 2002.128; Pl.VIII (2-3) 2002.129-130).
This variety is found in Amaravati hoard on 74 coins (2401-2474); Karimnagar hoard – 2 coins; Gulbarga hoard – 3 coins; Raichur hoard – 2 coins; Mambalam hoard – 4 coins; Bhimalipatan hoard – 3 coins; Venne hoard – 1 coin; Bahal hoard – 15 coins; Bhandara hoard – 1 coin; Kasarawad hoard – 1 coin; Taxila hoard (BHU-No. 1) – 1 coin; Gorakhpur hoard – 1 coin; Rairh hoards (I) – 1 coin, (II) – 2 coins, (IV) – 2 coins and (V) – 3 coins; Kausambi hoard – 1 coin; Gokulvan hoard – 2 coins; Mathura hoards – 2, 1, 2 coins; U.P.T.T.R. No. 28/1916 hoard – 1 coin; Patraha hoard – 11 coins; Machuatoli hoard – 32 coins; Gorhoghat hoard – 1 coin; and Barwani hoard – 24 coins (71.548/ 2191-2214).

(viii) Va. III. A. (8 coins) (S. no. 45, Fig. 11, 2002.136; Pl.VIII (2-5) and Pl. IX (6-8) 2002.131-135, 137-138).
This variety is noticed in Amaravati hoard on 118 coins (3834-3951); Karimnagar hoard – 2 coins; Gulbarga hoard – 2 coins; Mambalam hoard – 4 coins; Vembavur hoard – 3 coins; Vizagapatam hoard – 4 coins; Veersigmani hoard – 2 coins; Bhimalipatan hoard – 1 coin; Bahal hoard – 6 coins, Akkalkot hoard (Maharashtra) – 1 coin; Baroda hoard – 1 coin, Rairh hoards (I) – 4 coins, (IV) – 1 coin and (V) – 7 coins; Taxila hoard (BHU-No. 2) – 1 coin; Peshawar hoard – 1 coin; Lalganj hoard – 4 coins; Gorakhpur hoard – 4 coins; Allahabad hoards (No. 1) – 1 coin and (No. 2) – 1 coin; Gokulvan hoard – 7 coins; Mathura hoard – 4, 2, 1 coins; U. P. T. T. R. No. 28/1916 hoard – 3 coins; Patraha hoard – 38 coins; Machuatoli hoard – 36 coins; Gorhoghat hoard – 2 coins; and Barwani hoard – 32 coins (71.548/3108 - 3116, 3129-3134, 3144-3160).

(ix) Va. IV. A. (1 coin) (S. no. 46, Fig. 11, 2002.332).
Amaravati hoard contains 39 coins (3966-4004) of this variety; Karimnagar hoard – 1 coin; Bahal hoard – 1 coin; Rairh hoards (IV) – 1 coin and (V) – 1 coin; Gokulvan hoard – 7 coins; Gorakhpur hoard – 1 coin; Mathura hoard – 1 coin; Patraha hoard – 8 coins; Machuatoli hoard – 17 coins; Tregna hoard – 8 coins; and Barwani hoard – 6 coins (71.548/3252-3257).

(x) Va. V. A. (1 coin) (S. no. 47, Fig. 12, 2002.139).
This variety is noticed in Amaravati hoard on 15 coins (3791-3805); Karimnagar hoard – 2 coins; Bhimalipatan hoard – 1 coin; Bahal hoard – 3 coins; Lalganj hoard – 1 coin; Hathuma hoard – 1 coin; Gokulvan hoard – 1 coin; U. P. T. T. R. No. 28/1916 hoard – 1 coin; Patraha hoard – 3 coins; Machuatoli hoard – 4 coin and Barwani hoard – 9 coins (71.548/ 2492-2500).

(xi) Va. V. A1. (2 coins) (S. no. 48, Fig. 12, 2002.140; Pl. IX (2) 2002.333).
This variety is seen in Amaravati hoard on 16 coins (3806-3821); Vembavur hoard – 1 coin; Bahal hoard – 4 coins; Rairh hoards (I) – 1 coin, (IV) – 3 coins and (V) – 3 coins; Patraha hoard – 1 coin; and Barwani hoard – 1 coin (71.548/2108).

(xii) Va. VI. A. (5 coins) (S. no. 49, Fig. 12, 2002.143; Pl. IX (2-5) 2002.141-142, 144-145).
This variety is noticed in Amaravati hoard on 45 coins (3633-3677); Karimnagar hoard – 7 coins; Gulbarga hoard – 3 coins; Bhimalipatan hoard – 1 coin; Bahal hoard – 4 coins; Rairh

hoard (V) – 1 coin; Taxila hoard (BHU-No. 2) – 1 coin; Gokulvan hoard – 13 coins; Harha hoard – 1 coin; Mathura hoard – 1 coin; Machuatoli hoard – 19 coins; and Patraha hoard – 6 coins.

(xiii) Va. VII. A. (3 coins) (S. no. 50, Fig. 12, 2002.148; Pl. IX (2- 3) 2002.146, 147).
This variety is found on 63 coins (2568-2630) in Amaravati hoard; Karimanagar hoard – 2 coins; Gulbarga hoard – 6 coins; Raichur hoard – 1 coin; Mambalam hoard – 5 coins; Vembavur hoard – 6 coins; Kauniankuttai hoard – 1 coin; Bhimalipatan hoard – 1 coin; Venne hoard – 1 coin; Bahal hoard – 10 coins; Akkalkot hoard – 1 coin; Umrer hoard – 2 coins; Thathari hoard – 1 coin; Rairh hoards (I) – 1 coin and (V) – 1 coin; Taxila hoard (BHU- No. 2) – 2 coins; Peshawar hoard – 1 coin; Lalganj hoard – 2 coins; Kausambi haord – 1 coin; Gokulvan hoard – 3 coins; Mathura hoards 2, 1, 1 coins; Patraha hoard – 14 coins; Machuataoli hoard – 22 coins; Bhalana hoard (Bihar) – 1 coin; and Barwani hoard – 14 coins (71.548/2012-2025).

(xiv) Va. VIII. A. (4 coins) (S. no. 51, Fig. 13, 2002-152; Pl. IX (2-4) 2002.149-151).
This variety is seen in Amaravati hoard on 103 coins (3452-3554); Karimnagar hoard – 4 coins; Gulbarga hoard – 2 coins; Mambalam hoard – 2 coins; Vembavur hoard – 2 coins; Vizagapatam hoard – 3 coins; Bahal hoard – 9 coins; Umrer hoard – 1 coin; Thathari hoard – 1 coin; Bhandara hoard – 1 coin; Baroda hoard – 1 coin; Rairh hoards (I) – 3 coins, (II) – 2 coins, (IV) – 2 coins and (V) – 6 coins); Lalganj hoard – 2 coins; Gorakhpur hoard – 3 coins; Gokulvan hoard – 12 coins; Mathura hoards – 6, 2 coins; Patraha hoard – 32 coins; Machuatoli hoard – 34 coins; Gorhoghat hoard – 1 coin; and Barwani hoard – 39 coins (71-548/2422-2460).

Series Vb: (55 coins) constitute 11 varieties.

(i) Vb. I. A. (9 coins) (S. no. 52, Fig. 13, 2002.164; Pl. X (2-9) 2002.153, 161, 163, 166-167, 169, 171-172).
Seven hundred coins (2631-3296, 3298-3330) in Amaravati hoard belong to this variety; Karimnagar hoard – 16 coins; Gulbarga hoard – 13 coins; Raichur hoard – 3 coins; Mambalam hoard – 15 coins; Vembavur hoard – 7 coins; Vizagapatam hoard – 2 coins; Veersigamani hoard – 1 coin; Kauniankuttai hoard – 2 coins; Bhimalipatan hoard – 6 coins; Venne hoard – 6 coins; Bahal hoard – 73 coins; Bhandara hoard – 4 coins; Umrer hoard – 9 coins; Rairh hoards (I) – 29 coins, (II) – 1 coin, (IV) – 22 coins and (V) – 4 coins; Taxila hoard (BHU-No. 1) – 12 coins and (BHU- No. 2) – 11 coins; Peshawar hoard – 1 coin; Gorakhpur hoard – 23 coins; Allahabad hoards – 6 and 1 coin; Hathuma hoard – 3 coins; Gokulvan hoard – 72 coins; Harha hoard – 1 coin; Mathura hoards – 33, 5, 13, 2 and 1 coins; U. P. T. T. R. No. 28/1916 hoard – 5 coins; Patraha hoard – 52 coins; Machuatoli hoard – 283 coins; Gorhoghat hoard – 3 coins; Bhalana hoard – 6 coins; Ramna hoard – 1 coin; and Barwani hoard – 117 coins.

(ii) Vb. I. A1. (7 coins) (S. no. 53, Fig. 13, 2002.176; Pl. X (2-4) and Pl. XI (5-7) 2002.177-182).
This variety is noticed in Amaravati hoard on 31 coins (3332-3337, 3339-3363) and Barwani hoard – 11 coins.

(iii) Vb. I. A2. (3 coins) (S. no. 54, Fig. 13, 2002.185; Pl. XI (2-3) 2002.183-184).
This variety is seen in Amaravati hoard on 19 coins (3338, 3364-3381) and Barwani hoard on 34 coins.

(iv) Vb. I. A3. (14 coins) (Unattributed) (S.no. 55, Fig. 14, 2002.156; Pl. XI (2-10) and Pl. XII (11-14) 2002.154-155, 157-160, 162, 165, 168, 170, 173, 174).

On these coins, the fifth symbol, i.e. stag before a twig, with an object at its back, is not clear. In most of the cases, it is either out of flan or seen partly. Hence, the variety of such coins cannot be determined. These coins are grouped together and classified as unattributed variety. Numbers of such coins in this variety are more in other hoards also. Seventy-six such coins have been noticed in Barwani hoard, where the object at the back of stag is out of flan or only partly seen.

(v) Vb. II. A. (1 coin) (S. no. 56, Fig. 14, 2002.186).
Amaravati hoard contains 60 coins (3555-3614) of this variety; Mambalam hoard – 1 coin; Bahal hoard – 5 coins, Bhandara hoard – 2 coins; Umrer hoard – 1 coin; Rairh hoards (I) and (IV) – 3 coins each; Lalganj hoard – 1 coin; Allahabad hoard – 1 coin; Hathuma hoard – 1 coin; Gokulvan hoard – 14 coins; Mathura hoard – 6 coins; U. P. T. T. R. No. 28/1916 hoard – 1 coin; Patraha hoard – 13 coins; Machuatoli hoard – 26 coins; and Barwani hoard - 14 coins.

(vi) Vb. II. A1. (1 coin) (S. no. 57, Fig. 14, 2002.187).
This variety is noticed in Amaravati hoard on 7 coins (3615-3621) and in Barwani hoard on 6 coins (71.548/2502-2503, 2506-2508, 2512).

(iii) Vb. II. B. (3 coins), (S. no. 58, Fig. 14, 2002.190; Pl. XII (2-3) 2002.188- 189).
41 coins (3744-3784) of this variety are present in Amaravati hoard on Karimnagar hoard – 5 coins; Gulbarga hoard – 2 coins; Mambalam hoard – 5 coins; Vembavur hoard – 1 coin; Bahal hoard – 6 coins; Akkalkot hoard – 1 coin; Bhandara hoard – 1 coin; Rairh hoards (I) – 3 coins, (IV) – 3 coins and (V) – 2 coins; Kausambi hoard – 2 coins; Gokulvan hoard – 3 coins; Mathura hoard – 2 coins; Patraha hoard – 9 coins; Machuatoli hoard – 18 coins; and Barwani hoard – 1 coin (71.548/2510).

(i) Vb. II. B1. (2 coins) (S. no. 59, Fig. 15, 2002.191; Pl. XII (2) 2002.192).
This variety is noticed in Amaravati hoard on 70 coins (3622-3632, 3685-3743); Karimnagar hoard – 2 coins; Gulbarga hoard – 2 coins; Vizagapatam hoard – 2 coins; Bahal hoard – 1 coin; Bhandara hoard – 2 coins; Umrer hoard – 1 coin; Thathari hoard – 1 coin; Bilaspur hoard – 1 coin; Kasarwad hoard – 1 coin; Rairh hoards (I) – 2 coins, (II) – 2 coins, (IV) – 1 coin, (V) – 3 coins; Taxila hoards (BHU-No. 1) – 1 coin and (BHU-No. 2) – 1 coin; Gokulvan hoard – 5 coins; Hathuma hoard – 1 coin; Mathura hoard – 1 coin; U. P. T. T. R. No. 28/1916 hoard – 1 coin; Patraha hoard – 5 coins; Machuatoli hoard – 2 coins; and Barwani hoard – 9 coins (71.548/731-739).

(ii) Vb. III. A. (2 coins) (S. no. 60, Fig. 15, 2002.194; Pl. XIII (2) 2002.193).
Sixteen coins (2502-2517) belong to this variety in Amaravati hoard; Bahal hoard – 1 coin; Gokulvan hoard – 4 coins; Machuatoli hoard – 8 coins; Patraha hoard – 3 coins; and Barwani hoard – 12 coins (71.548/2461-2472).

(iii) Vb. IV. A. (1 coin) (S. no. 61, Fig. 15, 2002.195).
This variety is noticed in Amaravati hoard on 4 coins (3829-3832 in Barwani hoard – 6 coins (71.548/2945-2950).

(iv). Vb. V. A. (2 coins) (S. no. 62, Fig. 15, 2002.196; Pl. XII (2) 2002.197).
This variety is seen in Amaravati hoard on 7 coins (3958-3964); Bahal hoard – 1 coin; Vizagapatam hoard – 1 coin; Patraha hoard – 1 coin (814a); and Barwani hoard – 1 coin (71.548/2951).

Series VI: (133 coins).

Series, VIa. (16 coins) constitute 4 varieties.

(i). VIa. I. A. (1 coin) (S. no. 63, Fig. 16, 2002.198).
This variety is noticed in Amaravati hoard on 2 coins (3953-3954); Karimnagar hoard – 4 coins; Patraha hoard – 3 coins; and Barwani hoard – 5 coins (71.548/3268 – 3270, 3277-3278).

(ii) VIa. II. A. (9 coins) (S. no. 64, Fig. 16, 2002.199; Pl. XIII (2-9) 2002.200-207).
This variety is seen on 89 coins (5558, 5561-5648) in Amaravati hoard; Nasthulapur hoard (Hyderabad) – 1 coin; Bhandara hoard – 1 coin; Bahal hoard – 6 coins; Baroda hoard – 1 coin; Rairh hoard (V) – 9 coins; Taxila hoards (BHU-No. 1) – 2 coins and (BHU-No. 2) – 1 coin; Peshawar hoard – 1 coin; Gorakhpur hoard – 1 coin; Mathura hoards – 6, 3 coins; U. P. T. T. R. No. 28/1916 hoard – 1 coin; Patraha hoard – 23 coins; Machuatoli hoard – 34 coins; Mayurbhanj hoard – 1 coin; and Barwani hoard – 1 coin (71.548/3054).

(iii) VIa. II. A1. (2 coins) (S. no. 65, Fig. 16, 2002.208; Pl. XIII (2) 2002.209).
This variety is seen in Amaravati hoard on 77 coins (5481-5557); Karimnagar hoard – 4 coins; Bhandara hoard – 3 coins; Taxila hoard (BHU-No.1) – 3 coins; Allahabad hoard – 1 coin; Mathura hoards – 2, 1, 2 coins; Patraha hoard – 20 coins; Machuatoli hoard – 15 coins; Gorhoghat hoard – 1 coin; Mayurbhanj hoard – 1 coin; and Barwani hoard – 33 coins (71.548/3055, 3057 – 3074, 3076 – 3089).

(iv) VIa. II. A2. (4 coins) (S. no. 66, Fig. 16, 2002.210; Pl. XIII (2-4) 2002.211-213).
Amaravati hoard contains 71 coins (5665-5735) of this variety; Venne hoard – 1 coin; Bahal hoard – 4 coins; Bhandara hoard – 1 coin; Gorhoghat hoard – 1 coin; Machuatoli hoard – 1 coin; Hathuma hoard – 1 coin; and Barwani hoard – 40 coins (71.548/3090-3101, 3117-3128, 3135-3143, 3161-3166, 3194).

Series VIb: (117 coins) constitute 10 varieties.

(i) VIb. I. A. (19 coins) (S. no. 67. Fig. 17, 2002.219; Pl. XIV (2-13) and Pl. XV (14-19) 2002.214-218, 220-232).
This variety is noticed in Amaravati hoard on 196 coins; Karimnagar hoard – 8 coins; Gulbarga hoard – 12 coins; Raichur hoard – 1 coin; Mambalam hoard – 19 coins; Vembavur hoards (No. 1) – 2 coins and (No. 2) – 1 coin; Vizagapatam hoard – 3 coins; Veersigmani hoard – 14 coins; Bhimalipatan hoard – 1 coin; Tondamanatham hoard (South Arcot) – 5 coins; Dharapuram hoard – 2 coins; Venne hoard – 2 coins; Gudivada hoard – 3 coins; Bahal hoard – 27 coins; Bhandara haord – 4 coins; Thathari hoard – 2 coins; Kasarwad hoard – 7 coins; Baroda hoard – 1 coin; Palanpur hoard – 2 coins; Rairh hoards (I) – 4 coins, (III) – 1 coin, (IV) – 4 coins and (V) 12 coins; Taxila hoards (BHU-No. 1) – 18 coins and (BHU-No. 2) – 13 coins; Peshawar hoard – 1 coin; Gorakhpur hoard – 4 coins; Allahabad hoard – 4 coins; Mathura hoards – 5, 3, 4 coin; U. P. T. T. R. No. 28/1916 hoard – 2 coins; Hathuma hoard – 14 coins; Patraha hoard – 43 coins;

Machuatoli hoard – 78 coins; Bhalna hoard – 37 coins; and Barwani hoard – 16 coins (71.548/ 2046, 2959-2971, 3056, 3246).

(ii) VIb. I. A1. (43 coins) (S. no. 68, Fig. 17, 2002.248; Pl. XV (2-9) Pl. XVI (10-21), Pl. XVII (22-33) and Pl. XVIII (34-43) (2002.233-247, 248-274).
Ninety-two coins (4217-5206, 6708, 7513) of this variety are found in Amaravati hoard; Karimnagar hoard – 9 coins; Gulbarga hoard – 14 coins; Mambalam hoard – 10 coins; Vembavur hoards (No. 1) – 1 coin and (No. 2) – 1 coin; Vizagapatam hoard – 3 coins; Veersigamani hoard – 6 coins; Bhimalipatan hoard – 3 coins; Bhandara hoard – 1 coin; Umrer hoard – 5 coins; Thathari hoard – 1 coin; Rairh hoards (I) – 16 coins, (II) – 4 coins, (IV) – 9 coins and (V) – 102 coins; Taxila hoards (BHU- No. 1) – 53 coins and (BHU- No. 2) – 2 coins; Peshawar hoard – 5 coins; Sialkot hoard – 5 coins; Gorakhpur hoard – 2 coins; Allahabad hoards (No. 1) – 13 coins and (No. 2) – 2 coins; Kausambi hoard – 1 coin; Harha hoard – 2 coins; Mathura hoards – 39, 2, 17 coins; U. P. T. T. R. No. 28/1916 hoard – 4 coins; Patraha hoard – 143 coins; Machuatoli hoard – 385 coins; Gorhoghat hoard – 11 coins; Jalloy hoard (Darbhanga, Bihar) – 2 coins; Bhalna hoard 18 coins; and Barwani hoard – 93 coins (71.548/ 2215- 2306, 2957).

(iii) VIb. I. B. (18 coins) (S. no. 69, Fig. 17, 2002.282; Pl. XIX (2-15) and Pl. XX (16-18) 2002.275-281, 283-293).
This variety is noticed in Amaravati hoard on 69 coins (5368-5436); Bahal hoard – 6 coins; Taxila hoard (BHU-No. 1) – 14 coins; Machuatoli hoard – 32 coins; Ahraura hoard – 1 coin; and Barwani hoard – 633 coins (71.548/190-459, 989-991, 993, 995-1221, 1223-1352, 1608, 2958).

(v) VIb. I. C. (4 coins) (S.no. 70, Fig. 17, 2002.294; Pl. XX (2-4) 2002.295- 297).
This variety is noticed in Amaravati hoard on 32 coins (6420-6426, 6428-6452); Karimnagar hoard – 3 coins; Mambalam hoard – 1 coin; Bahal hoard – 6 coins; Rairh hoards (I) – 5 coins; and (V) – 5 coins; Gorakhpur hoard – 1 coin; Patraha hoard – 6 coins; Machuatoli hoard – 16 coins; Bhalna hoard – 1 coin and Barwani hoard – 56 coins (71.548/3306-3361).

(v) VIb. I. C1. (6 coins) (S. no. 71, Fig. 18, 2002.298; Pl. XX (2-4) and Pl. XXI (5-6) 2002.299-303).
This variety is noticed in Amaravati hoard on 207 coins (6116-6161, 6163-6193, 6195-6322, 6854, 6855); Karimnagar hoard – 1 coin; Gulbarga hoard – 5 coins; Rothulapalam hoard (Vizagapatam) – 1 coin; Vizagapatam hoard – 1 coin; Veersigamani hoard – 1 coin; Venne hoard – 1 coin; Bhandara hoard – 1 coin; Baroda hoard – 2 coins; Rairh hoards (I) – 10 coins, (II) – 3 coins, (IV) – 4 coins and (V) – 15 coins; Taxila hoards (BHU-No. 1) – 2 coins and (BHU-No. 2) – 8 coins; Gorakhpur hoard – 2 coins; Allahabad hoard – 2 coins; Hardoi hoard – 2 coins; Mathura hoards – 10, 1, 7, 1 coins; U. P. T. T. R. No. 28/1916 hoard – 1 coin; Patraha hoard – 64 coins; Machuatoli hoard – 67 coins; Bhalna hoard – 2 coins; and Barwani hoard – 1 coin (71.548/2953).

(vi) VIb. I. C2. (5 coins) (S. no. 72, Fig. 18, 2002.306; Pl. XXI (2-5) 2002.304-305, 307).
This variety is present in Amaravati hoard on 99 coins (6492-6590); Karimnagar hoard – 3 coins; Mambalam hoard – 2 coins; Kauniankuttai hoard – 1 coin; Venne hoard – 1 coin; Bahal hoard – 1 coin; Bhandara hoard – 2 coins; Umrer hoard – 1 coin; Bilaspur hoard – 1 coin; Rairh hoards (I) – 1 coin, (II) – 1 coin, (IV) – 2 coins and V) – 4 coins; Mathura hoards – 4, 8 coins; Patraha hoard – 9 coins; Machuatoli hoard – 14 coins; Bhalna hoard – 1 coin; and Barwani hoard – 103 coins (71.548/ 2515-2616, 3197).

(vii) VIb. I. C3. (1 coin) (S.no. 73, Fig. 18, 2002.309).
This variety is noticed in Amaravati hoard on 66 coins (6605-6670); Machuatoli hoard – 1 coin; and Barwani hoard – 30 coins (71.548/43-71, 2144).

(viii) VIb. I. D. (9 coins) (S. no. 74, Fig. 18, 2002.313; Pl. XXI (2-5) and Pl. XXII (6-9) 2002.310-312, 314-318).
Two hundred and six coins (5768-5924, 5925-5969 and 5970-5973) belong to this variety in Amaravati hoard; Gulbarga hoard – 2 coins; Kondapur find – 1 coin; Bhandara hoard – 2 coins; Thathari hoard – 2 coins; Baroda hoard – 1 coin; Rairh hoards (I) – 4 coins, (II) – 1 coin and (V) – 12 coin; Taxila hoards (BHU-No. 1) – 4 coins and (BHU-No. 2) – 5 coins; Sialkot hoard – 1 coin; Lalganj hoard–2 coins; Gorakhpur hoard – 1 coin; Allahabad hoard – 3 coins; Hathuma hoard – 2 coins; Mathura hoards – 7, 1, 6, 1 coins; Patraha hoard – 41 coins; Machuatoli hoard – 50 coins; Bhalna hoard – 12 coins; and Barwani hoard – 23 coins (71.548/2116-2118, 2122, 2124-2126, 2128- 2139, 2141, 2143, 2145, 3244).

Coins of this group have been listed in Amaravati Hoard with slight variations in the forms of 5th and 2nd symbols and grouped - VI.III.H.1a, 1b, and 1c. Gupta classified this variety into three sub-varieties – VI. III. H. 1a (157 coins, 5768-5924), VI. III. H. 1b (45 coins, 5925-5969) and V. III. H. 1c (4 coins, 5970-5973), mentioned unnoticed. He further noticed this variety on another 114 coins (5974-6087) but here the front part of the bull is mostly out of flan and hence, not possible to attribute them to any of these varieties. He also noticed 28 such coins (6088-6115) where the fifth symbol is not clear and it is difficult to say if they belonged to any of these sub-varieties. Either they had a quite different fifth mark and constitute a different variety or these coins can be arranged under any of this variety a, b or c (*Am,* 100-101).

He classified such coins into these sub-varieties because he found slight variatons in the form of fifth symbol on these coins. He also proposed that since this hoard has a large number of coins, it could be possible to delete the two forms (*Am,* 100).

Gupta classified all the coins belonging to these varieties, in Amaravati hoard, into three sub-varieties (VI. III. H. Ia-c), grouped them together and found the total number of coins as 206. However, in his latest work with Hardaker, he merged these three sub-varieties into one variety (*AISPMC,* VI. IV. E. 27, 571).

(ix) VIb. I. E. (10 coins) (S. no. 75, Fig. 19, 2002.324; Pl. XXII (2-8) and Pl. XXIII (9-10) 2002.319-323, 325-327).
This variety is noticed in Amaravati hoard on 58 coins (5250-5307); Bahal hoard – 8 coins; Rairh hoard (I) – 2 coins; Gorakhpur hoard – 1 coin; Mathura hoards – 1, 1 coins; Machuatoli hoard – 14 coins; Patraha hoard – 18 coins; Mayurbhanj hoard – 2 coins; and Barwani hoard – 134 coins (71.548/1613-1745, 3421).

(x). VIb. I. E1. (2 coins) (S. no. 76, Fig. 19, 2002.329; Pl. XXIII (2) 2002.330).
This variety is seen in Amaravati hoard on 20 coins (5308-5327); Bahal hoard – 1 coin; Rairh hoard (I) – 1 coin; Mathura hoard – 1 coin; Machuatoli hoard – 5 coins; Gorhoghat hoard – 2 coins; Tregna hoard – 1 coin; and Barwani hoard – 18 coins (71.548/2042-2045, 2091, 2093-2105).

Part IV
APPENDICES

I

Weights and Measures

Table 8. Weights and Measures.

S. No.	Series Acc. No.	wt. (gms.) / sz. (cms.)	Thickness (cms.)	No. of coins
1.	**II.I.A**			
	2002.1	3.2383 / 2.10 x 1.40	0.15	1
2.	**II.II.A**			
	2002.2	3.2815 / 2.23	0.11	1
3.	**III.I.A**			
	2002.3	3.1705 / 2.30 x 1.70	0.10	1
4.	**III.II.A**			
	2002.5	3.0863 / 2.05 x 1.90	0.15	7
	2002.8	3.2522 / 2.06	0.15	
	2002.4	3.2120 / 2.30 x 2.14	0.10	
	2002.6	3.2427 / 2.10	0.15	
	2002.7	3.2624 / 2.40	0.15	
	2002.9	3.2885 / 2.40 x 1.25	0.20	
	2002.10	3.1499 / 1.30 x 2.41	0.15	
5.	**III.III.A**			
	2002.11	3.2145 / 2.23 x 1.36	0.12	1
6.	**III.III.A1**			
	2002.14	3.2114 / 2.05 x 1.40	0.18	6
	2002.12	3.1360 / 2.00 x 1.40	0.18	
	2002.13	3.2546 / 2.05 x 1.44	0.15	
	2002.18	3.2675 / 2.15 x 1.40	0.15	
	2002.17	3.2672 / 1.33 x 2.12	0.12	
	2002.16	3.2497 / 2.40 x 1.25	0.12	

S. No.	Series Acc. No.	wt. (gms.) / sz. (cms.)	Thickness (cms.)	No. of coins
7.	**III.III.A2**			
	2002.19	3..2547/ 1.45 x 1.40	0.15	2
	2002.15	3.2308 / 2.00 x 1.50	0.15	
8.	**IVb.I.A**			
	2002.20	3.3130 / 1.90 x 1.40	0.15	1
9.	**IVb.I.A1**			
	2002.21	3.3329 / 1.92 x 1.95	0.15	1
10.	**IVc.I.A**			
	2002.22	3.4189 / 1.76 x 1.20	0.21	1
11.	**IVc.II.A**			
	2002.23	3.3047 / 1.60	0.20	1
12.	**IVd.I.A**			
	2002.24	3.4673 / 1.30	0.30	1
13.	**IVd.I.A1**			
	2002.26	3.4346 / 1.60 x 1.50	0.19	2
	2002.25	3.3329 / 1.60 x 1.30	0.19	
14.	**IVd.I.B**			
	2002.27	3.3373 / 2.20 x 1.40	0.12	1
15.	**IVd.I.C**			
	2002.28	3.3186 / 2.10 x 1.20	0.19	1
16.	**IVd.I.C1**			
	2002.29	3.3530 / 1.80 x 1.40	0.19	1
17.	**IVd.I.D**			
	2002.36	3.3093 /1.86	0.12	16
	2002.31	3.4152 /1.82	0.15	
	2002.34	3.3601 / 1.86	0.15	
	2002.32	3.2638 / 1.96	0.15	
	2002.33	3.2257 / 1.86	0.15	
	2002.35	3.3057 / 1.94	0.15	
	2002.37	3.2697 / 1.82 x 1.33	0.15	
	2002.45	3.3613 / 1.76 x 1.60	0.17	
	2002.38	3.4423 / 1.70 x 1.45	0.20	
	2002.39	3.2753 / 1.73 x 1.40	0.19	
	2002.30	3.2874 / 1.95 x 1.27	0.19	
	2002.42	3.2260 / 1.90 x 1.44	0.15	
	2002.44	3.2959 / 1.76 x 1.34	0.15	
	2002.41	3.3719 / 1.90 x 1.44	0.15	
	2002.40	3.3747 / 2.35 x 1.23	0.15	
	2002.43	3.1626 / 1.82 x 1.50	0.15	
18.	**IVd.I.D1**			
	2002.46	3.4350 / 1.75 x 1.46	0.19	1

S. No.	Series Acc. No.	wt. (gms.) / sz. (cms.)	Thickness (cms.)	No. of coins
19.	**IVd.I.D2**			
	2002.47	3.4229 / 1.73 x 1.40	0.20	1
20.	**IVd.I.D3**			
	2002.49	3.2347 / 2.10 x1.80	0.10	2
	2002.48	3.3298 / 2.02	0.10	
21.	**IVd.I.D4**			
	2002.51	3.2772 / 2.30 x 1.20	0.12	3
	2002.52	3.3976 / 2.20 x 1.50	0.15	
	2002.50	3.1951 / 2.20	0.12	
22.	**IVd.I.D5**			
	2002.53	3.3908 / 1.95 x 1.42	0.12	2
	2002.54	3.2606 / 1.84 x 1.40	0.12	
23.	**IVd.I.D6**			
	2002.56	3.3833 / 1.90	0.15	6
	2002.55	3.3700 / 1.52	0.19	
	2002.57	3.3797 / 1.64	0.21	
	2002.60	3.3666 / 1.73 x 1.25	0.20	
	2002.58	3.4407 / 1.62 x 1.32	0.20	
	2002.59	3.3158 / 1.80	0.20	
24.	**IVd.I.D7**			
	2002.62	3.4068 / 1.75 x 1.34	0.20	2
	2002.61	3.3342 / 1.72 x 1.60	0.15	
25.	**IVd.I.D8**			
	2002.63	3.4031 / 1.70	0.20	1
26.	**IVd.II.A**			
	2002.67	3.3689 / 2.10x 1.20	0.20	5
	2002.68	3.2916 / 2.15 x 1.20	0.20	
	2002.64	3.1891 / 2.10 x 1.45	0.18	
	2002.65	3.2250 / 1.90 x 1.40	0.20	
	2002.66	3.2465 / 1.64 x 1.45	0.15	
27.	**IVd.II.A1**			
	2002.331	3.2193 / 1.23 x 1.35	0.13	1
28.	**IVd.II.A2**			
	2002.69	3.3899 / 2.25 x 1.50	0.15	1
29.	**IVd.III.A**			
	2002.70	3.2320 / 2.10 x 1.60	0.15	3
	2002.71	3.3288 / 2.25 x 1.50	0.15	
	2002.72	3.4120 / 2.00	0.19	
30.	**IVd.III.A1**			
	2002.73	3.3345 / 1.75	0.15	1

S. No.	Series Acc. No.	wt. (gms.) / sz. (cms.)	Thickness (cms.)	No. of coins
31.	**IVd.III.A2**			
	2002.74	3.3206 / 2.25 x 1.25	0.19	1
32.	**IVd.IV.A**			
	2002.77	3.3015 /1.73 x 1.36	0.19	4
	2002.75	3.3016 / 1.85 x 1.35	0.19	
	2002.76	3.3048 / 2.07 x 1.15	0.19	
	2002.78	3.3077 / 1.76 x 1.36	0.19	
33.	**IVd.IV.A1**			
	2002.79	3.2276 / 1.85	0.15	1
34.	**IVd.V.A**			
	2002.80	3.4347 / 1.80 x1.40	0.19	1
35.	**IVd.V.A1**			
	2002.81	3.3916 / 1.76	0.15	1
36.	**IVd.VI.A**			
	2002.82	3.5271 / 1.20 x 1.02	0.14	1
37.	**IVd.VII.A**			
	2002.83	3.4750 / 1.50 x 1.25	0.35	1
38.	**Va.I.A.**			
	2002.90	3.4189 / 1.80 x 1.20	0.25	7
	2002.85	3.3234 / 1.60 x 1.30	0.35	
	2002.89	3.4500 / 1.26	0.30	
	2002.84	3.3827 / 1.34	0.30	
	2002.87	3.4274 / 1.60	0.35	
	2002.88	3.4683 / 1.63 x 1.40	0.21	
	2002.86	3.3819 / 1.70	0.30	
39.	**Va.I.A1**			
	2002.92	3.4301 / 1.62	0.20	2
	2002.91	3.3447 / 1.72 x 1.32	0.19	
40.	**Va.I.A2**			
	2002.98	3.4382 / 1.80 x 1.42	0.15	8
	2002.93	3.3818 / 1.84	0.15	
	2002.94	3.4178 / 1.73	0.15	
	2002.95	3.2646 / 1.76	0.15	
	2002.96	3.3977 / 1.70	0.15	
	2002.97	3.4178 / 1.80	0.15	
	2002.99	3.4559 / 1.60 x 1.42	0.19	
	2002.100	3.3584 / 1.60	0.15	
41.	**Va.I.A3**			
	2002.101	3.4357 / 1.66	0.15	2
	2002.102	3.2910 / 1.85 x 1.36	0.19	

S. No.	Series Acc. No.	wt. (gms.) / sz. (cms.)	Thickness (cms.)	No. of coins
42.	**Va.I.A4**			
	2002.103	3.4038 / 1.73 x 1.43	0.15	20
	2002.111	3.3130 / 1.80 x 1.00	0.21	
	2002.106	3.4022 / 1.65 x 1.00	0.27	
	2002.113	3.4242 / 1.50 x 1.20	0.25	
	2002.108	3.3696 / 1.75 x 1.05	0.21	
	2002.109	3.1915 / 1.73 x 1.14	0.20	
	2002.107	3.5974 / 1.72 x 1.10	0.21	
	2002.114	3.0910 / 1.20	0.20	
	2002.104	3.4218 / 1.40 x 1.2	0.21	
	2002.112	3.3587 / 1.22	0.21	
	2002.110	3.4007 / 1.20	0.25	
	2002.105	3.3815 / 1.23	0.25	
	2002.116	3.4061 / 1.43	0.21	
	2002.121	3.3434 / 1.70	0.20	
	2002.122	3.4736 / 1.60	0.20	
	2002.115	3.4340 / 1.74	0.26	
	2002.117	3.2826 / 1.40	0.21	
	2002.118	3.4531 / 1.34	0.21	
	2002.120	3.2447 / 1.36	0.29	
	2002.119	3.3300 / 1.46	0.25	
43.	**Va.I.A5**			
	2002.127	3.3894 / 1.82	0.15	5
	2002.126	3.3291 / 2.00	0.15	
	2002.123	3.3784 / 1.60	0.15	
	2002.124	3.4211 / 1.80 x 1.35	0.15	
	2002.125	3.4427 / 2.25 x 1.35	0.15	
44.	**Va.II.A**			
	2002.128	3.4342 / 1.56 x 1.24	0.21	3
	2002.129	3.3523 / 1.64 x1.04	0.21	
	2002.130	3.4170 / 1.83	0.21	
45.	**Va.III.A**			
	2002.136	3.4114 / 1.50 x 1.30	0.20	8
	2002.137	3.4158 / 1.30	0.21	
	2002.133	3.3240 / 1.75 / 1.20	0.21	
	2002.132	3.4540 / 1.42 x 1.20	0.25	
	2002.134	3.4047 / 1.64 x 1.20	0.21	
	2002.135	3.4013 /1.40 x 1.20	0.25	
	2002.138	3.4419 / 1.50	0.29	
	2002.131	3.3931 / 1.60	0.25	
46.	**Va.IV.A**			
	2002.332	3.4055 / 1.80	0.20	1

S. No.	Series Acc. No.	wt. (gms.) / sz. (cms.)	Thickness (cms.)	No. of coins
47.	**Va.V.A**			
	2002.139	3.4707 / 1.40 x 1.15	0.21	1
48.	**Va.V.A1**			
	2002.140	3.4846 / 1.36 x 1.25	0.20	2
	2002.333	1.6790 / 1.00 x 0.86	0.20	
49.	**Va.VI.A**			
	2002.143	3.4569 / 1.35	0.21	5
	2002.144	3.4266 / 1.50	0.21	
	2002.142	3.4481 / 1.60	0.21	
	2002.141	3.4626 / 1.37	0.25	
	2002.145	3.4097 / 1.30	0.25	
50.	**Va.VII.A**			
	2002.148	3.2749 / 1.96 x 1.30	0.15	3
	2002.147	3.2770 / 1.60 x 1.36	0.19	
	2002.146	3.4727 / 1.50	0.21	
51.	**Va.VIII.A**			
	2002.152	3.4997 / 1.64	0.25	4
	2002.150	3.4837 / 1.45	0.29	
	2002.151	3.3850 / 1.56	0.25	
	2002.149	3.4052 / 1.40	0.21	
52.	**Vb.I.A**			
	2002.164	3.4188 / 1.40 x 1.30	0.20	9
	2002.161	3.4478 / 1.30	0.25	
	2002.167	3.2128 / 1.35 x 1.25	0.20	
	2002.153	3.3900 / 1.65 x 1.03	0.21	
	2002.166	3.4366 / 1.53 x 1.25	0.20	
	2002.163	3.4340 / 1.56	0.20	
	2002.171	3.3681 / 1.60	0.25	
	2002.172	3.4586 / 1.55	0.25	
	2002.169	3.4588 / 1.45	0.25	
53.	**Vb.I.A1**			
	2002.176	3.4137 / 1.43 x 1.15	0.29	7
	2002.179	3.4153 / 1.56 x 1.05	0.25	
	2002.177	3.4516 / 1.80 x 1.00	0.25	
	2002.178	3.4293 / 1.32 x 1.15	0.25	
	2002.181	3.4225 / 1.5	0.21	
	2002.180	3.4808 / 1.30 x 1.13	0.29	
	2002.182	3.5202 / 1.45	0.25	
54.	**Vb.I.A2**			
	2002.185	3.3944 / 1.40	0.29	3
	2002.184	3.2723 / 1.64	0.21	
	2002.183	3.3169 / 1.55	0.25	

S. No.	Series Acc. No.	wt. (gms.) / sz. (cms.)	Thickness (cms.)	No. of coins
55.	**Vb.I.A3**			
	2002.156	3.5255 / 1.32 x 1.16	0.25	14
	2002.162	3.4808 / 1.14	0.30	
	2002.158	3.3794 / 1.16	0.35	
	2002.157	3.4939 / 1.35	0.29	
	2002.155	3.4898 / 1.30	0.21	
	2002.168	35485 / 1.33 x 1.23	0.25	
	2002.165	3.4805 / 1.60 x 1.10	0.21	
	2002.159	3.4481 / 1.45 x 0.90	0.30	
	2002.154	3.4481 / 1.35 x 1.00	0.21	
	2002.160	3.5612 / 1.36 x 1.05	0.30	
	2002.175	3.4434 / 1.46	0.29	
	2002.173	3.4001 / 1.50	0.25	
	2002174	3.4510 / 1.45	0.30	
	2002.170	3.3623 / 1.40	0.25	
56.	**Vb.II.A**			
	2002.186	3.4192 / 1.35	0.20	1
57.	**Vb.II.A1**			
	2002.187	3.5071 / 1.60	0.20	1
58.	**Vb.II.B**			
	2002.190	3.4959 / 1.50	0.20	3
	2002.188	3.4936 / 1.60	0.20	
	2002.189	3.4114 / 1.60 x 1.30	0.20	
59	**Vb.II.B1**			
	2002.191	3.4518 / 1.52	0.25	2
	2002.192	3.4740 / 1.40	0.25	
60.	**Vb.III.A**			
	2002.194	3.3952 / 1.35	0.20	2
	2002.193	3.3849 / 1.45 x 1.30	0.21	
61.	**Vb.IV.A**			
	2002.195	3.3224 / 1.50 x 1.30	0.20	1
62.	**Vb.V.A**			
	2002.196	3.4159 / 1.36	0.20	
	2002.197	3.5006 / 1.30 x 1.10	0.25	2
63.	**VIa.I.A**			
	2002.198	3.5750 / 1.40 x 1.10	0.25	1
64.	**VIa.II.A**			
	2002.199	3.4742 / 1.35 x 1.05	0.30	9
	2002.203	3.4326 / 1.35	0.30	
	2002.204	3.5016 / 1.40	0.30	
	2002.205	3.3197 / 1.40	0.30	
	2002.206	3.4195 / 1.50	0.30	

S. No.	Series Acc. No.	wt. (gms.) / sz. (cms.)	Thickness (cms.)	No. of coins
	2002.202	3.4237 / 1.37	0.30	
	2002.207	3.4569 / 1.52	0.29	
	2002.201	3.4881 / 1.46 x 1.16	0.25	
	2002.200	3.4866 / 1.34 x 1.14	0.30	
65.	**VIa.II.A1**			
	2002.208	3.4682 / 1.17 x 1.10	0.30	2
	2008.209	3.4544 / 1.25 x 1.05	0.30	
66.	**VIa.II.A2**			
	2002.210	3.4493 / 1.5 x 1.14	0.25	4
	2002.211	3.4719 / 1.42	0.29	
	2002.213	3.5018 / 1.22 x 1.13	0.30	
	2002.212	3.3264 / 1.16 x 1.32	0.25	
67.	**VIb.I.A**			
	2002.219	3.4441 / 1.45 x 1.23	0.25	19
	2002.224	3.5077 / 1.33	0.25	
	2002.225	3.4690 / 1.40 x 1.20	0.25	
	2002.227	3.5747 / 1.22	0.25	
	2002.216	3.4960 / 1.32 x 1.15	0.35	
	2002.215	3.4879 / 1.55 x 1.36	0.25	
	2002.214	3.5495 / 1.60 x 1.10	0.30	
	2002.229	3.4858 / 1.50 x 1.30	0.25	
	2002.217	3.4552 / 1.65 x 1.06	0.30	
	2002.223	3.4940 / 1.40 x 1.40	0.25	
	2002.221	3.4349 / 1.35 x 1.23	0.30	
	2002.218	3.5349 / 1.14	0.35	
	2002.222	3.4792 / 1.30 x 1.04	0.31	
	2002.228	3.4578 / 1.55 x 1.00	0.35	
	2002.226	3.4395 / 1.44 x 1.04	0.30	
	2002.230	3.4417 / 1.44 x 0.94	0.30	
	2002.220	3.4985 / 1.46 x 1.00	0.30	
	2002.232	3.5098 / 1.45	0.20	
	2002.231	3.4686 / 1.35	0.30	
68.	**VIb.I.A1**			
	2002.248	3.4386 / 1.55 x 1.33	0.25	43
	2002.238	3.2935 / 1.50 x 1.14	0.25	
	2002.233	3.2568 / 1.50 x 1.00	0.25	
	2002.267	3.5421 / 1.42 x 1.00	0.31	
	2002.243	3.3314 / 1.50 x 1.00	0.25	
	2002.249	3.4534 / 1.56 x 1.00	0.25	
	2002.268	3.4079 / 1.42 x 1.10	0.25	
	2002.271	3.3539 / 1.64 x 1.30	0.21	
	2002.275	3.3675 / 1.35 x 1.10	0.25	

S. No.	Series Acc. No.	wt. (gms.) / sz. (cms.)	Thickness (cms.)	No. of coins
	2002.240	3.5258 / 1.64 x 0.90	0.25	
	2002.241	3.4685 / 1.40 x 1.00	0.30	
	2002.262	3.3828 / 1.45 x 1.05	0.25	
	2002.254	3.4925 / 1.36 x 1.06	0.25	
	2002.253	3.5126 / 1.32 x1.00	0.25	
	2002.264	3.3845 / 1.25 x 1.10	0.30	
	2002.265	3.5379 / 1.24 x 1.10	0.30	
	2002.266	3.4693 / 1.25 x 1.05	0.30	
	2002.260	3.4580 / 1.20	0.30	
	2002.259	3.3647 / 1.24 x 1.10	0.25	
	2002.258	3.4649 / 1.20	0.30	
	2002.274	3.4998 / 1.20	0.30	
	2002.257	3.3696 / 1.35 x 1.23	0.30	
	2002.250	3.3657 / 1.26 x 1.12	0.25	
	2002.247	3.4485 / 1.26 x 1.14	0.25	
	2002.261	3.3733 / 1.30 x 1.12	0.35	
	2002.242	3.4735 / 1.22	0.30	
	2002.252	3.4659 / 1.00 x 1.20	0.25	
	2002.239	3.2950 / 1.23	0.30	
	2002.251	3.3132 / 1.35 x 1.10	0.25	
	2002.237	3.4013 / 1.20	0.25	
	2002.255	3.4706 / 1.24 x 1.06	0.30	
	2002.236	3.4587 / 1.16 x 1.05	0.25	
	2002.272	3.4432 / 1.35	0.31	
	2002.273	3.4348 / 1.45	0.30	
	2002.244	3.5408 / 1.55	0.30	
	2002.234	3.2909 / 1.41	0.25	
	2002.245	3.3581 / 1.30	0.30	
	2002.235	3.5723 / 1.44	0.30	
	2002.246	3.4246 / 1.45	0.25	
	2002.256	3.3055 / 1.40	0.25	
	2002.269	3.3994 / 1.30	0.30	
	2002.263	3.2384 / 1.40	0.25	
	2002.270	3.4191 / 1.35	0.25	
69.	**VIb.I.B**			
	2002.282	3.4883 / 1.20	0.30	18
	2002.277	3.5118 / 1.35 x 1.10	0.30	
	2002.292	3.4258 / 1.20 x 0.96	0.35	
	2002.293	3.4992 / 0.96 x 1.30	0.30	
	2002.281	3.2391 / 1.25 x 0.90	0.35	
	2002.280	3.3836 / 1.20 x 1.00	0.30	
	2002.284	3.4037 / 1.25 x 1.00	0.39	
	2002.287	3.4398 / 1.43 x 1.10	0.29	

S. No.	Series Acc. No.	wt. (gms.) / sz. (cms.)	Thickness (cms.)	No. of coins
	2002.278	3.3240 / 1.20	0.30	
	2002.286	3.3743 / 1.32 x 1.10	0.30	
	2002.276	3.4162 / 1.30 x 1.06	0.30	
	2002.285	3.4199 / 1.10	0.35	
	2002.283	3.4122 / 1.50 x 1.60	0.30	
	2002.279	3.3685 / 1.30 x 1.00	0.31	
	2002.288	3.4319 / 1.33	0.35	
	2002.290	3.3613 / 1.50	0.30	
	2002.289	3.3812 / 1.50	0.35	
	2002.291	3.3692 / 1.43	0.30	
70.	**VIb.I.C**			
	2002.294	3.5262 / 1.33	0.30	4
	2002.296	3.3422 / 1.36 x 1.26	0.25	
	2002.297	3.3669 / 1.30 x 1.20	0.25	
	2002.295	3.2734 / 1.44	0.25	
71.	**VIb.I.C1**			
	2002.298	3.4337 / 1.30	0.21	6
	2002.299	3.4516 / 1.40	0.21	
	2002.300	3.4950 / 1.43 x 1.20	0.20	
	2002.301	3.4648 / 1.62	0.20	
	2002.302	3.4431 / 1.73	0.20	
	2002.303	3.3337 / 1.60	0.20	
72.	**VIb.I.C2**			
	2002.306	3.5346 / 1.86 x 1.14	0.25	5
	2002.308	3.5485 / 1.25	0.29	
	2002.307	3.4888 / 1.20 x 1.07	0.30	
	2002.304	3.4373 / 1.36	0.30	
	2002.305	3.4078 / 1.30	0.30	
73.	**VIb.I.C3**			
	2002.309	3.3999 / 1.30	0.25	1
74.	**VIb.I.D**			
	2002.313	3.4059 / 1.30	0.21	9
	2002.311	3.4967 / 1.64 x 0.94	0.25	
	2002.315	3.3739 / 1.40 x 1.20	0.21	
	2002.314	3.4578 / 1.35 x 1.24	0.25	
	2002.317	3.4521 / 1.20	0.20	
	2002.318	3.5497 / 1.30	0.25	
	2002.316	3.4790 / 1.30	0.21	
	2002.312	3.4790 / 1.60 x 0.90	0.25	
	2002.310	3.4497 / 1.46	0.29	

S. No.	Series Acc. No.	wt. (gms.) / sz. (cms.)	Thickness (cms.)	No. of coins
75.	**VIb.I.E**			
	2002.324	3.4874 / 1.60 x 1.00	0.25	10
	2002.327	3.4596 / 1.45 x 1.05	0.29	
	2002.328	3.4845 / 1.20 x 1.10	0.35	
	2002.323	3.5242 / 1.40 x 1.10	0.25	
	2002.322	3.4586 / 1.42 x 1.10	0.25	
	2002.326	3.4423 / 2.00 x 1.35	0.25	
	2002.321	3.4270 / 2.10 x 1.10	0.20	
	2002.325	3.4614 / 1.34 x 1.24	0.20	
	2002.320	3.4336 / 1.40	0.25	
	2002.319	3.4117 / 1.46	0.25	
76.	**VIb.I.E1**			
	2002.329	3.4333 / 1.20	0.25	2
	2002.330	3.4580 / 1.15	0.25	

II

A Note on the Chemical Analysis and Fabrication Technique of Some Coins Found in the Hoard

Gold, silver and copper are known to be the most important metals used for minting coins in the early and medieval India. However, punch-marked coins are mostly made out of silver and few in copper. Numerous sources of silver and copper are known in the Indian sub-continent. Metals for minting coins were procured from indigenous sources. Chemical analysis of coins discovered from various important sites shows that the silver used for coins was alloyed with copper. It may suffice to mention here that addition of alloying elements (copper) to the punch-marked coins, up to about 15 per cent, may be attributed to technical reasons for providing sufficient strength to the flexible white metal, i.e. silver to sustain the wear and tear during minting of coins. The known results so far show that the coins of different periods have different grades of alloy. The amount of alloying additions in these coins also depends on political and economic factors.

Almost all the coins in this hoard under study are in well-preserved condition. However, a few coins show traces of brownish patina indicating higher percentage of copper. Those coins showing black or brownish stains represent the impurities in the metal. It is not possible to ascertain the exact composition of the bulk coinage alloy, unless advanced non-destructive techniques are employed, using non-destructive surface analysis techniques. However, an attempt has been made to know the coinage alloy composition by Energy Dispersive Spectroscopy (EDS).[1]

However, reports of several assays are available of the similar type coins of the contemporary period, published by scholars from time to time. Smith has reported them to be containing 80 per cent silver and 20 per cent copper.[2] Cunningham has given the assays of 113 coins that show the metal contents varying from 75.2 per cent to 86.2 per cent silver and 24.80 to 13.8 per cent copper.[3] However, other metals or impurities are not determined. Ramchandran has reported on the analysis of two samples of Mambalam hoard, 75.23 per cent and 74.37 per cent silver and 24.84 per cent and 25.31 per cent of copper respectively and 0.38 per cent other impurities.[4]

The coins of Series I from Golakpur hoard show 82 per cent silver, 15 per cent copper and 3 per cent other impurities.[5] According to Durga Prasad, the coins belonging to Series III and IV contain 80 per cent to 72 per cent silver in different coins.[6] Shreenivasan reported 76.36 per cent of silver and 23.65 per cent of copper in one coin of the same series, from Karimnagar hoard.[7] The coins of Series VI contained 79 per cent to 68 per cent silver and 20 per cent to 28 per cent copper, as reported by Durga Prasad.[8] A few coins of this period from Barwani hoard by Gairola show 67.01 per cent silver, 29.36 per cent copper and 3.59 per cent lead.[9] Another coin from Karimnagar hoard also shows the contents as 51.59 per cent silver and 49.41 per cent copper.[10] Prakash and Rawat reported 76.80 per cent to 84.71 per cent silver, 21.81 per cent to 14.64 per cent copper and 0.65 to 1.42 per cent other impurities in 4 coins from Kausambi.[11] These results show the admixture or other impurities in the silver-copper alloy varies from 13.8 per cent to 50 per cent. Walsh quotes the analysis of two silver punch-marked coins from Bhir mound hoard (1924), Taxila, reported only silver and copper – 40.3 per cent and 75.3 per cent respectively.[12] According to Bhardwaj, "The analysis looks to be wrong probably it is misquoted: 75'3 per cent silver and 40.3 per cent copper. Two coins from Taxila (BHU) show the result of analysis – (thick coin) 84.14 per cent silver, 13.01 per cent copper and other metals 3.25 per cent and (thin coin) 74.87 per cent silver, 22.40 per cent copper and 1.96 per cent other metals.[13] Bhardwaj concludes by these analysis that "admixture of copper (or debasement) in silver copper alloy varies from 13.8 per cent to 50 per cent. Hence, the coins can be classified into various grades according to copper content."[14]

Ten coins of the present hoard analyzed by SEM-EDS technique show 84.07 per cent, silver, 11.47 per cent copper and 1.74 per cent lead (Series II), 90.68 per cent silver, 4.33 per cent copper and 1.90 per cent lead (Series III), 85.79 per cent silver, 10.45 per cent copper and 0.72 per cent lead (Series Va), 82.97 per cent silver, 14.19 per cent, copper and 0.56 per cent lead (Series Va), 81.79 per cent silver, 12.78 per cent copper and 0.88 per cent lead (Series, Va) and 83.97 silver, 10.79 per cent copper and 0.88 per cent lead (Series Va), 87.50 per cent silver, 7.84 per cent copper and 0.83 lead (Series Va), 82.43 per cent silver, 13.10 per cent copper, 0.76 per cent lead (Series Vb), 92.17 per cent silver, 3.87 per cent copper, 0.86 per cent lead (VIb) and 62.67 per cent silver, 31.40 per cent copper and 0.61 per cent lead, respectively (Series VIb) (Table 9).

FABRICATION TECHNIQUE

Punch-marked coins were fabricated through distinct processes. The metal was first hammered to flat sheets of required thickness. The sheets were then cut into strips of varying width in proportion to the thickness of the sheets. Finally, blanks of desired weight were cut and punched with impressions. The coins manufactured by this technique are circular, oval, elliptical, square and rectangular. However, the irregular edges found in these coins seem to have been resulted from cutting or clipping the edges in order to adjust the weight standards. The coins produced by this cut sheet method are represented in all the series. Such coins vary in their shape, size and thickness. They are as broad as 1.25" and as small as 04" in size or diameter. The thickness varies between 0.02" and 0.125". The broad coins are thin and the small-sized ones are thick.[15]

The thin and broad coins represent Series I and II. A few coins of Series III are also of thin and broad flan. The coins of medium thickness (about 0.08") belong exclusively to the coins of Series III and IV. Few coins of thin fabric are also noticed in Series III and thick ones in Series IV.

(2002.326, VIb.I.E, pl.XXII, 6)

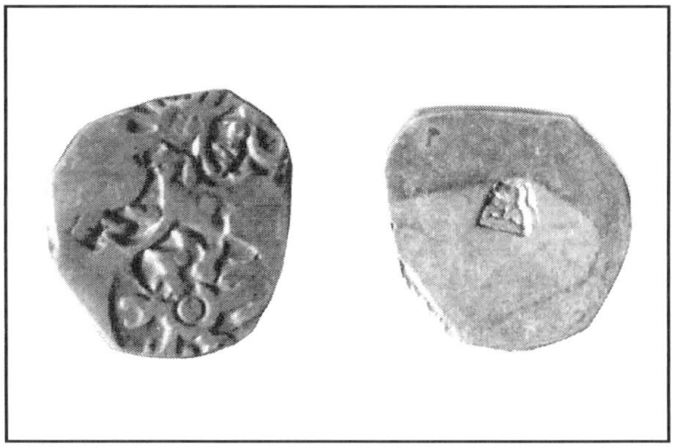

(2002.145, Va.VI.A, pl.IX, 5)

In Series V, the coins of medium as well as thick fabric are found together. The coins belonging to Series V to VII are exclusively made of thick fabric.

The other possible method employed for making coins includes the production of blank pieces by flattening the metal globules formed possibly by molten metal droplets. The cracked edges of the coins indicate that these metal globules were hammered to flatten them. Such coins are also of two types – thick, dumpy, and comparatively thin and broad. This method of fabricating coins was possibly adopted for utilizing the scrap clippings of the coins manufactured through the cut sheet process.[16] All these coins are punched mainly with five symbols. The symbols are quite flat and free from any kind of relief except for the punching depressions (incuse).

A solitary example (2002.326, VIb.I.E, pl.XXII,6) of the second fabrication technique, i.e. globule make in this hoard is elliptical in shape. Generally, the coins produced by the droplet technique are round in shape and are either thick and dumpy or flat and broad. Another coin (2002.145, Va.VI.A, pl. IX, 5) minted in droplet technique shows a peculiar feature: instead of rounded edge, it has straight ones. It appears that the edges were clipped probably to adjust the weight. Three such specimens (2485, 2510 and 4204) were alo reported in Amaravati hoard.[17]

The coin blanks or planchets were produced either by cutting from sheets or by droplet technique. Rajgor (2001) and Bhandare (2009) proposed the minting process of droplet coins.

> In this process, silver pieces were placed in a crucible in the following manner: Bottom of the crucible was filled with a layer of charcoal. Onto the bed of charcoal silver pieces of required weight were placed at an equal distance. This bed of silver pieces was followed by another bed of charcoal that in turn was followed by the next layer of silver pieces. In this way, the crucible was filled to the top by the alternate layers of charcoal and silver pieces. The bed of charcoal between the two layers of silver ingots is required to keep separate the silver layers when the crucible is heated up. The equal distance between the ingots is necessary to segregate the molted drops of silver.
>
> Thereafter, the crucible was transferred into earthen furnace. In the furnace the crucible was fully covered with the dishes of cow-dung, and was left for slow heating. After a few hours, silver pieces get melted down and assumed the shape of drops. Then the crucible was taken out of the furnace and the silver ingots were passed onto a person whose job was to flatten them. In turn, these pieces were struck with different punches having symbols. This technique can also be called 'Bed of Charcoal Process'.[18]

Bhandare disagrees with Gupta and other scholars and says, ...

> While commenting on the Sultanpur coins Gupta has envisaged a process in which the metal was stamped with the punch bearing the symbol while still being in a 'semi-molten' state, similar to sealing wax. He further comments that this has caused the edges of the coins to bulge upward in a rounded fashion, giving them their distinct scyphate shape. This explanation is metallurgically and technically inaccurate. Metals do not exhibit a 'plastic' state while they convert from liquid to solid form. At best they exhibit an increased malleability that varies directly with the temperature, as the metal cools down it become harder. So there is no room for a metal to remain in a 'semi-molten' stage. Moreover, in case of the Sultanpur hoard type coins, recent discovery of restruck pieces showing vestiges of the previous punch on the reverse clearly demonstrate that Gupta's view is not tenable. As regards the formation of 'droplets' or 'globules' it has been observed that a pre-weighed piece of metal like silver, if fired in a free standing manner, automatically assumes a spherical form when molten. If this sphere is allowed to cool naturally, a globule is formed that can then be flattened to yield a coin blank. Globules of silver according to various weight requirements are even today made by placing pre-weighed pieces of silver wire on a charcoal bed, and arranging many such beds in layers in a kiln which can be then fired to melt the pieces. As the kiln is allowed to cool, the molten silver solidifies giving globules, which are then separated from the charcoal simply by sifting. The technical and industrial efficiency of this process leaves no doubt that the manufacturing of globules to yield blanks of archaic PMCs was indeed undertaken by the same process in ancient India.[19]

NOTES AND REFERENCES

1. Mr. Gugalani, Scientific Officer in the department, has carried out the work in the Deptt. of Metallurgical Engineering, Institute of Technology, Banaras Hindu University, Varanasi.
2. V.A. Smith (1906), *IMC*, 133.
3. *Journal of Indian Museum Calcutta*, XIII, 16.
4. P.L. Gupta (1963), *Am*, 3.
5. *NS*, XLV, 14.
6. *Ibid.*, 58-59.
7. *ARANDH* (1928-29), 43.
8. *NS*, XLV, 59.
9. *AI* (1951), No. 7, 79-80.
10. *ARANDH* (1928-29), 43.
11. Satya Prakash and N.S. Rawat (1965), "Chemical Study of Some Indian Archaeological Antiquities", 70, Sr. No. 2.
12. Walsh, "Punch-marked coins from Taxila", *MASI*, No. 59, 32.
13. H.C. Bhardwaj (1966), "Bearing of Chemical Composition and Metallography on the Chronology of the Punch-marked Coins", *The Chronology of the Punch-marked Coins,* Dept. of A.I.H.C. & Archaeology, BHU, Varanasi, 58.
14. *Ibid.*, 59.
15. P.L. Gupta (1963), *Am*, 6. The metallurgical analysis of these coins shows that Copper contents in the alloy was not less than 20 per cent and as high as 60 per cent. *Arthaśāstra* of Kauṭilya also states for alloying 25 per cent copper and one *mā a* i.e. 6.1/4 per cent of other base metal with silver for making coins. *Arthaśāstra*, II. XII, text I, 205 (tr.90).
16. A few coin moulds of later period, found at Bhambor and Bahamanbad Mansura in Sindh, have a large number of round depression of definite depth. It appears that molten metal was poured in the depressions and blank pieces of desired weight were prepared. *ASIAR* (1903-04) 137.

17. According to P.L. Gupta, some similar method might have been employed for these coins. (1963) *Am*, 5.
18. Dilip Rajgor (2001), *Punch-marked Coins of Early Historic India*, 12. See also – (1993) *JNSI* (LV), "Droplet Technique of Archaic Indian Coins", 1-5.
19. Shailendra Bhandare (2009), "The Archaic Indian Punch-marked Coins: Approaches to Classification", http//www215.pair.com/Sacoins/public_htm/shailenspaper.htm. (7. Feb. 2009).

III

SEM-EDS Analysis

Numismatics requires the determination of alloy composition to understand the genuine fineness of coins, for which they call to analytical physicists, as traditional methods of numismatics cannot serve the purpose. Elemental composition of ancient coins provides valuable information in relation to different aspects of life: political, social, cultural, economy and metallurgy of minting. Minting is a government monopoly and the composition of coins reflects economic trends and occasionally political attitudes. The economic history of nations can be traced through changes in the composition of their coinage. Debasement—the reduction in fineness of the coining alloy—is an indication of economic decline. Collectors and the museum's authorities are, understandably, reluctant to allow permanent damage to coins due to the value or uniqueness of the object, which precludes the use of destructive methods of analysis. Emergence of non-destructive techniques has brought great changes in metallic analysis, as a large number of coins can be analyzed without destructing them. X-Ray Fluorescence (XRF), Electron Probe Micro Analysis (EPMA), Particle Induced X-Ray Emission (PIXE), Scanning Electron Microscopy with Energy Dispersive Spectrometry (SEM-EDS), Fast Neutron Activation Analysis (FNAA), Proton Activation Analysis (PAA) and Particle Induced Gamma-ray Emission (PIGE) are some of the non-destructive techniques widely used for this purpose. While XRF, EPMA, PIXE and SEM - EDS are recognized as surface methods since only surface layer of limited depth can be analyzed, FNAA and PAA offer the advantageous means of obtaining access to the bulk composition. Many difficulties are encountered when one has to draw conclusions based on the results of such analyses. Between the minting of the coin and its present state, the chemical composition of the coin may have suffered important changes. Even the cleaning techniques employed can cause alterations. For example, the cleaning of silver and copper coins to obtain a metallic surface causes superficial enrichment in silver due to oxidation of the grains of copper and relief of silver grains on the surface. Therefore, the results obtained greatly depend on the more or less alterations of the surface, while employing surface analytical methods. This disadvantage can be overcome if one adopts bulk analysis techniques.

Ten silver coins in the hoard under study belong to the period of c. 3rd century BCE to 2nd century BCE. These were analyzed using quantitative SEM-EDS technique in the Department of Metallurgical Engineering, Institute of Technology, Banaras Hindu University. SEM-EDS analysis is only limited to a few micrometres up to a few tens of micrometres from the surface. The advantages of SEM-EDS include the high spatial resolution and the ability to analyze small sample area. However, the detection limits of SEM-EDS are approximately 0.1wt. per cent depending on the atomic number and the matrix composition. The various elements present in the silver coins analyzed with their weight percentages are tabulated below.

Table 9. Results of SEM-EDS analysis of ancient sliver coinage samples (I-III).

Sample No.	Silver (Wt%)	Copper (Wt%)	Lead (Wt%)	Cadmium (Wt%)	Silicon (Wt%)	Aluminium (Wt%)
(I) / 1.11.	84.07	11.47	1.74	1.77	0.82	0.13
2.	90.68	4.33	1.90	1.78	1.31	—
3.	85.79	10.45	0.72	1.63	1.10	0.31
(II) / 4.	82.97	14.19	0.56	2.08	0.26	—
5.	81.79	12.78	0.88	1.86	2.69	—
6.	83.97	10.79	0.88	3.45	0.65	0.26
(III) / 7.	87.50	7.84	0.83	3.33	0.50	—
8.	82.43	13.10	0.76	3.42	0.29	—
9.	92.17	3.87	0.86	2.16	0.83	0.11
10.	62.67	31.40	0.61	4.73	0.38	0.21

It is clear from Table 9 that all the coin samples contain silver and copper in major proportions along with lead, cadmium and silicon in minor quantities. Aluminum is also present in trace amounts in some of the samples. From this one can conclude that these coins are silver-rich silver-copper alloys with minor elements accounting for impurities entered by the way of the processing technology employed and the ores used for the extraction of the primary metals. Coin silver as is known, is one of the antiquity alloys containing 75-95% silver and 25-5% copper. As silver is a soft ductile metal, copper is added to enhance its strength. All the samples analyzed lie in this antiquity alloy group with the exception of sample III (Sr. VIb.I.C1), containing about 62% silver.

The composition of the surface of objects made of ancient noble metal alloys is often different from that of the interior. The compositional alteration, known as surface enrichment, usually takes the form of enrichment of the principal alloy component. It follows that analysis of noble metal alloys by non-penetrating methods, such as the one used in the present study (SEM-EDS) is inadequate for determining the composition of the bulk. Silver forms eutectic with copper at 72% silver – 28% copper. In silver-copper alloys with more than 72% silver, the surface composition tends to follow the composition of the silver-rich primary phase (silver - 92%), i.e., in equilibrium conditions the composition given by the phase diagram. For silver-copper alloys with less than 72% silver, the trend is towards eutectic composition (72% silver). At very low silver content (15-20% silver), the silver proportion seems to be too low for forming a continuous eutectic layer. The enrichment phenomenon of debased silver alloys may be due to corrosion and subsequent leaching of the less noble metal (copper in this case). The minting practice employed, involving casting buttons of silver-copper alloy, heating leading to formation of copper oxide and revealing of silver phase and finally hammering causing the spread of the silver-rich phase, which is responsible for such surface enrichment. As already mentioned before, the surface cleaning methods employed too can lead to surface enrichment.

To conclude, the silver coins belonging to the period of c. 3rd century to c. 2nd century BCE are made of the antiquity alloy Coin Silver (silver-copper alloy). However, the surface analysis carried out by way of SEM-EDS is not adequate to establish the bulk composition of the coins, especially while dealing with the noble metal alloys, which are known for their tendency towards surface enrichment. In either case, all the samples with the exception of one (Sample III -VIb.I.CI) must be containing silver above 72%, as the surface layers contain more than about 80% silver. These results clearly agree with those reported elsewhere showing above about 72% to 80% silver.

(Contributed by Mr. K.V.U. Praveen, Research Scholar in the Department of Metallurgy, Engineering, (IT), Banaras Hindu University, Varanasi.)

Sample No. 1 (a)

Element	Line	Weight%	K-Ratio	Cnts/s	Atomic%
Al	Ka	0.26	0.0017	4.34	0.96
Si	Ka	0.82	0.0063	16.08	2.87
Cu	Ka	10.90	0.1155	35.47	16.85
Ag	La	83.96	0.8164	953.61	76.46
Cd	La	2.34	0.0224	25.19	2.04
Pb	Ma	1.72	0.0144	31.06	0.82
Total		100.00			

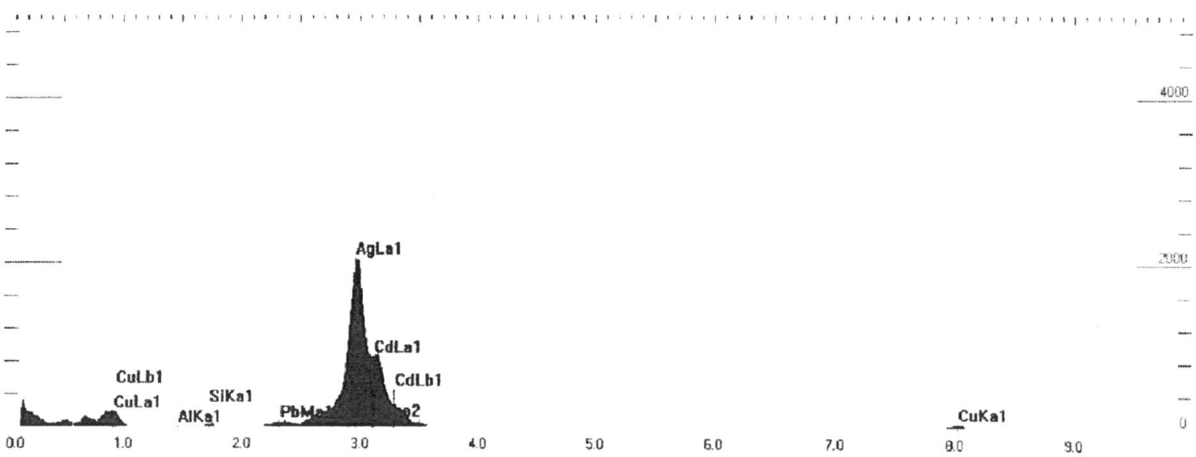

SEM Analysis

Sample No. 1 (b)

Element	Line	Weight%	K-Ratio	Cnts/s	Atomic%
Si	Ka	0.81	0.0062	16.20	2.82
Cu	Ka	12.03	0.1274	40.14	18.60
Ag	La	84.19	0.8178	979.41	76.68
Cd	La	1.21	0.0116	13.40	1.06
Pb	Ma	1.76	0.0146	32.41	0.83
Total		100.00			

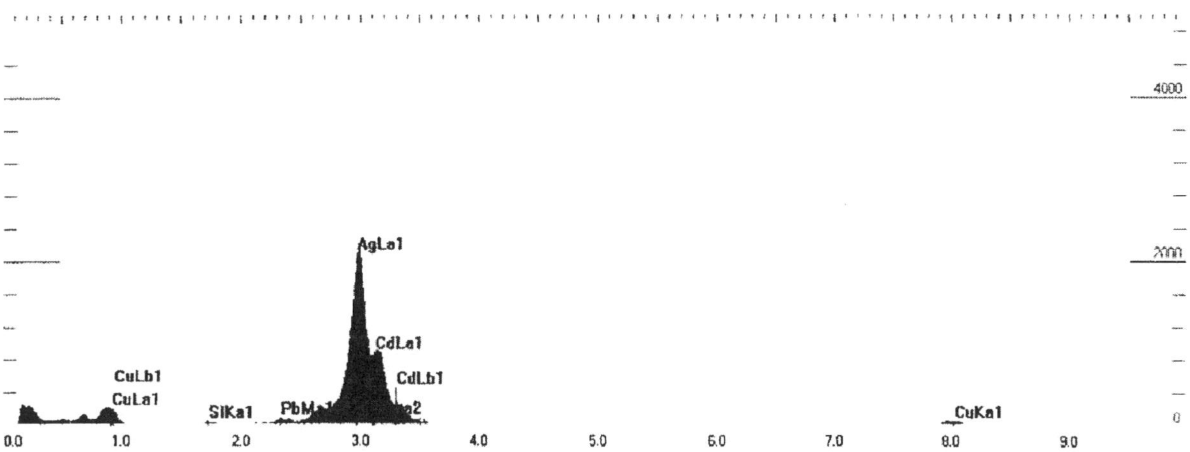

SEM Analysis

Sample No. 2 (a)

Element	Line	Weight%	K-Ratio	Cnts/s	Atomic%
Si	Ka	1.35	0.0107	29.83	4.88
Cu	Ka	5.02	0.0534	18.01	8.02
Ag	La	89.10	0.8736	1120.16	83.78
Cd	La	2.67	0.0258	31.89	2.41
Pb	Ma	1.85	0.0157	37.10	0.91
Total		99.99			

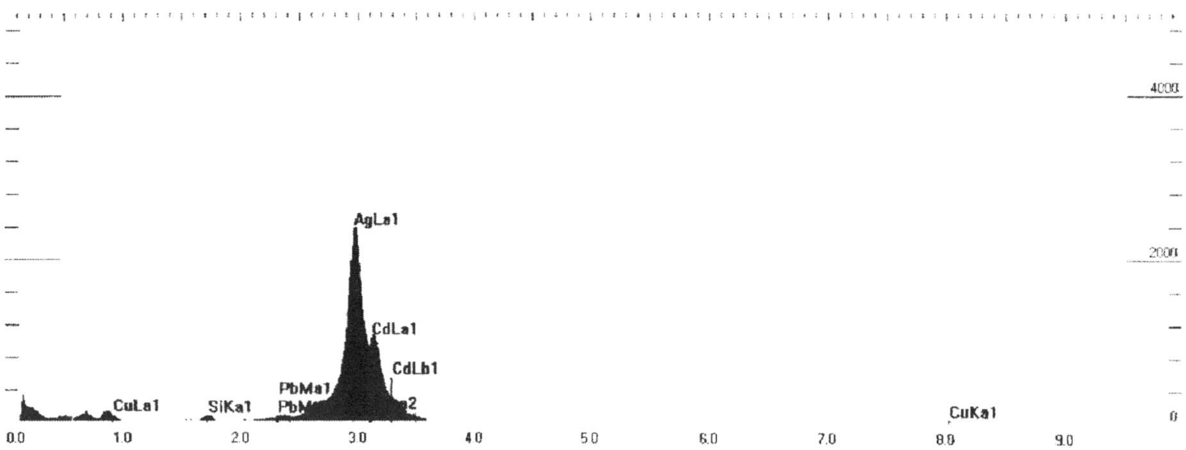

SEM Analysis

Sample No. 2 (b)

Element	Line	Weight%	K-Ratio	Cnts/s	Atomic%
Si	Ka	1.28	0.0102	27.00	4.67
Cu	Ka	3.64	0.0387	12.42	5.87
Ag	La	92.26	0.9064	1105.61	87.69
Cd	La	0.90	0.0087	10.20	0.82
Pb	Ma	1.93	0.0164	36.92	0.95
Total		100.01			

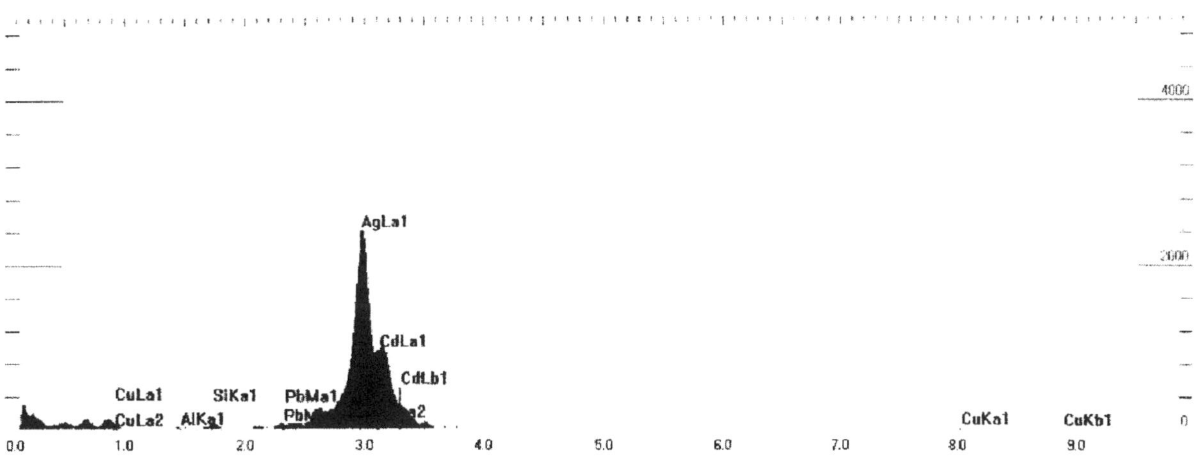

SEM Analysis

Sample No. 3 (a)

Element	Line	Weight%	K-Ratio	Cnts/s	Atomic%
Al	Ka	3.07	0.0171	59.39	8.54
Si	Ka	3.07	0.0211	70.95	8.20
Cu	Ka	37.75	0.3867	157.35	44.59
Ag	La	43.38	0.3987	616.84	30.18
Cd	La	12.73	0.1159	172.73	8.50
Total		100.00			

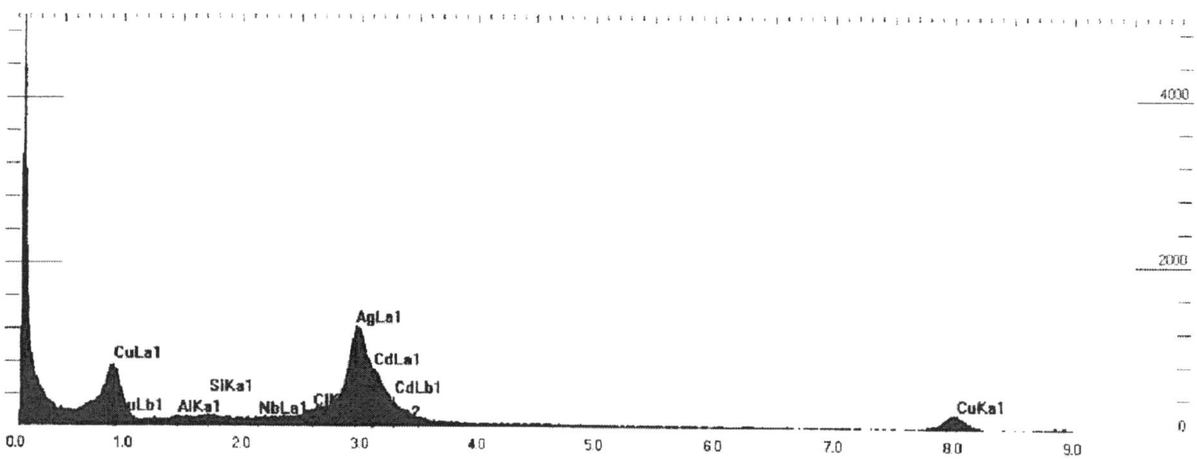

SEM Analysis

Sample No. 3 (b)

Element	Line	Weight%	K-Ratio	Cnts/s	Atomic%
Al	Ka	0.21	0.0012	3.52	0.68
Si	Ka	0.38	0.0027	7.68	1.18
Cu	Ka	31.40	0.3278	113.19	43.30
Ag	La	62.67	0.5923	777.64	50.90
Cd	La	4.73	0.0442	55.85	3.68
Pb	Ma	0.61	0.0048	11.76	0.26
Total		100.00			

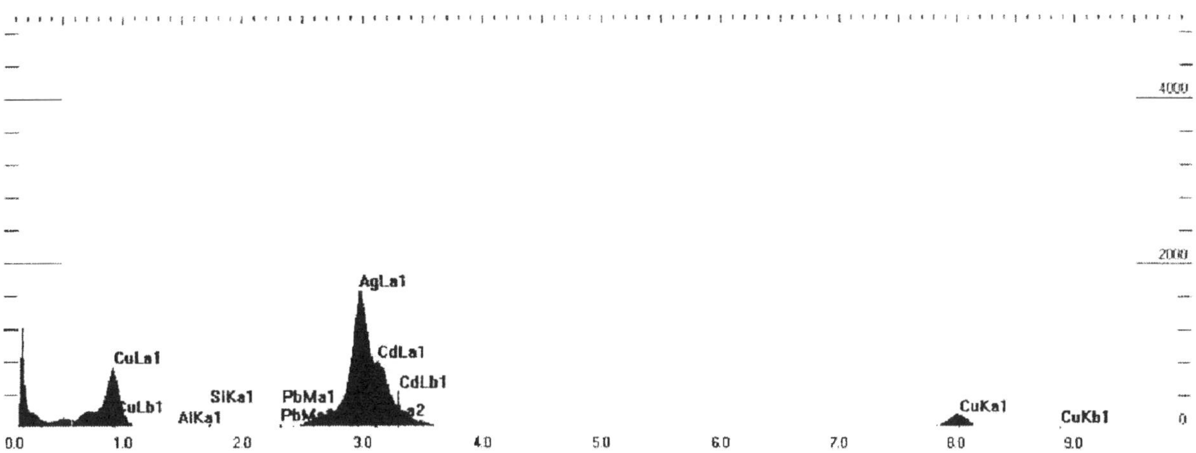

SEM Analysis

Sample No. 4 (a)

Element	Line	Weight%	K-Ratio	Cnts/s	Atomic%
Al	Ka	0.26	0.0016	4.22	0.94
Si	Ka	0.65	0.0050	12.72	2.28
Cu	Ka	10.79	0.1143	34.99	16.72
Ag	La	83.97	0.8195	954.02	76.62
Cd	La	3.45	0.0332	37.23	3.02
Pb	Ma	0.88	0.0074	15.85	0.42
Total		100.00			

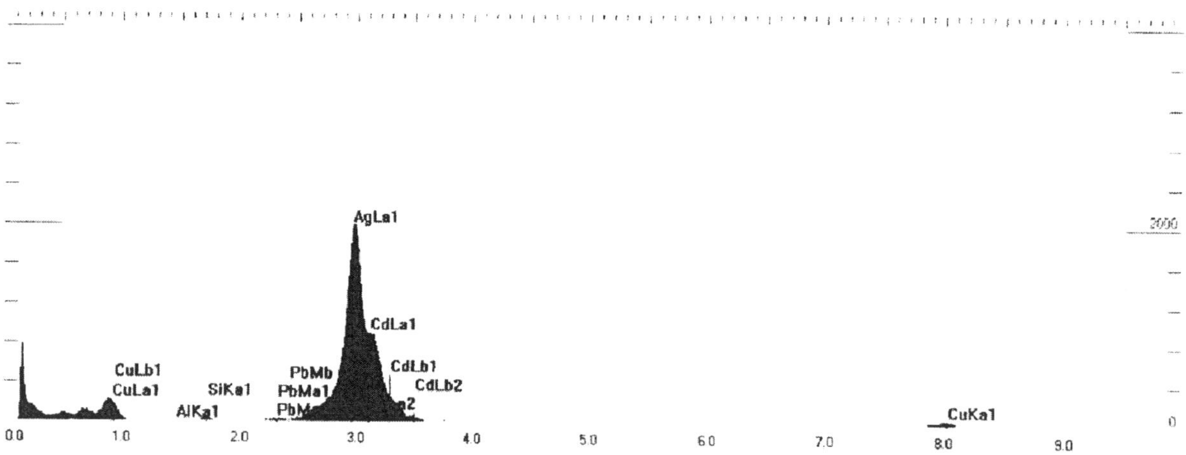

SEM Analysis

Sample No. 4 (b)

Element	Line	Weight%	K-Ratio	Cnts/s	Atomic%
Al	Ka	0.00	0.0000	0.00	0.00
Si	Ka	1.97	0.0154	37.37	6.89
Cu	Ka	7.15	0.0758	22.25	11.08
Ag	La	77.62	0.7588	846.77	70.85
Cd	La	12.19	0.1176	126.34	10.68
Pb	Ma	1.07	0.0090	18.52	0.51
Total		100.00			

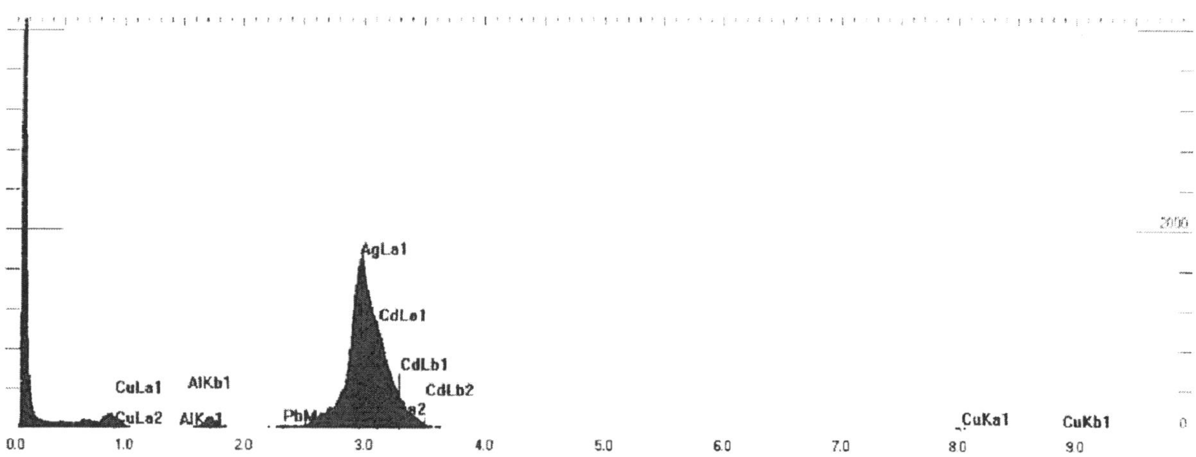

SEM Analysis

Sample No. 5 (a)

Element	Line	Weight%	K-Ratio	Cnts/s	Atomic%
Si	Ka	1.01	0.0077	19.38	3.50
Cu	Ka	11.76	0.1244	37.60	18.06
Ag	La	83.00	0.8082	929.01	75.07
Cd	La	3.48	0.0334	37.02	3.02
Pb	Ma	0.75	0.0063	13.29	0.35
Total		100.00			

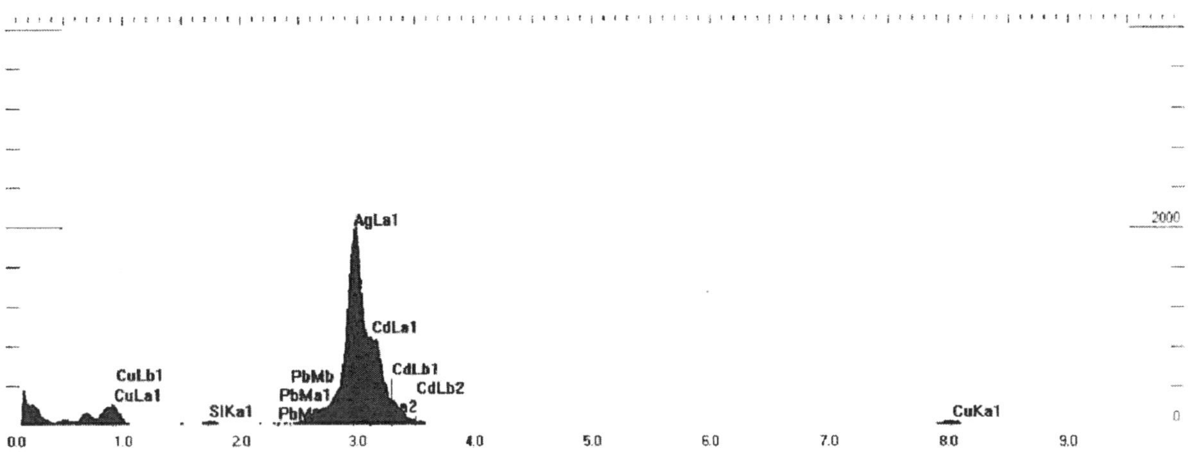

SEM Analysis

Sample No. 5 (b)

Element	Line	Weight%	K-Ratio	Cnts/s	Atomic%
Si	Ka	0.00	0.0000	0.00	0.00
Cu	Ka	3.93	0.0419	12.66	6.52
Ag	La	92.00	0.9116	1047.03	90.03
Cd	La	3.19	0.0312	34.51	3.00
Pb	Ma	0.88	0.0075	15.90	0.45
Total		100.00			

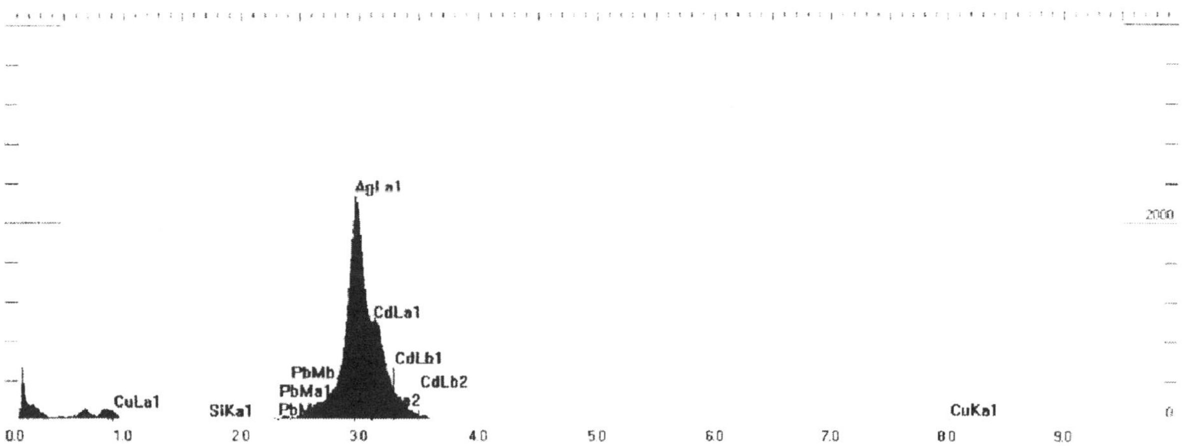

SEM Analysis

Sample No. 6 (a)

Element	Line	Weight%	K-Ratio	Cnts/s	Atomic%
Si	Ka	0.35	0.0027	6.40	1.21
Cu	Ka	17.03	0.1796	51.92	25.69
Ag	La	79.99	0.7746	851.31	71.11
Cd	La	1.97	0.0189	19.96	1.68
Pb	Ma	0.66	0.0054	11.02	0.30
Total		100.00			

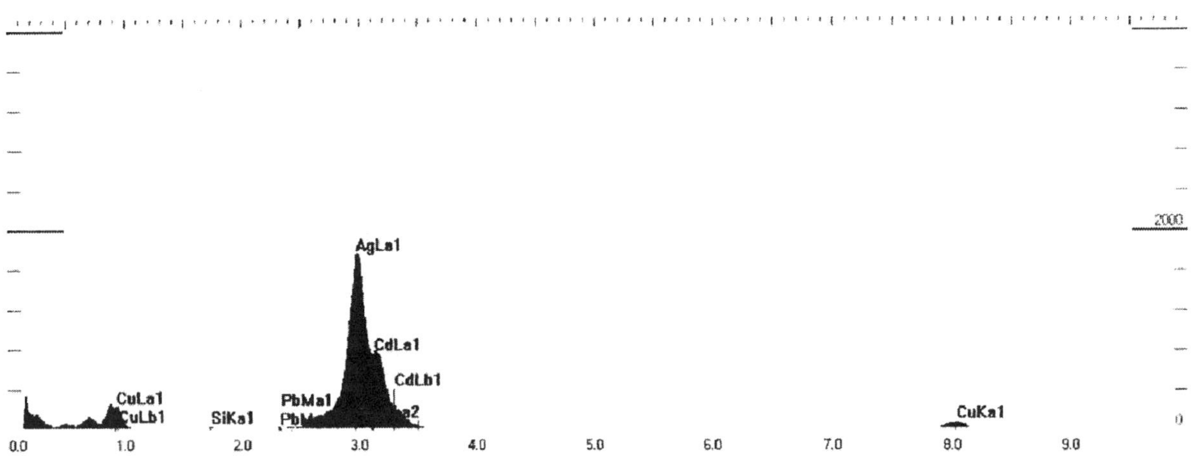

SEM Analysis

Sample No. 6 (b)

Element	Line	Weight%	K-Ratio	Cnts/s	Atomic%
Si	Ka	0.24	0.0018	4.69	0.86
Cu	Ka	9.18	0.0976	30.06	14.64
Ag	La	84.86	0.8328	975.75	79.70
Cd	La	4.87	0.0472	53.24	4.39
Pb	Ma	0.84	0.0071	15.35	0.41

Total 99.99

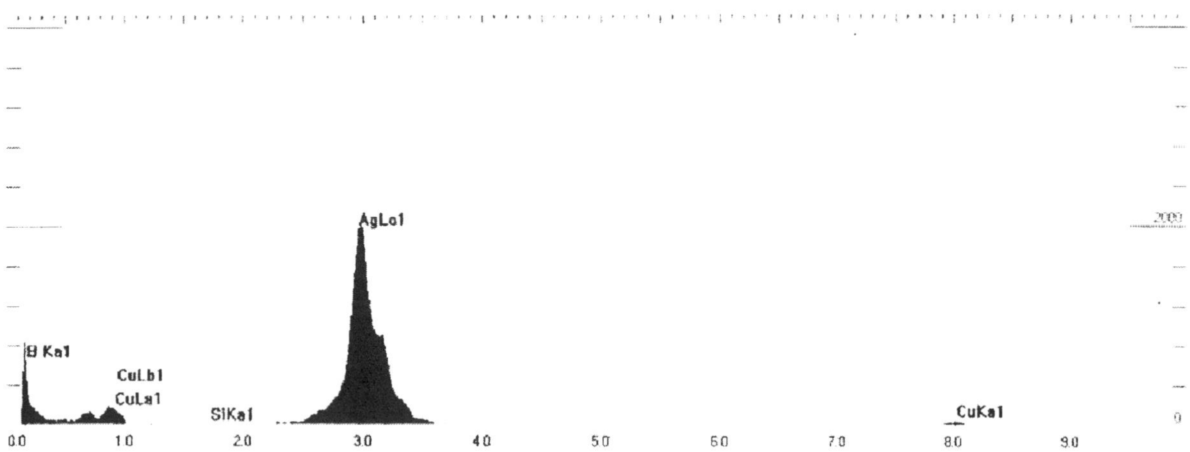

SEM Analysis

Sample No. 7 (a)

Element	Line	Weight%	K-Ratio	Cnts/s	Atomic%
Al	Ka	0.22	0.0014	3.70	0.83
Si	Ka	0.78	0.0062	15.82	2.86
Cu	Ka	3.24	0.0345	10.66	5.26
Ag	La	92.26	0.9115	1070.50	88.20
Cd	La	2.63	0.0256	28.99	2.41
Pb	Ma	0.87	0.0074	16.00	0.43
Total		100.00			

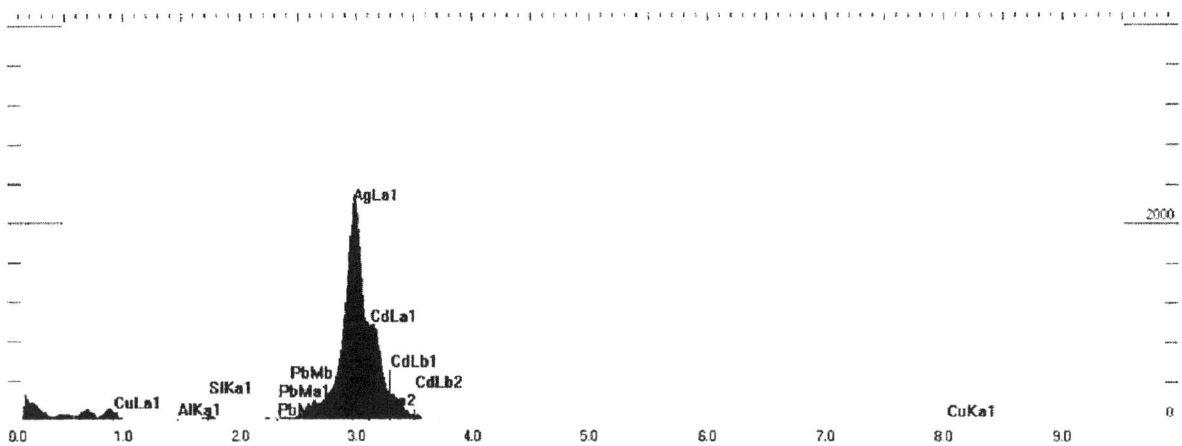

SEM Analysis

Sample No. 7 (b)

Element	Line	Weight%	K-Ratio	Cnts/s	Atomic%
Si	Ka	0.89	0.0071	18.33	3.26
Cu	Ka	4.49	0.0478	15.00	7.25
Ag	La	92.09	0.9081	1083.43	87.53
Cd	La	1.69	0.0165	18.91	1.54
Pb	Ma	0.84	0.0071	15.64	0.41
Total		100.00			

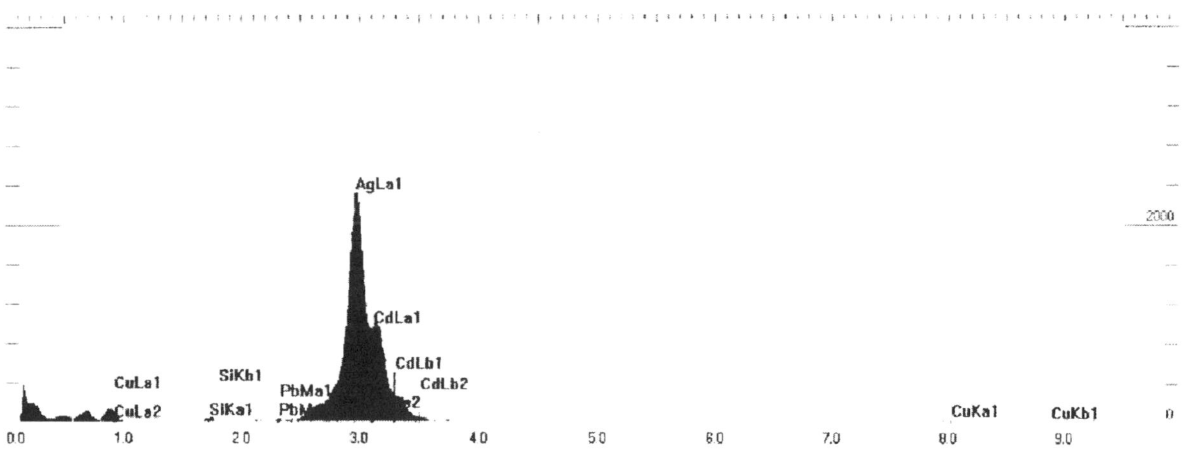

SEM Analysis

Sample No. 8 (a)

Element	Line	Weight%	K-Ratio	Cnts/s	Atomic%
Si	Ka	0.77	0.0059	11.94	2.71
Cu	Ka	10.62	0.1125	27.28	16.53
Ag	La	85.71	0.8368	771.64	78.56
Cd	La	2.02	0.0195	17.28	1.78
Pb	Ma	0.88	0.0074	12.58	0.42
Total		100.00			

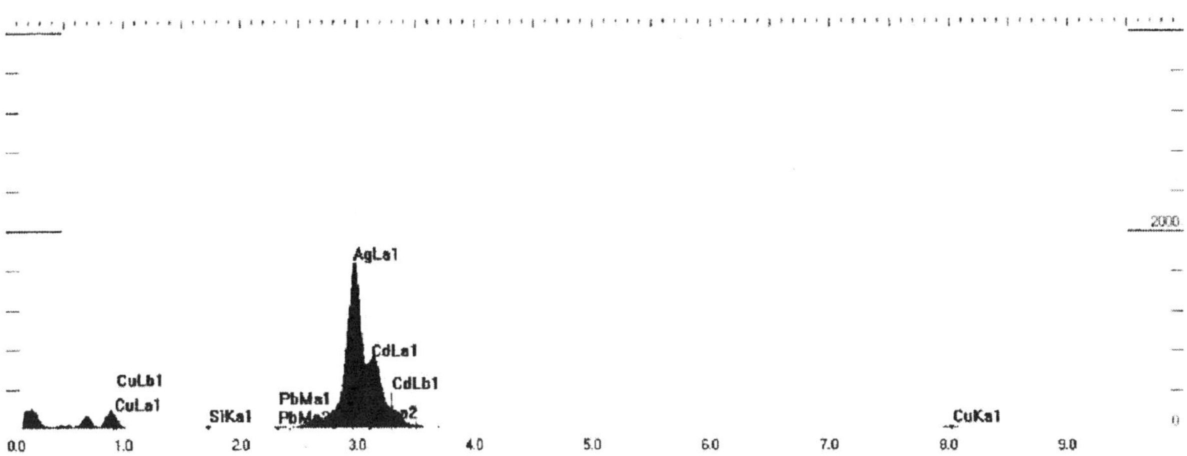

SEM Analysis

Sample No. 8 (b)

Element	Line	Weight%	K-Ratio	Cnts/s	Atomic%
Si	Ka	4.62	0.0352	44.22	14.41
Cu	Ka	14.93	0.1558	23.66	20.60
Ag	La	77.85	0.7423	428.62	63.27
Cd	La	1.71	0.0161	8.98	1.34
Pb	Ma	0.88	0.0072	7.64	0.37
Total		99.99			

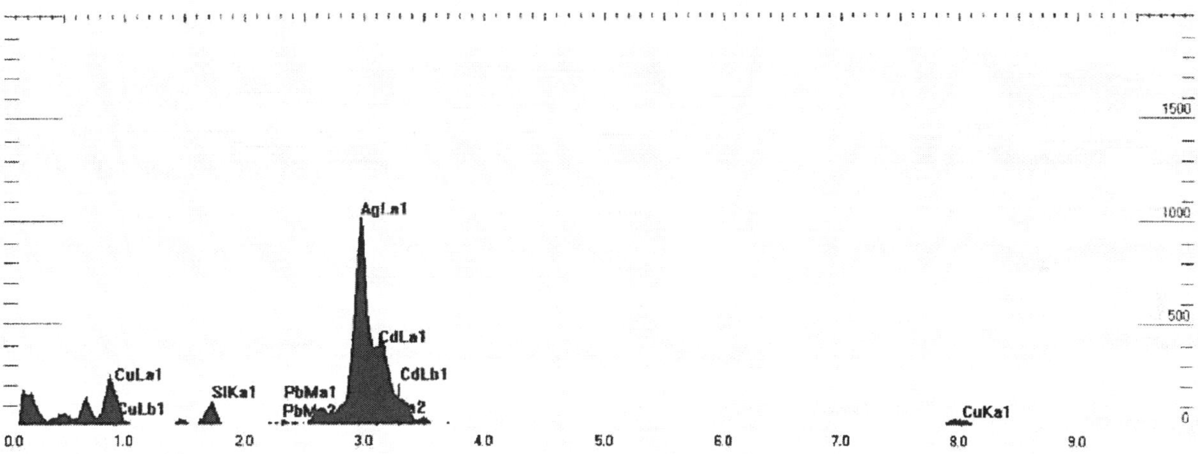

SEM Analysis

Sample No. 9 (a)

Element	Line	Weight%	K-Ratio	Cnts/s	Atomic%
Si	Ka	0.26	0.0020	3.65	0.90
Cu	Ka	14.19	0.1500	33.71	21.84
Ag	La	82.91	0.8070	689.45	75.18
Cd	La	2.08	0.0200	16.47	1.81
Pb	Ma	0.56	0.0047	7.37	0.27
Total		100.00			

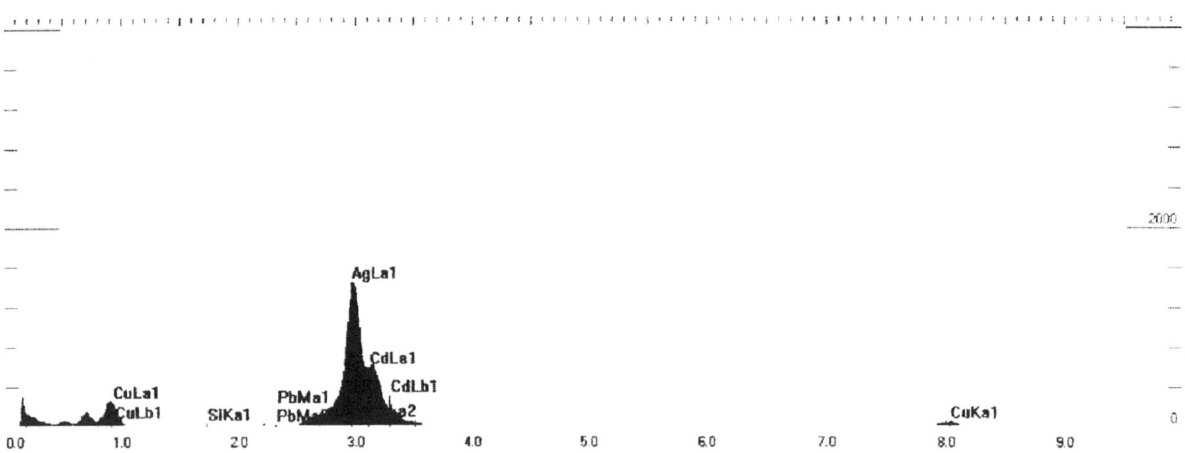

SEM Analysis

Sample No. 9 (b)

Element	Line	Weight%	K-Ratio	Cnts/s	Atomic%
Cu	Ka	12.95	0.1370	20.10	20.19
Ag	La	86.62	0.8459	471.83	79.60
Cd	La	0.00	0.0000	0.00	0.00
Pb	Ma	0.43	0.0036	3.71	0.21
Total		100.00			

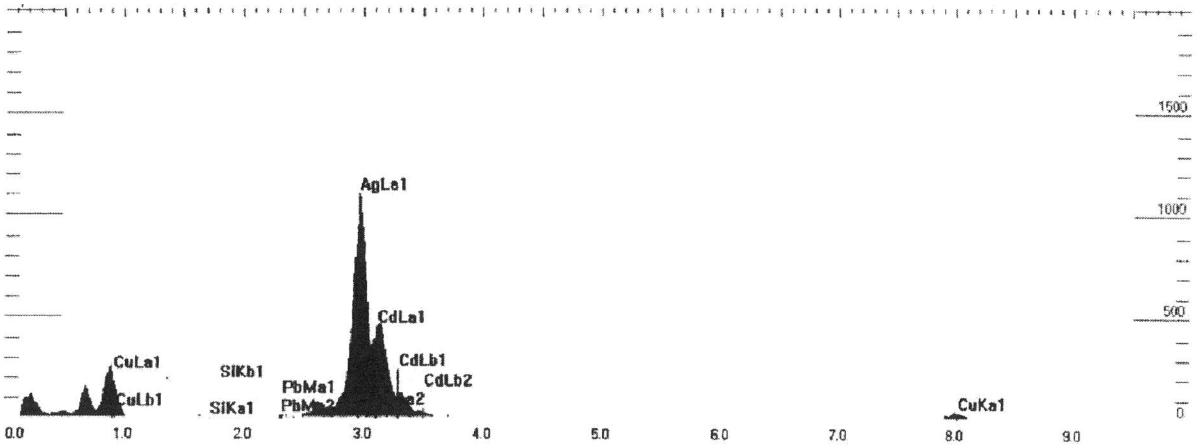

SEM Analysis

Sample No. 10 (a)

Element	Line	Weight%	K-Ratio	Cnts/s	Atomic%
Al	Ka	0.63	0.0039	4.75	2.18
Si	Ka	1.35	0.0103	12.26	4.52
Cu	Ka	13.91	0.1464	21.09	20.54
Ag	La	81.67	0.7895	432.48	71.04
Cd	La	1.63	0.0155	8.19	1.36
Pb	Ma	0.81	0.0067	6.78	0.37
Total		100.00			

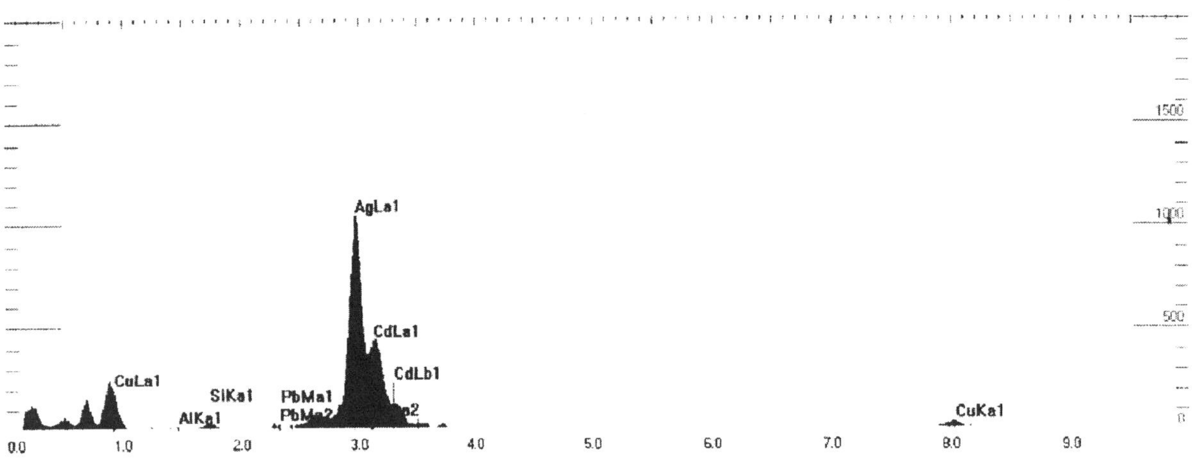

SEM Analysis

Sample No. 10 (b)

Element	Line	Weight%	K-Ratio	Cnts/s	Atomic%
Si	Ka	0.85	0.0067	8.42	3.06
Cu	Ka	6.98	0.0740	11.30	11.07
Ag	La	91.55	0.8994	522.20	85.57
Pb	Ma	0.62	0.0052	5.60	0.30
Total		100.00			

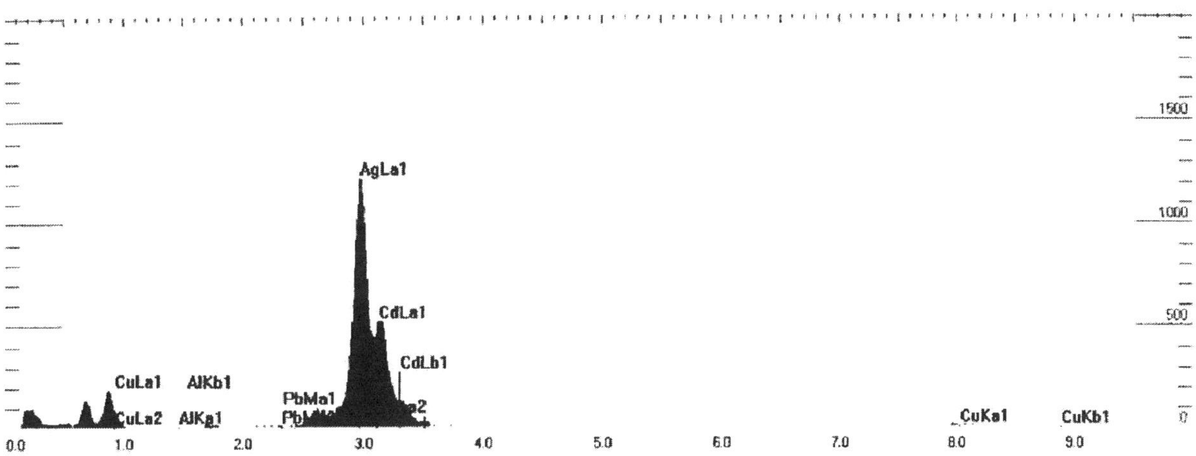

SEM Analysis

SEM Photo Micrograph of Coins

I

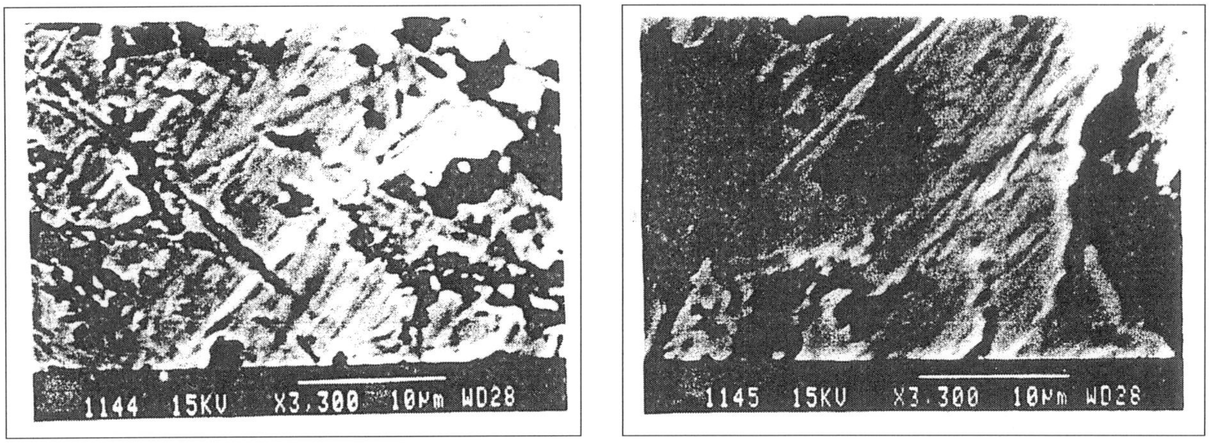

Sr.II.I.A-2002.1

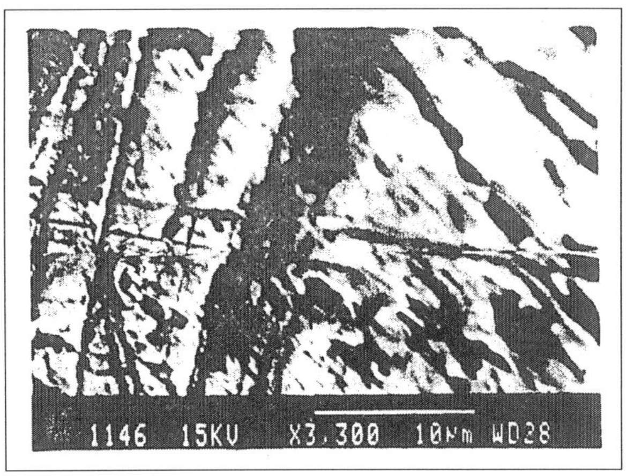

Sr.III.I.A-2002.3

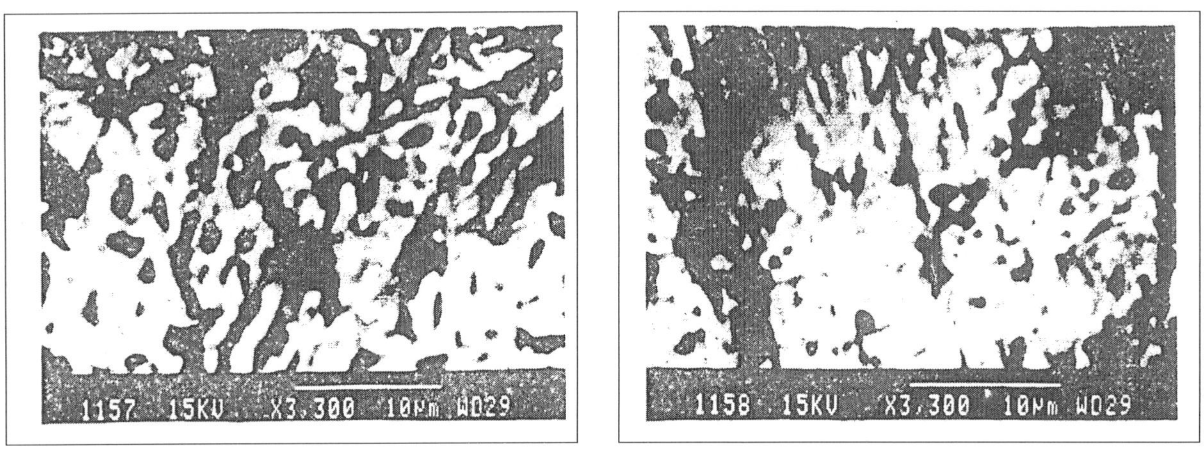

Sr.Va.I.A1-2002.92

II

Sr.Va.I.A5-2002.125

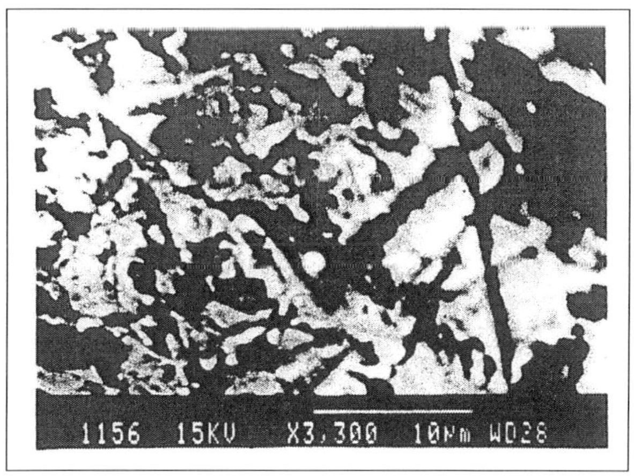

Sr.Va.I.A4-2002.116

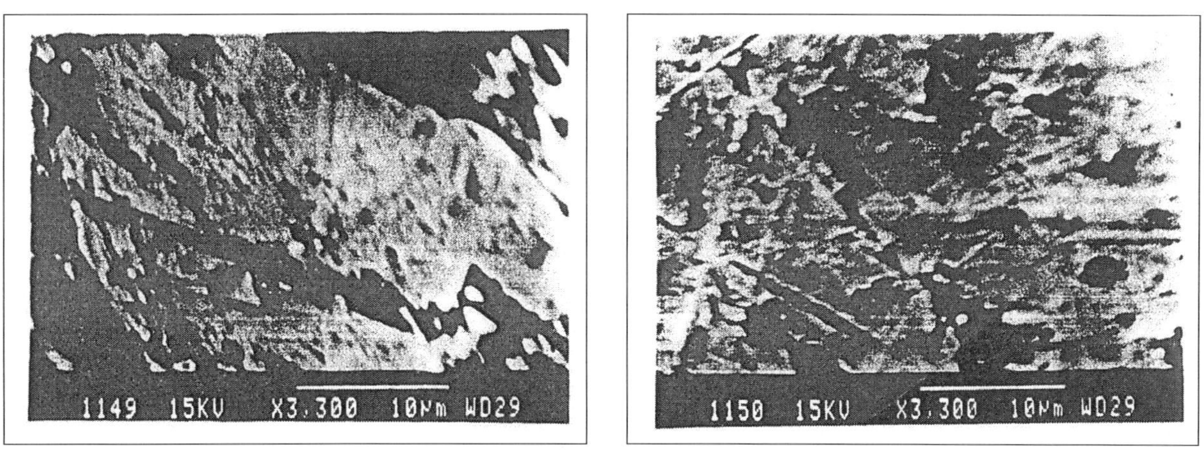

Sr.Va.I.A5-2002.127

III

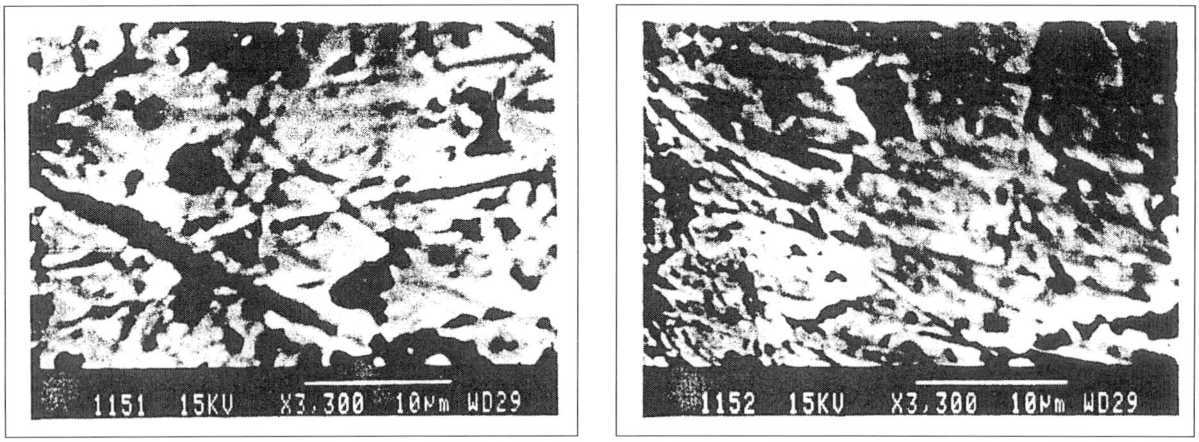

Sr.Va.VIIA-2002.148

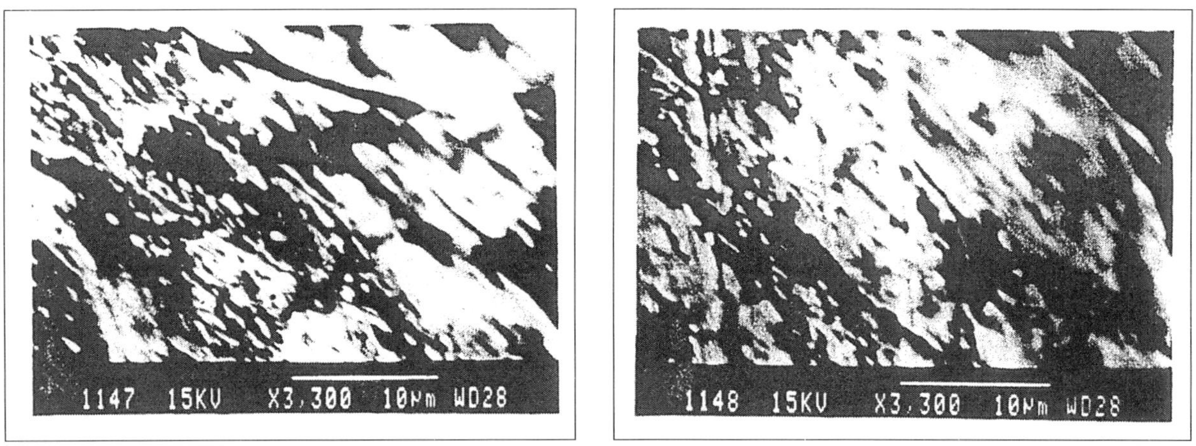

Sr.Vb.I.A-2002.164

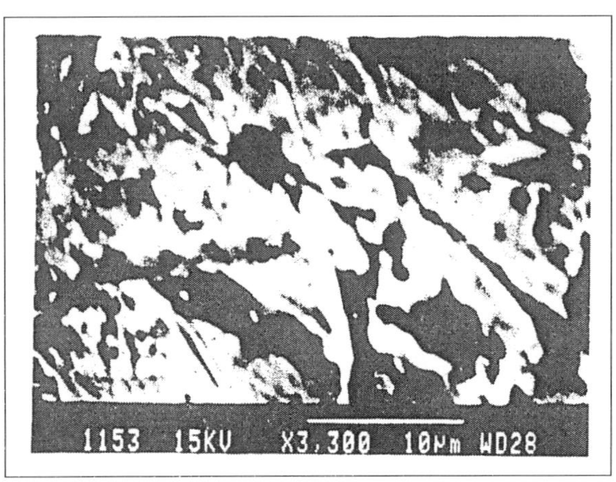

Sr.VIb.I.C-2002.299

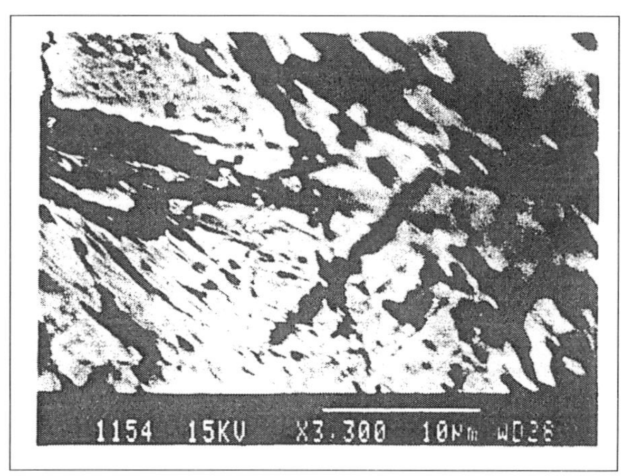

Sr.VIb.I.CI-2002.303

List of Hoards

AFGHANISTAN, N.W.F. & THE PUNJAB

Afghanistan (1910) (?) (44 coins) Asiatic Society of Bengal, Calcutta, *NS* (1910) 75; *NNM*, No. 2, 1.

AI Khanum hoard (677 coins) (6 Drachms of Agathocles).

Bajaur hoard (1942) (between Chitral and Swat rivers) (700 coins) (6 coins—Major General Houghton's collection); rest in trade; *JNSI* (1942) IV, 61; *NNM*, No. 2, 2.

Begram hoard (35 coins) (500 total from Masson).

Bhir mound hoard (Taxila, 1912) (No. 1) (176 coins, 1 coin - Diodotus, silver) Taxila Museum, Taxila; Central Asian Antiquities Museum, New Delhi; Walsh, 'Punch-marked coins from Taxila', *AI*. 1 (1945); *NNM*, No. 2, 3.

Bhir mound hoard (Taxila, 1924) (No. 2) (1167 coins, 33 Bent-bars, 79 minute punch-marked coins, 1055 coins—punch-marked coins; 2 coins- Alexander and 1 coin—Philip Arideaus) Taxila Museum, Taxila; Central Asian Antiquities Museum, New Delhi; Walsh, 'Punch-marked coins from Taxila'; *MASI*, No. 59; *JNSI*, XI and XII; *NNM*, No. 2, 4.

Bhir mound hoard (Taxila, 1945) (No. 3) 18 Bent-bars silver; some gold and silver jewellery, gems and beads; *AI*, 1, 27; in trade; *NNM*, No. 2, 5.

Chaman Hazouri hoards (Kabul, Afghanistan) (1933) (43 coins; some Athenian and Achemanian coins) Kabul Museum, Kabul (Afghanistan) *NC* (1954) 163; *NNM*, No. 2, 6.

Darora hoard (Dhir state, N.W.F.) (583 coins) *ASI* (1947).

Kangara hoard (Punjab) (1853) (Coins (?) silver with Antimachus II, Philoxenos, Lysias, Antialkidas and Menander) in trade; *NC* (1873) 209; *NNM*, No. 2, 7.

Mirzakah hoard (I) **(**40 miles east of south Kabul, Afghanistan) (1948) (5000 coins) (87 punch-marked coins along with Bactrian, Indo-Greek, Indo-Scythian, Indo-Parthian and Kushan coins, numbering more than 4000 coins) Kabul Museum, Kabul; Schlumberger, *Tresore Monetaires d' Afghanistan*; *NNM*, No. 2, 8.

Mirzakah hoard (II) (837 coins) (R. Tye) (640 coins) R. Senior (1966), Newsletter, No. 150 (autumn).

Nishan-I-Karuna (1948) (Tangi-da-Maira, Maira, Charsadda, Distt. Rawalpindi) (several 100 coins (?) bent-bars, punch-marked and mashakas) 43 coins—National Museum, New Delhi; rest in trade; *NNM*, No. 2, 9.

Peshawar hoard (Government House) (1905) (61+ coins) in trade; *ASIAR* (1905-06) 150-5.

Shahpur hoard (Punjab) (1895) (14+ coins) 4 coins—British Museum, London, 5 coins—Central Museum, Nagpur and 5 coins—Bombay Branch of Royal Asiatic Society, Bombay, *Proceedings of BBRAS* (1896) XII; *NNM*. No. 2, 11.

Sialkot hoard (Punjab) (?) (31+ coins) 20 coins—Central Museum, Nagpur, 11 coins—Government Museum, Madras; *NNM*, No. 2, 12.

Sugh Village hoard (?) (Ambala, Distt. Haryana) (28 coins) 26 coins—punch-marked; 2 coins-Indo-Greek, Menander and Antimachus Nikephoros (excavation conducted by the Deptt. of Ancient Indian History Culture & Archaeology, Punjab University, Chandigarh); *JNSI*, XXXV (1973) 39-47.

Taxila hoard (BHU, No. 1) (549 coins) College of Indology, BHU, *JNSI* (I) (1951) XIII, 53-68, *NNM*, No. 2, 14.

Taxila hoard (BHU, No. 2) (318 coins) College of Indology, BHU; *NNM*, No. 2, 15.

Thatta hoard (Distt. Attock, Punjab) (1926-27) (9 coins+ 1 silver coin—Philoxenos) in trade; *ASIAR* (1926-27), 229; *NNM*, No. 2, 13.

BANGLADESH

Mahasthan hoard (79 coins).

Baigacha hoard (33 coins) (B. Birch, Soteby'13/12/78, Lot 32, 241 coins).

RAJSTHAN

Bairat hoard (Distt. Jaipur) (1936-37) (33 coins) 8 silver punch-marked coins; 25 Indo-Greek coins—Heliokles, Apollodotus, Menander, Antialkidas and Hermaeus (Archaeological Remains and Exacavations at Bairat) Jaipur Museum, Jaipur, *JNSI* (1946) VIII, 24.

Rairh hoards (I-V) (Distt. Jaipur—1938-39 and 1939-40) I - 326 coins; II - 99 coins; III - 132 coins; IV - 1535 coins; V - 1938 coins) Puri, *Excavations at Rairh,* Department of Archaeology and Historical Research, Jaipur State.

Sikar hoard (Jaipur) (1918) (?) (7 + coins, Indian Museum, Calcutta; remaining coins—Sikar Museum, Sikar (Rajasthan).

UTTAR PRADESH

Ahraura hoard (Distt. Mirzapur) (1931) (500 coins) 220 coins—Shri Nath Shah, Banaras; *NS*, XLV, Pl. XLVII, 73; *NNM*, No. 2, 25.

Allahabad hoard (128 coins) *NNM*, No. 2, 26, in trade.

Amethi hoard (Distt. Sultanpur) (1917) (37 coins) 4 coins—State Museum, Lucknow, rest in trade; U.P.T.T.R. No. 12, 1917-18; *NNM*, No. 2, 60; *JNSI*, IV, Srivastava, Entry No. 662.

Aurihar hoard (Distt. Gazipur) (1952) (534 coins) 404 coins—State Museum, Lucknow; 111 coins—Patna Museum, Patna; 19 coins—BKB (Acc. Nos. 548-566); *NNM*, No. 2, 27.

Azamgarh hoard (Distt.) (1913-14) (60 coins) in trade; *NNM*, No. 2, 29.

Azamgarh hoard (Distt.) (1918) (16+ coins) 16 coins—State Museum, Lucknow; *NNM*, No. 2, 30.

Azamgarh hoard (Distt.) (1948) (280 coins) R.S. Rawat, Azamgarh (subsequently stolen, probably have been thrown in the river, *NNM*, No. 2, 31; *JNSI* (1948) X, 46.

Basaha hoard (Pargana kurub, Tehsil Sirathu, Distt. Allahabad) (1908-09) (127 coins) in trade, U. P. T. T. R. No. 9; in trade, Srivastava, Entry No. 437.

Ballia hoard (1886) (164 coins) Proceedings *ASB*, 1886, 68, in trade; *NNM*, No. 2, 36.

Ballia hoard (1894) (44 coins) (punch-marked coins 7 and 37 coins of Shah Alam II), Srivastava, Entry No. 120.

Bhatti hoard (Rohania Police Station, Distt. Banaras) (1904-05) (134 coins) U. P. T. T. R. No. 25, Srivastava, Entry No. 327, in trade; *NNM*, No. 2, 33.

Burhanpur hoard (Captanganj, Distt. Basti) (1913-14) (88 coins) 26 coins—State Museum, Lucknow, 62 coins in trade, U. P. T. T. R. No. 32, Srivastava, Entry No. 537; *NNM*, No. 2, 34.

Cookngar hoard (Pargana Budhapur, Distt. Gonda) (1913-14) (50 coins) 19 coins—State Museum, Lucknow, rest in trade (U.P.T.T.R. No. 24) Srivastava, Entry No. 551 (Gupta reported a hoard from Distt. Gonda containing 19+ coins, year 1913, disposition—State Museum, Lucknow, probably refering the same hoard) *NNM*, No. 2, 39.

Deorapatti hoard (Tehsil Phulpur, Distt. Azamgarh) (1937-38) (? Several thousand coins in a big earthen trough. Melted down by the finder) *NNM*, No. 2, No. 35.

Dilwarpur hoard (Tehsil Bikapur, Distt. Fyzabad) (1896) (83 coins) (670/11.11. 96) in trade, Srivastava, Entry No. 150.

Etawah hoard (1886) (141 coins) (?) Proceedings *ASB* (1886), 67, in trade; *NNM*, No, 2, 37.

Farrukhabad hoard (1891) (203 coins) (Lucknow, 397/10.11.92) in trade; Srivastava, Entry No. 80.

Gokulvan hoard (Tehsil Amethi, Distt. Sultanpur) (1967- 68) (179 coins, along with one copper cast coin) (Lucknow, F.10/78/68; IV. 1968) State Museum Lucknow (Acc. Nos. 34788-34966) Srivastava, Entry No. 1113; *NNM*, No. 2, 38.

Gorakhpur (Distt.) hoards (No. 1) (1912) (7+ coins) State Museum, Lucknow, *NNM*, No. 2, 40; (No. 2) (1913-14) (50 coins) *NNM*. No. 2, 41, in trade; (No. 3) (1926-27) (16 coins) 7 coins—State Museum, Lucknow, 9 coins in trade, U. P. T. T. R. No. 20, Srivastava, Entry No. 759; *NNM*, No. 2, 44.

Gulariha Bazar (Distt. Gorakhpur) (1915-16) (8 coins) in trade, *NNM*. No. 2, 43 U. P. T. T. R. No. 11, Srivastava, Entry No. 610.

Hardoi hoard (1882) (14 coins) (Lucknow, 237/28.7.1882), Srivastava, Entry No. 1.

Hardoi (city) hoard (1944) (22 coins) Shri Jineswar Das Jain, Allahabad, *JNSI* (1946), VIII (I) 34-35; *NNM*, No. 2, 45.

Harha hoard (P.S. Atrola, Distt. Hardoi) (1953-54) (20 coins) State Museum, Lucknow, U.P.T.T.R. No. 9, Srivastava, Entry No. 1025; *NNM*, No. 2, 46.

Hathuma hoard (Tehsil Derapur, Distt. Kanpur) (1954-55) (39 silver coins and 1 copper coin of Ayodhya) U.P.T.T.R. No. 17, Srivastava, Entry No. 1405; *NNM*, No. 2, 47.

Hulas Khera hoard (Distt. Lucknow) (80 coins)—7 silver punch-marked coins and 73 copper Kushana coins, Uttar Pradesh State Archaeology Department, Lucknow (unpublished).

Ismailpur hoard (Uttar Pradesh) (73 coins), *JRAS* (1974-75).

Jagdishpur hoard (Tehsil Karchchana, Distt. Allahabad) (1966-67) (30 coins) U.P.T.T.R. No. 30, Srivastava, Entry No. 1093.

Jajmau Tila (Distt. Kanpur) (2008) (780 coins) Found from late NBPW Phase, discovered during excavations by Uttar Pradesh State Archaeology Department, Lucknow (unpublished).

Jaunpur hoard (1947) (?) (32+ coins) 5 coins—College of Indology (Dept. of Ancient Indian History Culture & Archaeology) BHU, Varanasi; *JNSI*, IX, 1; 20 coins—State Museum, Lucknow; 7 coins—BKB.

Kaharpur or Khanpur hoard (Tehsil Maharajaganja, Distt. Gorakhpur) (1891) (46 coins) (Lucknow, 1084/12.6.91), Srivastava, Entry No. 84.

Kausambi hoards (1937-38), *JNSI*, XII, 74.

Khatauli hoard (Pargana Atraulia, Distt. Azamgarh (1903-04) (44 coins) U.P.T.T.R. No. 8, 1903-04, in trade; Srivastava, Entry No. 294; *NNM*, No. 2, 28.

Lotapur hoard (Distt. Unnao) (1967-68) (1347 coins) (Lucknow, F.10/78/68. IV. 1968, Acc. Nos. 34967-36313), State Museum, Lucknow, Srivastava, Entry No. 1114 (P.L. Gupta, recorded 1251 coins, year not known, *NNM*, No. 2, 50, *NS*, XLVII, 55.

Malipur hoard (Tehsil Akabarpur, Distt. Faizabad) (1950) (6+ coins), Baldeva Prasad Agrawala, Tatheri Bazar, Banaras; *NNM*, No. 2, No. 51.

Marjadpur hoard (Distt. Banda) (1897) (341 coins) 291 coins—State Museum, Lucknow (200 *Karshapana* and 141 *Pana* or *Mashaka* coins) rest in trade; 253/2.10.97, Srivastava, Entry No. 163.

Mirzapur hoard (Distt.) (1894) (8+ coins), British Museum, London; *BMC*, Introduction xlix; *NNM*, No. 2, 52.

Mathura Museum hoards (lot no. 461) (172 coins) and (lot no. 489) (100 coins) *JNSI* (1997), LIX (I-II) and LVIII (I-II).

Nagava hoard (Varanasi city) (1940) (?) 4 coins in BKB; rest of the coins thrown in the Ganges by the finder for the fear of evil spirit; *NNM*, No. 2, 53.

Nesrauli hoard (P.S. Rudrapur, Distt. Gorakhpur) (1913-14) (15 coins) U.P.T.T.R. No. 28, Srivastava, Entry No. 533; *NNM*, No. 2, 44.

Nizamabad hoard (Distt. Azamgarh) (1913-14) (18 coins) 4 punch-marked and 14 gold coins—Govind Chandradeva, U.P.T.T.R. No. 60, Srivastava, Entry No. 562; in trade; *NNM*, No. 2, 30.

Paila hoard (Distt. Lakhimpur Kheri) (1912) (1014 coins), Lucknow, F.78/68; IV-1968 (Acc. Nos, 33532-34545), Srivastava, Entry No. 1111; *JBBRAS*, XXII, 262; *JNSI* (1940) II, 15-78 and III (1941) 1-20.

Parasa Dayarama hoard (Distt. Gorakhpur) (167 coins), *JNSI* (1964) XXVI.

Pindakhpur hoard (Pargana, Gonda) (1897) (838 coins) (Lucknow, 22/2.7.97) in trade; Srivastava, Entry No. 167.

Rae Bareli hoard (No. 1) (1887) (Lucknow, 371. IX. 9. 11. 87) (13 coins—6 silver punch-marked and 7 coins—Vigrahpala), Srivastava, Entry No. 22.

Rae Bareli hoard (No. 2) (1898) (15 coins) in trade; Lucknow, 82/17. 3. 98, Srivastava, Entry No. 190.
Rajghat hoards (Varanasi) (?).
Ramnagar hoard (Marhiahu, Distt. Jaunpur) Badlapur (1940) *JNSI*, III, 5.
Rauduli hoard (Distt. Barabanki) (1950-51) (75 coins) State Museum, Lucknow; *NNM*, No. 2, 56.
Sahet-Mahet hoard (Distt. Baharaich) (1935-36) (500 coins) 3 coins in British Museum, London, rest in trade; *NNM*, No. 2, 57, (*BMC*, Introduction, lxix; *JNSI* (1958) XX (I) 62-64).
Samdhin hoard (Distt. Farrukhabad) (1913) (16 coins) State Museum, Lucknow; *NNM*, No. 2, 58.
Sariawan hoard (Bela Police Station, Distt. Etawah) (1905-06) (42 coins) 6 coins, Central Museum Nagpur, rest in trade; U.P.T.T.R. No. 2, 1905-06, Srivastava, Entry No. 345.
Shamiwala hoard (Distt. Bijnore) (1920) (137 coins; 4 blank pieces and some fragmantry pieces of silver scrap, State Museum, Lucknow (F.10/78/68; IV-1968, Acc. Nos. 34651-34787) *NNM*, No. 2, 59; *JNSI* (I) (1939) 1-4, *JNSI* (II) (1940) 79, Srivastava, Entry No. 1112.
Sitapur (Distt.) hoard (1886) (142 coins) in trade; Lucknow, 355/X/24.10.86, Srivastava, Entry No. 4.
Unknown provenance of Uttar Pradesh (1916) (105 coins) (U.P.T.T.R. No. 29 of 1916) (Lucknow, F.10/78/68, Acc. Nos. 34546-34650); *JNSI* (1941) III, 1-20; XIII (1967-68) 3; Srivastava, Entry no. 1115.

BIHAR

Bhagalpur hoard (Distt. Shahbad) (found in a subterranean passage) (early part of 19th century) (7+ coins), some coins in British Museum, London, *BMC*, Introduction, xlvii; *CSAR*, V, 31; *NNM*, No. 2, 63.
Bhalna hoard (Distt. Gaya) (1948) (129 coins) Patna Museum, Patna; *NNM*, No. 2, 64.
Chakramadas hoard (Distt. Muzaffarpur, Vaishali) *ASIAR* (1954-55) 61.
Gohada hoard (Distt. Monghyr) (1942) (611 coins) Patna Museum, Patna; *NNM*, No. 2, 66.
Golakpur hoard (Patna City) (1918) (108 coins) Patna Museum, *JBORS* (1919) 463; *NNM*, No. 2, 67.
Gorhoghat hoard (P.S. Baragaon, Distt. Bhagalpur) (58 coins) *JBORS* (1919) 463; *NNM*, No. 2, 65.
Jalloy hoard (Distt. Darbhanga) (1927) (38 coins) 25 coins: 11 coins—Patna Museum; 2 coins—Indian Museum; Calcutta, 4 coins—State Museum, Lucknow; 4 coins—Central Museum, Nagpur; 2 coins—Prince of Wlaes, Bombay; 2 coins—Government Museum, Madras; rest in trade; *NNM*, No. 2, 68.
Machuatoli hoard (Patna city) (1937) (2232+ coins) Patna Museum, Patna; *JBORS*, XXV, 91; XXVII, 1; *NNM*, No. 2, 69.
Madhipur hoard (Distt. Bhagalpur) (1925) (54+ coins) Indian Museum, Calcutta; *BMC*, *Introduction*, lxxix.
Patna hoard (Patna Distt.) (1935) (33 coins) in trade; *ASIAR* (1935-36) 134.
Patraha hoard (P.S. Dhamdaga, Distt. Purnea) (1925) (2873 coins) 2760 coins—Patna Museum, Patna; 11 coins—Indian Museum, Calcutta; 9 coins—Prince of Wales Museum, (Chhatrapati Shivaji Maharaj Vastu Sangrahalaya), Mumbai, *MASI*, No. 62; *JNSI* (IV) 81.

Ramna hoard (Patna city) (1935) (45 coins) Patna Museum, Patna; *JBORS*, XXV, 91; *NNM*, No. 2, 73.

Rajgir hoard (1962) (14 coins) Patna Museum, Patna.

Singhbhum hoard (Chaibasa) (1885) (1191 coins) 12—Central Museum Nagpur, rest in trade; Proceedings, *ASB* (1885), 126.

Supaul hoard (Distt. Bhagalpur) (1909) (15 coins) Indian Museum, Calcutta; *NNM*, No. 2, 75.

Tregna hoard (Distt. Patna, Masurali) (1925) (254 coins?) 243 coins—Patna Museum, Patna; 8 coins—Indian Museum, Calcutta; 6 coins—State Museum, Lucknow; 5 coins—Central Museum, Nagpur; 5 coins—Chhatrapati Shivaji Maharaj Vastu Sangrahalaya, Mumbai; 2 coins—Bombay Branch of Royal Asiatic Society, Bombay, rest in trade; *NNM*, No. 2, 76.

Uziaraghat hoard (256 coins) (2002) *ND* (2003-2004), Vols. 27-28.

Vaisali hoard (Basarh, Distt. Muzaffarpur) (1953) (52 coins) *Vaisali Sangha*, Basarah, *Indian Numismatic Chronicle* (1961) (II) Patna; *NNM*, No. 2, 77.

BENGAL (BANGLADESH & WEST BENGAL)

Brahmaputra hoard (on the bank of an old course in northeast corner of Dacca Distt.) (1937) (?) only 9+ coins in Dacca Museum, rest in trade; *ARDM* (1937-38). Catalouge of the coins of Taifoor Collection in Dacca Museum, Dacca; *NNM*, No. 2, 78.

Chandraketugarh hoard (Berachampa) (1955) *ASIAR* (1955-56).

Phetagram hoard (P.S. Manda, Distt. Rajshahi) (1932) (35+ coins, exact number of coins not known). 21 coins—Museum Varendra Reasearch Society, Rajshahi; 9 coins—Indian Museum; 5 coins (?) probably in Dacca Museum, Dacca (the latter were presented to H.R. Stapleton) *NNM*, No. 2, 79.

Tamluk hoard (Distt. Midnapur) (19th century) (exact number of coins not known; included copper casts and a copper coin of Huvishka) in trade; Proceedings, *ASB* (1882), 112; *NNM*, No. 2, 80.

ORISSA

Asurgarh hoard (1966) (Distt. Kalahandi) (exact numbers not known; however, as reported, several thousand silver punch-marked coins) *OHRJ*, XIV, 25ff; *JNSI* (1970) XXXII 111-30.

Bahalda hoard (Distt. Bhubaneshvara) *JNSI*, II, 123; *NS* (1937) XLVII 106 ff.

Jagamara hoard (Khandagiri Hills, Puri Distt.) (1955) *ASIAR* (1955-56) 62.

Jharpada hoard (Distt. Bhubaneshvara) *JNSI* (1981) XLIII, 35-36.

Mayurbhanj hoard (1940) (192 coins, in a river-bed) Orrisa Museum, Bhubaneshvara, *NNM*, No. 2, 81.

Pandia Village hoard (1970) (Distt. Ganjam) (334 coins), Orissa Museum, Bhubaneshvara, *JNSI* (1981) XLIII 35-40.

Salepur hoard (Distt. Cuttuck) (1964) (376 coins) *OHRJ*, XII, No. 3 (1964) 125-160; *JNSI* (1979), XLI.

Samantaraipur Village hoard (1978) (about 3 kms from Bhubaneshvara) (360 coins), Orissa State Museum, Bhubaneshvara, *JNSI* (1981) XLIII, 35-40. Hoards from several other places have also been reported. Findspots not properly recorded, which are now preserved in Orissa State Museum, Bhubaneshvara, *JNSI*, XLIII, 36.
Sonepur hoard, *JNSI*, XIII, 92; XIV, 22; XV, 54.

MADHYA PRADESH

Barwani hoard (Distt. Nimar) (1945) (3420 coins) National Museum, New Delhi; *JNSI*, X, 146 and XIV, 93; *ND* (1992) Vol. 16, (*NNM*, No. 2, 23, reported the number of coins as 3450. However, the exact number of coins are 3420; personally examined the coins).

Bhandara hoard (1878) (65+ coins), Central Museum, Nagpur; *NNM*, No. 2, 85.

Bilaspur hoard (1907) (9+ coins), Central Museum Nagpur; *NNM*, No. 2, 85.

Dhapewara hoard (Distt. Balaghat) (1893) (92 coins) 21 coins—Central Museum, Nagpur, rest in trade; *NNM*, No. 2, 86 Balaghat District Gazetteer, 69; *JNSI* (1949) XIX, 109.

Karchulha hoard (Tehsil Murwara, Distt. Jabalpur) (1908) 80 silver punch-marked coins + 15 copper cast and 3 copper coins of Hoshangshah of Malwa (?) 5 coins—Central Museum, Nagpur; remaining coins returned to the finder, J.S. Butler of Budha Danga, Asansol, West Bengal; *NNM*, No. 2, 87.

Kasrawad hoard (Distt. Indore) (?) (36 coins) *JNSI*, X, 146; XIV (I) 93-98.

Mamdar hoard (Sidhi, Distt. Rewa, Vindhya Pradesh) 54 coins (41 coins, 13 fragments), *ASI*, New Delhi; *NNM*, No. 2, 83.

Thathari hoard (Tehsil Janjgir, Distt. Bilaspur, Akaltara) (1925) (253 coins; of them 85 coins were minute *mashka* coins) 54 coins—Central Museum, Nagpur; 20 coins—Indian Museum, Calcutta; 8 coins—State Museum, Lucknow; 4 coins—Hyderabad Museum, Hyderabad; 8 coins—Rajputana Museum, Ajmer; 8 coins—British Museum, London; 8 coins—Patna Museum, Patna; 8 coins—Chhatrapati Shivaji Maharaj Vastu Sangrahalaya, Mumbai; Punjab Museum, Lahore; 7 coins—Government Museum, Madras; 8 coins—Assam Museum, Shillong; 8 coins—Peshawar Museum, Peshawar; 7 coins—Rangoon Museum, Rangoon; 7 coins—Dacca Museum, Dacca; 7 coins—Bombay Branch of Royal Asiatic Society, Bombay; 20 coins—returned to the finder, rest in trade; *NNM*, No. 2, 90. *JNSI* (1949) XIX, 110.

MAHARASHTRA

Akkalkot hoard (Distt. Sholapur) (1914) (12+ coins) 4 coins—Indian Museum, Calcutta; 2 coins—Bombay Branch of Royal Asiatic Society, Bombay; 4 coins—Chhatrapati Shivaji Maharaj Vastu Sangrahalaya, Mumbai; 2 coins—Government Museum, Madras; *NNM*, No. 2, 92.

Bahal hoard (Chalisgoan, Taluka of East Khandesh) (1943) (655 coins + 5 fragments), Chhatrapati Shivaji Maharaj Vastu Sangrahalaya, Mumbai, *JBBRAS*, XX (*NS*) 83ff; *JNSI*, VII, 65ff and VIII (II) 119 ff; *Ante. A.*, VIII, 63; *NNM*, No. 2, 93.

Kalawan hoard (Distt. Nashik) (1899) (2+ coins), 1 coin—Bombay Branch of Royal Asiatic Society, Mumbai; 1 coin—Central Museum, Nagpur; *NNM*, No. 2, 96.

Konkan (?) (9+ coins), British Museum, London; *BMC*, 9; *NNM*, No. 2, 97.

Malegaon hoard (Basim, Distt. Akola) (1921-22) (2+ coins), Central Museum, Nagpur; *NNM*, No. 2, 88.

Mana hoard (Distt. Akola) (86 coins) *ND* (1992) Vol. 16.

Mangrul hoard (Hinganghat, Distt. Wardha) (1923-24) (221 coins—174 coins recovered, 47 coins—melted down) 10 coins—Central Museum, Nagpur; 4 coins—Indian Museum, Calcutta; 7 coins—Baroda Museum, Baroda; 4 coins—Hyderabad Museum, Hyderabad; 2 coins—State Museum, Lucknow; 2 coins—Rajputana Museum, Ajmer; 2 coins—British Museum, London; 2 coins—Patna Museum, Patna; 2 coins—Chhatrapati Shivaji Maharaj Vastu Sangrahalaya, Mumbai; Punjab Museum, Lahore; Government Museum, Madras; 2 coins—Assam Museum, Shillong; 2 coins—Peshawar Museum, Peshawar; 2 coins- Rangoon museum, Rangoon; 2 coins—Bombay Branch of Royal Asiatic Society, Bombay; rest in trade; *JNSI*, XIX; *NNM*, No. 2, 89.

Shinhi hoard (Kurveerpetta, Distt. Kolhapur) (1871) (192 coins along with a gold ring with the inscription *Nadihagasa* in Ashokan script) in trade, Proceedings, *JBBRAS* (1872), XII, xxi-xxii; *NNM*, No. 2, 98.

Salebhatti hoard (Umrer hoard) (Umrer, Distt. Nagpur) (?) (138 coins) 45 coins—Central Museum, Nagpur, rest in trade; *NNM*, No. 2, 91.

Sultanpur hoard (Wai, Distt. Satara) (1876) (4+ coins), British Museum, London; *JBBRAS* (1876) 400; *BMC*, 68; *NNM*, No. 2, 99.

Ratangiri hoard (1867) (59 coins) *NNM*, No. 16.

GUJARAT

Ahmedabad hoard (Sanaud) (1875) (20 coins).

Banaskantha hoard (Depadar, Vadia, Distt. Palanpur) (1917) (101 coins), *ASIAR* (1917-18) I, 30.

Baroda hoard (Old Baroda State) (19th century) (58+ coins), Baroda Museum, Baroda; Baroda Museum Bulletin; *NNM*, No. 2, 94.

Vadia hoard (Taluka Depdar, Distt. Palanpur) (1917) (72+ coins) 11 coins—British Museum, London; 21 coins—Indian Museum, Calcutta; 10 coins—Bombay Branch of Royal Asiatic Society, Bombay; 15 coins—Chhatrapati Shivaji Maharaj Vastu Sangrahalaya, Mumbai; 6 coins—Central Museum, Nagpur; 9 coins—Patna Museum, Patna; *NNM*, No. 2, 100; *ASIAR* (1917-18) I, 30.

KARNATAKA

Dharwar hoard (1938) (?) (11 coins) Mysore Archaeological Department, Mysore; *ARMAD* (1938), 73-76.

ANDHRA PRADESH

Amaravati hoard (1953) (7668 coins); *Am.* (1963).

Bhimalipatan hoard (Distt.Vizagapatam) (1897) (172 coins) 74 coins—Government Museum, Madras; 9 coins—British Museum, London; 8 coins—Bombay Branch of Royal Asiatic Society, Bombay; 8 coins—Central Museum, Nagpur; 8 coins—Department of Archaeology, Mysore; *MMAR*, 1897, 5; *BMC*, Introduction, liv; *NNM*, No. 2, 106.

Dharnikot hoard (Distt. Amaravati) (1953) (8000 coins); *ASIAR* (1953-54), 39.

Gulbarga hoard (Village Habbal, Hyderabad State) (1940-41) (225 coins) Hyderabad Museum, Hyderabad; *APGM*, 16-22; *NNM*, No. 2, 101.

Kamanchi hoard (Distt. Kurnool, Pattikonda) (1925-26) (27 coins) (?).

Karimnagar hoard (Hyderabad State) (1920-21) (367 coins) *APGM*, 4-15.

Nasthulapur hoard (Distt. Karimnagar, Hyderabad State) (1952) (47 coins: 8 silver punch-marked coins and remaining 39-Roman silver coins), Hyderabad Museum, Hyderabad; *APGM*, 27 28; *NNM*, No. 2, 103.

Raichur hoard (Hyderabad State) (1935-36) (63 coins), *APGM*, 23-26; *NNM*, No. 2, 104.

Rothulapalam hoard (Taluka Bhimalipatan, Distt. Vizagapatam) (21 coins) 8 coins—Government Museum, Madras, rest in trade; *NNM*, No. 2, 118.

Venne hoard (Srungavarapukota, Distt. Vizagapatam) (1927) (81 coins) 42 coins—Government Museum, Madras, rest in trade; *NNM*, No. 2, 124.

Vizagapatam hoard (1910-11) (61 coins) (?) Government Museum, Madras; *NNM*, No. 2, 125.

TAMIL NADU

Alampalyam hoard (Kolathupalayam, Dharapuram, Distt. Koimbatore) (1948) (63 coins) 5 coins—Government Museum, Madras, rest of the coins in trade; *NNM*, No, 2, 105.

Bodinaikkanur hoard (Pariyakulam, Distt. Madura) (1940) (1138 coins + 4 pieces of gold, not coins), *JNSI* (VI), 1; *JBBRS, XXVI*, 214. *NNM*, No. 2, 107.

Chavadipalayam hoard (Savadipalayam, near Palladam, Distt. Coimbatore) (?) (1807) in trade; *MLJS* (1857), 228; *NNM*, No. 2, 108.

Gudivada hoard (Distt. Krishna) (1924) (53 coins) 12 coins—Government Museum, Madras, rest in trade; *NNM*, No. 2, 113.

Kauniankuttai hoard (Distt. Salem) (1919-20) (17 coins) 14 coins—Government Museum, Madras, rest in trade; *MMAR* (1919-20), 6; *NNM*, No. 2, 115.

Mambalam hoard (Madras) (?) (770 + coins (?), with a Roman coin of Augustus) 1 coin in each museum—Chhatrapati Shivaji Maharaj Vastu Sangrahalaya, Mumbai; Baroda Museum, Baroda; Sardar Museum, Jodhpur. However, Madras Museum reported 808 coins, probably, mixed up with other coins or reported wrongly; *NNM*, No. 2, 116.

Penrar hoard (Distt. Coimbatore) (1803) (?) *MJLS*, 1857, 228. A pot full of coins along with a silver dinarius of Augustus; (?) in trade; *NNM*, No. 2, 117.

Tondamanatham hoard (Distt. South Arkot) (1916) (27 coins along with 6 Roman gold coins—3 aurei - Tierius, 1 - Claudius, 1 - Agrippina and 1 - Nero) 10 coins—Government Museum, Madras, rest in trade; *NNM*, No. 2, 120.

Veersigmani hoard (Taluka Sankarankoli, Distt. Tinnevelly (1953) (287 coins) Government Museum, Madras; *NNM*, No. 2, 121.

Vellanpur hoard (Taluka Pemambalur, Distt. Trichnapolly) (346 coins), *JNSI* (1979) XLI.

Vembavur hoard (No. 1) (Taluka Pemambalur, Distt. Trichnapolly) (1907) (991 coins) 572 coins—Dacca Museum, Dacca; 27 coins—Patna Museum, Patna; 21 coins—Indian Museum, Calcutta; 10 coins—Bombay Branch of Royal Asiatic Society, Bombay; 10 coins—State Museum, Lucknow;

10 coins—Central Museum, Nagpur; 2 coins—Hyderabad Museum, Hyderabad; 10 (?) coins—British Museum, London; 8 coins—Chhatrapati Shivaji Maharaj Vastu Sangrahalaya, Mumbai; 175 in various private collection and 164 coins in trade; *NNM*, No. 2, 122.

Vembavur hoard (No. 2) (1925) (1375 coins) 166 coins—Government Museum, Madras, rest in trade; *NNM*, No. 2, 123.

Kerala hoard (Eyyal, 22 miles of North West of Trichur) (1945) *AI*, No. 2.

A.K. Srivastava (1980), *Coin Hoards of Uttar Pradesh* (1882-1979), State Museum, Lucknow.

Elizabeth Errington (2003), "A Survey of Late Hoards of Punch-marked Coins", *The Numismatic Chronicle*, The Royal Numismatic Society, London.

J. Allan (1936), *Catalouge of the Coins of Ancient India, British Museum*, London.

P.L. Gupta (1955), A *Bibliography of the Hoards of Punch-marked Coins of Ancient India, Numismatic Notes and Monograph*, No. 2. The Numismatic Society of India, Chhatrapati Shivaji Maharaj Vastu Sangrahalaya, Mumbai (*NMM*, No. 2).

——, *Unpublished thesis* (1959), Banaras Hindu University, Varanasi.

——, *Bibliography of Indian Numismatic* (I) Ancient Periods up to 1960; (II) 1961-1970.

Bibliography

Agrawala, V.S. (1953), *India as Known to Pāṇini*, Lucknow.

—— (1953), "Ancient Coins as Known to Pāṇini", *JNSI*, XV (I), 27-41.

—— (1969), *Pāṇinikālīna Bhāratavarṣa* (*Hindi* – Reprint), Varanasi.

Allan, J. (1936), *Catalogue of the Coins of Ancient India in the British Museum*, London.

Altekar, A.S. (1937), *History of Benares*, Benares Hindu University, Benares.

—— (1953), "Origin and Early History of Coinage in Ancient India", *JNSI*, XV (I), 1-21.

Altekar, A.S. & C.R. Singhal (1951), "Numismatic Discoveries and Researches during 1941-1950", *JNSI*, XIII (I), 1-21.

Aṅguttar Nikāya (1885, 1900), R. Morris & E. Mardy (eds.), P.T.S., London.

Aṣṭādhyāyī (of Pāṇini) (1932), Nirnaya Sagar Press Bombay; S.C. Vasu (ed.), (1962), Delhi.

Barker, D.A. (1913), *The Theory of Money*. (The Cambridge Manuals of Science and Literature).

Bhandarkar, D.R. (1913-14), "Excavations at Besnagar", *ASR*, 210.

—— (1921), *Lectures on Ancient Indian Numismatics* (The Carmichael Lectures, Calcutta University, Calcutta).

—— (1984, reprinted), *Ancient Indian Numismatics*, Calcutta.

Bhandare, Shailendra (2009), "The Archaic Indian Punch-marked Coins: Approaches to Classification", http//www.215.pair.com/Sacoins/public_htm/Shailenspaper.htm (7. Feb. 2009).

Bhardwaj, H.C. (1966), "Bearing of Chemical Composition & Metallography on the Chronolgy of the Punch-marked Coins", *Seminar Papers on the Chronology of the Punch-marked Coins*, A.K. Narain (ed.), College of Indology, Banaras Hindu University, Varanasi.

Bhattacharya, P.N. (1940), "A Hoard of Silver Punch-marked Coins from Purnea (Patraha)", *MASI*, No. 62, Delhi.

Bulletin of the Prince of Wales Museum (1955-57), No. 5.

Chakrabortty, S.K. (1931), *A Study of Ancient Indian Numismatics*, Calcutta.

—— (2004, reprinted), *Indian Numismatics: From the Earliest Times to the Rise of the Imperial Guptas*, Delhi.

Chaudhuri, S.B. (1955), *Ethnic Settlement in Ancient India*, Calcutta.

Chatterjee, C.D. (1931), "Some Numismatic Data in Pali Literature", *Buddhistic Studies*, B.C. Law (ed.), Calcutta.

Chopra, S.N. (1973), "A Hoard of Punch-marked Coins from Sugh", *JNSI*, XXXV, 39-47.

Cribb, Joe (1983), "Investigating the Introduction of Coinage in India—A Review of Recent Research", *JNSI*, XLV, 81-101.

—— (2005), *The Indian Coinage Tradition: Origins Continuity and Change*, IIRNS, Anjaneri, Nashik.

Cunningham, A. (1891), *Coins of Ancient India*, London. (Reprint, 1971, Delhi).

Curiel, R. & D. Schlumberger (1953), *Trésore Monétaires d' Afghanistan*, *Memoire de le Delegation Archeologique Francaise en Afghanistan*, Paris.

Dani, A.H. (1955), "Punch-marked Coins and the Evidence from Taxila", *JNSI*, XVI (II), 27-32.

—— (1958), "Taxila Evidence on the Dating of the Punch-marked Coins", *JNSI*, XIX (II), 180-81.

Das, A.C. (1925), *The Ṛgvedic Culture*, Calcutta.

Deo, P.K. (1970), "Punch-marked Coins from Asurgarh Fort (Orissa)", *JNSI*, XXXI (II), 111-30.

Dhavalikar, M.K. (1975), "The Beginning of Coinage in India", *World Archaeology* (VI) No. 3, 330-38.

Dikshit, M.G. (1964), "Punch-marked Coins from Nevari, Umrer (Distt. Nagpur)", *JNSI*, XXVI (I), 91-95.

Diskalkar, D.B. (1948), "Kasrawad Hoard of Silver Punch-marked Coins", *JNSI*, X (II), 146.

Elliot, Sir Walter (1886), *Coins of Southern India* (The International Numismata Orientalia), *Encyclopaedia Britannica*, (XVII) Ninth Edition.

Errington, Elizabeth (2003), "A Survey of Late Hoards of Indian Punch-marked Coins", *NC*, London, 69-121.

Gairola, T.R. (1951), "The Weight of Punch-marked Coins from Barwani", *AI*, No. 7.

—— (1954), "Density and Percentage Composition of Metals in Coins Struck in Alloys", *JNSI*, XVI (II), 268-69.

Gazetteers of India (1965), *Uttar Pradesh*, Varanasi.

Gopal, L. (1966), "Source of Silver for the Punch-marked Coins", *The Chronology of the Punch-marked Coins*, A.K. Narain (ed.), College of Indology, Banaras Hindu University, Varanasi, 64-76.

Gupta, P.L. (1948), "A Unique Hoard of Silver Punch-marked Coins", *JNSI*, X, 46-49.

—— (1949), "Silver Punch-marked Coins from Taxila (The Hoard of 1924, A Critical and Comparative Study)", *JNSI*, XI (II), 114-46.

—— (1950), "Some Observations on the Punch-marked Coins Based on the Study of Taxila Hoard of 1924", *JNSI*, XII (II), 136-50.

—— (1951), "A New Hoard of Silver Punch-marked Coins from Taxila", *JNSI*, XIII (I), 53-68.

—— (1952), "Some Observations on the Punch-marked Coins of Kasrawad Hoard", *JNSI*, XIV (I), 83-98.

—— (1953), "The Silver Punch-marked Coins from Taxila" (Bhir mound hoard, 1912-13) *JNSI*, XV (II), 172-77.

—— (1954), "The Punch-marked Coins from Hyderabad", *JNSI*, XVI (I), 51-54.

—— (1954), "A Unique Hoard of Silver Punch-marked Coins", *JNSI*, XVI, 61.

—— (1954), "Notes and News: Treasure Troves from Uttar Pradesh", *JNSI*, XVI (II), 111.

—— (1955), "A Bibliography of the Hoards of Punch-marked Coins of Ancient India", *JNSI*, XVII (II) Appendix; Numismatic Notes & Monograph (No. 2), Varanasi.

—— (1957), "Nasthulpur Hoard of Silver Roman and Punch-marked Coins", *JNSI*, XIX (I), 1-4.

—— (1957), "Evidence from Taxila on the Dating of Silver Punch-marked Coins", *JNSI*, XIX (I), 5-8.

—— (1958), "Sahet-Mahet Hoard of Silver Punch-marked Coins", *JNSI*, XX (I), 62-65.

—— (1959), The Punch-marked Coins of Ancient India, Ph.D. thesis (unpublished).

—— (1959), "On the Chronology of Silver Punch-marked Coins", *JNSI*, XXI (I), 1- 8.

—— (1959), "The Dates of the Taxila Hoard of Punch-marked Coins", *JNSI*, XXI (I), 114-19.

—— (1960), *Punch-marked Coins in the Andhra Pradesh Government Museum* (Andhra Pradesh Government Museum Series (No. 1), Hyderabad.

—— (1960), "Numismatic Data in *Arthaśāstra* of Kauṭilya", *JNSI*, XXII, 13-37.

—— (1963), *The Amaravati Hoard of Silver Punch-marked Coins*, Hyderabad.

—— (1965), "Some Observations on Parsa Dayaram Hoard of Silver Punch-marked Coins", *JNSI*, XXVII (I), 1-20.

—— (1966), "The Chronology of Punch-marked Coins", *The Chronology of the Punch-marked Coins*, A.K. Narain & L. Gopal (eds.), College of Indology, Banaras Hindu University, Varanasi, 1-15.

—— (1992), "Barwani Hoard of Silver Punch-marked Coins", *ND* (16), 6-23.

Gupta, P.L. & Durga Prasad (1954), "Clay-moulds of Punch-marked Coins from Mathura", *JNSI*, XVI (II), 166-76.

Gupta, P.L. & T.R. Hardaker (1985), *Ancient Indian Silver Punch-marked Coins of the Magadha-Maurya Kārshāpana Series*, IIRNS, Anjaneri, Nashik.

Kauṭilya Arthaśāstra (1962), Gairola, Vachaspati (*Hindi*, Vidya Bhavan Series), Varanasi; *Arthaśāstra* (of Kauṭilya), (tr.) R. Shamasastry (1920).

Kosambi, D.D. (1940), "A Statistical Study of the Weights of Old Punch-marked Coins", *NIA*, IV, 1-35.
—— (1940), "A Note on Two Hoards of Punch-marked Coins found at Taxila", *NIA*, III (1940-41), 156-59.
—— (1941), "On the Origin and Development of Silver Coinage in India", *Current Science*, 10 (9), 395-400.
—— (1941), "On the Study of Metrology of Silver Punch-marked Coins", *NIA*, IV, 1-35, 48-76.
—— (1946), "Silver Punch-marked Coins with Special Reference to the East Khandesh Hoard", *JNSI*, VIII, 63-65.
—— (1949), "Chronological Order of Silver Punch-marked Coins" (part-I), *JBBRAS*, XXIV-XXV (1948-49), 33-47.
—— (1951), "Chronological Order of Silver Punch-marked Coins" (part II), 'The Bondenayakanur Hoard', *JBBRAS*, XXVI, 214-18.
—— (1981), *Indian Numismatics*, Delhi.
Lahiri, A.N. (1976), "Complexities of the Silver Punch-marked Coins", *JNSI*, XXXVIII (II), 1-34.
Mahābhāṣya (of Patañjali) (1892, 1909), F. Keilhorn (ed.), 3 vols., Bombay.
Mahajan, Nupam & R. Balasubramaniam (1998), "Scanning Electron Microscopy Study of an Ancient Silver Punch-marked Coin with Central Pentagonal Mark", *ND*, Vols. 21-22 (1997-98), 153-67.
Majumdar, R.C. (ed.) (1953 & 1990, 2nd & 6th edition), *The History and Culture of the Indian People*, Vol. II: *The Age of Imperial Unity*, Bhārtiya Vidyā Bhavan Series, Bombay.
Manusmṛiti, V.N. Mandlik (ed.) (1886), Bombay; (tr.) G. Buhler (1886) *SBE* (XXV) Oxford; (tr. with notes) G. Jha (1922-29), 5 vols., Calcutta.
Marshall, J. (1931), *Mohenjodaro and the Indus Valley Civilisation*, London.
—— (1951), *Taxila: An Illustrated Account of Archaeological Excavations Carried Out at Taxila Under the Orders of Government of India Between the Years 1913 and 1934*, 3 vols., London.
McCrindle, J.W. (1901), *Ancient India as Described in Classical Literature* (translated and copiously annotabled by McCrindle), Westminister.
Mitra, P. (1923), *Pre historic India*, Calcutta.
Mitchiner, Michael (1973), *The Origins of Indian Coinage*, London.
—— (1978), *Ancient and Classical World*, London.
—— (2004), *Ancient Trade and Early Coinage* (Vol. 2), London.
Mookerji, R.K. (1953 & 1990), "Rise of Magadha Imperialism", ch. II, 18-37; "Chandragupta and the Maurya Empire", ch. IV, 54-69; "Aśoka the Great", ch. V, 71-90 and ch. VI, "The Rise of the Magadhan Empire", ch. VI, "The Śuṅgas", 95, *The Age of Imperial Unity* (2nd & 6th edition).
Narain, A.K. (1957), "Notes on the Chronology of Punch-marked Coins", *JNSI*, XIX, 99.
Nath, B.N. (1952), "Punch-marked Coins from Sonepur", *OHRJ*, Vol. I (2), 27.
Patnaik, S. (1979), "A Note on the Salepur Hoard of Silver Punch-marked Coins", *JNSI*, XLI, 124.
Prasad, Durga (1934), "Classification and Significance of the Symbols on the Silver Punch-marked Coins of Ancient India", *NS*, XLV, 5.
—— (1937), *Observations on Silver Punch-marked Coins and Their Age*, Banaras.
—— (1939), "Shamiawala (Bijnor, District) Hoard of Silver Punch-marked Coins", *JNSI*, (I).
Prasad, Maheshwari (1966), "Literary Evidence on the Chronology of the Punch-marked Coins", *The Chronology of the Punch-marked Coins*, A.K. Narain (ed.), College of Indology, Banaras Hindu University, Varanasi, 164.
Prakash, Jai (1961-62), "Parallel Accounts of the Origin of Kingship in Judea and India", *Bharati*, Dept. of A.I.H.C. and Archaeology, Banaras Hindu University, Varanasi, No. 5 (I) 56-61.
—— (1966), "The Bearing of Trade and Commerce on the Chronology of the Punch-marked Coins", *Seminar Papers on the Chronology of the Punch-marked Coins*, A.K. Narain (ed.), College of Indology, Banaras Hindu University, Varanasi, 82-84.
Puri, K.N. (1938-39, 1939-40), *Excavations at Rairh*, Department of Archaeology and Historical Research, Jaipur State.
Rajgor, Dilip (1996), "Minting Technique of Punch-marked Coins of India", *JNSI*, LVIII, 115-21.
—— (1997), "Droplet Technique of Punch-marked Coins", *Numismatic Studies* (Vol. 5), 1-5.
—— (2001), *Punch-marked Coins of Early Historic India*, Wagle Estate, Thane.

Ray, S.C. (1959), *Stratigraphic Evidence of Coins in Indian Excavations and Some Allied Issues*, The Numismatic Society of India, Varanasi.

—— (1966), "Archaeological Evidence on the Date of Punch-Markaed Coins", *Seminar Papers on the Chronology of the Punch-marked Coins,* A.K. Narain (ed.), College of Indology, Banaras Hindu University, Varanasi.

Rapson, E.J. (1968, reprint), *Indian Coins* (1898, Stressburg).

Ray, P. (1956), *History of Chemistry*, Calcutta.

Rhys, David (1903), *Buddhist India*; (1897), *History of Indian Buddhism*; (1926), *Buddhism: Its History and Literature* (New Edition) London.

Raychaudhuri, Hemachandra (1923), *Political History of Ancient India,* Calcutta.

Schoff, W.H. (1922), *The Periplus of the Erythraean Sea.*

Senior, R.C. (1996), "Punch-marked Coins from Mir Zakah Hoard II", *ONS, Newsletter*, No. 150.

—— (1997), "Ancient Coins of Chaman-i-Hazouri Type", *ONS, Newsletter*, No. 154.

Sharma, R.S. (1976), "Coins and Problems of Early Indian Economic History" (Seminar on Coins as a Source of Economic History of Ancient India, 1969, Patna), *Memoirs Series*, No. 6, The Numismatic Society of India, 7.

Sircar, D.C. (1968), *Studies in Indian Coins*, Delhi.

Sharma, Savita (1990), *Early Indian Symbols: Numismatic Evidence*, Delhi.

Shastri, A.M. (1966), "Literary Evidence Bearing on the Chronology of the Punch-marked Coins", *The Chronology of the Punch-marked Coins,* A.K. Narain (ed.), College of Indology, Banaras Hindu University, Varanasi.

Singh, S. (1964), "Parasa Dayarama Hoard of Silver Punch-marked Coins", *JNSI*, XXVI, 131-56.

Smith, V.A. (1906) *Indian Museum Catalogue* (I), Oxford; *Coins of Ancient India, Catalogue of the Coins in the Indian Museum Calcutta*, Varanasi.

Spooner, D.B. (1905-06), "A New Find of Punch-marked Coins", *ASIAR*, 150-64, Peshawar Government House Hoard.

Srivastava, A.K. (1980), *Coin Hoards of Uttar Pradesh* (1882-1979), State Museum, Lucknow.

Tandon, Pankaj (2007), "Some Magadha Series I Overstrikes from Sasaram", *ND* (31), 17-45.

The Chronology of the Punch-marked Coins (1966), A.K. Narain & L. Gopal (eds.), Deptt. of Ancient Indian History Culture & Archaeology, College of Indology, Banaras Hindu University, Varanasi, (1-18; 26-38; 56-63; 64-76; 77-80; 81-85; 112-20; 161-70).

Thomas, Edward (1858), *Princep's Essays on Indian Antiquities*, London. (*Essays on Indian Antiquities, Historic, Numismatic and Paleographic* on the Late James Prinsep by Edward Thomas) (reprinted 1971), 2 vols., edited with notes and additional matter, Delhi.

—— (1874), *Ancient Indian Weights*, London.

Theobold, W. (1890), "Notes on Some of the Symbols Found on Punch-marked Coins of Hindustan and Their Relationship to the Archaic Symbolism of Other Races and the Distance Lands", *JASB,* LIX (I), No. 3.

—— (1890), "A Revision of the Symbols of the Karshapana Coinage Described in Vol. LIX, *JASB* (I) No. 3, 182 and 'Description of Many Additional Symbols", (1901) *JASB,* LXX, 73.

Verma, T.P. (1988), "On Minting of Punch-marked Coins: A New Suggestion", *JNSI,* L, 144-46.

Walsh, E.H.C. (1917), "Punch-marked Coins, Their Standard Weight, Age and Minting", *JRAS*, 393.

—— (1924), "Indian Punch-marked Coins", *JRAS* (Centenary Supplement).

—— (1939), "A Find of Punch-marked Coins in Patna City" (An examination of a find of punch-marked coins found in Patna city with reference to the subject of punch-marked coins generally), *JBORS* (II), 172.

—— (1939), *Punch-marked Coins from Taxila, MASI*, No. 59, Archaeological Survey of India, New Delhi.

—— (1939), "Notes on Two Hoards of Silver Punch-marked Coins (Ramna hoard and Machuatoli hoard)", *JBORS*, XXV, 91-117.

—— (1939), "Some Notes Regarding Marks on the Silver Punch-marked Coins found at Golakpur in Patna and at Gorhoghat, *JBORS,* XXV, 6.

—— (1940), "Paila Hoard of Punch-marked Coins", *JNSI* (II), 15-78.

—— (1940), "A Note on the Shamiawala (Bijnore District) Hoard of Silver Coins", *JNSI* (II), 79.

—— (1941), "Examination of a Hoard of 105 Silver Punch-marked Coins Found in the United Provinces in 1916", U.P. Treasure Trove No. 28 of 1916, *JNSI* (III), 1-20.

—— (1951), "Two Hoards of Silver Punch-marked Coins found in the Bhir mound at Taxila", Chapter 40 in John Marshall, *Taxila*,London, pp. 843-52.

Index